Published with
the financial assistance of
the Zion Research Foundation

The Third Campaign at Tell el-Fûl: The Excavations of 1964

The Annual of the American Schools of Oriental Research

Volume 45

Edited by
David Noel Freedman

The Third Campaign at Tell el-Fûl:
The Excavations of 1964

The Third Campaign at Tell el-Fûl:
The Excavations of 1964

Edited by
Nancy L. Lapp

With Contributions by
John A. Graham, Howard M. Jamieson, Nancy L. Lapp,
and Walter E. Rast

Published by
American Schools of Oriental Research

Distributed by

American Schools of Oriental Research
126 Inman St.
Cambridge, MA 02139

The Third Campaign at Tell el-Fûl:
The Excavations of 1964

Edited by
Nancy L. Lapp

With Contributions by
John A. Graham, Howard M. Jamieson, Nancy L. Lapp,
and Walter E. Rast

Library of Congress Cataloging in Publication Data

The Third campaign at Tell el-Fûl.

    (The Annual of the American Schools of Oriental
Research ; v. 45)
    Bibliography: p. 151.
    Includes index.
    1. Fûl, Tell. I. Lapp, Nancy L., 1930- .
II. Graham, John Allen. III. Series: Annual of the
American Schools of Oriental Research ; v. 45.
DS101.A45   vol. 45   [DS110.F83]   933   81-3659
ISBN   0-89757-045-6   AACR2

Printed in the United States of America
1   2   3   4   5

Table of Contents

Preface

This is the second excavation report that I have attempted to compile from my late husband's excavations in Jordan during our years of residence there, 1960-68. Unlike the first, the Wâdī ed-Dâliyeh cave clearances, where much of the material was in rough draft form, almost no preliminary study of the Tell el-Fûl excavation materials had been done at the time of Paul's death. Shortly after the excavation in 1964 he wrote a short preliminary report, distributed first as a Newsletter of the American Schools of Oriental Research (1963-64, no. 6) and then published in the *Biblical Archaeologist* (1965: 2-10). This report, his field diary and pottery book, a few letters and notes, and the field books of the area supervisors and plans of the architects have served as the basis for this report.

The choice of Tell el-Fûl as the second major project to undertake was a logical one for me. Since Paul's death I have served as Curator of the James L. Kelso Bible Lands Museum at Pittsburgh Theological Seminary and adviser to archeological students. Tell el-Fûl was a joint undertaking of Pittsburgh Theological Seminary and the American Schools of Oriental Research. The cooperation and encouragement of the seminary could be expected. There were also some seminary students who were looking for archeological projects.

In the spring of 1971, John A. Graham was interested in an archeological study for his Master of Theology thesis at Pittsburgh Theological Seminary. Jack had been a student of Paul's and a member of the first Idalion expedition where Paul lost his life. Jack continued archeological studies with me, and he has since become a colleague in his quests and contributions. Through funds provided by the generosity of Professor Emeritus J. L. Kelso of Pittsburgh Theological Seminary, Mr. Graham spent four weeks in Jerusalem in the summer of 1971 preceding the second season at Idalion. He made a preliminary survey and assembly of the Tell el-Fûl materials still at the Albright Institute in Jerusalem.

In the spring of 1972, I received a grant from the Penrose Fund of the American Philosophical Society for the study of the pottery in Jerusalem and the preliminary preparation for its publication. In the meantime, Jack Graham undertook a thorough study of the Tell el-Fûl archeological evidence from the three campaigns (1922, 1933, and 1964), particularly as it related to the biblical stories at the time of the Judges and the United Monarchy. His study resulted in his masters thesis, "Saul's Fortress at Tell el-Fûl," in the spring of 1975 and ultimately became the main body of material in chaps. 1, 3, and 4 of this report.

Dr. Howard Jamieson, now pastor of Tustin Presbyterian Church, Tustin, California, served as an Area Supervisor and representative of Pittsburgh Theological Seminary. He has been of constant aid and encouragement in the preparation of this manuscript and has told the story of the 1964 excavation in chap. 2. Through his efforts, I also received a grant from the Murdy Foundation in California to aid in the preparation of this volume.

Professor James L. Kelso served as President of the 1964 excavation and has continued to be our link with the earlier campaigns. He has prodded us on when work went slowly and helped us on occasion with financial aid.

My study and research in Pittsburgh has been hampered considerably by the fact that the Tell el-Fûl pottery and artifacts must still be housed in the Albright Institute in Jerusalem because of the political situation. Pottery drawings and descriptions had to be completed after I left Jerusalem in 1972. An apology is in order for the inconsistencies and incompleteness of the ware descriptions — the work of several people at different stages of the publication process. I am grateful for the efforts of a number of friends in

Jerusalem who willingly expended undue energy across the seas. Special thanks are due to Professors Walter Rast and Thomas Schaub while they were residents in Jerusalem, Professor William Dever, Director of the Albright Institute while I was working on the material from 1972 to 1975, Mr. Elia Kahvedjian, our unfailing photographer, Mrs. Jean Boling, whose constant efforts in the past year have aided the completion of unfinished projects, and Mr. Shibley Kharman and Dr. Michael Coogan, who filled in during the emergency.

As in the case in each of my husband's excavations, we are appreciative of the permission and cooperation of the Department of Antiquities of the Hashemite Kingdom of Jordan and of the Royal Jordanian Army for work in a strategic area. Personal encouragement in the publication task came from the late G. Ernest Wright, and more recently, Frank M. Cross and David Noel Feedman, President and Vice President of the American Schools of Oriental Research. The work would have been impossible without assistance from the Penrose Fund of the American Philosophical Society, the Murdy Foundation, and a grant by the Fairchild Foundation through the American Schools of Oriental Research for work on the publication of the excavations of Paul W. Lapp.

The original drawings were the work of Mr. Bishara Zoghbi and his staff, and the architect was Mr. Oliver Unwin. Paul Lapp took all the field photographs, and Elia Kahvedjian took those of the pottery and artifacts. Jack Graham has been of assistance throughout the preparation of this report, often helping with preliminary research and offering suggestions on the editing of the material; finally, his work is the final preparation and assembling of all the line drawings — the plans, figures in the text, and pottery plates. The task would have been impossible without him.

I can only be grateful that Paul's records were so complete and that he encouraged his field supervisors in their efforts in clear and precise reporting. My thanks are due them. Paul's preliminary report in the *Biblical Archaeologist* has been basic to this report. Except for some small details, further research has reinforced his conclusions. It is for him and in his memory that this work is presented.

Pittsburgh, Pa.   Nancy L. Lapp
August 5, 1976

Postscript

Due to unfortunate circumstances, the manuscript completed in August, 1976, has been delayed in publication. With renewed promises that it will soon be printed, I thought it necessary to make some revisions particularly in relation to recent studies of the late Iron II period and the renewed excavations at Lachish. I have attempted to incorporate some new material, but I fear there may be inconsistencies and omissions that time does not permit me to correct. I only hope the evidence from Tell el-Fûl may become a part of the on-going archeological research of Palestine.

Pittsburgh, Pa.   Nancy L. Lapp
March 15, 1978

LIST OF PLANS

1. Excavated remains from three campaigns.

2. Excavated areas and sections of the 1964 campaign.

3. Topographical map of the vicinity of Tell el-Fûl.

4. Topographical map of Tell el-Fûl showing excavated remains of the three campaigns.

5. Section n-s. North-south section on the west side of the mound.

6. Section a-b. West-east section of Areas XV, XI, VI, north face.
   Section c-d. East-west section of Trench T.

7. Section e-f. East-west section west of Period II tower.
   Section g-h. East-west section northwest of Period II tower.

8. Section j-k. East-west section south of Hellenistic Tower through Rooms B and C.

9. Section l-m. West-east section north of Hellenistic Tower.

10. Cisterns 1 and 2 plans and sections.

11. Silo sections.

12. Silo sections and caps.

13. Iron I excavated remains.

14. Period III excavated remains.

15. The Coins from the 1964 campaign.

LIST OF PLATES

LIST OF FIGURES IN TEXT

LIST OF ABBREVIATED TITLES

ᶜAfûla   M. Dothan. The Excavations at ᶜAfûla. Pp. 19-70 in *Atiqot* 1, English Series. Jerusalem: Hadassah Apprentice School of Printing, 1955.

ᶜAlâyiq   J. B. Pritchard. *The Excavation of Herodian Jericho, 1951*. Annual of the American Schools of Oriental Research 32-33 (1952-54). New Haven: American Schools of Oriental Research, 1958.

AS IV   E. Grant and G. E. Wright. *Ain Shems Excavations, IV (Pottery)*. Biblical and Kindred Studies 7. Haverford: Haverford College, 1938.

AS V   E. Grant and G. E. Wright. *Ain Shems Excavations, V (Text)*. Biblical and Kindred Studies 8. Haverford: Haverford College, 1939.

Ashdod II-III   M. Dothan. *Ashdod II-III: The Second and Third Seasons of Excavations, 1963, 1965 (Text and Plates)*. Atiqot 9-10, English series. Jerusalem: Department of Antiquities, et al., 1971.

Atiqot V   B. Mazar, T. Dothan, and I. Dunayevsky. *En-Gedi: The First and Second Seasons of Excavations, 1961-1962*. Atiqot 5, English Series. Jerusalem: Department of Antiquities, et al., 1966.

Beersheba I   Y. Aharoni. *Beer-sheba I: Excavations at Tel Beer-sheba, 1969-1971 Seasons*. Jerusalem: Tel Aviv University Institute of Archaeology, 1973.

Bethany   S. J. Saller. *Excavations at Bethany (1949-1953)*. Jerusalem: Franciscan, 1957.

Bethel   J. L. Kelso et al. *The Excavation of Bethel (1934-1960)*. Annual of the American Schools of Oriental Research 39. Cambridge, MA: American Schools of Oriental Research, 1968.

BMC   *British Museum Catalogue.*

BZ II   O. R. Sellers et al. *The 1957 Excavation at Beth-zur*. Annual of the American Schools of Oriental Research 38. Cambridge, MA: American Schools of Oriental Research, 1968.

CBZ   O. R. Sellers. *The Citadel of Beth-zur*. Philadelphia: Westminster Press, 1933.

CPP   J. G. Duncan. *Corpus of Palestinian Pottery*. London: British School of Archaeology in Egypt, 1930.

Ex. Gezer I-III   R. A. S. Macalister. *The Excavations of Gezer: 1902-1905 and 1907-1909*. 3 vols. London: John Murray, 1912.

Gerar   Wm. F. Petrie. *Gerar*. Publications of the British School of Archaeology in Egypt 43. London: British School of Archaeology in Egypt, 1928.

Gezer I   W. G. Dever, H. D. Lance, and G. E. Wright. *Gezer I: Preliminary Report of the 1964-66 Seasons*. Annual of the Hebrew Union College Biblical and Archaeological School in Jerusalem 1. Jerusalem: Keter, 1970.

Gezer II   W. G. Dever et al. *Gezer II: Report of the 1967-70 Seasons in Fields I and II*. Annual of the Hebrew Union College/Nelson Glueck School of Biblical Archaeology 2. Jerusalem: Keter, 1975.

Gibeon   J. B. Pritchard. *Winery, Defenses, and Soundings at Gibeon*. Museum Monographs. Philadelphia: University Museum, University of Pennsylvania, 1964.

Hazor I, II, III-IV   Y. Yadin et al. *Hazor I, II, III-IV*. 3 vols. Jerusalem: James A. de Rothschild Expedition at Hazor, 1958, 1960, 1961.

HE I, II   G. A. Reisner, C. S. Fischer, and D. G. Lyon. *Harvard Excavations at Samaria, 1908-1910*. 2 vols. Cambridge, MA: Harvard University, 1924.

JW   F. Josephus. *The Jewish War*. Trans. J. St. J. Thackeray. Cambridge, MA: Harvard University, 1950.

Lachish III   O. Tufnell. *Lachish III: The Iron Age*. London: Oxford University, 1953.

Lachish V   Y. Aharoni. *Investigations at Lachish: The Sanctuary and the Residency*. Tell Aviv: Gateway, 1975.

Meg. I   R. S. Lamon and G. M. Shipton. *Megiddo I: Seasons of 1925-34, Strata I-IV*. Oriental Institute Publications 42. Chicago: University of Chicago, 1939.

Meg. II	G. Loud. *Megiddo II: Seasons of 1935-39.* Oriental Institute Publications 62. Chicago: University of Chicago, 1948.
MT	P. L. O. Guy. *Megiddo Tombs.* Oriental Institute Publications 33. Chicago: University of Chicago, 1938.
PCC	P. W. Lapp. *Palestinian Ceramic Chronology, 200 B.C.—A.D. 70.* New Haven: American Schools of Oriental Research, 1961.
Revue Numism.	*Revue Numismatique.*
RR I	Y. Aharoni et al. *Excavations at Ramat Raḥel I: Seasons 1959 and 1960.* Serie archaeologica 2. Rome: Centro di studi semitici, 1962.
RR II	Y. Aharoni et al. *Excavations at Ramat Raḥel II: Seasons 1961 and 1962.* Serie archaeologica 6. Rome: Centro di studi semitici, 1964.
Shiloh	M-L. Bull and S. Holm-Nielson. *Shiloh: The Danish Excavations at Tell Sailūn, Palestine, in 1926, 1929, 1932 and 1963.* Copenhagen: National Museum of Denmark, 1969.
SS I	J. W. Crowfoot, K. M. Kenyon, and E. L. Sukenik. *The Buildings at Samaria.* Samaria-Sebaste 1. London: Palestine Exploration Fund, 1942.
SS II	J. W. and G. M. Crowfoot. *Early Ivories from Samaria.* Samaria-Sebaste 2. London: Palestine Exploration Fund, 1938.
SS III	J. W. Crowfoot, G. M. Crowfoot, and K. M. Kenyon. *The Objects from Samaria.* Samaria-Sebaste 3. London: Palestine Exploration Fund, 1957.
TBM I	W. F. Albright. *The Excavation of Tell Beit Mirsim, I: The Pottery of the First Three Campaigns.* Annual of the American Schools of Oriental Research 12 (1930-31). New Haven: American Schools of Oriental Research, 1932.
TBM II	W. F. Albright. *The Excavations of Tell Beit Mirsim, II: The Bronze Age.* Annual of the American Schools of Oriental Research 17 (1936-37). New Haven: American Schools of Oriental Research, 1938.
TBM III	W. F. Albright. *The Excavation of Tell Beit Mirsim, III: Iron Age.* Annual of the American Schools of Oriental Research 21-22 (1941-43). New Haven: American Schools of Oriental Research, 1943.
TDA I	H. J. Franken. *Excavations at Tell Deir ʿAllā; I, A Stratigraphical and Analytical Study of the Early Iron Age Pottery.* Documenta et monumenta orientis **antiqui** 16. Leiden: Brill, 1969.
TFL I	W. F. Albright. *Excavations and Results at Tell el-Fûl (Gibeah of Saul).* Annual of the American Schools of Oriental Research 4 (1922-23). New Haven: American Schools of Oriental Research, 1924.
TFL II	L. A. Sinclair. An Archaeological Study of Gibeah (Tell el-Fûl). Part 1 (Pp. 1-52) in *Annual of the American Schools of Oriental Research 34-35 (1954-56).* New Haven: American Schools of Oriental Research, 1960.
TN I	C. C. McCown. *Tell en-Naṣbeh, I: Archaeological and Historical Results.* Berkeley: Palestine Institute of Pacific School of Religion, 1947.
TN II	J. C. Wampler. *Tell en-Naṣbeh, II: The Pottery.* Berkeley: Palestine Institute of Pacific School of Religion, 1947.

Abbreviations used throughout text: C = Cistern; L = Locus; S = Silo. Ware descriptions refer to the *Munsell Soil Color Charts,* Baltimore: Munsell Color Company, 1971 edition. Abbreviations used: ext. = exterior; int. = interior; incl. = inclusions; ml = medium levigation; fl = fine levigation; ffl = fairly fine levigation; cl = coarse levigation.

TABLE OF THE CHRONOLOGY OF TELL EL-FÛL

Period	1964 Campaign	1933	1922
I Iron I A	1200 - 1150 B.C. (pre-Fortress)	ca. 1100 B.C. (pre-Fortress)	end 13th cen. B.C. to end 12th cen. B.C. (Fortress I)
II Iron I C	1025 B.C. to 950 B.C. (Fortress I & II)	1020-1000 B.C. (Fortress I) 1000-990 B.C. (Fortress II)	ca. 1030 B.C. to David/Solomon (Fortress II)
III Late Iron II	ca. 700 B.C. (Mid-Field silo deposits; Fortress III A?) 650-587 B.C.　　　Phase A (Fortress III B)	8th cen. B.C. (Fortress III A) 7th cen.-597 B.C. (Fortress III B)	ca. 900-800 B.C. (Fortress III A) ca. 800-733 B.C. (Fortress III B) 7th cen. B.C.
Exilic	587-538 B.C.　　　Phase B		
			through
IV		350 - 200 B.C. (Fortress IV)	
Late Hellenistic	175-135 B.C.　　　Phase A 135-100 B.C.　　　Phase B 100-63 B.C.　　　Phase C		2nd cen. B.C. (Fortress IV)
V Early Roman	ca. A.D. 70	1st cen. B.C. through 1st cen. A.D.	Early Roman

Chapter 1

Previous Excavations at Tell el-Fûl:
A Survey of Research and Exploration

John A. Graham

Location and Description of the Site

The Nablus Road traverses the western slope of Tell el-Fûl 5 km (just under 3 miles) north of the Damascus Gate in Jerusalem. While Tell el-Fûl is part of the ridge which becomes Mt. Scopus and the Mt. of Olives to the south, the mound is rather isolated, with no other comparable promontories close by (see plan 3).

From the watershed plateau which extends from Shafat northward to Ramallah, Tell el-Fûl rises to a respectable elevation of 862 m above sea level.[1] The magnificent view from the top in all directions suggests that this has been a key to Tell el-Fûl's strategic location. To the southeast, the Dead Sea is visible on a clear day, although the Jordan Valley is blocked by Tell ꜥAsur to the east. The view northeast toward Jebaꜥ and Mukhmas is extensive. The higher Ramallah ridge to the northwest limits visual range in that direction. The famous landmark, Nabi Samwîl, lies to the northwest. The deep Wâdī Beit Hannînā winds to the southwest, dropping some 2500 feet to the Mediterranean, 36 air miles away. Tell el-Fûl has an impressively commanding view of Jerusalem sprawled over the hillsides to the south, although the Old City itself is obscured by the Shafat ridge. Thus, it is easy to understand why the mound has played a strategic military role in the defense of Jerusalem in some periods of history.[2]

Tell el-Fûl is situated on the crest of the watershed, with deep wadis cutting toward the east and west to create a spine with narrow ribs. With the slopes of many of the wadis being 30° and more, north-south travel is extremely difficult except along the spine. As it is today, the ancient north road from Jerusalem went along the base of Tell el-Fûl and north along the crest of the watershed. With its command over the main north-south route of central Palestine, the site has had a doubly-prestigious position.

The mound itself rises roughly 100 feet. Its terraced slopes are quite steep in the east, north, and west sides (fig. 2); there is a more gradual slope to the south (plan 2; pls. 1a-b). The relatively level top surface is approximately 150 m north-south and 90 m east-west (cf. pl. 1d). The northwest corner is the highest part of the mound. A number of geographical formations in the immediate vicinity of Tell el-Fûl are shown in plan 3 as recorded by William F. Albright in the publication of his first excavation at the site in the early 1920's (*TFL I*: 2). The mound is bounded on the northeast by a field called Merj el-Qonbar, which deepens as one goes east into the Karm Abû Rîšeh (or Šiꜥb, Ḥallet) and eventually becomes the Wâdî Zimrī. Tell el-Fûl is similarly bounded on the south by the Wâdî Abû Zureig which deepens on the east to become the Wâdî ꜥAnâtā.

A strong Mediterranean wind has left only a thin layer of topsoil on the mound to cover the thick layer of whitish clay *ḥuwar* that comprises the hill. *Ḥuwar*, a calcareous marl, is a geologically late limestone deposit in Palestine and quite common to Judean hills. It is soft, enabling the easy hewing out of silos and pits but too porous to hold water and serve for cisterns. The *ḥuwar* does support a meager crop of wheat, as one may usually observe on the southeastern slope of the mound, but Albright notes that it is not suitable for grain or deciduous trees. It does support coniferous trees quite well. As the first fortress of Gibeah made use of coniferous trees, Albright has suggested that the site may have supported these trees at the beginning of the 1st millennium B.C.[3]

The name, "Tell el-Fûl," is related to the vegetation that supposedly flourished on the site. It means "Mound of Horse-Beans," a name given because the marly soil of this mound was particularly suited for the cultivation of this kind of bean.[4] Obviously, it is not strictly a "tell," since the layers of occupation are relatively shallow on the natural hill.

Tell el-Fûl is located along the Judah-Gilead anticlinal axis and just west of two major geological faults along the Dead Sea. These faults are part of the great rift created by the collapse of the Afro-Arabian platform. Since excavations were begun on the site, there have been two substantial earthquakes, one on July 11, 1927 (when Tell el-Fûl experienced an intensity of 9 on a 10-point scale), and another on September 13, 1954, leaving behind collapsed walls.

All of these factors have played a significant role in the occupational history of Tell el-Fûl. It saw no permanent settlement until the beginning of the Iron Age. While the site was easily defensible and it enjoyed a strategic command over the surrounding area, its occupation was limited by the availability of water (annual rainfall is 20-24 inches and there are no springs on the hill itself), the supply of building materials (*mizzī* stones, more suitable for building, were quarried from nearby ridges), the suitability of the climate (the west wind makes the site cool in the summer and bitterly cold in winter), and the availability of living space and food supply. While Tell el-Fûl was on the main trade route, its own commercial contribution was apparently minimal, although the many silos, channels, and basins which have been unearthed do suggest industrial activity. The population size and occupied area of this ancient city are not known, as ruins and any occupational remains have disappeared through wind erosion and recent urban expansion near the site. If the city had achieved really significant size, there would probably be some indication of this; yet, the lack of such does not reduce the importance of this site for archeologists today.

Early Exploration of Tell el-Fûl

Tell el-Fûl captured the curiosity of Palestine's earliest modern explorers, geographers, and archeologists. On May 15, 1838, Edward Robinson, in the course of his survey of the ancient remains of Palestine, visited Tell el-Fûl. He spent a half hour on the mound, and writes (1874: 577):

> We now left the road again, in order to pass over the high Tell on the left, called Tuleil el-Fûl, "Hill of Beans," six or eight minutes from the path, with a large heap of stones upon it. We reached the top at 11 o'clock. There seems to have been here originally a square tower, fifty-six feet by forty-eight, built of large unhewn stones and apparently ancient; this has been thrown down, and the stones and rubbish falling outside, have assumed the form of a large pyramidal mound. No trace of other foundations is to be seen. The spot is sightly and commands a very extensive view of the country in all directions, especially towards the east; in this respect it is second only to Neby Samwîl.

The square tower that Robinson observed was the fortress which Albright excavated in 1921.

Thirty years later, Tell el-Fûl withstood its first archeological assault. Charles Warren interrupted his work at Robinson's Arch excavations in Jerusalem to send a group of laborers to Tell el-Fûl for a period of two weeks in May of 1868. Only a very brief description of his work appeared (Warren 1869-70: 66):

> Tuleil el-Fûl (Hill of Beans). — Generally regarded as Gibeah-of-Saul, is a rounded hill with a mound on the top, through which walls appear on the east and west. Excavations were made from north to south to determine the nature of these ruins, which were found to consist of the foundations of a rectangular tower (forty-eight feet by fifty-seven) with a berm

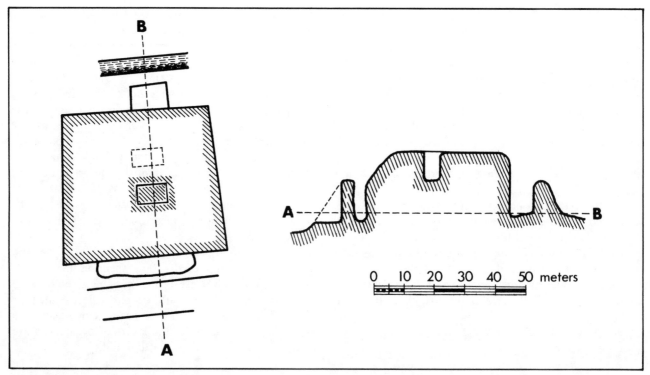

Fig. 1. Plans of Warren's Fortress excavations.

nine feet wide and a second exterior wall; this latter has to the north a similar batter to that at the Jaffa Gate Tower. The walls were composed of roughly-squared stones and of rubble. In the centre of the town [*sic*, probably tower] there is a shaft seven feet square with masonry sides, and at the depth of twenty eight feet a stone with a circular opening in it about eighteen inches in diameter, which is an entrance to a small cavity scooped out of the natural soil (marl); cavity three feet nine inches high and four feet in diameter. The walls in each case were bared below the foundation, and were found to rest on the marl. Some pieces of hard wood were found sticking in the walls at a depth of twelve feet. A sketch plan and section is forwarded.

Warren's plans were published by Conder and Kitchener (1883: 159) and are reproduced here in fig. 1. Judging from what he found when he excavated the fortress in 1922, Albright believes that Warren dug trenches along the north and south sides and sank a small pit on the summit; however, he did not penetrate more than 3 m into the little mound and did not reach the remains of the third fortress (*TFL I*: 3). The shaft with masonry sides, having what is obviously a silo at the bottom, appears to be part of Albright's Room A of the fortress; yet this silo does not appear on later top plans. Warren claims to have excavated to bedrock and reports that he found hard wood sticking out from the walls at a depth of 12 feet; he seems to have dug deeper than Albright realized. Nevertheless, Albright's judgment stands: that Charles Warren "did not prosecute his operations long enough to do any serious damage" (*TFL I*: 3).

When C. R. Conder visited Tell el-Fûl on December 14, 1874, he noted the excavations carried out there some six years earlier (1883: 158-59): there was

a building 30 feet high, measuring 50 feet east and west, by 46 feet north and south at the top, the walls being sheer, and a cross wall running through the middle east and west. The building is not rectangular. There appears to have been two chambers in the top, each 10 feet by 6 feet, and 9 feet deep.

On the north and south there are two lower outer walls which have a sloping outer revetment. The monument measures therefore 71 feet north and south at the bottom, but on the east and west there are no outer walls. Possibly flights of steps may have led up on these sides. The slope of the revetment is about 60°.

The whole of the walls, which are 7 or 8 feet thick and 15 feet high, including revetment, are composed of stones of good size, rudely hewn and undressed. The joints are packed with smaller stones. Some of the corner stones are not squared. The stones in the scarp are slanted, so as to form the sloping face. The masonry resembles some of that used by the Crusaders. The face-stones are set in mortar.

Albright notes that Conder's measurements are inexact and the dimensions of the northern chambers of the fortress correspond only vaguely to what he found (*TFL I*: 3). Warren's reference to the tower's similarity to the Jaffa Gate Tower and Conder's conjecture that

the tower at Tell el-Fûl was "Crusading" were errors that were perpetuated for decades and contributed substantially to the confusion and debate over the ancient identity of the site.

The 19th- and Early 20th-Century Debate Over the Location of Gibeah

After Conder's visit to the site in 1874, subsequent visits by scholars were almost completely related to the question of what ancient city had once existed there. Lively debate over the location of Gibeah of Saul waged for over 80 years, the matter being largely settled with the publication of Albright's excavation in 1924 (*TFL I*: 3). Since the linking of the fortress and related artifacts to a historical place and person (such as Gibeah of Saul) has had an important place in biblical studies, the debate over the identification of Gibeah is worth recounting.

In the first edition of his *Biblical Researches*, in 1841, Edward Robinson identified Gibeah with modern Jeba[c] (fig. 2). The fact that Gibeah is the feminine form of Geba, coupled with the certainty that the two sites are only 6 km apart, has complicated the identity of both sites. Furthermore, there are several passages in the Old Testament where the context demands that Gibeah be changed to Geba and vice versa (*TFL I*: 31). Thus, Robinson's identifying Gibeah with Geba was problematical.

It was in a review of *Biblical Researches* in 1843 that a young theologian at Calov in Württemberg, a Mr. Gross, won the distinction of first identifying Tell el-Fûl as the site of ancient Gibeah (Gross 1843: 1082). Gross took the position that Gibeah must have been south of Ramah (modern er-Ram) and Geba (modern Jeba[c]; fig. 2). He elaborated his argument in a letter to Edward Robinson, finding most support from Judg 19:11-14: "we find named in succession, on the great road from south to north, Jerusalem, Gibeah, and Ramah. The Levite does not reach Ramah, but only Gibeah; which therefore lay on the great road between Jerusalem and Ramah" (Robinson 1844: 599). According to Robinson, Gross also placed considerable stock in the order of names of cities, such as Isa 10:28-32, seeing geographical significance in their sequence — a practice which Robinson called into serious question (1844: 599).

The letter from Gross persuaded Robinson to change his mind. In an article in *Bibliotheca Sacra* in 1844 (598-602) and in the second edition of the *Biblical Researches* in 1856 (577-79) Robinson advanced what he saw to be an even more convincing argument for situating Gibeah at Tell el-Fûl based on the evidence of a passage in Jerome and Josephus. Jerome, in narrating the journey of Paula, describes her journeying to Jerusalem by way of Lower and Upper Beth-horon; on her right side she sees [c]Ajâlon and Gibeon.

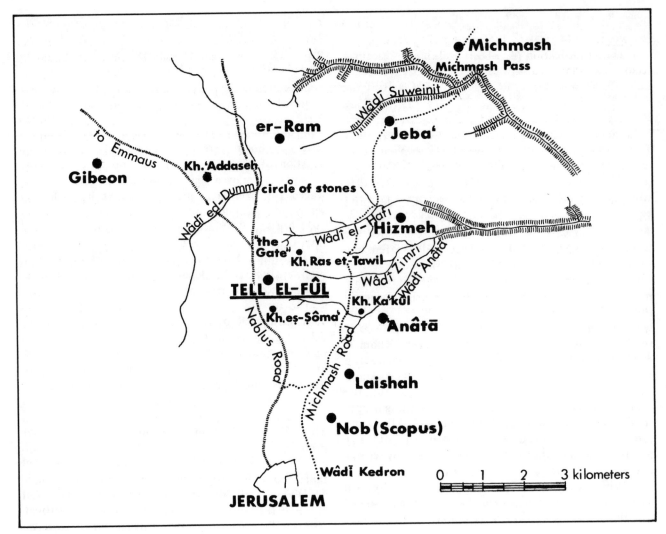

Fig. 2. Map of sites near Tell el-Fûl.

She stops a little at Gabaa (Gibeah), then leveled to the ground, remembering the ancient crime and the concubine cut in pieces; then leaving the mausoleum of Helena on her left, she enters Jerusalem (Robinson 1844: 600). This account would place Gibeah along the road between Gibeon and Jerusalem, and Tell el-Fûl is the only suitable candidate, Jebaᶜ being much too far northeast out of the way.

Josephus has two references to Gibeah. In *Antiquities of the Jews*, which relates the story of the Levite and his concubine, the Levite was unwilling to remain in Jerusalem but chose to go 20 stadia farther to lodge in a town belonging to his countrymen; he lodged at Gibeah. Robinson finds this reference to 20 stadia inexact, reading it as "some 20 stadia further" from where he was (Robinson 1844: 600). The other passage in Josephus is more explicit. His description of the march of Titus from Samaria to besiege Jerusalem is as follows (*JW* 5.2.1 §§50-52):

Leading his army forward in this orderly array, according to Roman usage, Titus advanced through Samaria to Gophna, previously captured by his father and now garrisoned. After resting here one night he set forward at dawn, and at the end of a full day's march encamped in the valley which is called by the Jews in their native tongue "Valley of Thorns," close to a village named Gabath Saul, which means "Saul's Hill," at a distance of about thirty furlongs from Jerusalem. From here, with some six hundred horsemen, he rode forward to reconnoiter the city's strength and to test the mettle of the Jews. . . .

A translator's note suggests that the "Valley of Thorns" may be the Wâdī Suweinît, which means "valley of the little acacias" (Thackeray 1927 [*JW*]: 216). The Wâdī Suweinît is several miles northeast of Tell el-Fûl. Judging that it was the Roman encampment that was 30 stadia away from Jerusalem and only a short distance from "Gabath Saul," the only hill (*lophos*) that would qualify as the place of Gibeah is Tell el-Fûl (Robinson 1844: 600-1; 1856 and 1874: 578).

The identification of Gibeah as Tell el-Fûl seemed secure. In 1858, Valentiner independently proposed that Gibeah was Tell el-Fûl; this was followed by the same affirmation by Guerin in 1874 (*TFL I*: 28). However, several years later Conder resurrected some old arguments, again suggesting that Gibeah was really Jeba[c]. The Arabic *fûl*, he reasoned, is preserved in the name "ophel," meaning "bean hill"; thus, Tell el-Fûl is probably the site of Ophni of Benjamin (1877: 104). Conder went on to say that Jeba[c] was a much better candidate for Gibeah because 1) Tell el-Fûl was only 22 stadia from Jerusalem; 2) the feminine form Gibeah likely refers to the country around Jeba[c] (Geba) — hence "Gibeah of the fields" in Judg 20:31; 3) the watchmen of Gibeah (1 Sam 14:16) could see and hear the sound of battle at Michmash across the Wâdī Suweinît (Tell el-Fûl would be too far away to see and hear); 4) there is a reference in Judg 20:33 to a large cave, but there is no cave at Tell el-Fûl as there is at Jeba[c] (1877: 104-5).

In the same issue of the *Palestine Exploration Fund Quarterly Statement*, W. F. Birch rebutted Conder's assertions, pointing out that in Josephus, 30 stadia referred to the place of the Roman encampment and that Jeba[c] was too far away from the main road to be Titus' campsite (1877: 204-5). Four years later, Conder retorted that "Tell el-Fûl is an isolated monument (probably a beacon) and not a city at all." Birch then changed his mind and proposed that Gibeah was actually situated at Khirbet [c]Addâseh (*TFL I*: 29),[5] a position that he doggedly held for the next 30 years.

The debate gathered momentum in 1911, when Birch again argued passionately that Khirbet [c]Addâseh (fig. 2) was the site of Gibeah. He set forth two basic "proofs" for his position. The first was based on the Levite bound for Shiloh in Judg 19:14. If from the north road the Levite saw the sun set beside Gibeah, then Gibeah would have to be west of the road, and Khirbet [c]Addâseh was the only hill near the Wâdī ed-Dumm that could qualify.[6] Second, Birch felt that Titus' camp was in the Wâdī ed-Dumm, 30 stadia from Jerusalem. The massacre of the Benjamites occurred in a "hollow place" — for which the Wâdī ed-Dumm best qualifies (1911: 107).[7]

To settle the Gibeah debate (Tell el-Fûl vs. Khirbet [c]Addâseh), Duncan Mackenzie visited both sites on February 10, 1911. His survey at Tell el-Fûl led him to conclude that ". . . the fort on top . . . could not by any possibility be Crusading, and that it had every appearance of being an early Jewish fort. Much of the pottery was characteristically Jewish" (1911: 98).[8] From his visit to Khirbet [c]Addâseh, he said, "The inevitable conclusion was that [c]Addâseh could not possibly be

Gibeah, for the very simple reason that, as far as the data were concerned, *it was not a pre-Christian site*. There was nothing earlier than Byzantine at [c]Addâseh" (1911: 99). This marked the first helpful archeological contribution to the discussion. E. W. G. Masterman followed up with a visit to both sites and concluded, after sinking a trial pit to bedrock, that Khirbet [c]Addâseh contained nothing except Roman pottery; Tell el-Fûl, he reaffirmed, had a great quantity of pottery belonging to the Hebrew period (1914: 118).

Clearly, Tell el-Fûl had become the accepted site for Gibeah of Saul, with support particularly from the German school. There were proposals that Gibeah should be located elsewhere (*TFL I*: 29-30; Birch 1911: 107), but for the most part these gained very little credence. It was in the wake of these later discussions that Gustaf H. Dalman approached William F. Albright of the American Schools of Oriental Research and urged him to excavate at Tell el-Fûl in order to provide more substance for the discussion of the identification of the site.

W. F. Albright's Excavation of the Fortress: The Campaigns of 1922-23 and 1933

The rather crude excavations carried on at Tell el-Fûl by Charles Warren in 1868 give the site the distinction of being one of the first in Palestine to be excavated. The turn of the century saw some slight maturation in archeological method with some refinement in chronology. Acknowledging his indebtedness to the German school for their advancement in topographic method, W. F. Albright directed an initial campaign at Tell el-Fûl in 1922-23. His prompt publication of the excavation results in the 1924 *Annual of the American Schools of Oriental Research* marks a respectable contribution in topographical and geographical discussions as well as archeological method and ceramic dating evidence, particularly in view of the fact that the site is not a large one.

Operating from a budget of $1100, Albright began excavating on top of the mound in March of 1922. He ran into immediate difficulty over the land negotiations with the 36 shareholders who had control over the mound. In a suit against the Director, some troublesome landowners were asking 400 pounds Egyptian for the poor land around the fortress; the government finally fixed the figure at 7 pounds Egyptian (*TFL I*: 4-5).

Excavations were carried on over a 17-month period from March, 1922, through August, 1923, although Albright reports that there were actually only about 40 digging days during this period (*TFL I*: 6), employing an average of 40 regular workers, mostly from the nearby village of Beit Hannînā.

Work was concentrated on the tumulus on the summit, i.e., the fortress ruins. Albright began by running five trenches radially from the fortress; after several days of digging, he had determined the parameters of the fortress. A trial trench indicated that an earlier fortress lay under the top one, Fortress IV (*TFL I*: 5). The excavation from July 27 to September 2, 1922, proved to be the most extensive and concentrated effort of the first campaign. Albright began by clearing the fortress and digging some trenches around the late Iron II glacis. By the end of July he had removed the remains of the fourth fortress (Hellenistic), and in the early part of August, he had removed much of the debris from the third fortress (Iron II). He left substantial walls of the fortresses standing. Next Albright began to remove some of the remains of the second fortress and by the end of August he had uncovered some of the first fortress. He reports (*TFL I*: 6) that the intermittent digging in November and in the spring of 1923 brought further work on the first fortress. Two final weeks in August of 1923 were spent "clearing up obscure points" (*TFL I*: 6).

In a glowing review of the excavation report (*TFL I*), E. W. G. Masterman noted that Albright's work "may be said to have settled the question" of the identity of the site (1925: 46). But the discovery of the successive fortresses raised new questions about their history and what else was to be found at Tell el-Fûl. The plans of the earliest fortresses were still rather obscure, partly because Albright had left many of the walls of later periods standing. The severe earthquake of 1927 toppled many of these, making further exploration into the remaining walls of the earlier periods possible and desirable. Continuing refinement of ceramic chronology invited reevaluation of the findings of the first campaign. Consequently, Albright returned to Tell el-Fûl for a second campaign of digging in September of 1933. Three goals established for the work were: 1) clearance of half of the outside of the fortress; 2) excavation of the untouched earth left in the inside of the fortress; and 3) examination of the eastern edge of the hill (Albright 1933: 6). The 1933 campaign lasted about a month, with an average work force of 60 laborers. Unlike the first campaign, the 1933 season saw several decades before the final report was published. All the records of the 1933 excavation were made available to a graduate student of Albright's at Johns Hopkins University, Lawrence A. Sinclair, who worked them into a dissertation in 1959 and published this in 1960 (*TFL II*). Sinclair also published a summary article of the 1933 campaign in *The Biblical Archaeologist* (1964: 52-64).

The discoveries of the first and second campaigns will be reviewed as a unit, since the 1933 season represents largely a clarification and revision of the 1922-23 excavation. Frequent reference will be made to the chronological table (p. xvii) outlining the occupational chronology developed from the respective excavations. It graphically indicates the changing interpretation of the discoveries as well as the refinement of a constructed chronology based on new evidence.

Prefatory to the discussion of the findings of Albright's two campaigns, it is useful to review the terminology used for the types of rock found at the site or used in the buildings at Tell el-Fûl:

ḥuwar   a calcareous limestone, having the consistency of clay or hard earth, and too soft to serve as building material.

nârī   a dull, white limestone, refractory to fire (i.e., capable of withstanding heat), tends to split, soft for carving silos, does not hold water, used in the building of Fortress I.

melekī   a harder limestone, easily hewn and carved (often into door sockets), not so brittle, soft when first dug up but hardens as it dries out, imported to Tell el-Fûl, quarried near Beit Hannînā and er-Ram, used in the building of Fortresses III and IV.

mizzī   a local hard limestone, brittle, used in Fortress II.

sûwan   a hard flint, used in making tools.

Period I: The Pre-Fortress Remains

It is shown in the chronological table (p. xvii) that initially Albright dated the first fortress in the Iron IA period, but after the 1933 campaign, he dated it to the time of Saul, ca. 1020 B.C. In this reinterpretation, a new awareness of a pre-fortress occupation of the site emerged. From a very few maceheads and potsherds, Sinclair (*TFL II*: 11) judged that the earliest occupation at Tell el-Fûl was Middle Bronze; there are no building remains and no further descriptions of the evidence or conclusions drawn about the Middle Bronze occupation.

Substantially more evidence for a 12th-century occupation was unearthed. The building of the fortress and the housing on the eastern edge of the mound destroyed most of the pre-fortress evidence, except what could be found in pockets in the bedrock. It is possible that some of the silos were cut in this period, but they were reused in later periods, rendering a date for most of them impossible. A summary of the pre-fortress evidence uncovered by Albright is as follows:

(1) the stone installation in Room A of the fortress (*TFL II*: 11; pls. 28, 30, 32);

(2) the diagonal wall (running NE to SW in Room F) (*TFL I*: 77; pl. 22);

(3) the north-south wall at the west of Room H (*TFL I*: 77; pl. 22); this is never discussed, except

possibly where Albright refers to "walls under the citadel foundations to the north and northeast of the tower" (1933: 7);

(4) "a few fragmentary remains of housewalls" (*TFL II*: 11), unmapped; these are associated with potsherds, particularly collar-rim storage jar fragments (*TFL II*: 16);

(5) a rubble wall in Room A, west of the stone installation (*TFL II*: 11), unmapped;

(6) ash destruction in Rooms B (North) and B (South) (*TFL II*: 10).

Fig. 3 is a reconstruction of the pre-fortress remains, relying on *TFL I* for the wall plans and *TFL II* for the plan of the stone installation.

The only evidence of the pre-fortress period discussed in the publications is the stone installation in Room A. In fig. 3, "a" is identified as "rock terrace" by Sinclair (*TFL II*: 11) and is almost certainly bedrock. In a kind of niche that is 40 cm deep, stones "b," "c," "d," and "e" are placed end to end, with probably another stone to the east of "b"; these stones vary from 35 to 70 cm in height. They are around the lip of a shallow basin 90 x 100 cm and 20 cm deep. Stone "e" lies under the north wall of Room A, and the southeast

edge of the cut bedrock extends under the south wall of Room A. In an attempt to explain the function of this installation, Sinclair suggests that it may have been a grave cleaned out before the fortress construction, although it is curious that the stones were not disturbed or removed in such a clearing. The installation remains enigmatic.

Period II: Fortresses I and II

The 1933 campaign distinguished a pre-fortress period and redated the first fortress to the last decades of the 11th century, attributing it to King Saul. In the relatively short 30-year duration assigned to Period II, Albright and Sinclair distinguish two separate fortresses; furthermore, Fortress II underwent a rebuilding phase. The plans of the two fortresses are rather complicated, and the differentiating characteristics of the fortresses and phases will be set forth in as much detail as possible.

The Period II, Fortress I evidence is summarized as follows:

(1) the fortress walls and tower of rubble masonry as seen in fig. 4; the tower is not bonded to the main fortress walls;

Fig. 3. Plan of Period I remains from the 1922 and 1933 campaigns. Cf. *TFL I*: pl. 22; *TFL II*: pl. 32.

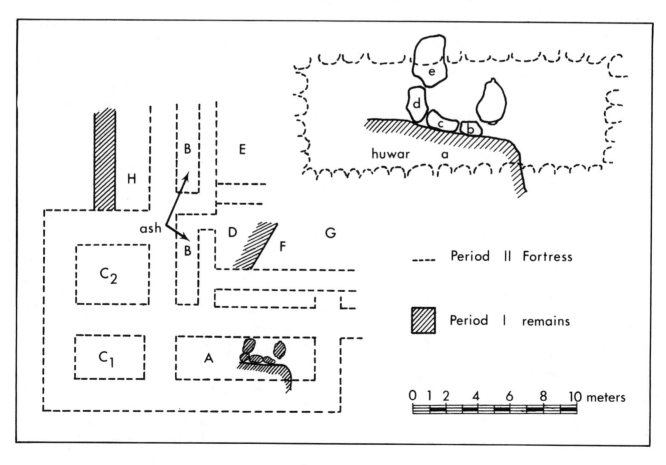

(2) the partition wall in Room A, the west side of which is faced (*TFL II*: 11, pl. 3);

(3) an apparent floor level above the stone installation in Room A, although this is not designated in any plans or sections;

(4) a doorway, 85 cm wide, leading into Room B (South) (*TFL I*: 8);

(5) possibly many of the silos were cut during this period; note especially the silo in Room B (North) (*TFL II*: pl. 28);

(6) pottery of fine quality and diversity: cooking pots (slanted, rounded, and concave rims), hand-burnished saucers and bowls, jugs, ring and disc bases, some painted pottery (one white Painted I Cypriote import), handles (bar-handles, ridged, and knob), black burnished juglet; objects: spinning whorls, bone scrapers, two bronze arrowheads, sling stones, whetstone, and an iron plow tip (from Room A) (*TFL I*: 9-17; *TFL II*: chap. 3, pp. 46-47);

(7) a substantial amount of destruction containing pine and cypress ash, likely part of a second story (*TFL I*: 7).

As can be seen in fig. 4, Fortress I has a main outer wall that is generally 1.20 m thick and an inner wall that is a narrower 1.00 m thick. The meter-wide interstice between these walls forms several small rooms, notably B (North) and B (South). The tower walls are considerably thicker: 2.00 m (*TFL II*: 11) to 2.15 m (Albright 1933: 7). The south wall of the tower is 17.80 m long and the west wall 11.60 m. Two partition walls abut the corner of the fortress wall, creating three rooms in the tower, A, C_1, and C_2. The outer walls and tower walls were preserved to a height of 1.80 to 2.20 m, while the inner walls remained about 1 m high.

Fig. 4. Plan of Fortress I. Cf. *TFL I*: pl. 22.

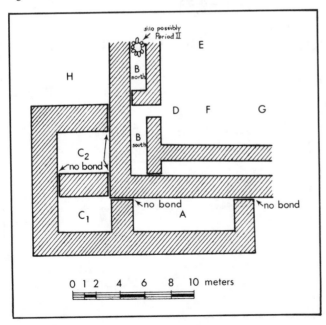

Fortress I was made of large rubble masonry. *Mizzī* and *nārī* blocks, in roughly equal proportions (*TFL I*: 9), were laid in horizontal courses, with small stones in the interstices between the stones. Albright gives the representative size of these blocks as 70 x 30 cm, 65 x 45 cm, and 45 x 35 cm (*TFL I*: 7). One of the more significant aspects of Fortress I is that the tower is not bonded to the outer wall of the fortress. There are straight joints where the east and west walls of Room A meet the north wall and the north walls of Rooms C_1 and C_2 meet the outer wall of the fortress. As Sinclair points out (*TFL II*: 11), the tower was apparently constructed after the main building was completed, yet as part of the original plan.

The most controversial aspect of Albright's interpretation of Fortresses I and II concerns his reconstruction of a major citadel (Albright 1933: 8) of which the tower in fig. 4 is the southeast corner. Sinclair only notes that the citadel was a casemate and repeats Albright's reasoning for the dimensions of the whole fortress (*TFL II*: 12). That reasoning depends primarily upon the contours of the hill and length of the towers. Assuming that the length of the fortress lay in an east-west direction, the maximum length was set at 65 m because the edge of the mound dropped sharply beyond that point. It was assumed that the distance between the southern towers would be at least as great as the length of the south wall of the tower, that is, almost 18 m; thus the minimum length would be about 52 m. From this, the fortress was reconstructed as shown in fig. 5 (Albright 1933: 7-8).

Fortress I ended in destruction. The excavator found a layer of ash 20-50 cm thick in Rooms B, D, E, F, G, and H. In the tower rooms, A, C_1, and C_2, there was as much as 2 m of burn debris. The large amount of ash and carbonized material indicated considerable wood construction. Analysis of these cinders by John Dinsmore showed them to be carbonized cypress and pine (*TFL I*: 7). The conclusion was that the tower was composed of at least two stories (Sinclair, *TFL II*: 14, suggests possibly a third) made of timber cut from cypress and scrub pine forests in the vicinity of the mound.

Fortress II is a rebuilding of the destroyed first fortress. It was the most elaborate and carefully constructed of all the fortifications at Tell el-Fûl. Albright even noticed an improvement in the quality of the pottery with the second fortress (*TFL I*: 8). The rebuilding (fig. 6) closely followed the plan of Fortress I, with its walls resting on the walls of the former fortress, yet with significant difference in construction technique.

The Period II, Fortress II evidence is summarized as follows:

(1) rebuilding of fortress walls using the walls of the first fortress as foundations (*TFL II*: 14);

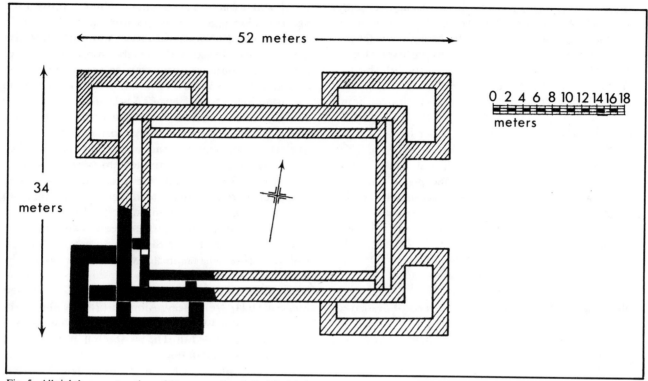

Fig. 5. Albright's reconstruction of Fortresses I and II. Cf. Albright 1933: 7.

(2) dressed masonry blocks smaller than those of Fortress I, made mostly of *mizzī* stone and laid in courses (*TFL I*: 9; Albright 1933: 10; *TFL II*: 14, 15);

(3) two building phases (*TFL I*: 8-9):
   IIA - doorway in northeast corner of Room B (South) sealed shut with masonry (*TFL II*: 15); stairs to a second story constructed east of the doorway; collapse of stairway;
   IIB - retaining wall built against the debris of II A; platform built over the steps and debris masonry platform built between Rooms F and G;

(4) tower bonded to the main fortress wall, yet there are straight joints in the middle of two of the tower walls (*TFL II*: 14-15);

(5) ten apertures through the tower walls allowing light and air to filter into the cellar rooms (*TFL I*: 9);

(6) no ceramic distinction between the two phases and the two fortresses (but cf. *TFL I*: 8);

(7) no destruction evidence of Fortress II (*TFL I*: 9).

As in Fortress I, Fortress II appears to be constructed according to the casemate principle (*TFL II*: 12), with Rooms B (North) and B (South) serving as narrow chambers between the inner and outer walls of the casemate, as well as the undesignated chamber north of Room A.

There is a discrepancy reported in the thickness of the fortress walls, but it seems likely that the outer wall

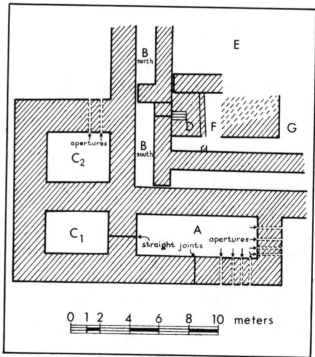

Fig. 6. Plan of Fortress II. Cf. *TFL I*: pl. 22.

was about 1.60 m and the inner wall ca. 1.20 m.[9] The other dimensions given for Fortress I seem to be the same as for Fortress II.

The masonry of Fortress II is considerably better than that of Fortress I. The stones are usually about half the size of those used in the earlier fortress; they are hammer dressed and laid in courses. Fig. 7 illustrates the masonry characteristic of the two fortresses. The most curious feature is the straight joints. The Fortress I tower formed straight joints where it abutted the outer wall of the main fortress wall. In contrast, the Fortress II tower is bonded into the main fortress wall, so that they are one unit. Yet, right in the middle of the south and west walls of Room A (*TFL I*: figs. 8, 9, 11) and possibly the east wall as well, there are straight vertical joints. (Sinclair designates pl. 33A as the "inside face of the east wall of Room A" although the top plans do not indicate a straight joint there.) Sinclair (*TFL II*: 14) notes that these are quite uncommon in Palestinian architecture, and we can only guess as to their function. Perhaps they were to prevent the main fortress wall from collapsing if the tower wall was breached or destroyed.

Fortress II may be divided into two phases, the second representing a minor repair and alteration of the first. This is seen in the interior of the fortress (cf. fig. 8). In Fortress I, there was a doorway in the north end of Room B (South). In Phase A of Fortress II, this doorway was sealed shut. In Room D, just east of Room B (South), a stairway was constructed — ostensibly to a second floor. The steps were of stone, 1 m wide and 25 cm high (*TFL I*: 8-9). The stairway collapsed along with other rubble from Fortress II, Phase A. Phase B is the hasty repair of this collapse. The stairs (two steps and part of a third were unearthed by Albright) were left where they had fallen along with the other Phase A debris. A retaining wall was constructed in a north-south direction in Room F to hold back the debris. A masonry platform was then constructed on top of the Phase A steps and debris. A similar platform was constructed between Rooms F and G, with a narrow, meter-wide passageway on the west, south, and possibly east sides. Almost no description of these platforms is given, and their function is far from clear. Albright (*TFL I*: 9) thought they connected with the upper story, although any lower story was filled in. The passageway was either for communication or storage.

Another interesting feature of the second fortress was the apertures that let air and light into the interior rooms of the tower. There were four square apertures in the east wall of Room A; and in the south wall of that room, there were four more, partly square and partly triangular. Two more triangular apertures, in the north wall of Room C_2, are reconstructed in fig. 9 from the photographs. Albright notes that these apertures are generally 20-25 cm wide and 35-50 cm high. Sinclair (*TFL II*: 14) mistakenly relates the apertures to the first fortress and says that they are on the east, south, and west sides. The plans and Albright's description show no apertures on the west, and Albright's more elaborate descriptions and photographs clearly indicate that the apertures are part of Fortress II (see especially *TFL I*: figs. 10, 12).

The second fortress was not destroyed by fire. Its massive walls were left standing to a height as much as 3 m (*TFL I*: 9). In places, the walls were dismantled and the masonry reused in other buildings. It fell into disuse sometime during the reign of David or Solomon.

Fig. 7. The masonry of Fortresses I and II. Cf. *TFL II*: pl. 33A.

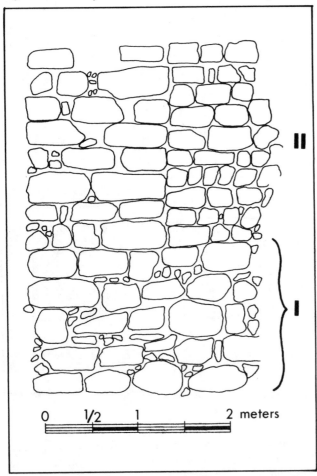

Fig. 8. Reconstructed top plan of Fortress II.

Fig. 9. Reconstructed section along x-y of fig. 8. Cf. *TFL I*: 8-9, figs. 10, 12-14; *TFL II*: 14, pl. 6.

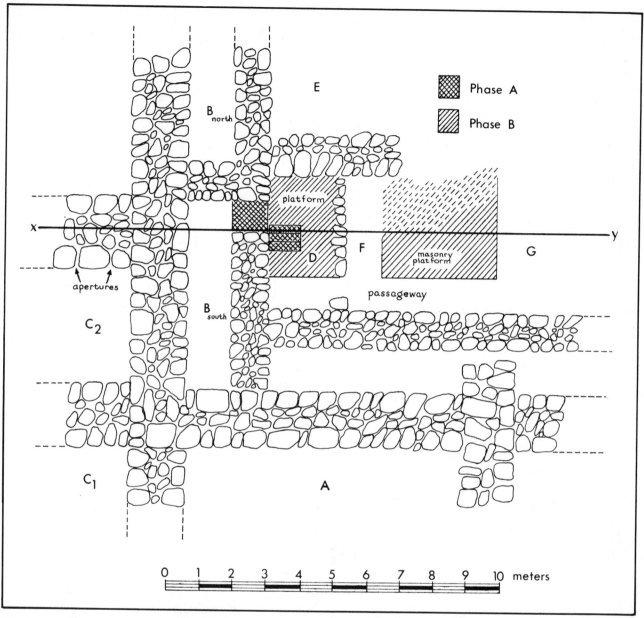

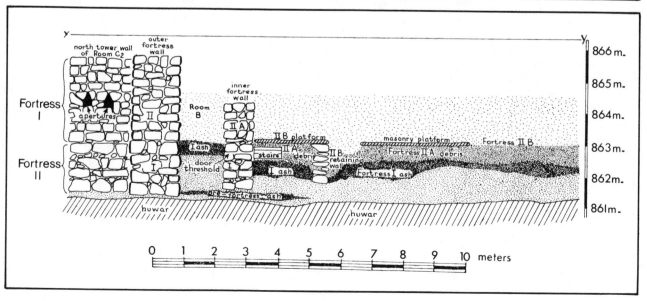

Period III: Fortress III

Almost three centuries passed before the site was again occupied and fortified. The date of the third period of occupation underwent substantial modification with each season of excavation (see the chronological table). In 1922, Albright judged that the third fortress was built about 900 B.C. and sustained destruction about 800 B.C.; a second phase of the third fortress dated to the 8th century, ending with the destruction during the Syro-Ephraimite War (*TFL I*: 52-53). After the second campaign, the refinement in ceramic chronology led Albright to redate Fortress III, Phase A to the 8th century and Phase B to the 7th century, with an end in the Babylonian destruction of 597 B.C. (Albright 1933: 7). Paul Lapp's 1964 campaign

indicated widespread late 7th-century remains, with two or three groups of late 8th-century pottery with which it may be possible to associate the first use of Fortress III.

Fortresses III and IV were quite different in plan from the earlier fortresses. The Period III builders found a tumulus of debris 4 m deep (*TFL I*: 18); a glacis was constructed around the base of the tower which was built on top of the earlier debris.

The Period III, Fortress III evidence is summarized as follows:

Phase A
(1) walls of the tower itself, many of which were built on top of the Fortress II walls, forming a slight trapezoid (see fig. 10);

Fig. 10. Plan of Fortress III. Cf. *TFL I*: pl. 23; *TFL II*: pls. 28, 31.

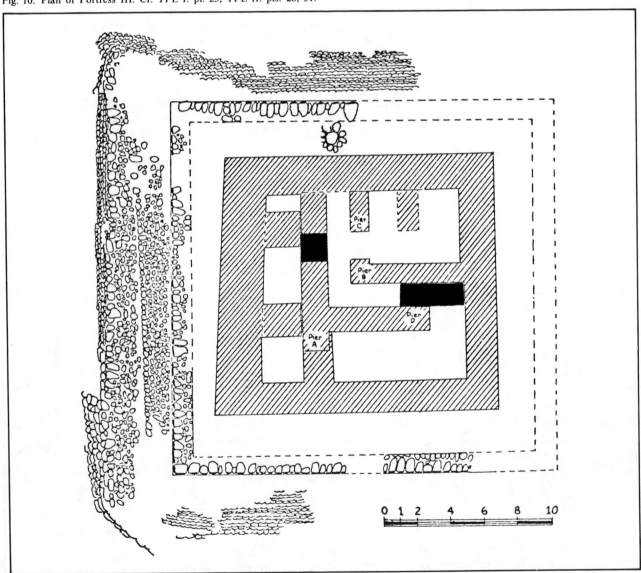

(2) piers A, B, C, D, and indications of as many as five more piers on the interior of the tower used to support a floor (*TFL II*: 27-28);

(3) masonry roughly hewn, carelessly laid, and comprised of reused *melekī* stone (*TFL I*: 20);

(4) a thin outer wall a little more than 2 m from the tower (*TFL I*: 18-19);

(5) a masonry glacis set against the thin outer wall, presumably on all four sides of the tower, although it was removed by subsequent builders on the west side and unexcavated on the east side (*TFL I*: 19);

(6) two vertical drains between the tower wall and the outer wall on the northern side (*TFL I*: 21);

(7) pottery not distinguished between Phase A and B, although the royal stamped jar handles may belong to Phase A (cf. below, p. 000) rather than Phase B as previously thought (*TFL II*: 33);

Phase B

(8) interior walls (piers) repaired — Pier A filled in west of Pier B, and space between east end of Pier B and Pier D filled in; see fig. 10 (*TFL I*: 21);

(9) pottery and objects more homogeneous with much less variety than Period II; bowls with ring burnishing on the inside and rim predominant; also represented are cooking pots, smaller saucers, holemouth jars, ribbed handles, a bull's head handle; objects include numerous rubbing stones, buttons, fibulae, iron nails, and loop pins (*TFL I*: 23-25; *TFL II*: 29-33);

(10) 2 m of destruction debris (*TFL I*: 20, 53).

Albright's assertion that Fortress III was a typical Palestinian *migdal* (*TFL I*: 17) has not been called into serious question. Certainly this structure was the primary fortification of Period III. Paul Lapp did uncover a late Iron II casemate wall running north from the *migdal* glacis and again extending along much of the eastern side of the mound (see below, chap. VI). Sinclair (*TFL II*: 27) describes the tower as "a modified casemate arrangement," with the outer wall being the stone revetment, about 1.10 m thick. There is an interstice of a uniform 2 m, with no cross-walls. The inner wall ranges in thickness from 2 m on the south and southeast to 3 m on the north and west.

The tower is slightly trapezoidal in shape, with the south wall measuring 17 m in length, the north wall 16 m, and the east and west walls measuring 14.70 m in length. In the interior of the tower, the pier structures are complex and difficult to reconstruct completely. Piers B and C were found to be 2 m high, while Pier A was only 0.75 m high (cf. *TFL I*: figs. 23-26). Sinclair (*TFL II*: 28) suggests that there were more piers, with probably two piers on either side of C, one west of B, another at the east part of B, and possibly another pier parallel to C and B supporting D. Fortress III A may have had nine piers in all.

The south and west walls of the tower, as well as a number of the piers, were built using the walls of

Fortress II as foundations (cf. fig. 11); however, the west wall of the tower almost missed the west tower wall of the earlier fortress. In the north and northeast, the tower was not built on earlier walls, accounting for the fact that they are as much as a meter thicker here. Even though the *melekī* blocks are hammer dressed, they are rather crude and carelessly laid, necessitating the thickness. Sinclair suggests that the high "proportion" of the length to the width and thickness is a Solomonic characteristic (*TFL II*: 27).

The glacis unearthed on the north, west, and south sides of the tower presumably surrounded the *migdal* (*TFL I*: fig. 17; *TFL II*: pl. 5B). The remains on the west are coarse and uneven, having been removed by later builders (*TFL I*: 19; *TFL II*: pls. 7-9). The foundation stones of the glacis are larger than the upper stones. Rising obliquely at a 60° angle, the glacis reaches a height of 4.60 m and is estimated to have reached 6.50 m. Two drains in the northern glacis, 5.40 m long and 55-60 cm inside diameter, allowed rainwater to be carried to the *ḥuwar* (*TFL I*: 21, figs. 21-22).

Fortress III was destroyed twice, dividing it into two phases. The first phase fortress was restored not long after its destruction. The inside walls, poorly made in the first place, were repaired. The northern end of Pier A was filled in, as was the space between Piers B and D near the east wall of the tower (see fig. 10).

Fig. 11. Plan of Fortress III superimposed on plan of Fortress II.

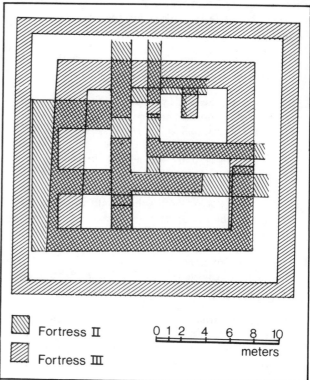

| | Fortress II |
| | Fortress III |

0 1 2   4   6   8   10

meters

Both Albright and Sinclair state that Fortress III B was probably destroyed by the Babylonians (Albright 1933: 10; *TFL II*: 33). Destruction was indicated by 2 m of stone slivers, charred sherds, and cinders within the central chambers of the watchtower. According to Albright, the analysis of the ash indicates that Fortress III had a second story constructed of almond wood beams, suggesting that the conifer forests that had supplied wood for the building of Fortress I may have disappeared by the Iron II period (*TFL I*: 20). Evidence from the third campaign that the destruction should be associated with the second Babylonian conquest will be discussed in chap. V.

Period IV: Fortress IV

Three and a half centuries passed before Tell el-Fûl again saw any substantial inhabitation and fortification. The mid-4th through the 3rd-century date given to Period IV by Albright and Sinclair (Albright 1933: 10; *TFL II*: 36) has been revised by the results of the 1964 excavation. Paul Lapp has shown that, with the exception of a few 3rd-century potsherds, the ceramic evidence of Period IV is to be dated from 175 to 100 B.C. (Lapp 1965: 7; see the chronological table for the phasing of this period).

The Hellenistic builders of Fortress IV followed the basic exterior lines of Fortress III, reusing the earlier glacis and revetments with some modifications. The interior of the fortress followed entirely new lines, forming three small chambers. According to Albright and Sinclair (*TFL I*: 26; *TFL II*: 7), the Hellenistic fortress was again probably a watchtower or *migdal*.

The Period IV evidence from the 1922-23 and 1933 campaigns is summarized as follows:

(1) repair and reuse of the Iron II glacis; most significantly, the top of the glacis was left about a meter lower (*TFL I*: 25);

(2) several buttress walls were constructed to shore up the earlier fortifications, notably:

   (a) a buttress wall at the southeast corner of the tower (*TFL II*: 34);

   (b) a small masonry wall against the south glacis (*TFL II*: 34; pl. 10);

   (c) buttress walls against the west glacis of the tower (Lapp clarified these walls in 1964); see fig. 12;

(3) three small chambers in the interior of the tower, which probably serve as a kind of "basement" (*TFL I*: 26);

(4) column fragments (*TFL I*: 26; *TFL II*: 35, pl. 35);

(5) a water spout (*TFL II*: 35);

(6) door sockets (*TFL I*: 26);

(7) grain pits, around the edges of the revetment; one rather large with an arched doorway and flight of steps (not plotted on any plans or photographs), probably dug before Period IV but in use in Hellenistic times (*TFL I*: 27);

(8) pottery, including lamps, "hole-mouth jars," cooking pots, short-necked amphorae, and a pilgrim flask; objects included three stone bowls, coins, a bronze handle, and iron knives (*TFL II*: chap. VII, pp. 46-47);

(9) 600 sq m of house walls belonging to the Hellenistic village along the eastern edge of the mound; following the contour of the hill, the walls were built of roughly dressed coursed stone (Albright 1933: 10; *TFL II*: 35);

(10) many silos and cisterns, particularly on the eastern side of the mound (*TFL II*: 35).

The plan of the interior of Fortress IV is not very clear. Except for the sketchy and incomplete plan given by Albright (*TFL I*: 78), there is no top plan of the Hellenistic fortress. Fig. 12 represents a reconstruction of the top plan gleaned from the text and Albright's sketchy plan. Fortress IV was removed early in the 1922 campaign. In an unpublished letter to James Kelso on May 27, 1964 (Kelso was then participating in the third campaign), Albright was revising his thoughts about the fourth fortress, saying, "there was probably much less of Fortress IV preserved than I had thought in 1924."

Particularly problematical are the three interior chambers. On Albright's plan there is a suggestion of a wall dividing the larger chamber. Actually, the walls of these chambers are the inner face of a mass of masonry and debris as much as 6 m thick. Aside from the chambers, the rest of the area of the Fortress III tower was filled in with debris. On top of the debris, which was about 50 cm above the top of Pier B of Period III, a pavement of flat stones was laid. It served as a platform on which the watchtower was erected. Some of the walls were still preserved in 1922 more than 2 m above their foundations (*TFL I*: 26). The masonry of Fortress IV was generally inferior and careless, suggesting haste in construction. The builders reused materials from Fortress III. *Melekī* stones were used, and some of them were quite large; the largest measured 100 x 70 x 40 cm. The north inner wall of Fortress IV rose 3.5 m above its foundations (*TFL I*: 25-26).

The buttress between the outer wall and against the southeast corner of the tower was constructed to strengthen the sagging Fortress II wall serving as a foundation for Fortress III and IV walls (*TFL I*: figs. 19, 20). It was originally considered to be part of the Fortress III rebuilding, but Sinclair states that the excavator changed his mind after restudying the buttress (*TFL II*: 34). The *melekī* blocks were dressed on all four sides and laid as headers to maintain lateral strength. The outside of the buttress was dressed after the blocks were laid, and then earth was packed all around it (*TFL II*: 34).

Only cursory treatment is given to the house remains and occupational evidence on the eastern half of the mound (Albright 1933: 13; *TFL II*: 25-35; pls. 11-12). No destruction evidence for the end of Period IV was found; it was probably abandoned at the end of the 2nd century, according to Lapp's chronology.

Period V: Early Roman Occupation

A fifth period of occupation was identified in both campaigns (*TFL I*: 27; Albright 1933: 10). Reoccupation of the mound in the Early Roman period was demonstrated by pottery dating from the 1st century B.C. to the 1st century A.D. This evidence was not found in the tower but in the grain pits and latest floor levels of the housing installations. Apparently, the fortress was not in use when Titus arrived at the site in A.D. 70.

The following evidence of Early Roman occupation is cited (*TFL II*: 46; pls. 13, 14):

(1) Early Roman pavement in Room 2 and Room 6;
(2) pottery above pavement in Rooms 2 and 6, homogeneous pottery from Rooms 1, 3, and 5, and sherds from Rooms 4, 10 (upper level), and 12;
(3) the contents of Silo 5 in Room 6;
(4) the north wall and probably upper levels of Room 13;
(5) masonry walls at the base of the north revetment of the tower;
(6) a manger from Room 13, a broken Roman millstone of lava from Room 2, and two ovens in Rooms 18 and 14.

The Identification of Gibeah with Tell el-Fûl

Particularly since the publication of the 1933 campaign, the identification of Tell el-Fûl with Gibeah

Fig. 12. Reconstructed plan of Fortress IV. Cf. *TFL I*: pl. 23.

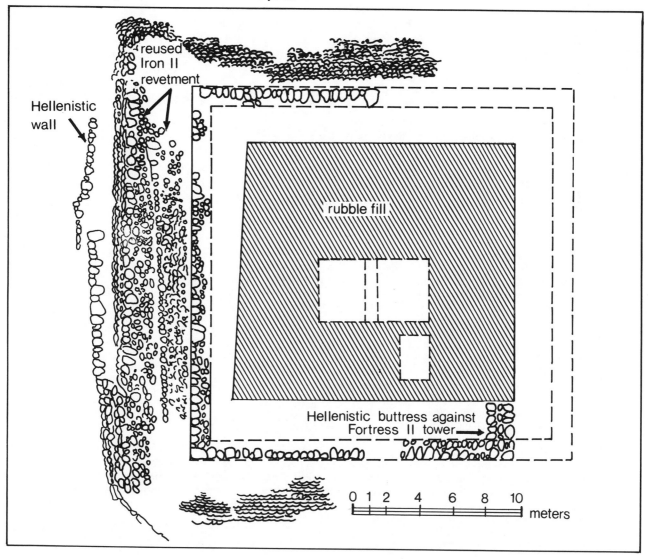

of Saul has again been questioned. In many respects this is justified, and advances in archeology and textual criticism demand renewed consideration.

The publication of the third archeological report is not the place to go into a detailed study of the textual problems. In the remainder of this volume, the results of the third campaign of archeological excavation at Tell el-Fûl will be reported, and the contributions here presented are independent of the written sources and are important regardless of whether Tell el-Fûl is to be identified with Gibeah of Saul. Recently, the textual problems have been given considerable attention by J. Maxwell Miller (1974, 1975) and Aaron Demsky (1973). Miller attempts to identify both biblical Geba and Gibeah with modern Jeba^c, and although he has thoroughly reviewed the textual evidence, it is necessary that further attention be given to his assumptions. Demsky presents some interesting suggestions concerning Geba, Gibeah, and Gibeon, and they too need further consideration.

The publication of the results of the second campaign (*TFL II*) tended to raise more questions concerning the archeological evidence than it solved. The limitations of the report caused a number of scholars to be skeptical of earlier conclusions.[10] Was there really a fortress at Tell el-Fûl which dated to the time of Saul? Were the Tell el-Fûl fortifications actually a citadel or simply a tower (*migdal*)? Was Albright correct in his orientation and suggested dimensions of Fortress II? Tell el-Fûl seemed to present one of the earliest casemates in Palestine and this needed further clarification. Was there any evidence for domestic dwellings at Tell el-Fûl earlier than Hellenistic times? Did the site have any industrial significance?

These and other questions occasioned the third campaign at Tell el-Fûl by Paul W. Lapp in 1964. This last excavation did clarify a number of the questions scholars were asking, and it did call for some modification of the conclusions of the earlier campaigns. These matters will be considered in future chapters, and the results are significant. As shall be seen, the archeological evidence points to an impressive occupation at the time of Saul, and Albright's attribution of a fortress to this period is justified. Earlier occupation could be associated with the pre-Saul biblical stories. Early Roman occupation corresponds to the time of Titus, as mentioned by Josephus. There are no Byzantine remains, corresponding to Jerome's description where Paula says Gibeah was "a town destroyed to the ground." The archeological evidence strongly supports the identification of Gibeah as Tell el-Fûl.[11] As Paul Lapp wrote shortly after the conclusion of his campaign at Tell el-Fûl: "While it is therefore not categorically proved that the fortress belonged to Saul, the identification rests on evidence about as strong as archaeology is ever able to provide — especially in light of the comparably strong case for the identification of Tell el-Fûl with Gibeah of Saul" (1965: 3).

NOTES

[1] There seems to be some discrepancy over the elevation of Tell el-Fûl. W. F. Albright (*TFL I*: 1) cites the figure of the Survey of Western Palestine as 2754 feet (or 839 m). A British Army map of the British Mandate records the elevation at 2758 feet (or 840 m); plan 3 is based on this map. The figure of 862 m (or 2827 feet) is based on the highest elevation recorded on the 1964 excavation top plan.

[2] Robinson (1874: I, 544, n. 2) provides the following bearings from Tell el-Fûl: er-Ram is N. 10 E.; Nabi Samwîl is N. 70 W.; and Jerusalem is S. 10 W. See *TFL I*: figs. 3 and 4 for views to the west and east in 1924, and *TFL II*: pl. 1 for an aerial view of the mound.

[3] John Dinsmore, a botanist, identified Fortress I cinders as cypress and pine; these trees have been extinct for centuries in this part of the country.

[4] *TFL I*: 1 provides additional information on the etymology of Tell el-Fûl and variant names of this site.

[5] Albright notes that there are two names: Khirbet ^cAddâseh is the important ruins northwest of Tell el-Fûl and east of Gibeon; Khirbet el-^cAdaseh is the ruins of a small village just northeast of Tell el-Fûl, also called Beit Lijjeh. The two are confused and the former often misspelled; Birch's spelling is corrected to read Khirbet ^cAddâseh.

[6] In a later article, Birch elaborates this thesis with a recording of the exact degrees of sunsets in May (1914: 42-44).

[7] Birch also plays with the word "Gidom" (opposite Khirbet ^cAddâseh) which he says was regarded as "Gai-Dummim" in Hebrew at the time of Josephus; "Gai-Dummim" or "Valley of Blood" was translated into Greek *aimatōn* (blood) and then miscopied to read *akanthōn* (thorns) in the Josephus text.

[8] Professor Dalman had visited Mackenzie and talked of Tell el-Fûl as a "Crusading" fort. Dating chronology was quite primitive and imprecise. As presented by Bliss and Macalister (1902), the following chronology was in use at the time:

Early pre-Israelite	— pre-Mycenean, pre-Phoenician, pre-1500 B.C.
Late pre-Israelite	— Mycenean and Phoenician, ca. 1500-800 B.C.
Jewish	— period of Mycenean decline
Seleucidan	— ca. 300 B.C.
Roman	— ca. 100 B.C. - 350 A.D.

By 1912, Macalister had considerably refined chronology in his publication of *Gezer*. Late pre-Israelite became Second Semitic (to end of 18th Egyptian Dynasty) and Third Semitic (to establishment of Hebrew Monarchy); Jewish became Fourth Semitic (1000-500 B.C.) and Persian and Hellenistic; Byzantine was given the dates A.D. 350-600.

[9] Sinclair (*TFL II*: 12) says that the outer fortress walls are 1.20 m thick. Albright (*TFL I*: 8) gives the figure of the outer wall as

between 2.00 and 2.30 m thick, but he is apparently referring instead to the tower walls. As Franken notes (1963: 85), the top plans do not correspond to these figures. The plans suggest a width of the outer walls in the vicinity of 1.60 m and the inner wall 1.20 m. As will be seen in chap. III, Lapp's excavation suggests that the top plan figure is the most accurate.

[10]For example, Franken wrote in 1963: 85:

The identification of Tell el-Fûl with biblical Gibeah is generally accepted. In fact, this is the only basis for the identification of the building and its history with the history of Saul and of the village. (N.B. No remains of an early Iron Age village have been found at Tell el-Fûl. The earliest remains of a village are Hellenistic according to Sinclair.) It is by no means possible to accept as close a dating as Albright-Sinclair give on the archeological evidence. There is also no evidence that the "fortress" was originally or later more than just a small stronghold which may or may not have been used by King Saul and his father as a palace. Every serious reconstruction has to be based on material evidence, and in this case it is lacking.

[11]Miller (1975: 162-64) was limited by the confusing report of the second campaign and the availability of only the preliminary report of the third campaign, but he tends to misunderstand or misuse the archeological evidence to support his conclusions rather than to let the evidence speak for itself. The evidence for the pre-fortress occupation and the Period II fortress is more substantial than he will admit, and the quantity of pottery from the five periods of occupation, together with the almost complete absence of earlier pottery, represents material evidence which cannot be pushed aside easily. On the other hand, Iron I remains of any kind never have been reported at Jeba[c].

Chapter 2

The Story of the 1964 Campaign

Howard M. Jamieson

The third campaign at Tell el-Fûl in 1964 was a "salvage campaign." King Hussein of Jordan had rented a home on the western slope of the mound. The home, which served as a West Bank palace, was strategically located for his majesty, since it is only 3 miles north of Jerusalem and a few miles south of the city airport. The view from the crown of the hill is delightful: on a clear day the Mediterranean can be seen in the west; Nabi Samwîl dominates the northwestern horizon. While the elevation of the hill is not impressive (pl. 1a), from the top of Tell el-Fûl one looks down on Jerusalem and has the definite impression that the Old City is lying at the feet of the viewer. The panorama to the east is extensive, as the Dead Sea and the hills of Moab and Ammon are clearly visible on most days. The desirability of the location of Tell el-Fûl is unquestionable.

When rumors circulated that King Hussein was planning to build his own structure at the top of the mound (cf. pl. 1b), archeologists became concerned. Any building would destroy the evidence that had been preserved for centuries from prior occupations. This evidence would be most important in either confirming the conclusions of the first campaigns at Tell el-Fûl or in forcing their revision.

Fully aware of the talk about the king's plans for the hill, Paul W. Lapp, Director of the American School of Oriental Research at Jerusalem in 1964, was eager to excavate Tell el-Fûl. James L. Kelso of Pittsburgh Theological Seminary had written Lapp about the possibility of continuing the tradition of joint excavations between the Jerusalem School and the Seminary. When Kelso suggested a site near Jerusalem with Hellenistic and Early Roman remains, Lapp suggested a "salvage campaign" at Tell el-Fûl. The project was quickly given the enthusiastic support of William F. Albright. Original plans from the first two campaigns were made available by Albright. Other assistance, generously and freely given, proved to be very helpful.

The strategic location of Tell el-Fûl was appreciated by the army of the Hashemite Kingdom of Jordan. The whole hilltop was under the strict control of the military authorities. While a permit for excavating the site was granted by the Jordanian Department of Antiquities, negotiations had to take place with the commander of the army post at Beitin. After agreement had been reached with the military, there was the usual frantic search for landowners and the establishment of reasonable compensation for use of the land. Securing an approach to the tell from the north proved to be the most difficult problem. The army officials were most helpful so that the delays and irritations encountered by Albright in the twenties and thirties were not repeated. The representative from the Jordanian Department of Antiquities was also most cooperative in securing signatures on all the required documents. Photographic work and visiting privileges were curtailed by the military, but the requirements were reasonable.

Trucks with equipment and cars with personnel were allowed to proceed about halfway up the mound on the north slope. At the point where the army defense trenches were located, the vehicles were parked. Then the supplies had to be carried the remainder of the way to the field headquarters. The technical men, Nasir Dhiab Mansoor, Jabr Muhammed Hassan, Muhammed Hussein, Abd er-Rahman Hussein, and the driver-foreman, Aboud Dhib Nasif, erected a small camp and headquarters at the northeast corner of the hill. There they guarded the equipment 24 hours a day in addition to their duties in the excavation process. The budget was slightly over $3,000: one-third came from the regular archeological budget of the Jerusalem School; two-thirds came from Pittsburgh Theological Seminary's Kyle-Kelso Fund for Archaeological Research.

On May 3, the squares for the excavation were laid out. As the architect and the technical men assisted Lapp in the process, the question arose whether there was anything at the site worth salvaging. The question about the wisdom of the effort was prompted by Albright's conclusion at the end of the 1933 campaign. He wrote, "It is hardly probable that the returns would warrant another campaign."

An examination of the surface of Tell el-Fûl seemed to suggest that Albright's judgment was correct. There was almost nothing to indicate that the site would be productive. It had been observed that the proximity of the mound to the city of Jerusalem and the encroachment of houses on the west slope had made the hill a favorite walking area for school boys and others interested in strolling about. Even with the military presence, students could be seen sitting either on the top of the exposed revetment or on top of the tower. Each student had the badge of safe conduct in hand, an open textbook. With such heavy pedestrian traffic, all surface material had been carefully scrutinized and most of it removed. It would have been surprising to find anything of interest on the surface of Tell el-Fûl. What was more disconcerting was the absence of any significant stratigraphical evidence in the balks of the trenches dug by the military.

The work force, which averaged 55 workers per day, began excavation under the leadership of Paul W. Lapp, the Director, and the Field Supervisors: Delbert Flora, John Holt, Howard Jamieson, George Nickelsburg, and C. Umhau Wolf. John Zimmerman and Mrs. Betty Wolf were the registrars. The supervisors were all associated with the American School of Oriental Research in Jerusalem. John Zimmerman was on the staff of St. George's Cathedral. The laborers came from the villages near the mound, Beit Hannînā, Hizmeh, and ʿAnâtā. Oliver M. Unwin of England was the surveyor. James L. Kelso of Pittsburgh Seminary served as the President of the excavation (cf. pl. 1c). The excavation at Tell el-Fûl was the 16th archeological project in which Pittsburgh Seminary was a participant in Palestine.

The actual excavation began on May 4, 1964 (cf. pl. 1d), and continued for six weeks, ending on June 13. While the technical men lived on the site, the rest of the staff returned each evening to Jerusalem. A five-day week was the pattern with special recording, checking, and photography being pursued on the sixth day.

The strategy followed in the third campaign was dictated primarily by questions which had arisen over the published results of the first two expeditions. First, the size and orientation of the fortress structure had to be investigated. Albright's proposed reconstruction of the fortress required an extension eastward beyond the limits of the mound as it stands today. Second, the dates for the military defense structures had to be checked. What hard data were there for the proposed

dating? Third, the occupational history of the entire site had to be established, if possible.

In addressing these three considerations, the actual excavation moved ahead in three areas. On the first day, squares were opened immediately north of the sloping revetment which Albright had studied carefully. These squares were productive, so additional squares were opened within a few days. These were in an area about 25 m north of the revetment. By the end of the six weeks, all the area between the northern squares and the defense wall had been cleared. An east-west trench was cut along the northern end of the mound. This provided a means for connecting the stratigraphy of the east and west sides of the site. It also revealed that the deposit 25 m beyond the revetment was very thin. Bedrock was reached within 0.5 m or less.

A second area of excavation was established approximately 20 m north of Albright's 1933 work on the east side of the mound. When the initial probes uncovered important data, the work in the area of the northeast summit was expanded.

A third area of concentrated work was opened in an east-west trench at the northwest corner of Albright's Period II fortification. This effort provided material by which the chronology of the construction could be checked.

The staff did not expect to uncover as many underground pits, cisterns, and silos as were discovered. In all, 23 silos were cleared out, and two plastered cisterns were carefully studied with very positive results. During the last two weeks of work, the mound seemed to be half deserted by the crew, for half the men worked in the installations cut into bedrock.

The amount of work done by the workmen was impressive. The total area excavated was 801.25 m². This area is comparable to the total area excavated in the first two campaigns. Such a remarkable achievement was possible because the technical men were experienced and had worked with Lapp on several previous excavations. They were knowledgeable men and could proceed with both reasonable speed and disciplined carefulness. Likewise, the staff generously expended itself tirelessly in seeking to achieve the maximum possible within the six-week time frame.

Since the spring of 1964 was wet (the rainiest winter in "40 years"), the working conditions were a bit uncomfortable. The major discomfort came from the strong winds which began to blow around noon from the west. By quitting time, which was 4:15 P.M., a regular gale was in progress. This was hard on the eyes and made recording most difficult. Occasionally, the situation became intolerable and work had to be stopped early. Tape measuring was impossible and the workmen talked of striking. Official action preserved the dignity of the situation!

The catalog of objects recovered during the six weeks records some 300 objects from the excavation. More than 70 of the items are ceramic pieces from the late 6th century B.C. Twenty-five coins, including five silver pieces, were discovered. Twenty-five lamps (12 Hellenistic, 13 6th-century) were a part of the material taken to the American School in Jerusalem for careful study and storage. More than 20 bone artifacts and 12 animal or human figurines add to the wealth of the finds. Stamped jar handles, several bearing Hebrew inscriptions, provided their contribution to the history of Tell el-Fûl. As the work was finished on the site, it was noted that most of the objects came from the silos and cisterns. Plans and photographs preserve the variety of architectural structures and complexity of home and industrial installations.

By June 13, 1964, no doubt as to the value of the "salvage dig" at Tell el-Fûl remained. Visitors to the mound, such as Roland de Vaux, Pierre Benoit, Jean Parrot, and Kathleen Kenyon, concurred that the effort was significant in its results.

Events following June, 1964, proved that Lapp's concern about the availability of Tell el-Fûl for future archeological work was well founded. In 1965, work began on King Hussein's West Bank Palace. The structure was not completed by 1967 (pl. 1b), but the preparation of the site for building purposes had destroyed its historical record.

Chapter 3

New Light on the Fortress: Periods I and II

John A. Graham

One of the principle objectives of the third campaign was to check the date of the fortifications. A 5-m-wide trench (plan 2, Area XIII) was laid out where the west wall of Room C_2 of the Period II tower excavated by Albright joins the north wall of that same room. This trench was gradually extended down the western slope of the mound a total distance of 10 m, uncovering four revetment walls in the process (pl. 4c).

The undisturbed debris against the north face of the Period II tower and its foundation trench (L. XIII-10, 11, 12) yielded a clear Iron IC pottery horizon (cf. pl. 2a and the pottery, pl. 48; loci descriptions and the pottery found and published from each are listed in Appendix B). This evidence, pottery exclusively from the post-Philistine phase of Iron I, definitely dates the tower to the time of Saul, as Albright had maintained. If the identification of Tell el-Fûl with ancient Gibeah can be accepted, it is reasonable to say that this tower belonged to King Saul.

As can be seen in the photographs and the section drawing of the northwest corner of the tower (plan 7, pl. 2a-b), the tower was composed of large *nârī* blocks, roughly hewn (yet squared off) and laid in courses. Smaller rocks fill the interstices between the blocks. A number of the large blocks appear to have fractured or split, perhaps the result of earthquake activity. Comparing these stones with masonry characteristics of the first and second fortresses of the earlier campaigns, the tower masonry uncovered by Lapp can be said to be the same as Fortress I (cf. fig. 7, p. 10).

Plan 7, section g-h (cf. pl. 2a-b) shows the foundation trench for Saul's tower. It was cut through the softer *huwar* into the *nârī* bedrock. Within the foundation trench were a number of large stones packed against the west face of the tower at the northwest corner, buttressing the sagging tower at this point. Two large stones capped the buttress above the foundation trench. The outer wall of the Iron II (Period III) revetted

tower had been built over a loose 20 cm of fill above the buttress. The buttress itself contained pottery (L. XIII-15; cf. pl. 48) similar to that found in strata packed against the lowest levels along the north face of the tower. Thus, the buttress is seen as a repair of the tower during its Iron IC use. The tower probably would have collapsed if the buttress had been removed, so the buttress was indeed necessary and left intact by the excavators.

Fig. 13, a drawing from a northwesterly photograph (pl. 2b) of the buttress, further illustrates the need for a buttress. The foundation of the Period II tower just to the south of where the buttress abuts it consists of both large and small stones, poorly dressed and inadequately laid in courses (cf. pl. 2c). In places, there was no dirt between stones at all. Stones higher up were projecting farther out than the stones forming the foundation. For such a monumental fortification, the tower had a poor, precarious foundation indeed.

As will be seen in chap. V, the buttressing of the fortification in Iron I was not sufficient for later use. In Period III an outer wall for the late Iron II tower was built on Iron I debris against Saul's tower wall (L. XIII-2; cf. pottery, pl. 48). A sloping revetment was built further out with a mid-wall between. Presumably, a masonry glacis covered these revetment walls. A still lower wall was hastily constructed in Period IV (see chap. VII; cf. pl. 4c; plan 7, sec. e-f; figs. 10, 12).

The third campaign substantiated Albright's dating of Fortress I. Evidence from the second campaign indicated that after a major destruction, Fortress I underwent a substantial rebuilding which employed distinctly different masonry technique. Repairs on the interior of this second, rebuilt fortress suggested additional phasing of Fortress II (cf. the chronological table, p. xvii). It is impossible to link the buttressing of the corner of the tower that Lapp uncovered with the rebuilding identified by Albright.

The construction of the buttress, crude like the tower, bears little resemblance to that of Fortress II with its smaller, dressed stones. Thus, the buttress is simply a repair of the original fortress. The results of the third campaign neither confirm nor deny Albright's conclusions relating to two successive fortresses being built during the Iron I occupation.

Perhaps the most controversial aspect of Albright's earlier campaigns at Tell el-Fûl has been his assertion that in Period II an entire fortress, with the tower he unearthed serving as the southwest corner, was built; Albright claimed that similar towers were built on the **other corners of the casemated fortress (cf. fig. 5, p. 9).**[1] Competent scholars from England and France raised fundamental objections: 1) that the contours of the mound did not permit a fortress to be extended as far east as Albright maintained; 2) that the fortress was not a casemate; or 3) that there was no fortress at all at Tell el-Fûl, only a small defensive tower. Such basic objections needed to be checked.

In the third campaign, excavation was continued north of the tower. At a point roughly 12 m north of the revetment, Lapp came upon a 3-m-long fragment of the wall, designated Wall S, which he determined to be part of the west wall of Saul's fortress (plan 13; pl. 3a). The

following conclusions were reached (cf. Lapp 1965: 4): (1) Wall S is composed of large, semi-dressed stones (pl. 3c) of the very same character as Albright's "outer casemate wall" in the tower. Even the large boulders forming the foundations are similar. (2) Wall S has the same 1.50 m width as Albright's "outer casemate wall." (3) Wall S is nearly on a line with the west wall, extending north from the tower. In his Diary (p. 16), Lapp noted that Wall S lay eastward on a slight step. The top plans (plans 1, 13) locate Wall S about 1.5 m out of line to the west from the line of the "outer casemate wall." This discrepancy may be significant, but it could be due to the contour of the hill. At a point 2.75 m to the south of Wall S, three other stones were unearthed and proved to be in line with Wall S and part of the same wall (pl. 4a). In addition, a deposit of earth with Period II sherds was found on bedrock at the base of the Iron II revetment built against the tower (L. II-46) on line with the fortress wall (pl. 5a). (4) Strata of earth against Wall S (L. XVII-12, VII-3b; cf. plan 6, sec. c-d; pls. 2d, 3a) contained large body sherds and collar rims that dated ca. 1000 B.C. (Period II; cf. pl. 48). Later dismantling of this wall confirmed a date of around the time of Saul (L. VII-3b, 21; pl. 3c). (5) Wall S and the tower were built on a 30-cm deposit of clay *ḥuwar* (plan

Fig. 13. The northwest corner of the Period II tower.

North face of Per. II tower

West face of Per. II tower

Outer wall of Per. III revetted tower

Poor foundation of Per. II tower visible

Foundation trench for Per. II tower

Iron I C buttress repair

6; pl. 3c). Unlike the tower, however, the wall was built directly on the thin layer of soil and did not have a foundation trench. This clay above bedrock represents the pre-fortress phase of occupation at Tell el-Fûl. A few sherds of the 1200 B.C. horizon (Period I; cf. pottery, pl. 47) were found just above bedrock (L. XVII-14, VII-20, 22; pl. 3b) and on a floor beyond the wall to the east (L. XVII-8, pl. 2d).

It was indeed fortunate that this small segment of the west wall of the fortress was preserved. With the exception of the several stones south of Wall S identified as also part of the fortress wall and the small deposit at the base of the revetment (L. II-46), the entire area between Wall S and the tower revetment was cleared to bedrock by late Iron II operations. Similarly, on the north, Hellenistic constructions cleared away all traces of the fortress wall as the Period IV builders also sought to ground their buildings in bedrock. Iron II and Hellenistic remains were found to the east and west of Wall S as well. Nowhere else on the mound were the excavators able to locate other fragments of Period II fortification walls.

Iron I sherds were found mixed with later debris in many places on the mound, but other stratified or homogeneous Period I and II deposits were few. A deeply excavated cavity in bedrock (L. XXIII-12, 13), just northwest of Albright's excavations on the east, contained a pure Period I deposit. The north revetment of the southwest Iron II tower was built over the

remains of a wall which ran diagonally to the northeast in the lower levels of Room E. The early date for the wall was confirmed by the ashy deposit on bedrock between the five large stones and the revetment (L. I-44; pl. 11a) which contained only Iron I body sherds. The silt deposit on the floor of Silo 24 (L. XIX-3ext.), south of the Northeast III Building, contained Period II sherds. The silo lay beneath the subsurface debris and scree which contained principally Period III material. The stony rubble had broken the opening to the silo, and the top material contained III A sherds. Although no cap was found, a kind of shelf for a cap can be seen in the section (plan 11), and the silo was probably not used after Iron I times. Of the 44 silos from the three campaigns at Tell el-Fûl, an indeterminate number of them were probably cut out of bedrock in the Iron I period and cleared out and reused in later periods (Lapp 1963-64: 3; see below, pp. 59-62).

Albright's assertion that there was an Iron IC fortress at Tell el-Fûl is vindicated. But Albright also maintained that the fortress was of the casemate type. The matter is crucial in that Tell el-Fûl was frequently cited as having the earliest datable casemate in Palestine (for example, *TBM III*: 14; De Vaux 1965: 235). No evidence of an inner casemate wall east of Wall S was uncovered in 1964 (Lapp 1965: 4). While it is possible that the inside casemate wall could have been built in segments at only certain places of the fortress (a noncontinuous casemate), or that it could

Fig. 14. Wall S superimposed on Albright's reconstruction of the Period II fortress.

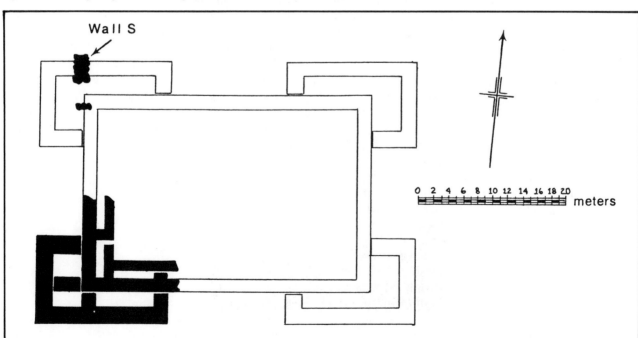

have been built at a higher level which was subsequently destroyed, Lapp discounts these possibilities as being quite unlikely (1963-64: 3). In private correspondence with Paul Lapp (dated Aug. 14, 1964), Albright notes further that the inner casemate walls at the southwest corner of the fortress were not bonded to the outer casemate wall but form straight joints (see fig. 4). In the true casemates, the inner and outer walls are bonded together through the partitions separating the inner and outer walls. Although he then argued that Tell el-Fûl had a secondary casemate system, Lapp records that Albright finally agreed that the Period II fortress could not be a casemate (1965: 4). There is no evidence of an early casemate construction at Tell el-Fûl.

Consideration must now be given to the orientation of the fortress. As was noted in chap. I, Albright suggested that the length of the fortress lay in an east-west direction; the maximum length was 65 m (the sloping contours of the mound precluded more than this) and the minimum length was 52 m. (The distance between the towers would logically be at least as great as the length of the tower walls.) The width is determined on the basis of the regular proportions of the tower, making it not less than 34 m wide. The fragment of the western wall of the fortress, Wall S, is located north of the north wall of the fortress as suggested by Albright (cf. fig. 14).

This discovery indicates that the north-south axis of the fortress was longer than Albright had proposed, evidence by which Lapp concludes that the north-south axis was the longer axis of the fortress (1965: 4). Furthermore, the mound itself is more elongated north-south than east-west. It was seen in the trench excavated against the southwest tower that the builders followed the natural contours of the mound, so it would seem much more reasonable to propose a north-south orientation.

Conclusions in reconstructing a complete fortress, however, remain quite tentative. That there were a number of corner towers is suggested by a number of Israelite fortresses from late Iron I and Iron II which had corner towers; these will be examined in chap. VI. Without any evidence of other towers at Tell el-Fûl, suggesting a complete fortress is quite conjectural. However, at least some corrections of former plans can be made (cf. fig. 15). The dimensions and location of the southwest tower are known, and with the support of other parallels, the remaining towers of the fortress must have had similar proportions. Furthermore, the discovery of Wall S enables us to locate the west wall of the fortress. Since Wall S is slightly west of the extension of the west fortress wall projected by Albright, it seems likely that the fortress walls are not exactly at right angles to one another.

The topographical map suggests additional limitations to positioning the corner towers. The eastern edge of the mound begins to slope steeply east of the 859-m contour line. With the southeast corner tower at a point 65 m east of the southwest corner, the slope would probably have necessitated substantial revetment walls down the slope; no such evidence has been found. Locating the southeast tower at a point ca. 62 m east of the southwest corner seems more plausible and more consistent with the construction on the southwest. Locating the northeast tower is even more difficult. Concerning the excavations on the northeast part of the mound where a casemated late Iron II fortification was unearthed, Lapp writes, "It is tempting to suggest that there was a revetted tower similar to the one at the southwest on the northeastern corner of the summit, but the vestiges so far unearthed make it impossible to go beyond suggestion" (1965: 6). Once more the contours of the mound would preclude the construction of a tower more than 10 m north of the northeast excavations. We are inclined to locate the northeast tower in the vicinity of the Northeast Hellenistic House, where late Iron II and Hellenistic builders would have dismantled all traces of an earlier tower.

On the basis of such speculation, the fortress would resemble the hypothetical plan in fig. 15. The distance between the corner towers on the south is 62 m, and the distance between the corner towers on the east is approximately 57 m. Thus, the fortress was roughly square. The lack of architectural evidence in the center of the mound does not suggest that the dimensions would be drastically smaller than those suggested. The Period II fortress, then, is rather large, covering most of the summit.

In conclusion, we are able to say that the archeological evidence indicates that there was a fortress at Tell el-Fûl, the date of which suggests identification with King Saul. Furthermore, we are able to conclude (1) that the Iron I fortress was probably not casemated, (2) that its date is post-Philistine, and (3) that it was probably larger, at least from north to south (if there was more than a southwest tower) than Albright proposed.

NOTES

[1] Albright's fortress theory captured the imagination of other writers. Cf. the imaginative reconstruction and explanation in Wright 1974: 155.

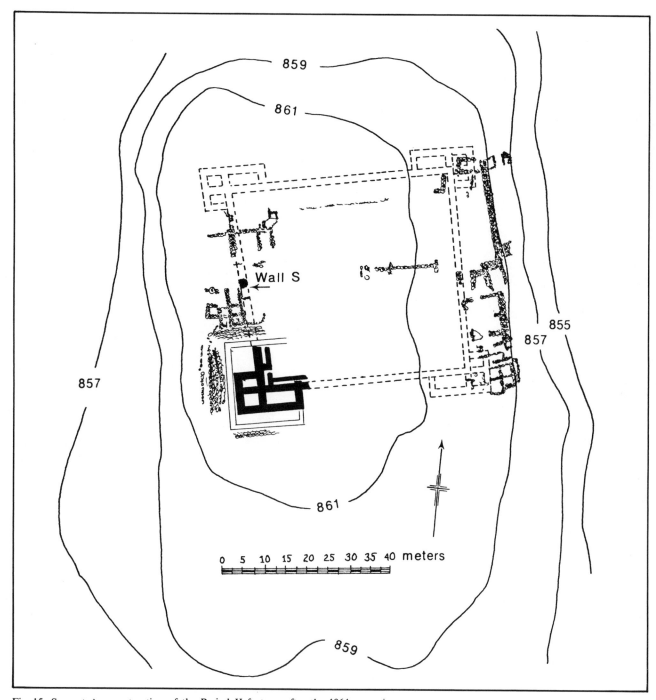

Fig. 15. Suggested reconstruction of the Period II fortress after the 1964 campaign.

Chapter 4

Iron I at Tell el-Fûl:
Some Historical Considerations

John A. Graham

The contribution of archeology to the understanding of the occupational history of Tell el-Fûl does not fundamentally contradict the picture provided by known written records. The archeological evidence indicates occupation at the beginning of the 12th century with some suggestion that it ended in destruction. There was a gap in occupation until the last quarter of the 11th century, when a fortress was built on the site at the time of King Saul. Soon after the death of Saul, occupation at Tell el-Fûl ended until the last half of the 7th century. At the time of the Babylonian conquest, the site was heavily fortified, and it continued as a flourishing town until the end of the Exilic period. Several centuries later, Tell el-Fûl saw renewed occupation during the 2nd century B.C. and campsite use near the time of the fall of Jerusalem in A.D. 70. This archeological history of Tell el-Fûl is in accord with the written records, that is, Judges 19-20 (the ravishing of the concubine and the destruction of Gibeah), the biblical accounts of Saul and Jonathan, Josephus' account of Titus' encampment at Gibeah, and Jerome's narration of the journey of Paula and her finding Gibeah in ruins. Still, the archeological evidence raises some historical questions. In this chapter, we will consider some matters related to Iron I at Tell el-Fûl.

As the historian looks at the first two periods of occupation, the 12th century and the late 11th and early 10th centuries B.C., questions arise: Can one identify the settlers of the pre-fortress period? Could they be the ancestors of Saul? To what historical event would one attribute the abandonment of the site during the Philistine period? How does the settlement of Tell el-Fûl tie in to expansion of the tribe of Benjamin? Even more pressing questions concern the relation of the Philistines to the site. The excavators have shown that there was no Philistine presence at the site. How

does this fact affect present understanding of where the Philistines settled and how Saul and David confronted them? Where was the headquarters of the Philistine garrison?

Tell el-Fûl and Philistine Settlement and Expansion

G. Ernest Wright, in an article "The Phenomenon of American Archaeology in the Near East," discusses W. F. Albright's and Paul Lapp's work at Tell el-Fûl. Wright concludes, "The only difficult question is whether the Philistines built the fort for a garrison, or whether Saul himself erected it, instead of taking it over from those whom he defeated" (1970: 25). This very issue has been debated since Albrecht Alt proposed in 1930 that Gibeah (Tell el-Fûl) was the site of the Philistine garrison (1953: 30-31; 1959: 259).

Many scholars have maintained that Fortress I of Period II at Tell el-Fûl found its origins in Philistine occupation prior to King Saul's arrival. Following Alt's lead, B. Mazar maintains that the fortress was erected by the Philistines as a residence for the Philistine governor (1964: 13 and n. 19). Albright felt that the original fortress was part of a network of outposts which were part of a Philistine monopoly of trade routes on land (Albright 1966: 33). Mazar says that Saul's first victory over the Philistine administrative and military center for the hill country located at Gibeah brought an end to Philistine domination of the tribe of Benjamin. The Philistine fortress was subsequently destroyed by the Israelites in the battle at Michmash. Saul then rebuilt the fortress along the Philistine plan and made improvements, that is, Period II Fortress II as set forth by Albright's excavations (Mazar 1964: 13). In the final publication of the 1933 campaign, Sinclair links the destruction of Fortress I at the hands of the Philistines with the death of Saul at

Mount Gilboa (*TFL II*: 6, 26). Fortress II is thus post-Saul. Later, Sinclair maintained that Fortress I was Philistine, that Saul captured and destroyed it during the battle of Michmash, and that Saul later rebuilt it as our Fortress II (1964: 56); however, Sinclair recently has returned to his former position (1976: 445). Biblical commentators and dictionary-writers have generally linked the fortress and the Philistines (Caird 1953: 946; Gray 1963: 327-28; Mitchell 1962: 466; Myers 1962: 229; Avi-Yonah 1969: 67). Suffice it to say, the Iron I fortress(es) at Tell el-Fûl has sustained a predominant identification with the Philistines.

One of the primary reasons that the Philistines are linked with Tell el-Fûl is to support the biblical references to "Gibeah-haelohim" in 1 Sam 10:5 and to "Geba" (or Gibeah) in 1 Sam 13:3. For those scholars who believe that the Philistines were responsible for the introduction of iron and casemate fortifications into Palestine, the discovery of an iron plow tip in the Iron IC tower and the erroneous belief that this fortress was a casemate bolstered their assertion that this fortress belonged to the Philistines (Sinclair 1964: 57; Mazar 1964: 6).[1]

Against this interpretation, the results of Lapp's 1964 excavations are clear: not a trace of Philistine occupation at Tell el-Fûl was found. The pottery from the pre-fortress occupation is given a 1200-1150 B.C. horizon. There is a definite gap in occupation during the period of Philistine ascendancy. Lapp concludes, "There seems to be no evidence to recommend the view that Saul's fort had been originally Philistine construction" (1965: 4).

The extent of Philistine expansion has been the subject of considerable discussion over the past decade. To what extent were they able to gain a foothold in the hills of Ephraim, the Jordan Valley, and Transjordan? How does Tell el-Fûl's lack of evidence contribute to this picture? The thesis in the following discussion holds that the probable reason for the lack of Philistine occupation at Tell el-Fûl is that the Philistines never really gained a firm foothold in the hills of Judah, Benjamin, and Ephraim; that is, they were confined to the Shephelah and possibly the Jordan Valley and did not effectively penetrate east of the western crest of the Judean hills. To document this, we will need to survey the migrations, settlement, and expansion of the Sea Peoples, particularly the Philistine group.

The end of the Bronze Age saw tremendous social upheaval and the migrations of masses of people for reasons unknown. This movement brought the Gauls to France, the Galatians to Asia Minor, the Thracians to Greece, the Arameans into southern and eastern Syria. It saw the end of the Mycenean world, the fall of Troy, the collapse of the Hittite and Hurrian empires, and the decline of Egypt; Assyria was the one major world power that survived this upheaval. Palestine also felt the influx of new peoples: the Israelites, the Philistines and other Sea Peoples, the Arameans from the east, and the Ugarits from the north (Hallo and Simpson 1971: 117-24).

The breakup of the Aegean culture and the migrations of the various groups designated as Sea Peoples was a gradual event, lasting more than a century. In all likelihood, the appearance of the Philistines in southwestern Palestine sometime around 1170 B.C. does not mark the first appearance of Aegean immigrants to Egypt or Palestine. R. D. Barnett, in his chapter on "The Sea Peoples" for the *Cambridge Ancient History* (1969), documents earlier incursions of "Sea Peoples." A few instances can be mentioned. The Amarna Letters indicate that the Egyptians used Sherden mercenaries in the battle between Ramesses II and Muwatallish, king of the Hittites (Barnett 1969: 4). During the reign of Merneptah, ca. 1232 B.C., Sea Peoples amassed against Egypt by land from the west, that is, in Libya, but were repulsed. Another onslaught against Egypt came ca. 1200 B.C. in the aftermath of the overthrow of the Hittites; the records of Merneptah at Karnak and Athribis indicate that these attackers were the Akawasha, Teresh, Sherden (already Egyptian mercenaries), the Lukku, and the Sheklesh (Barnett 1969: 10-11). The Akawasha were probably the largest group; they were circumcised, a practice common to the Egyptians and Semites, but foreign to Greeks. The Akawasha were Mycenean Greeks. The Tursha or Teresh were bearded, wore a high headcloth and pointed kilt with tassels, and carried spears and armaments of leather or linen on their chests. The Sherden were, prior to the invasion, Egyptian mercenaries; they wore distinctive helmets with a chin strap and disc on top, carried a round shield and a two-edged sword, and were beardless. The Sherden were noted for their bronze-working. Others mentioned are the Lukku or Lukka and the Sheklesh or Shakalsha.

Albright attributes the fall of Ugarit, ca. 1230 B.C., to a wave of conquering by Sea Peoples (Wright 1966: 73, citing Albright; Barnett 1969: 14). Tell Sukas was permanently destroyed; Sidon, Tell Abu Hawam, and Kition (Cyprus) also fell. There seems to be a common pattern here, as Barnett observes — destruction followed by fresh settlers (1969: 14).

In Palestine, there is mounting evidence of pre-Iron Age Aegean settlement. Thirteenth-century Aegean evidence is found at Ashkelon, Tell el-Ḥesi, Tell el-ᶜAjjul, Tell Jemmeh, and Tell el-Farᶜah (S). Cretan seals have been found near Gaza indicating an Aegean colony there; Aegean weaponry has even been found in Iraq (Mitchell 1967: 411-13). As will be seen later in the discussion, the anthropoid clay coffins found in southern Palestine, the Jordan Valley, and

Transjordan show significant Egyptian and Aegean influence, and these predate the Philistines. Significantly, Sea Peoples other than the Philistines apparently actively settled Palestine.

Philistine presence in Palestine begins with the great battle of the Sea Peoples and Ramesses III. As Albright notes, it is difficult to fix the exact date of the invasion of the last wave of the Sea Peoples, partly because the date of the reign of Ramesses III is uncertain within a range of a generation and possibly a decade; the earliest and latest dates for his accession are 1205 and 1180 B.C. respectively (Albright 1966: 24). In the Shephelah there is evidence that there is a gap of a generation or more between the latest imports of Mycenean pottery and the introduction of Philistine pottery (p. 32). J. Swauger suggests that the Philistines who settled in the coastal plain may have been agents of this trade with Crete and Mycene prior to their own moving (1969-70), this pottery being imported via Cyprus by the same group of Sea Peoples who settled in southwestern Palestine.

At any rate, in the course of his reign, Ramesses III warred against the Libyans on his western border and against the Sea People confederacy. It seems, according to Barnett, that there may have been two battles with the Sea Peoples: the first in Syria against the land invaders, and the second in the Nile Delta against the sea raiders (Barnett 1969: 15). Egypt was able to defeat these invaders in a battle which is colorfully depicted in relief on the walls of the Medinet Habu temple in Egypt. To fight the Egyptians, the Sea Peoples formed a confederacy comprised of the Peleset, the Tjekker, the Sheklesh, the Denye, and the Weshesh. The Peleset were clean shaven and wore headgear of a circle of upright reeds or leather strips or horsehair with a horizontal band and a chin strap. They also wore a paneled kilt decorated with tassels, ribbed chest protectors, and carried a pair of spears. On land, they fought in Hittite manner, with a three-crew chariot (two warriors and a driver). Clearly, the Peleset had strong connections with Anatolia. They were masters of iron-working, evidenced by iron furnaces found at Tell Qasîle, ᶜAin Shems, and Tell Jemmeh. There also seem to be connections with Crete. The boats of the Peleset are unusual, powered by sail, not oars (Barnett 1969: 16-17). It is universally agreed that the Peleset are to be identified with the Philistines (Barnett 1969: 16).

With the precedent of Egypt's turning the Sherden into mercenaries, most scholars believe that Ramesses III settled the Peleset peoples as mercenaries in garrisons on the Egyptian Empire frontier to protect the Egyptian borders (Albright 1966: 26; Wright 1959: 65; 1966: 72; Hindson 1971: 118; T. Dothan 1957: 151). They were settled certainly in the existing cities of

Gaza, Ashkelon, and Ashdod. There is division among scholars over whether the Peleset peoples were settled in Beth-shean, Tell el-Farᶜah (Sharuhen, near Gaza), and Tell Deir ᶜAlla (see below).

Soon afterward, it seems that the Philistines expanded to the cities of Ekron and Gath (Wright 1966: 74; Mazar 1964: 10), whose exact whereabouts are not known. These five cities — Ashdod, Ashkelon, Gaza, Ekron, and Gath — became the capital cities of the Philistines and formed a kind of city-state confederacy called the Philistine Pentapolis (the Philistines never appear to be united under one king). With the decline of Egypt's power and ability to control her borders, the Philistines began to expand into the Shephelah before the end of the 12th century (Wright 1966: 74-77).

While economics was at the heart of Philistine expansion, it is difficult to say whether the primary ingredient in the confederacy of the Philistines and other Sea Peoples was their ethnic and cultural background or their economic aspirations. Apparently, the Sea Peoples came to Palestine with generations of seafaring experience. The Wenamon document refers to Badar, the Sikalite Prince of Dor, who dispatched eleven warships to detain Wenamon at Byblos (Mazar 1964: 3-4; Pritchard 1955: 27). The Tjekker Sea Peoples were settled into Dor, and it is abundantly clear that they in particular became masters of the sea. They also gained a foothold on Cyprus, although they were not the only Sea Peoples to do so (Barnett 1969: 20). The Tjekker in Dor had less farmland, and so they remained in the piracy racket until they were finally defeated by an alliance of Israel and Tyre (Albright 1966: 32). Warkatara, prince of Ashkelon (a Philistine city), formed a trading confederacy with Phoenician Sidon in the 11th century (Mazar 1964: 6). The Phoenicians and the Philistines struggled for maritime supremacy in the eastern Mediterranean in the wake of Egypt's decline in that area, the Philistines gaining this position and maintaining it until their defeat by Israel and Tyre. Two observations can be made: first, it seems that the Philistines sought to consolidate and develop their sea monopoly before developing control over the inland trade routes.[2] Second, we see in the nature of the alliances, such as the Philistines meeting with the Tjekker at Aphek (Albright 1966: 33), a certain autonomy of the different Sea Peoples.

Expansion from the coast into the Shephelah also began within a generation after the original settlement of the Philistines. Important deposits of Philistine evidence appear at the following sites before the conclusion of the 12th century: ᶜAfûla (IIIA), Megiddo (VIIA), Tell Qasîle (XII), Gezer (cemetery-9), Tell Jemmeh (181.00 and KY), and Tell el-Farᶜah (Sharuhen, cemetery, 364, YX) (Dothan 1967: 64). To

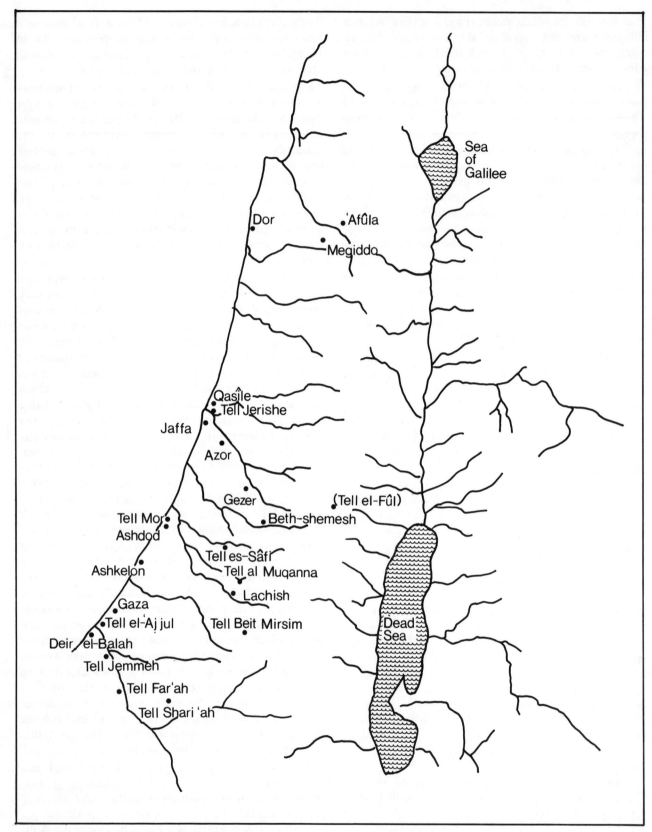

Fig. 16. Sites with Philistine (or Sea People) deposits.

this list, Wright adds Beth-shemesh (III), Tell Beit Mirsim (B₂), Tell eṣ-Ṣâfi, Tell Sippor, Khirbet al-Muqannaᶜ, Tell Melat, and Tell esh-Shelaf (Wright 1966: 74-77). In addition, Dothan finds Tell es-Zuweyîd, Tell el-ᶜAjjul, Tell Mor, Lachish, ᶜAzor, Jaffa, Tell Jerishe, and Dor helpful in determining Philistine expansion. (Most of these sites are located in fig. 16.)

Dothan also mentions three sites which are not acceptable as sites demonstrating Philistine expansion: Bethel, Tell en-Naṣbeh, and Beth-zur — the only sites from her list in the region consistently belonging to the Israelites. At Bethel there is simply not enough evidence to substantiate Philistine occupation. J. L. Kelso, the excavator of Bethel, writes, "Bethel seems to have escaped destruction in this crisis [the Philistine invasion of Israel]. There was only one place in the city where there was burning at this time. Most important of all, Philistine pottery was rare; none was found in the 1954 or 1960 campaigns. Bethel entered into an era of peace at the end of the Philistine crisis in the highlands" (*Bethel*: 50).

Tell en-Naṣbeh, excavated in 1926-29 and 1932 by W. F. Bade, yielded only 47 Philistine sherds, plus a dozen which were questionable from Stratum II (dated 11th century). The layer of debris between Stratum II and I does not permit us to conclude Philistine occupation preceded by destruction. There is the possibility of trade import to account for the small presence of Philistine pottery. At the time of the Philistines, Tell en-Naṣbeh was an insignificant village with very small city walls, no high place, and no Philistine pottery in early tombs (*TN I*: 61, 180-81; *TN II*: pl. 80).

Beth-zur, according to the excavator, O. Sellers, remained unoccupied between 1400 and 1100 B.C. The Iron I city was destroyed toward the close of the 11th century. The 1957 excavation did not turn up any evidence for Philistine presence (*BZ II*: 6-7).

As can be seen in the fig. 16 map, Philistine expansion went only as far as the western mountain ridge, where the western watershed began. The Philistines did not expand into Israelite territory. The major challenge to this limitation of Philistine expansion comes from Beth-shean, Tell Deir ᶜAlla, and Sahab. Let us turn to a consideration of each of these sites to see the evidence that links these cities with the Philistines.

The question at stake is: to what extent did the Philistines gain economic control of the trade routes? Can it be demonstrated that the Philistines gained control of the Via Maris and control over the caravan trade which used the Esdraelon, the Jordan Valley, and Transjordan?

To prove that Beth-shean was a Philistine stronghold would also be to identify this site in the Jordan Valley as the place where the beheaded body of Saul was displayed on the gates. The matter lies in positively identifying a sizable number of anthropoid clay coffins found in the Great Northern Cemetery as being distinctly Philistine. Just such a claim is made by T. Dothan. Her recent preliminary report on the discovery of anthropoid clay coffins at Deir el-Balah, near Gaza, provides valuable information on the history and use of these burial cases relevant to their appearance at Beth-shean (1973: 129-46). Anthropoid clay coffins have been found at a number of sites: Tell el-ᶜAjjul, Lachish, Megiddo, Sahab, Beth-shean, Tell el-Farᶜah (Sharuhen), and Deir el-Balah — these last three providing by far the most important evidence. Approximately 50 coffins have been found at Deir el-Balah, and probably an equivalent number from Beth-shean. (The collection at the University of Pennsylvania in Philadelphia consists of 40 coffins.) Dothan divides these into two groups: Group A are mummy-shaped coffins of traditional Egyptian concept; Group B consists of only the heads and shoulders, the dominant shape in Egypt and the only shape in Palestine until the Deir el-Balah discovery. Within Group B there are again two types, a natural terra-cotta mask of a face that was sculpted and added as a unit and a grotesque mask where the eyes, nose, mouth, and ears were applied separately (Dothan 1973: 130). Both types of Group B were found at Beth-shean.

It is the five grotesque coffins found at Beth-shean that interest us. These depict an applique headdress with horizontal bands and rows of knobs and zigzag patterns (to which there are no analogies from Canaan or Egypt). The same kind of headdress is seen in the relief at the Medinet Habu temple in Egypt depicting the battle of the Sea Peoples with Ramesses III. The headdresses in the relief were composed of a cap, diadem, horizontal band, and leather strips and were worn by the Peleset Sea Peoples, that is, the Philistines (Dothan 1973: 144). Parallels of anthropoid clay coffins found in Tell el-Yahudiyeh and Nebesheh in Egypt and a number of imported Egyptian vessels found with the coffins establish a definite link with groups from Egypt (Dothan 1973: 136, 141). In addition, the tomb architecture, consisting of a stepped dromos and a rectangular rock-cut tomb, reflects Mycenean burial customs (Waldbaum 1966: 331-40). Artifacts, such as seals, bronze and iron objects, and pottery also document Aegean influence in these burials (Dothan 1973: 143; 1967: chap. 4). Thus, identification of the Beth-shean coffins with the Sea Peoples, indeed, with the Peleset, is very strong.

There are, however, two problems. First, the Beth-shean coffins are early, the 13th century being the date for the earliest burials. This is before the Peleset had made their appearance in Egypt or Palestine. Dothan's response is that the Philistines took over this style of burial from earlier immigrants; at Beth-shean, the Philistines who were garrisoned by Ramesses III continued the burial practice of the Egyptians already there (Dothan 1973: 145; 1967: chap. 4). She also adds that the anthropoid burials in Egypt at Tell el-Yahudiyeh and Nebesheh have strong, non-Egyptian flavor; this type of burial in both Egypt and Palestine was used by non-Egyptian elements (Dothan 1973: 141). Were these earlier Sea Peoples?

The second problem is that there is absolutely no Philistine ware at Beth-shean. There is Philistine pottery with the anthropoid clay coffins at Tell el-Far ͨah (Sharuhen), but here the coffin lids lack the "feather crown" found on the lids at Beth-shean and identified with the Medinet Habu temple relief (Dothan 1967; 1973: 143). Admittedly, the correlations are strong, but not to the point where we must exclude some other Sea Peoples group, possibly cultural relatives of the Philistines, as the dwellers of Beth-shean and responsible for these burials. The distinctive, telltale evidence that says "Philistine" is missing.

F. W. James, who has published the excavation results related to this cemetery (1966), raises serious doubt whether the Philistines were at "Beisan" (Beth-shean). She notes that it has been thought that the coffin people belonged to the Sherden group at the time of Ramesses II, but the pottery indicates that this cannot be so. The group must represent a garrison detailed by Ramesses III after his victory over the Sea Peoples. The lack of Philistine pottery debars us from saying they were Philistines. The "coffin people" of Beth-shean, James concludes, are perhaps other people invading Egypt as well as the Philistines. The users of Philistine pottery in the south were not the group who held Beth-shean. She continues, there is no evidence for a temple of Dagon at Beth-shean (1966: 136-37).

E. Oren, in his recent work on the Northern Cemetery, reinforces James' conclusions:

> The conclusions arrived at in the foregoing pages that the coffin burials of Beth Shan actually represent a garrison group of Egyptians and a few troops of Aegean origin detailed by the pharaohs of the Nineteenth and Twentieth Dynasties, sometime between the late thirteenth and eleventh centuries, is well attested by the discoveries made on the Tell. . . . Both total absence of real Philistine ware in the Northern Cemetery or indeed in any of the Tell strata and the pre-Philistine date assigned to the earliest coffin burials prove conclusively that the Philistines of the Pentapolis, who are identified by a distinctive class of pottery which emerged at the earliest in the second quarter of the twelfth century, cannot in any way be identified with the coffin burials of either class, and were evidently never present at Beth Shan (Oren 1973: 47-48).

Oren suggests that the Aegean peoples possibly garrisoned at Beth-shean with the Egyptian mer-

cenaries may have been the Denye (Denyen) Sea Peoples (1973: 150). P. Lapp, in unpublished notes, also adds the following observation to this matter of the occupation of Beth-shean. Although James states that the Beth-shean Level VI is 12th century to possibly as late as 1075 B.C., the pottery, according to Lapp, is mostly 13th century with only an intrusive piece or two later than 1150 B.C. Level V is divided into upper and lower. The "lower" is the 11th century down to Shishak's invasion in 918 B.C.; the "upper level" of V dates the following century down to around 800 B.C. Although James argues that Level V began just after Level VI, there is a *major gap from 1150 to 1025 B.C.,* the period of Philistine ascendancy. Dothan has tried to explain the absence of Philistine pottery at Beth-shean by asserting that Philistine ware had pretty much disintegrated and been assimilated into local ware by the second half of the 11th century (1973: 144), and hence is unrecognizable. An absence in occupation at Beth-shean during the Philistine ascendancy and expansion certainly precludes their being there and strengthens James' and Oren's hypothesis that the "grotesque coffin people" were Sea Peoples other than the Philistines.

The discovery of "Philistine pottery" at Deir ͨAlla (Succoth) has led Albright and others to see Philistine penetration into Transjordan (Albright 1966: 32; Wright 1966: 74, 77). The excavator of Deir ͨAlla, H. J. Franken, recognized for his careful excavation and precise work, has this to say about the Philistine pottery found in Phases A-D (*TDA I*: 245):

> If one had to assume that this pottery reached Deir ͨAlla from Philistine centers of manufacture in the southwest of Palestine, and that it belongs to the distribution pattern as it is known up till now, then Phase A could not be dated earlier than 1150 B.C. Philistine pottery has not as yet been found east of the central mountain ridge of Palestine, and apparently did not even reach Beth Shan. As it is comparatively scarce at Deir ͨAlla, its presence can be explained by trade. However, Phases A-D are interpreted as industrial phases, typified by the melting and casting operations by an itinerant tribe of smiths. The "Philistine" pottery disappears from the scene with them; therefore it is quite possible that a) this material does not come from the southwest of Palestine, but from places where these smiths met other metal workers when obtaining their raw material, and b) these contacts may date from an earlier phase of the "trek" of the Peoples of the Sea. The meeting place could just as well have been Egypt as along the coast of Lebanon. Until these relationships can be traced properly, too much weight should not be put on the evidence of this pottery for dating purposes. At the moment, it seems rather as though it disappears at Deir ͨAlla just at the time it is beginning to penetrate into Palestine.

It cannot be said, therefore, that the Philistines were present at Deir ᶜAlla. And again, the evidence points to the possible activity of other groups of Sea Peoples, who, as at Beth-shean, preceded the Philistines.

In the remaining instance, Albright suggests that the influence of the Philistines on desert trade is illustrated by the discovery of an anthropoid clay coffin at Sahab, east of Amman (1966: 32; 1932a: 295). Dothan has dated all the Transjordanian instances of anthropoid clay coffins (that is, those at Amman and Dibon) as belonging to the 9th-7th centuries B.C. (1973: 138), much too late to attribute to Philistine culture.

In summary, the Philistines were highly motivated to develop control over land trade as much as they had over sea trade. Their expansion along the coast and into the Shephelah seems economically motivated. The claims that the Philistines controlled the desert and caravan trade inland and that they established strongholds in the Jordan Valley and the Transjordan are not easily substantiated. In his survey of the east Jordan Valley in 1975, Sauer did find solid evidence of Philistine ware, reviving the earlier Wright hypothesis that the Philistines may have moved east across the Esdraelon Valley and south along the Jordan Valley (personal conversation and cf. Ibrahim, Sauer, and Yassine 1976). Further definition of possible Philistine presence in these inland valleys, whether it be permanent settlement or evidence of commercial trade, must await future excavation.

In all probability, the picture of settlement in Palestine in the 13th through the 11th centuries B.C. has been vastly over-simplified. Reflecting on the excavations at Ai, Callaway (1976: 29-30) has suggested that between 1220 and 1125 B.C. a group of newcomers with considerable urban experience moved into the hill country from the west along the coast. With parallels at Bethel, Tell en-Naṣbeh, Beth-shemesh, El-Jîb, and Raddana, these settlements are characterized by lack of fortification walls, pier-constructed houses, cisterns, terraces, and cobbled streets. In the latter half of the 12th century, ca. 1150-1125 B.C., village life was interrupted by yet another group of newcomers with less refined urban development skill: they built silos destroying the cobbled streets, remodeled houses to accommodate more people, and used above-ground silo granaries. If there is evidence that the Israelites settled at Ai, then Callaway concludes that this latter group of the silo-granary phase, coming with a nomadic background, would be more suitable. At approximately the same time, not only the Philistines but also other Aegean relatives were moving into Palestine, some from the southwest, others from the north. Until additional evidence enables us to better identify and define these varied cultural groups, the nature of the Israelite and Philistine conquests and settlement patterns will remain confused.

It probably would not be too much to say that a primary ingredient in Israel's rise to power, her expansion, and battles with the Philistines and Arameans was also economic. As Mazar (1964: 4) suggests, there are a number of biblical references which suggest Sidonian incursions and clashes between Israel and the people of Sidon: Josh 13:6; Judg 10:2; 18:7-8, 28. We have not generally pictured Israel as competing with the major maritime powers. Any naval experience Israel had was not remembered as a part of her story. The downfall of the Philistines occurred as Sidon's power declined; Israel formed a *ḥubur* or trade alliance with Tyre, another maritime power which had also formed a *ḥubur* with Egypt. Israel thus served as a bridge between the Mediterranean and the Red Sea (Mazar 1964: 16) as the findings at Ezion-geber indicate. Similarly, on the eastern front of Israel, a confederation was formed between the Arameans and Ammonites, whom David defeated, and Israelite garrisons in Damascus testify to Israel's economic control over inland trade routes (Albright 1966: 51).

Since it cannot be shown that the Philistines had secured a foothold in the hill country, it comes as little surprise that there is no evidence of Philistine occupation at Tell el-Fûl. However, the biblical story involves Gibeah considerably in conflict with the Philistines, as well as a number of other cities of northern Israel. How can the absence of the Philistines in this area be reconciled with the biblical record?

At the outset, we cannot deny that in all probability clashes between Israel and the Philistines took place on Israelite soil. The battle traditions associated with Michmash, to choose an example, seem quite authentic. It would be likely that there were a number of Philistine incursions into Israelite territory, but these did not result in permanent settlement or more than a temporary territorial occupation.

We can further delimit the expansion of the Philistines. With few exceptions, the material evidence does not suggest that they extended northward along the coastal plain farther than Jaffa. K. Kenyon says that north of Jaffa the occupational evidence does not support more than trading with the Philistines (1970: 230-31). There is no evidence of Philistine pottery at Dor, where the Tjekker settled, or at Tell Abu Hawam at the foot of Mount Carmel. There is a small amount of Philistine pottery at Megiddo, probably as a result of trade. At ᶜAfûla, a significant deposit of Philistine pottery was found; M. Dothan correctly observes that this is a relatively large quantity of Philistine pottery compared with other excavations in northern Palestine, but there is hardly enough to document substantial Philistine occupation (ᶜ*Afûla*: 39).[3]

Where then is the frontier between Israel and the Philistines, the battlefront where the two nations fought for survival? With references to Mount Gilboa

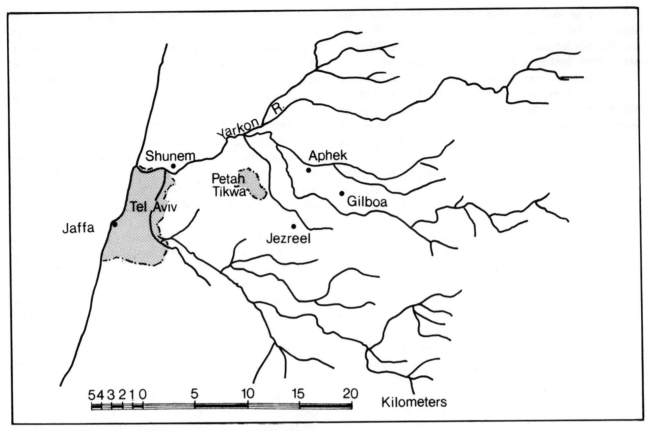

Fig. 17. Possible locations for Saul's final battles with the Philistines.

and Beth-shean as the sites where Saul's life ended, we have generally seen these final battles in Israel's territory. H. Bar-Deroma suggests that these battle-grounds are in Philistine territory along the coast and at the western edge of the Shephelah (1970: 129). The sites of Aphek, Jezreel, Shunem, and Mount Gilboa, where the biblical record says Israel and the Philistines clashed under Saul's leadership, are located in fig. 17, according to Bar-Deroma's thesis. He bases his justification for the location of these sites on logistic and story demands of the biblical account and by coordinating this with linguistic remnants of modern place names. Recognizing the lack of Philistine pottery at Beth-shean, Bar-Deroma looks elsewhere for the Beth-shean where Saul's body was displayed at his death. He notes that the "Beth-shean" of the tribe of Manasseh in the Jordan Valley is always spelled with an ʾalep, בית שאן. The town which saw Saul's death is spelled without an ʾalep, בית שן, and he maintains that the MT consistently spells the city Beth-shean in connection with the Saul story without an ʾalep. Accordingly, Bar-Deroma suggests the town of "Shen" (שן), mentioned in 1 Sam 7:12. Beth-shan (Shen) and Beth Dagon are one and the same place located in Philistia, south of Gath (Bar-Deroma 1970: 125-33).

The above locations cannot be accepted as conclusive. Nevertheless, to situate the battlefields between Saul and the Philistines in the Tel-Aviv region reasonably parallels the archeological and geographical evidence as it has been surveyed here.

To be fair to the archeological evidence and literary accounts, it cannot be conclusively stated that the Philistines did not penetrate farther north than the Tel-Aviv region; still, there is mounting evidence that they did not successfully inhabit the territory of Manasseh to the extent that they were able to build substantial defensive and domestic constructions. Their presence in this area was certainly quite limited.

Finally, it may be that Israel battled another Sea People group, such as the Tjekker, loosely confeder-ated with the Philistines. In this instance, Israel would not have made the distinction between the groups but lumped them all under the common enemy, "Pelese-tim" or Philistines. The other Sea Peoples, who seem to have made their presence felt at Beth-shean, Deir ʿAlla, northern Israel, and possibly Byblos and Ugarit, for the present remain anonymous. The notion is not far-fetched, for it certainly would make sense in explaining the archeological evidence. This does not mean that Israel did not come into bloody contact with the

Philistines as well, for that certainly seems to be the case.

The matter cannot be settled here. The quest to clarify the absence of Philistine occupation at Tell el-Fûl and surrounding sites has taken us somewhat afield as we have necessarily probed into the origins, settlement, and expansion of the Philistines and other Sea Peoples. Other questions remain about the Iron I occupation of Tell el-Fûl. While we cannot provide exhaustive treatment of these historical questions, it is appropriate that we once more return to Tell el-Fûl's role in the life of King Saul.

Gibeah and Saul

Assuming the identification of Tell el-Fûl with biblical Gibeah, one must ask why Tell el-Fûl was not inhabited before Saul's arrival there. By any projections, Saul died, not as a young man, around 1000 B.C. We have dated the Period II occupation of Tell el-Fûl as beginning not much before 1025 B.C. Obviously, Saul grew up elsewhere. To address this issue, one must first ask what happened to the 12th-century occupation. What brought Gibeah's humble origins to a halt around 1150 B.C.?

Several theories emerge. The Bible supplies ample evidence of the incursions of peoples such as Moabites, Edomites, Midianites, and others of this period (Kenyon 1970: 238), and it is possible that Tell el-Fûl was destroyed by one of these neighbors. Evidence, however, is lacking.

Civil war perhaps brought an end to Gibeah's short-lived, initial attempt for survival (Gray 1963: 327; an example of such civil war is cited in Judg 20:15-17). S. Yeivin, in an article titled "The Benjamite Settlement in the Western Part of Their Territory," notes that the process of occupying land belonging to other peoples creates hostilities (1971: 141-54). The territorial claims and formation of an amphictyonic confederation was no doubt far from peaceful.

The general concensus, however, has been to attribute the fall of Tell el-Fûl I to the events recorded in Judges 19-20, the story of Israel's revenge against Benjamin for the atrocity committed against the Levite's concubine at Gibeah (*TFL I*: 49; *TFL II*: 6). A. Demsky has expanded on this theory by suggesting that the details of Gibeah's destruction found in Judges 20 and 21 follow the pattern for the destruction of "a subverted city" (ᶜîr niddaḥat) (1973: 26-31). According to Deut 13:13-19, (1) one must gather the evidence against the accused city (Deut 13:15 and Judg 20:3-6); (2) the punishment must take the form of total destruction, with man and beast slain and the city burned (Deut 13:16-17 and Judg 20:37, 40, 48); and

finally, concern for repopulation must exist (Deut 13:18; Judg 21:14, 15, 22; Demsky 1973: 29). The archeological evidence does not provide a clue about the reason for the destruction of Tell el-Fûl I, but the literary evidence positing the destruction of Gibeah as "a subverted city" seems to give a reasonable explanation.

Demsky comments further that the "subverted city" was to remain in ruins forever, never to be rebuilt (Deut 13:17b). Even the name was to be permanently obliterated. Thus, when Saul arrived on the site at the time when he rose to power, he found the site barren and desolate, uninhabited for over a century (Demsky 1973: 29).

This leads to a further conclusion, that Gibeah was not the ancestral home of Saul. Saul was buried near Jabesh (1 Sam 31:13; 1 Chr 10:12); his father, Kish, was buried at Zelah, and Saul's bones moved there later (2 Sam 21:14); the location is unknown. The archeological evidence precludes any of Saul's ancestors living at Gibeah immediately prior to his rise to power. While the books of Samuel preserved accurately many traditions, on this point the Chronicler seems to have the more accurate version of Saul's ancestry, 1 Chr 9:35 locating Saul's ancestors at Gibeon (Yeivin 1971: 151-52; Demsky 1973: 27). Gibeon contains no remains of a Late Bronze Age settlement, but Saul's ancestors might have lived there, for the opening date of the Iron Age city at Gibeon is obscure, though probably early (Lapp 1967: 290).

If Gibeon was Saul's ancestral home, why did he leave it and go to Gibeah? Demsky and Yeivin each make interesting suggestions as to what prompted Saul to move. Demsky believes that Gibeon was the site of the Philistine garrison governing Benjamin. The center of administration and economy, it was located along the Emmaus Road, a major route from the hill country to the Shephelah. Since Gibeon was near both the north-south route along the watershed and along a good east-west artery, it was ideally suited for administrative and military control. Furthermore, Gibeon had a bāmâ, a high place, which Demsky feels qualifies the site to be identified as "Gibeah ha-elohim" (1973: 27). He conjectures that Saul left Gibeon because the Philistines simply would not have tolerated his political aspirations. He would never have been permitted to have a "coronation" as king of Israel (p. 28), and it would have been very difficult to raise an army from there. So Saul moved to a new location, near the Benjamites he knew; he moved to a strategic site along the main highway, a point from which he could move militarily with speed; he moved to Gibeah (Tell el-Fûl). A real problem with Demsky's thesis is that it is difficult to establish Philistine presence at Gibeon. As is the case in other Benjamite villages, no strong evidence of Philistine occupation can be found.

Yeivin attempts to describe Benjamin's occupation of the Canaanite territory. Penetration into a town took place in part through intermarriage, the Israelite man acquiring the rights of heritage and property to that place. No doubt, this practice was frowned upon by local inhabitants, for it undermined their control of their cities. The settlement of Benjamin very likely also occurred through violent means in places. The Israelite assimilation of Benjamin was apparently quite slow. Since Saul was probably a descendant of the "father of Gibeon" (three generations later, 1 Chr 9:35-39), his departure may be related to some atrocity or persecution perpetrated by his grandfather or great-grandfather. 2 Sam 21:1-9 records vengeance directed against Saul's descendants by the Gibeonites during David's reign, motivated by Saul (or possibly his ancestors) having put to death some Gibeonites, thus breaking a treaty. Whether it was Saul himself (as the passage suggests), or his ancestors (as Yeivin suggests), a definite feud existed between the house of Saul and the people of Gibeon (Yeivin 1971: 154). Saul had to go elsewhere; he was *persona non grata* in his hometown. And while Saul was king, with great military power at his disposal, reprisal by Gibeon against his house was not wise. After his death, however, the feud could be taken up with Saul's descendants. (Compare the allusion to his sons as captains of raiding bands in 2 Sam 4:2.) This rationale for Saul's leaving Gibeon for Gibeah is plausible.

Thus, Saul made his way to the desolate hill just north of the Jebusite enclave that David was to capture and make his capital. Saul and his followers, in the face of a tremendous threat from the Philistines, other Sea Peoples, and possibly his fellow Gibeonites, constructed a substantial fortress at Gibeah. Under military pressure, it was hastily constructed and probably with disregard for the "subverted city" curse. He named his new dwelling after himself.

It is not easy to evaluate the life of Saul, inasmuch as the biblical record disparages him to the benefit of David. Yet, two things can be said for Saul: first, Israel grieved deeply for him. Bar-Deroma has observed that the country did not disintegrate after Saul's death. The unifying institutions were strong enough to withstand the loss — indeed, strong enough to endure civil war and internal political struggle as David rose to the throne. Israel lost a brilliant warrior to the Philistines at Gilboa, but she did not lose herself (Bar-Deroma 1970: 135).

Second, Saul was probably far more astute as a politician than is often recognized. The Philistines were not able to penetrate his country. He organized a military power of very diverse elements to meet crises on several fronts. Apparently, as we have seen, he died not in his own backyard, but in enemy territory considerably to the west of his homeland. Saul emerges as more aggressive and enterprising than generally pictured. The successes of David and Solomon were surely built on the remarkable effort of Saul of Gibeah.

In conclusion, the definite absence of evidence for Philistine occupation at Tell el-Fûl, together with the demonstrable lack of Philistine penetration past the western edge of the hills of Israel, strongly suggests that the fortress found at Tell el-Fûl, attributable to Saul, was not built by the Philistines. This evidence also leads to new insights in interpreting the biblical record as we trace the course of Israel's war with the Aegean inhabitants who lived to the west. The clarification of the occupational history of Gibeah, through P. Lapp's work at Tell el-Fûl, also forces us to draw new conclusions about the origins of Israel's first king: Saul's ancestral home lies elsewhere.

We cannot move inductively from the few stones and potsherds unearthed during three seasons of excavation at Tell el-Fûl to support all the conclusions that have been drawn here. Yet, the attempts at reconstructing the political and social realities of the 12th and late 11th centuries B.C. make the archeological evidence found at Tell el-Fûl most understandable. The historian's task is by no means concluded. History is continually reborn in new understandings as new data come to light, as new connections are made with old artifacts. Although future excavation at this important site is useless, the evidence irretrievably destroyed by modern bulldozers and buildings, the quest to understand what Tell el-Fûl teaches about our past and ourselves has just begun.

NOTES

[1] Mazar lists the main material contributions of the Philistines as (1) their pottery, (2) the clay anthropoid coffins, (3) introduction of the casemate wall, (4) the three-room house, and (5) metallurgical development, especially iron.

[2] Wright (1966: 77) interprets 12th-century evidence from Tell Deir ʿAlla and Beth-shean as indicating Philistine presence and position designed to control a drive southward through the Jordan Valley. Albright (1966: 32) sees Philistines controlling land trade in the Esdraelon Valley (via Beth-shean) and Jordan Valley (via Deir ʿAlla) in the period preceding the invasion under Ramesses III. Against these views, Mazar (1964: 10) thinks that the confederation of Philistines and Tjekker formed at Ebenezer near Aphek in order to drive out the Israelites and gain control of the Via Maris did not coalesce until the mid-11th century. Sea control preceded land control, and the sea power was more effective than the land power for the Philistines.

[3] Only 18 out of 142 potsherd drawings shown in the plates are distinctively Philistine in decoration; it is difficult to tell how much is non-decorated Philistine ware. Other forms are standard Iron IB forms. The Philistine evidence is still relatively small and its occurrence at ʿAfûla is fairly localized — hardly enough to say that Stratum III A is wholly Philistine. Caution is necessary in asserting that there is Philistine presence at this site.

Chapter 5

The 7th-6th-Century Occupation: Period III

Nancy L. Lapp

Taking into account refinements in pottery chronology, it seems certain that the principal Period III occupation at Tell el-Fûl must be limited to the second half of the 7th and 6th centuries B.C. (see the **chronological table, p. xvii**). **It was probably during** Josiah's reign, 640-609 B.C., when he attempted to extend his kingdom and spread religious reform northward, that "Fortress III" was rebuilt over the remains of the Iron I tower, and a casemate wall was constructed. Pottery from the Period III houses and buildings of the 1964 excavations date to the last decades of Iron II (Lapp 1965: 4), and material from the earlier campaigns must be similarly dated.

It was presumed that Tell el-Fûl was destroyed at the time of Nebuchadnezzar's first campaign of 597 B.C. (Lapp 1965: 6; *TFL II*: 7). In accord with refined pottery chronology at Tell el-Fûl and other late Iron II sites, the division between Period III A and III B is better placed at 587 B.C., and the Fortress III destruction can be attributed to Nebuchadnezzar's second campaign against Jerusalem in 588-587 B.C. The earlier excavations found widespread evidence for destruction in the Fortress III area, but in 1964 the only evidence was found in the Northeast III Building which had over 20 cm of ashy destruction debris on a **floor (Lapp 1965: 6, and cf. below, p. 41). It is possible** that Nebuchadnezzar's forces destroyed the Period III fortress and produced limited damage elsewhere without causing extensive destruction throughout the village. Once the fortress was useless, the Babylonians may have had little concern for the remainder of the town's occupants and allowed them to live in peace.

After the 1922 excavation Albright had placed the final destruction of the third fortress toward the end of the 8th century (*TFL I*: 23). He revised the dating after the second campaign, placing the first destruction in the 8th century (ca. 735 B.C.), its rebuilding and occupation in the 7th century and the final destruction at the hands of the Chaldeans in 597 B.C. (Albright 1933: 10; *TFL II*: 7). The 1964 excavations indicate that the principal Iron II occupation (Period III A) was in the second half of the 7th century.[1] Only in some silos in the center of the mound (the "Mid-Field" silos) were there groups of pottery that should be dated about 700 B.C. The widespread destruction of the fortress revealed in 1922 (cf. above, p. 14) should be attributed to Nebuchadnezzar's 588-587 B.C. siege of Jerusalem. Thus, Albright's rebuilding of Fortress III dates to the 1964 Period III A, with Period III B being an (unfortified?) occupation elsewhere on the mound (cf. the chronological table, p. xvii).

In any case, after Nebuchadnezzar's destruction of the fortress, Tell el-Fûl continued to be occupied, and the population may have increased considerably. This is quite possible owing to the shifts in population following the destruction of Jerusalem. Perhaps refugees from the capital fled to such nearby villages as Tell el-Fûl, possibly intending to wait out the exile close at hand until they could return to Jerusalem.[2] The 1964 campaign testified to the extensive post-587 occupation (Period III B). In fact, after the first campaign it had been recognized that the settlement continued on the site. Albright thought occupation was continuous from the 7th or 8th century B.C. down to the 1st century A.D. (*TFL I*: 23); the gap in occupation was not recognized, a common mistake until Persian and Hellenistic pottery became better known in the 1960s (cf. the "EI III and H" pottery at Beth-zur, *CBZ*: 41).

A date near the time of the first return from the exile (538 B.C.) seems likely for the Period III B abandonment. The occupants may have joined the returnees and moved to Jerusalem; there is no evidence of a final destruction. As will be seen, common Persian pottery forms do not appear, and it is probable that Tell el-Fûl was abandoned before the period of Balâtah Stratum V (Lapp 1970: 179 and n. 2).

Albright had determined that the Iron II occupation at Tell el-Fûl included a *migdal*, or revetted tower, which had been built on top of the Iron I tower in the southwest portion of the mound. The Iron II date for the revetment enclosing the southwest tower was confirmed in the 1964 campaign. A newly discovered defensive element, an Iron II casemate, was uncovered on both the east and west sides of the mound. At least on the west side its use along with occupation outside the walls continued into Period III B, the Exilic period. At the northeast corner of excavations there was perhaps an Iron II sloping revetment with an attempt to shore up this revetment farther down the slope.

The earliest Period III deposits were in the Mid-Field silos which were filled in before the main occupation in Period III A. The Mid-Field excavations yielded quantities of Iron II sherds. The well-built Iron II construction identified as the Northeast III Building yielded remains of Period III A and B, as did lower deposits south of the building and in the southwest rooms. A few of the silos and a cistern had layers of silt with III A pottery or III A and B pottery on their floors. Cistern 1 had a layer of homogeneous III A and B pottery as well as a large quantity of III pottery in the upper layers mixed with Hellenistic material. The homogeneous III B deposit in the lower meters of Cistern 1 is of great significance for the knowledge of 6th-century Palestinian pottery. A nearby Pottery Cache also contained a good III B group. The widespread Period III B occupation was identified by the walls and pottery found to the southwest outside the casemate.

These Period III constructions and deposits will now be described. Some specific loci help date the Period III occupation and in turn contribute to the knowledge of pottery chronology (cf. plan 14 and Appendix B, pp. 126-31).

Revetment

Northwest Corner of Tower

To check the date of the fortifications, a trench (Area XIII) was cut at the northwest corner of the Iron I tower. Four revetment walls were uncovered in the process (plans 2, 7; pl. 4c). The most eastern wall was shown conclusively to be of Period II, including a buttressing repair at the corner (see above p. 23). The wall or "peel" next to it (pl. 4d) was the outer wall of the Period III tower, constructed a little more than 2 m from the Period III inner tower wall, against which the

glacis was built (cf. above pp. 12-13 and figs. 10, 11). At the corner the Period III outer tower wall was built on a loose fill over the Period II buttress repair. Elsewhere, this Iron II wall had been constructed on *nârī* bedrock with a foundation trench of its own and was left standing to a height of at least 1.80 m (plan 7; pl. 2b-c). The stones of this wall were smaller than the larger masonry blocks of the Fortress II tower and buttress.

A mid-wall with a great deal of scree emerged just to the west (plan 7, sec. e-f; pl. 4c). The fill with scree upon which the mid-wall was laid (L. XIII-2) yielded pottery that consistently dated to Period II (see above, p. 23). Less than 2 m to the west the outer wall of the sloping revetment was uncovered. This wall had a step roughly halfway up its remaining two-meter height (plan 7, sec. e-f). The wall was dismantled down to this step (pl. 3d), and pottery from the dismantled portion (L. XIII-8) dated to Period III A. Albright's basic conclusions concerning the sloping revetment were confirmed with the slight modification that the III A pottery should be dated to the late 7th-early 6th-century B.C. horizon rather than the 8th-7th century B.C. (Lapp 1965: 3).

North of Revetment

In the excavations which were carried on to the north of the tower (pl. 1d), deposits at the base of the sloping revetment were examined. Clearance against the north face (Area P, L. II-2E, 22 [pl. 5a; cf. fig. 28, p. 70]) and of adjacent deposits (Room E, L. 1-26 [pl. 11b] and the pit in Room F, L. I-49 [pl. 12c]) confirmed the Period III A dating. The revetment was actually built over a northeast to southwest wall segment represented in Room E by five large stones (see above, p. 25; plan 13, pl. 11a).

Casemate Walls

Walls of casemate construction were discovered going north from the fortress on the west and along much of the eastern edge of the mound (plan 14). On the western side the casemate was located slightly west of the west fortress wall of Period II. Keyed into the lowest courses of the tower revetment, the casemate extended 11 m north to Wall S; north of this point the Hellenistic builders had cleared away all traces of the Iron II casemate (cf. pls. 4a, 5b, 6c). Along the eastern slope of the mound a large wall was traced without a break for 20 m; presumably this continued south immediately to the east of Albright's 1933 excavations (Lapp 1965: 5). The eastern portion of this wall was the inner wall of the Iron II casemate; Hellenistic builders added to this wall, giving it the resultant 1.80 m width (cf. pl. 18d). The other casemate wall was founded on bedrock and in places was built against a vertical face cut into bedrock.

The outer wall of the casemate construction was usually about 80 cm wide, and the inner about 50 cm. The interstice between the walls varied from 1.5 to 2 m. Crosswalls still standing were spaced at varying intervals, from over 1 m to almost 3 m; however, these had often been disturbed, and later occupants had either added or taken away from the original construction. The Tell el-Fûl casemate and others of the Iron Age will be discussed further in chap. VI.

East Casemate

Evidence for the construction and use of the East Casemate is substantially limited to Period III A. Several stratified loci related to the walls have good pottery of the period: in the northern area excavated debris against the east face of the inner casemate (Room EC-2, L. V-89, 90 [pl. 18b]),[3] a pit in the northeast corner of Room C (L. V-45), occupational debris (L. V-50) associated with an Iron II wall (L. V-37) in the northern part of Room C, bedrock deposits west of the casemate in the southern part of Room C (L. VIII-16, 18, 19 [plan 8, sec. j-k; pl. 21:b-d]) and debris east of the outer casemate in the southernmost area excavated on the east side in 1964 (east of Room EC-3, L. XXIV-8-12 [pl. 4b; cf. Lapp 1965: 5-6]). Typical sherds recovered included hole-mouth and neckless rims, burnished-bowl fragments, double-ridged handles and ridged cooking pots with interior angles. Otherwise, the Hellenistic occupants had cleared out the areas around the East Casemate walls for their own constructions. Substantial evidence of Period III B occupation is absent, so it cannot be determined whether the exilic residents made use of the East Casemate walls.

West Casemate

Like the East Casemate, construction of the West Casemate was undoubtedly in the III A period, but the use of the walls and occupation within them continued past 587 B.C. (plan 5, sec. n-s; pl. 5b). The Period III occupation was evidenced in the lower layers of stratified debris in West Casemate Room L (L. II-29-31; 35-37, including Floors 30 and 36 [pl. 5c]), Room N (Floor II-19 and below — L. II-19, 27, 34 [pl. 5d]) and Room O (L. II-15, 17). Casemate Crosswall N/O (L. II-18) and the lower course of a northern section of the outer casemate wall (L. VII-5b [plan 6, sec. c-d; pl. 6a]) were dismantled and indicated Period III use. A 40-cm wall on the west side of Room L (L. II-32 [pl. 5c]) may have been an attempt to bolster the outer casemate wall next to the revetment sometime in Period III. From Period III B note especially the very high-rimmed cooking pot (pl. 69:14) from Room L (L. II-35) and a piece of chevron ware from the northern section of the outer wall (L. VII-5b; cf. pl. 65:5-7).

Cistern 2

In the northernmost preserved section of the West Casemate a plastered cistern was uncovered with a channel leading to it from the south (plan 10; pl. 6a-b). The channel and channel walls were beneath Hellenistic debris and yielded only Iron I and Iron II material (L. VII-15W). The cistern shaft yielded some Hellenistic sherds (L. VII-10a), but the lower levels (L. VII-10b) yielded 14 baskets of Iron I and Iron II pottery (Lapp 1965: 6), indicating it had not been cleaned out for later use. To be noted from the lower levels of the cistern are a rilled-rim cooking pot (pl. 67:14) and a concentric-circle stamped handle (pl. 29:5) which firmly date the deposit. Also recovered were several stone objects (pl. 25:7, 8; no. 155) and a decorative piece of bone inlay (pl. 27:7) which predates Period III A.

Northeast Revetment

Excavation at the northeast corner of the mound unearthed structures of defensive nature (plans 1, 8, 9). During Iron II this may have included a revetted tower similar to that on the southwest, but perhaps smaller. A stone revetment (L. V-91) was laid against the outer casemate, and a heavy wall below (L. V-49) strengthened the complex. However, the structures were apparently rebuilt and reused in Period IV, and Hellenistic material was found to bedrock. A "Hellenistic Tower" perhaps replaced earlier defensive elements (see below, p. 65; pl. 18a).

The casemate walls and the possibility of a northeast revetted tower suggested to P. W. Lapp (1965: 5-7) that the Period III defenses consisted of more than the *migdal* that Albright described (*TFL I*: 17). The usual picture of a *migdal* is that of an isolated watchtower. The characteristics of this "fortress" and its relation to other Iron Age fortifications will be discussed in chap. VI.

Northeast III Building

Inside the casemate in the northeast, what remained of a Period III building was uncovered (fig. 18). It was well built, with foundations cut nearly a meter into bedrock and walls about a meter thick (Lapp 1965: 6). The longest remaining segment was a north-south wall of 6 m, the west wall of Room NE. A parallel segment of 4 m was uncovered 2 m to the east. The 6-m segment turned to the west at the south end and extended another 2 m. Some of the rockfall to the south and north undoubtedly came from the walls.

The east foundation trench of the long wall yielded III A sherds (L. XVI-10, 14 [pl. 8a]). Black ashy destruction debris on bedrock in the northwest (sub L. IX-14 [pl. 8b]) and over fragments of a floor toward the south (L. XVI-9) may be evidence of the 587 B.C.

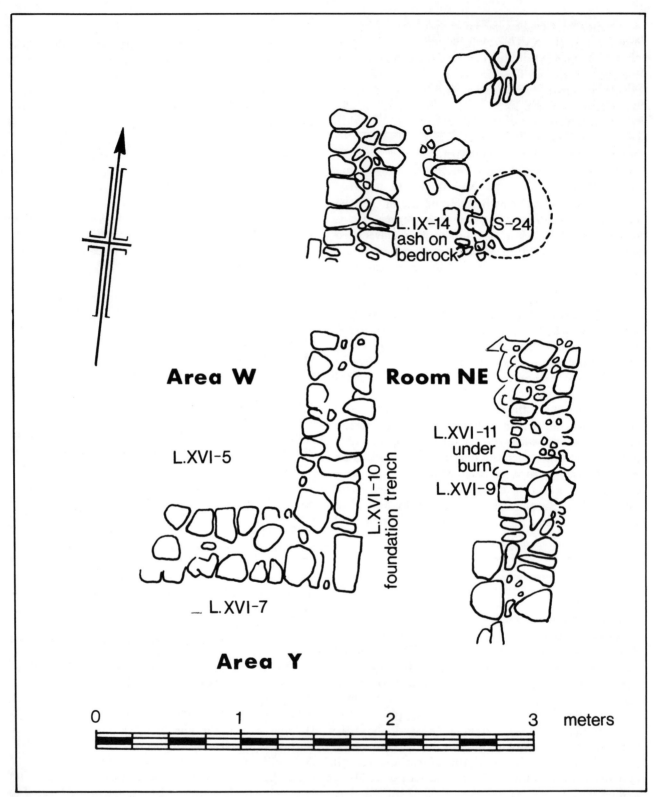

Fig. 18. The Northeast III Building.

destruction by Nebuchadnezzar (Lapp 1965: 6).[4] In the lower debris (L. XVI-11-13 in Room NE [pl. 8a], L. XVI-7 in Area Y), only pottery of III A appeared. Included were burnished-bowl and elongated-juglet sherds, an out-splayed rim of an Iron II bowl, cooking-pot fragments and a number of objects: loom weights (pl. 25:1), a bronze disc (pl. 26:14) and a bone spatula (pl. 25:17). Above the burn (L. IX-7, 14; XVI-4, 9), pottery of the III B' horizon occurred as well. Area W, to the west, around bedrock outcrop (L. XVI-5), and Area Y, above the floor (L. XVI-6), yielded important III B pottery also. Possible Exilic forms are a small open lamp, heavy-based lamps, high, straight-necked cooking pot rims, ridged-rim cooking pots with interior angle and rounded-rim jars with high necks.

Silo 28

In the northeast corner of Room NE of the Period III building the Hellenistic occupants disturbed the upper debris (L. IX-12) of Silo 28 (pl. 8b; cf. plans 8, sec. j-k, 11), but they apparently did not make use of the silo. The lowest layer of this relatively shallow pit (L. IX-13), as well as the packing at its base (L. IX-19 [pl. 8d]), contained only Period III pottery. In the soft, yellow-brown dirt were four nearly complete vessels: a cooking pot, an unburnished bowl of burnished-bowl form and two jar stands (pls. 8c; 64:17; 66:9, 10; 68:17); they all could belong to III B and indicate the deposit was laid near the end of Period III.

South of the Northeast III Building

South of the Northeast III Building and just to the north of Albright's excavations there was other evidence of the Period III occupation.

Stratified Debris

To the south of the Northeast III Building, bedrock debris (L. XIX-6) contained only III A sherds with one Period II sherd. Silo 25 (L. XIX-7) just south contained principally III B sherds; the few Hellenistic may have slipped in through the tilted cap (pl. 9c). Just northwest of Albright's excavations, stratified debris (L. XIX-2ext) contained considerable III A material as well as Iron I (Period II). Neckless jar rims and burnished-bowl fragments were typical. The presence of other unstratified III B sherds in the area indicate that there was probably Exilic occupation of the mound here inside the casemate walls. The debris in these deposits is undoubtedly related to the Period III use of the Northeast Building.

Silo 21

This silo was just north of the old excavations and in Albright's Room 17 (pl. 9a). Cut out of the hard floor of the room and into bedrock, it was sealed by a rectangular slab in the circular cap recess with the help of stone wedges (pl. 9b). The deposit in this silo consisted of a number of burnished-bowl sherds, a small, thin, unburnished Iron II-type bowl sherd, a globular cooking-pot fragment, part of a bronze pin and a couple of Iron I sherds. All probably predate 587 B.C.

Mid-Field

A trench was cut across the mound in the north in an attempt to relate the east and west excavations. Toward the center of the mound the trench was extended south, widened, and then taken east to connect with the eastern areas (plan 2). There was very little debris over bedrock, and wall remains were usually only one course high. The shallow debris contained much Period III pottery.

Gray Ash Deposit

Only one small area of stratified material can be singled out — a gray ash deposit just east of the center north-south wall of the eastern extension (L. XVIII-45). It illustrates the Period III B use of the area since among the sherds recovered was a cooking pot with very high rim (pl. 69:15).

Silos 36, 38 and 39

Five silos were uncovered in the Mid-Field excavations. Two, Silos 35 and 37, contained later deposits. Three, Silos 36, 38 and 39 (pl. 10d; plan 11; figs. 22-23), from the south extension had excellent pottery deposits which predated Period III A and were thus the earliest groups of Iron II pottery on the site. A great quantity of pottery came from Silo 36 (17 baskets), and the smaller amounts from Silos 38 and 39 were of a similar repertory. There were many common late Iron II forms — hole-mouth and neckless jars, three-handled jugs or jars with spouts, vertically elongated, burnished juglets, ring-burnished bowls with everted or flattened rims, rilled-rim cooking pots and saucer lamps. In addition there were a few forms which preceded the III A pottery in date not present in the stratified III A deposits: burnished bowls with rims thickened slightly on the interior; heavy, shallow cooking pots with grooved rims; plain, short-necked jars; an earlier type of hole-mouth; and rounded-shoulder hole-mouth-type jars. Absent were high-necked jars, ridged cooking pots with distinctive interior angles at the rim and heavy high-footed lamps — all common III A forms in the other deposits. These forms are all discussed further in chap. IX.

Southwest Rooms

The Exilic period following the destruction by Nebuchadnezzar in 587 B.C. evidently brought peaceful conditions to Tell el-Fûl (see above, p. 39). Period III B occupation was widespread. Rooms outside the West Casemate suggest that the political situation allowed occupation and construction outside the walls of Period III A. Substantial walls were laid on bedrock, but they were of smaller stones than those of the casemate walls and were not as well constructed (Lapp 1965: 6; pl. 11a).

Room E

In the western portion of Room E (L. I-41 and 42), the westernmost area of the mound excavated, even the latest surface sherds were from Period III B. Beneath, in burned debris to bedrock (L. I-45), homogeneous Period III pottery was found. East in Room E in sub-surface levels (L. I-24 and 25) most sherds were from Period III. Scree removal (L. I-26, 27 [pl. 11b]) yielded a few Iron II and Iron I sherds, and deposits beneath to bedrock were either sterile (L. I-46) or contained Iron I body sherds (L. I-44).

Room D

The debris in a depression north of Wall D/E (L. I-16 [pl. 11c]) yielded III A and B sherds. Walls D/G-E/F and D/E (pls. 11a-d, 12b) can be dated to Period III B both by construction and the pottery from foundation trenches and deposits in the rooms.

Rooms F and G

In Room F the pit next to the revetment (L. I-49 [pl. 12c]) with an Iron II deposit was mentioned above. The Hellenistic basins above the pit were supported by the Period III Wall F/G (L. I-50) on the north which separated Rooms F and G (cf. pl. 12b-c). Wall F/G was 70 cm wide and 65 cm high. Its north face was fairly even and formed the south face of a Period III basin complex in Room G (fig. 19; pl. 12a). This complex was built in the corner formed by Wall F/G and the west face of the outer West Casemate. A small dividing wall 25 cm wide and 66 cm high, extended 70 cm west from the casemate wall into Room G. The whole room was plastered although there were breaks and varying levels. A stone socket with most of the base intact and about half the rim was found on the floor near the north door of the room. The Room G debris (L. I-35) over and around the basin and plastered floor contained sherds dating the installation to Period III B.

Room J

There were two entrances to Room G from Room J to the north (pl. 12b): one, 65 cm wide, on the east next to the casemate (L. I-32), and one, 80 cm wide, on the west next to Wall D/G (L. I-34). These were reused in Hellenistic times (cf. pl. 13b and below, p. 72). In the southeastern part of Room J a plastered area, less than a meter wide and forming a kind of step, went along and up the side of the casemate more than 50 cm. Close by was a small, flat grinding(?) stone and a cup depression with some plaster in a stone block (see fig. 19). Just north was a small stone socket and evidence of burning in the area. A large flat stone, 50 x 50 cm and 12 cm high was found 5 m to the west on the same floor level (L. I sub-29 [pl. 13d]). It may also have been a grinding stone. The basin installation of Room G and the plastered areas and artifacts of Room J suggest some kind of industrial activity during Period III B.

The debris in Room J (L. I-29) down to the floor and occupation level contained Hellenistic sherds. L. I sub-29 with the basin installation in Room G belongs to Period III B (as can be seen in pl. 12b). Excavation did not go below Floor L. I sub-29.

Silo 40

To the north in Area K, the Hellenistic occupation continued to the depths excavated although earlier pottery always was found along with the Hellenistic and Roman sherds. Wall J/K was built over Silo 40 (L. XII-28 [cf. pl. 13d; plan 11]) and had broken its mouth, which had probably stood above the bedrock *nârî*. The silo contained a homogeneous Period III deposit. The debris consisted of a number of folded-over jar rims similar to those of the III B deposit of Cistern 1 and the III B Pottery Cache (see below, p. 46). Recovered were also rounded jar rims and cistern-type jug fragments, so it is possible that this was a homogeneous III B deposit.[5]

Northwest

As in some places to the south, in the northwest the Hellenistic people had cleared away most Iron II constructions. A huge Hellenistic wall, Wall H, replaced the West Casemate. Only a fragment of a Period III wall, Wall U-Uw/Z (pl. 14b-c), remained, similar to the walls of Period III B to the south. In Area U the latest pottery in a pit (L. XV-17 [pl. 15c]) was Iron II. Then in the northeastern section of this part of the mound very important evidence for Period III B was uncovered.

Cistern 1

This large, well-plastered cistern in the northwest rooms was cut 5.25 m into bedrock (plan 10, pls. 16d, 17a). A transverse partition wall 0.5 m thick was constructed in a northeast-southwest direction through the middle of the cistern. The partition, built of uncut stones with cobbles stuffed into the irregular interstices,

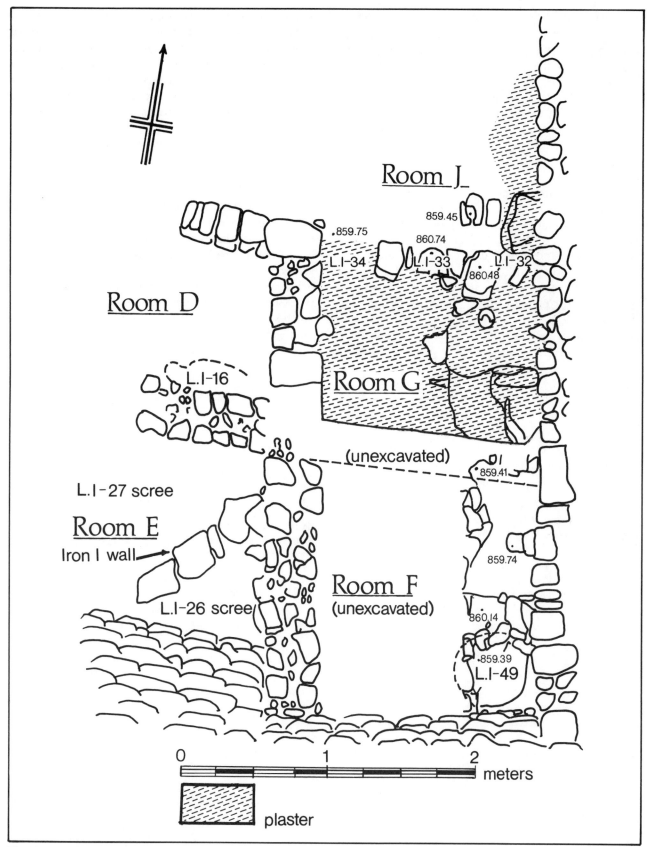

Fig. 19. The Period III basin complex.

was plastered. A passageway 1.7 m high and 0.80 m wide connected the two halves of the cistern (pl. 17b, c). Only the northwest half of the cistern was excavated, but it may be assumed that the other half was similar. The plaster on the bedrock sides of the cistern was 2.5 to 3 cm thick and extended to a height of over 4.20 m; the plaster on the crosswall was only 0.5 cm thick on the lower courses. There is evidence of patching on the bedrock side. Much pottery and many objects came from the cistern. Most important was the lowest silt layer, a deposit of over a meter in depth, from which came a homogeneous group of III B pottery (L. III-30-33; 32 and 33 came from a small clearance through the passageway in the partition wall [cf. Lapp 1965: 6; 1970: 179]). The pottery comes from a relatively unknown period in ceramic chronology. It was a large group with a great variety of forms, both sherds and whole vessels, and it all dates within a relatively short period of time. The many forms which appear in the deposit are important, but in addition, the absence of certain Iron II forms is strong evidence that they were no longer made in the Exilic period.

When the pottery forms are discussed in chap. IX, this homogeneous group is very significant. Special mention may be made here of the new evidence concerning folded-over jar rims; the many cistern-type jugs; flasks; craters and chevron ware; straight, high-rimmed cooking pots; short-necked cooking pots; elongated and globular juglets; and Exilic lamp forms.

Pottery Cache

Just to the west of Cistern 1 a north-south wall and "plaster lintel" may have been related to the cistern. P. W. Lapp referred to the wall or stone scree as a "fence," perhaps to hold back the transported garden soil to the west, in post-Period IV times (see **below, p. 75**). In any case, a distinctive pottery cache (L. X-8) was crushed beneath and in the stones of the north-south wall (cf. pl. 16c). This locus was a group of homogeneous Exilic pottery similar to that in the lowest layer of Cistern 1.

NOTES

[1]Stager (1975: 244-48) discusses the expansion of Judah and environs in the 7th century B.C.

[2]Contrast Noth 1958: 295, who believed the real nucleus of Judeans remained in Palestine, with Bright 1959: 325, who believes "Israel's true center of gravity had temporarily shifted from the homeland."

[3]Originally a date ca. 550 B.C. was given to L. V-89 and 90 (P. W. Lapp Pottery Book, p. 32). A number of typical III A sherds appeared as indicated below, but it was probably the ridged cooking

pots with interior angles that prompted the designation ca. 550 B.C. See the pottery discussion of this form, p. 96, to indicate its use at the end of Iron II as well as in the Exilic period.

[4]Cf. Fieldbook 4, p. 35; Lapp Diary, p. 51. The heavy destruction must have been concentrated in the area of the third fortress, cf. above, p. 14.

[5]At the time of excavation the deposit was considered to date about 600 B.C., but further study has shown that folded-over jar rims are not known in Iron II deposits but were present in the two Tell el-Fûl III B homogeneous groups.

Chapter 6

Tell el-Fûl and Some Iron Age Constructions

Nancy L. Lapp

The Casemate Construction at Tell el-Fûl and in Palestine

The identification of late Iron II casemate walls at Tell el-Fûl was one of the principal discoveries of the 1964 campaign (Lapp 1965: 4-5). The casemate belongs to Period III, constructed in the second half of the 7th century B.C. (Period III A). It was reused, but probably not for defensive purposes, during the Exilic period (Period III B, 587-538 B.C.), and again in the Hellenistic period (Period IV). Albright's contention that there was an Iron I casemate has to be abandoned; however, instead of having one of the earliest casemate constructions known in Palestine, Tell el-Fûl has one of the latest. It is now known that casemate constructions were fairly common through Iron II, though sometimes not of the substantial size and construction of earlier times. It is appropriate to review the known casemate walls in Palestine so that the purpose of Tell el-Fûl's wall construction can be assessed. Reference can be made to their location in fig. 20 and to some of their distinctive features in fig. 21.

Early Casemates

Until recently it was believed that the casemate construction originated in Late Hittite Asia Minor about the 15th century B.C. and reached Palestine through Syria several centuries later (Albright 1960: 120-22; Wright 1965: 151; Yadin 1963: 91-93, 289-90). Gibeah from the time of Saul (11th century, Period II) was believed to have the earliest casemate walls in Palestine (cf. *TBM III*: 14). Those who argued for the presence of the Philistines at Tell el-Fûl attributed the introduction of the casemate in Palestine to them (Mazar 1964: 6). Now several late MB IIC-LB I casemate constructions are known in Palestine, so neither a cultural lag nor a relation to the Philistines can be claimed.

At Taanach (Lapp 1969: 17-22), Hazor (Yadin 1972: 61), and Shechem (Dever 1973: 244-45) substantial casemate walls as a part of their late MB IIC fortifications have been uncovered. The earliest casemate at Taanach dated to the first half of the 16th century B.C. It was a rather flimsy effort, but in its second phase (second half of the 16th century B.C.), as well as the walls at Hazor and Shechem, there were substantial structures with total spans of 4.5 to 5.5 m (see plans, Lapp 1969: figs. 10-11). At Hazor and Shechem the casemate constructions were also substantial and in connection with city gates (Yadin 1972: fig. 13; Dever 1974a: figs. 2, 4; first half of the 16th century B.C.). Similar construction was noted at Taanach and Hazor (Lapp 1969: 22, n. 34).

A casemate construction which is attributed to the Philistines (11th century B.C.) has been uncovered at the coastal city of Ashdod according to the excavators (Dothan 1968: 253, and verbal communication with James Swauger). Details must await publication.

United Monarchy

Chronologically, the next well-dated casemates are known from Tell Beit Mirsim and Beth-shemesh (*TBM III*: 12-14, 37; *AS V*: 23-26). No evidence of a casemate wall has been uncovered at Tell en-Naṣbeh (contrast Yadin 1963: 290). Albright attributed the similarity in plan and construction of the Tell Beit Mirsim and Beth-shemesh walls to common supervision at the time of David (see plans, *TBM III*: pls. 1-3, 6; *AS V*: fig. 1). Aharoni (1959: 35-37) attempts to date them to Solomon along with the walls of Hazor and Gezer. But the similarity is not as close as he implies (see fig. 21), and building activity undoubtedly took place during David's reign. The dating of the original excavators is stratigraphically based and more acceptable. The walls were repaired and rebuilt by the first kings of the southern kingdom. The wall at Tell Beit Mirsim con-

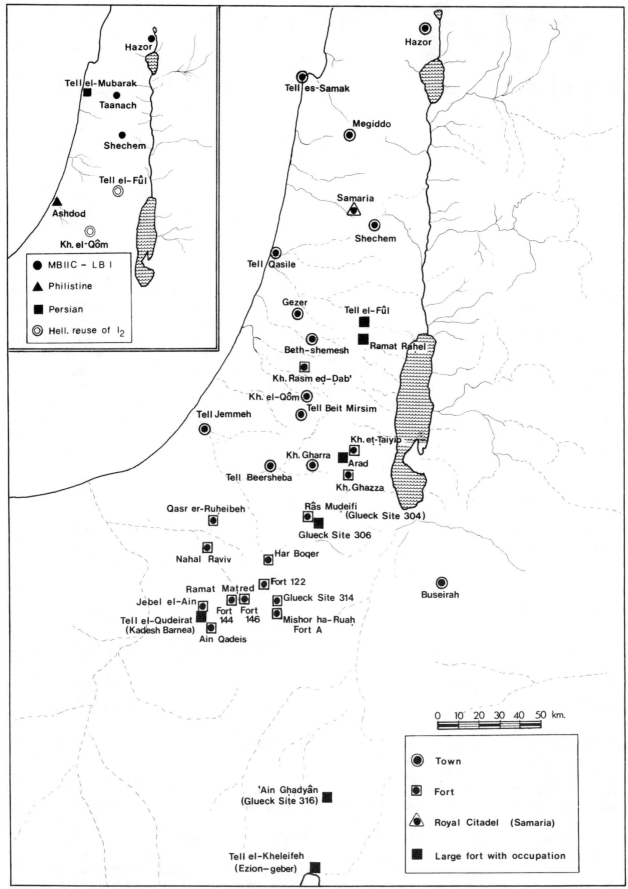

Fig. 20. Iron Age sites in Palestine with casemate constructions with insert showing later and earlier sites.

tinued in use down to the city's destruction, but Beth-shemesh was apparently unwalled after about 850 B.C.

Solomonic casemate walls in conjunction with the city gates have been identified at the strategic sites of Hazor, Gezer and Megiddo (Yadin 1972: 135-40, 147-64; *Gezer I*: 62-63; Yadin 1960: 67-68). Plans and dimensions of the gatehouses and walls are so similar that they can all be attributed to Solomon's engineers (1 Kgs 9:15; see plans, Yadin 1972: figs. 27, 31-37, 39, 40; *Gezer I*: plans 9, 12). Aharoni (1972: 302-11; 1974a: 13) does not associate the casemate wall at Megiddo with the Solomonic gate. However, Yadin, the excavator, maintains his position (1973: 330).

On the northern coast Solomonic casemates have been uncovered at Tell Qasîle, Stratum IX B (Maisler 1950-51: 73, 194-95, 200-2), and perhaps at Tell es-Samak (Elgavish 1969: 247; 1970: 229; 1972: 167). In the expansion southward during the United Monarchy a system of forts was constructed to protect developing trade routes and agricultural settlements. At Arad heavy casemate walls enclosed a fortress or citadel, 50 x 50 m, and there was also a typical Solomonic gateway with three guardrooms on either side (Aharoni 1967d: 270-71). At the southern extremity of Solomon's kingdom, a 45 x 45 m casemate construction at Tell el-Kheleifeh (Ezion-geber?) enclosed a "storehouse granary" which was strengthened by a sloping rampart of mud bricks (Glueck 1965: 81-83; plans, figs. 7, 9).

In the central Negeb region a number of forts may be a part of Solomon's defense system. An agricultural settlement on the Ramat Matred plateau has been surveyed (Aharoni et al. 1960: 23-36, 97-111, especially pp. 103-9). Four forts are located on the highway passing south of the plateau leading southwestward toward Kadesh-barnea, and at least three of them yield evidence of casemate constructions. They are all small with walls only one or two stones thick (cf. fig. 21; Aharoni et al. 1960: figs. 15-17). Fort 144, ca. 20 x 20 m, has three or four casemate rooms on each side. Fort 146 follows the shape of the elliptical knob on which it is located, 23 m long and 12 m wide at its widest point. To its west are more rooms with a second casemate wall some 15 m beyond the oval-shaped fort. Fort 122 is not casemated itself but has three casemated rooms to the north attached to the main fort by a kind of courtyard. The archeological surveyors considered the outside rooms of Forts 146 and 122 as a kind of khan for visitors. The pottery found around the forts was of the usual wheel-made 10th-century type as well as a handmade, roughly finished ware found throughout Iron II in the Negeb. This ware has not been closely dated, but its appearance here with 10th-century types has led the surveyors to date the agricultural settlement and the forts to the United Monarchy (Aharoni et al. 1960: 102). Their destruction

is attributed to Shishak's campaign of 920 B.C. (Aharoni et al. 1960: 110), and the settlements were not rebuilt or reused. The network of forts, however, was perhaps restored when later kings of Judah exerted their power to the south.

The oval-shaped fort on Ain Qadeis 15 km south of Kadesh-barnea dates to the 10th century, or perhaps somewhat later (Rothenberg 1961: 125, 137-38, fig. 15; Yadin 1963: 376). This fort and a number of others have been located and mapped but have not been systematically excavated (for example, Glueck's survey in the Negeb, 1956: 21; 1957: 23; cf. Aharoni 1967b: 3-11). Most of them cannot be dated to a particular period or reign, principally because the handmade Negeb pottery has not been stratigraphically delineated. Aharoni (1967b: 7) seems to want to limit this handmade pottery to the 10th century, but stratigraphical evidence is not cited and the date was still questioned at least as late as 1974 (Meshel and Sass 1974: 273-74). Whether these forts were originally built as a part of Solomon's defensive system, were constructed by later kings of Judah, or were used continually or intermittently throughout Iron II cannot be determined until excavation. Besides those discussed in the next section, the following can be mentioned: a square-like fort at Nahal Raviv, 19-22 m on each side (Aharoni 1967b: 5; Feldmann 1959: 102-4), and a large 40 x 30 m fort at Khirbet et-Taiyib (Aharoni 1967b: 8).

Divided Monarchy

Yadin has claimed that the casemate wall as a defensive element gave way, because of the introduction of a powerful type of battering-ram by the Assyrian army, to a more massive wall of formidable strength, commonly known as the type with salients and recesses, during the reign of Rehoboam (Yadin 1963: 289). Thereafter, he contends, casemate walls were abandoned as a type of construction in new city walls and were used in Iron II only for walls of the inner citadel or for isolated and independent fortresses where the chambers were used mainly for dwelling and storage. This may be the general development, but recent excavations point to several exceptions. At Shechem, Tell Beit Mirsim, Beth-shemesh and Tell Qasîle there is evidence of rebuilding or repair of old casemates as part of the defensive system. At Tell Beit Mirsim in Stratum A (918-587 B.C.) and Beth-shemesh, Stratum II B (950-825 B.C.), improvements were made in the earlier 10th-century walls. At Shechem the MB IIC wall near the Northwest Gate was rebuilt in a much cruder manner in the 10th-9th century (Stratum IX) according to recent excavations (Dever 1973: 244-45). The Tell Qasîle wall is clearest in its latest rebuilding, dated by the excavators to the Omri (Stratum VIII)

Fig. 21. Casemate constructions in Palestine.

SITE	STRATUM	DATE	AREA ENCLOSED
TAANACH		MB II C - LB I	Town
	1st phase	ca. 1600-1550	
	2nd phase	ca. 1550-1500	
HAZOR	Area K, Stratum 3	MB II C ca. 1600-1550	Town
	X-IX	Solomonic-875	Town - 6.5 acres (26,000 sq. m.)
SHECHEM		MB II C - 1540	Town
	IX	918-810	Town
ASHDOD	Area G, Stratum 12	11th century Philistine	
TELL BEIT MIRSIM	B₃	1000-918	Town - 7.5 acres
	A	918-587	Town - 7.5 acres
BETH-SHEMESH	IIa	1000-950	Town
	IIb	950-825	Town
GEZER	VII-1	Solomonic reused through 1st century B.C.	Town
MEGIDDO	V A-IV B	Solomonic-918	Town
TELL QASILE	IX, 1	Solomonic, 10th century	Town - less than 3.75 acres (15-16 dunans)
	VIII	9th century	less than 3.75 acres
	VII	8th-732	less than 3.75 acres
TELL ES -SAMAK		10th century	Town - 2500 sq. m. (4.5-5.0 x 4.5-5.0)
ARAD	XI	Solomonic-920	Citadels - 50 x 50 m. (2.5 dunans)
	VII	700-640	50 x 50 m.
	VI	640-early 6th century	50 x 50 m.
TELL EL-KHELEIFEH (EZION GEBER)	I	Solomonic-918	Around granary - 45 x 45 m.
RAMAT MAṬRED Fort 122		Solomonic - 850	Forts 10 x 28 m.
Fort 146			23 x 12 m. **casemate rooms to west**
Fort 144			20 x 20 m.
ᶜAIN QADEIS		10th-9th centuries?	Fort - 42 x 32 m.
NAḤAL RAVIV		Iron II	Fort - 19 x 22 m.
HAR BOQER		Iron II	Fort - 24 x 18 m.
KHIRBET EṬ-ṬAIYIB		Iron II	Fort - 40 x 30 m.
SAMARIA	Period II	870 or 840	Around palace 100 x 220 m. On north:
TELL BEERSHEBA	III	9th-8th centuries	Town - 70 x 100 m.
	II	8th-701	Town - 70 x 100 m.
KHIRBET GHARRA		8th-7th centuries	Town - 330 x 100 m. (6-7 acres)
KHIRBET GHAZZA		8th-7th centuries	Fort - 53 x 41 m.

OUTER	INNER	INTER-STICE	TOTAL	BUILDING MATERIAL	NOTES
1.5	0.5	1.5	3.5	stone	caps glacis and is flimsy
1.75	1.50-2.25	1.25	4.5-5.25	large stones	follows earlier
1.5	1.5	2.25	5.5	stone	by city gate
1.5-1.6	1.1	2.4-2.5	5.4	brick on stone foundation	Solomonic gate
1.55	1.5	1.55	4.6	stone	by city gate
1.55	1.5	1.55	4.6	stone	crude rebuild
				mudbrick	rebuild of LB fortress
1.5	1.0-1.1	1.5-2.0	4.0-4.5	stone	
1.5	1.0-1.1	1.5-2.0	4.0-4.5	stone	poorer rebuild
1.4-1.6	1.1	1.5-2.0	4.0-4.5	stone	
1.4-1.6	1.1	1.5-2.0	4.0-4.5	stone	reuse
	1.6-1.9		5.4	stone	by Solomonic gate - recent excavations inner wall only
1.0	1.0	2.0-4.0	4.0-6.0	brick on stone foundation	near Solomonic gate
				"kukar" stone	crossway rooms
				"kukar" stone	rebuild
		5.0	6.5	"kukar" stone	repair
1.9		1.9		stone	outer is 2 or 3 walls together with rubble
				ashlar masonry	Solomonic gate
3.0-4.0	1.3			stone	massive wall reuse, internal wall added
1.5-1.6	1.3	3.5	6.5	stone	massive wall not reused; casemate over sanctuary
1—	1—	2+	4.0	larger bricks	with salients and recesses; glacis of small bricks around granary
0.8	2.3	0.8	3.0	1 stone wide	3 casemate rooms line courtyard outside
0.4	1.8	0.4	2.5	1 stone wide	oval with casemate
0.8	1.3	0.8	3.0	1 stone wide	rooms to west
1.0	2.0	0.5	3.5	inner: 1 stone wide outer: 2 stones wide	
		1+	2.5	stone	oval
1.0	1.0	1.5	3.5	stone	
				stone	casemate rooms on all 4 sides
				stone	
2.0	1.0	2.0	5.0	hewn stone	expanded and used Period I wall;
2.0	1.5	6.5	10.0		1 m. partitions
1.6	1.05	2—	4+	bricks on stone foundations	constructed on solid wall
1.5	0.6	3.0	5.1	large undressed stones	stone glacis vs. outer wall
1.5	0.75	4.0	6.25	large undressed stones	towers: corners and center sides

SITE	STRATUM	DATE	AREA ENCLOSED
TELL EL-QUDEIRAT (KADESH-BARNEA)	Period II	9th/8th-early 6th centuries	Fort - 60 x 41 m.
KHIRBET RASM ED-DAB^c		8th-7th centuries	Fort - 30 x 40 m.
MISHOR HA-RUAḤ Fort A		Israelite III - 840-587	Fort - 20 x 20 m.
JEBEL EL-ᶜAIN		Iron II	Fort - 20 x 20 m.
GLUECK'S Site 314		Iron II	Fort - 21 x 16 m.
Site 306		Iron II	Fort - 80 x 40 m.
RÂS MUDEIFI (Glueck's site 304)		Iron II	Fort - 40 x 50 m.
QASR ER-RUḤEIBEH		Iron II	Fort - 20 x 23 m.
ᶜAIN GHADYAN		Iron Age	Fort - 64 x 40
BUSEIRAH		Iron II	Town
KHIRBET EL-QÔM		7th century (reused 3rd-2nd)	Town
TELL JEMMEH		Assyrian-late 7th century	Town
TELL EL-MUBARAK	II	mid & late Persian	Walled estate (100 x 80 m.)
RAMAT RAḤEL	V	8th-7th centuries	Citadel - 40 x 78 m.
TELL EL-FÛL	III A	7th-587	Village
	III B	587-538	62 x 57 m. ?
	IV	2nd century	

and Jehu (Stratum VII) dynasties (Maisler 1950-51: 73, 94-95, 200-2; plan, fig. 1).

At Samaria a casemate wall system was constructed around the royal quarters. It dates to the second building phase, Ahab's or Jehu's addition to Omri's construction. According to Kenyon this followed very soon after Omri's building (1970: 265), but according to Wright during Jehu's reign (1961: 100). The casemate wall is only on the summit surrounding the palace area, providing a kind of inner fortress. On the north side the casemate rooms were situated crossways, making the total width of the wall as much as 10 m (*SS I*: pl. 2; oblong rooms built next to one another were also found at Tell Qasîle, Maisler 1950-51: 202). On the other sides they were of the usual lengthwise construction with a width of about 5 m. The royal quarters were expanded on the north and west, but the beautifully constructed first-building-phase wall was used on the south and east. Although the walls may not have withstood battering rams as Yadin contends, they would have provided strong protection against assault troops (Yadin 1963: 289; Kenyon 1970: 263-65).

Population settlement of the Negeb continued during the Divided Monarchy, probably during the reigns of Jehosophat, 873-849 B.C. (2 Chr 17:12, "He built in Judah fortresses and store cities"), and Uzziah, 783-742 B.C. (2 Chr 26:10, "And he built towers in the wilderness, and hewed out many cisterns"). Casemate constructions have been excavated or traced at a number of sites. In the northern Negeb the excavations at Tell Beersheba have revealed the casemated town of the 9th-7th centuries, Strata III-I (Aharoni 1974b: 34-36; plan and sec., figs. 1, 2). The casemated walls topped the earlier solid wall. Twenty kilometers to the east is a large tell of 6-7 acres, Khirbet Gharra. It has not been excavated, but a casemated wall can be traced all around the slope (Aharoni 1958: 36-38; sec., fig. 3). A stone glacis bolstered the outer wall. Pottery included late Iron II sherds and a *le-melek* handle. This is a casemated, defended city toward the end of the Divided Kingdom.

In the same area is a small fort, Khirbet Ghazza, which can perhaps be attributed to Uzziah (Aharoni 1958: 33-35; plan, fig. 2). It is similar in size (53 x 41 m)

OUTER	INNER	INTER-STICE	TOTAL	BUILDING MATERIAL	NOTES
1.0	1.0	3.0	4-5.0	unhewn or crudely dressed stones	towers: corners and center sides; glacis surrounded
1.3	1.2	3.0	5.5		towers: corners and center sides
0.5	0.5	1.8	2.8	1 stone wide	
				crude limestone stone	"rooms vs. walls" "rooms vs. walls"
0.7	0.7	2.5	4.0	stone brick top	
				stone	
				rectangular bricks laid dressed stones filled with un-dressed	header & stretcher
1.1-1.5	1.1	2.8	5.0	dressed stone	
0.35-0.8	0.5	2.0	3.0	stone	
					reused with occupation outside

and plan to the one at ᶜAin el-Qudeirat (Kadesh-barnea), 60 x 41 m (Dothan 1965: 135-38; plan and sec., figs. 1 and 2). These two casemate-walled forts had eight towers, one at each corner and in the middle of each side. A smaller fort at Rasm eḏ-Ḏabᶜ on the road between Tell Zakariyeh (Azekah) and Tell el-Judeidah is similar, and perhaps all are part of a common system of King Uzziah (Rachmani 1964: 209-14; plan, fig. 2; Aharoni 1967c: 313-14; map 28; for a comparison of the towers see N. Lapp 1976: fig. 4). The fort (with towers) at Arad was constructed toward the end of the 8th century (Stratum VII) by adding a wall inside the solid wall used in the forts of Strata X-VIII (Aharoni 1967a: 244-46; plan, fig. 3). In Stratum VI (second half of the 7th century) the casemate walls completely replaced the older walls and were built over the Israelite sanctuary.

In the central Negeb the agricultural settlements of the Mishor ha-Ruaḥ plateau indicated 8th-century occupation (Evenari et al. 1958: 239; plan, fig. 5). Forts protected the road running through the plateau and attracted the farms. One small fort, 20 x 20 m, is casemated. It is comparable to one on Jebel el-ᶜAin, the ridge above ᶜAin el-Qudeirat (Rothenberg 1961: 41, 125; plan, fig. 6). In Nelson Glueck's survey of this area two other forts are described as casemated, Sites 314 and 306 (Glueck 1957: 22-23; 1959: 185-86; cf. Aharoni 1967b: 7). Neither has been excavated nor closely dated. Glueck's Site 304 at Râs Mudeifī was described by him as an open village, but closer examination revealed the foundations of an oblong casemated fort (Glueck 1957: 23; Aharoni 1967b: 7). Woolley and Lawrence (1914-15: 40-41) located a small fort at Qasr er-Ruḥeibeh which had wheel-burnished sherds among its pottery.

To the south and east two sites have been excavated which have not yet yielded precisely datable material. At ᶜAin Ghaḏyân (Glueck Site 316) which overlooks the west side of the Arabah, casemate rooms from the fort have been cleared, yielding the typical coarse handmade Negeb pottery (Meshel and Sass 1974: 273-74). At Buseirah (Bozrah) across the Arabah in Edom, a part of Judah in the days of Uzziah, a casemate wall has been excavated that surrounded the city during part of the Iron II period (Bennett 1974: 73-76).

Casemated walls have been reported in the preliminary notices of several excavations, but details have not yet been published. At Khirbet el-Qôm, west of Hebron, a casemate construction belonging to the 7th century was identified (Holladay 1971: 176). It was reused by the Hellenistic people in the 3rd and 2nd centuries as were the casemate walls at Tell el-Fûl. South of the Philistine coast at Tell Jemmeh, excavations have revealed a casemated wall constructed during the Assyrian period and in use until the late 7th century (Van Beek 1972: 246; 1974: 139). Excavations at Tell el-Mubarak just north of Caesarea have uncovered a casemate wall surrounding an administrative building or estate which covers the whole mound. It dates from the middle or late Persian period (Stern 1973: 256; 1974: 267).

Important for the study of the casemate walls at Tell el-Fûl is the casemated citadel at Ramat Raḥel, just south of Jerusalem (*RR I*: 10-12, 59-60; plan, figs. 10, 23). Pottery and seal impressions date the citadel to the 7th century, so at Ramat Raḥel there was a fortress which can be compared to Tell el-Fûl in date and location. Both sites must have served to some extent as outposts of Jerusalem for the kingdom of Judah before its fall to the Babylonians in 587 B.C. However, the Ramat Raḥel citadel was much the stronger. Its 5-m walls were comparable to the Davidic and Solomonic city walls of Tell Beit Mirsim, Beth-shemesh, Hazor, Gezer and Megiddo. But perhaps it could best be compared to the royal fortified quarters at Samaria, or even closer in date, to the late Iron II casemated citadels at Arad.

The Tell el-Fûl Fortifications

The Tell el-Fûl casemate was found to the north of "Saul's tower" keyed into the lower courses of the Iron II revetment which surround the Period III (Iron II) tower excavated in the earlier campaign (plan 14, fig. 5b). Approximately 12.5 m of the outer wall was uncovered and 11 m of the inner. Further north, Hellenistic constructions went down to bedrock, having cleared away all traces of the late Iron II casemate. The casemate was also found on the eastern side of the summit where the inner wall was traced over 20 m from the northeast southward. From there it is presumed to have continued on the eastern edge of the excavations of Albright's second campaign. Sections of the outer casemate were uncovered in the northeast (6 m; pl. 18b, d) and just to the north of Albright's excavations (2 m; pl. 4b). This outer wall was founded on bedrock and in places was built against a vertical face cut into bedrock. Its width varied between 75 and 35 cm because of the packing against bedrock. Where it was preserved above foundation, it was some 80 cm thick.

The casemate walls at Tell el-Fûl were not thick and heavy like the Solomonic and Davidic walls at other sites nor like some of the late casemates of the Divided Kingdom. The total span of the earlier walls with their interstices equalled 4-5.5 m. The 9th-7th-century fortress and city walls at Samaria, Tell Qasîle and Khirbet Gharra were 5 to 6.5 m thick. Even the Negeb fortresses of late Iron II at Kadesh-barnea, Khirbet Ghazza and Arad spanned over 5-6 m, and the Ramat Raḥel citadel walls of 5 m have been noted. Of the published casemate walls, Tell el-Fûl can only be compared in strength to the 2.5- to 3-m walls of some of the Negeb forts. In the latter the "casemate rooms" probably served more as guardrooms, storerooms or khans than as true defensive structures.

Tell el-Fûl's outer casemate wall was generally two stones wide, ca. 60-90 cm thick. The stones were unhewn and of varying sizes (cf. pls. 4b, 5b, 18b), nothing like the carefully laid header stones of equal length at Ramat Raḥel (*RR I*: 10; pl. 4). The inner wall was one stone thick, averaging 50 cm wide. The space between the walls was 1.5-2.0 m and the total span was ca. 3 m.

Occupation levels within the Tell el-Fûl casemate rooms indicated that they had been used for domestic purposes or storage. Within the West Casemate a plastered floor in tiny Room N (L. II-19) dated to **Period III A (pl. 5d; see above, p. 41), whereas a plaster installation in Room L dated to III B (pl. 5c; see above, p. 41). The particularly well-preserved, plastered floor and drain of Room M dated to the Hellenistic period (see below, p. 69). Room O in the West Casemate contained a cistern (pl. 6a-b; see above, p. 41).** Pottery from its lower levels was Iron I and Iron II. What was probably an Iron I cistern had been incorporated into the casemate construction, and it continued in use at least during Period III A. In the East Casemate, Room EC-1 contained a stone basin (pl. 18b) under which was found one of the many capped silos (pl. 18c). There was Hellenistic pottery as well as Iron II in the silo; it was often the case that the Hellenistic occupants made use of earlier constructions. Most probably the silo was in use in Period III within the casemate room.

Where crosswalls remained the rooms were small—2 x 2.5 m, but other rooms could have been larger to provide additional living or working space. On the other hand, frequent crosswalls would add to the defensive strength of the feeble north-south walls and lessen the difficulty of filling them during time of siege. Besides use of the casemate rooms, it has been noted that there was occupation outside the casemate walls particularly in the III B period after the Babylonian **conquest (see above, pp. 39-44). Then, as well as in the** Hellenistic period, political conditions were such that building and daily activity could take place outside the town walls. It is probable that the casemate type of construction was chosen with more than a defensive purpose in mind. The high winds that blow sand and dirt over the mound make protection desirable in any season of the year. Casemated rooms for domestic and industrial use would be an economical and easy way to lay out the small town for protection against the elements, for care of animals, and for living and storage. Further floors and rooms were probably laid against the inner wall, although the Hellenistic occupations erased all evidence.

Yet the casemate walls were built into the defensive system. Excavation showed that the rooms on the west were keyed into the Iron II revetted tower, and it has been suggested that there may have been such a revetted tower in the northeast also (Lapp 1965: 6), although erosion and Hellenistic rebuilding have destroyed substantial evidence. It is possible there were corner towers at Tell el-Fûl such as those at the Kadesh-barnea and Khirbet Ghazza forts although the feeble casemate walls which would connect the towers make this doubtful.[1] Of course, in case of attack the space between the walls could be filled with stones and dirt and a substantial wall would result. But there is no evidence this was ever done, and there are no signs of violent destruction within the walls.

The Revetted Tower

In the first campaign at Tell el-Fûl Albright excavated the Period III tower (*TFL I*: 17-20, pl. 23). Built on the foundations of the Period II tower (Iron I, about 1000 B.C. or the period of Saul), the Period III tower was removed by the excavators when the earlier tower was excavated. Plans and descriptions indicate that it was composed of an inner wall and rooms about 18 x 18 m surrounded by a thin outer wall about 2 m from the inner wall. The space between was filled with debris and a stone glacis was set against the outer wall on all four sides.

Since the Period III tower had been completely removed in the first campaign, it was impossible to check its plans or stratigraphy in 1964. However, it was possible to put a trench through the revetment at the northwest corner of the Period II fortress where the outer wall of the Iron II fortress was still standing (plan 2). Four revetment walls were uncovered in the process (plans 1, 7; pl. 4c). The most eastern was shown conclusively to be Period II ("Saul's wall"), including a buttress repair at the corner (pl. 2a-c). The thin wall or "peel" next to this (pls. 2b-c; 4d) is the outer wall of the Period III tower, constructed a little more than 2 m from the inner tower wall against which the glacis was **built (cf. figs. 10, 11; p. 12). At the corner the Period III** outer tower wall was built on a loose fill over the Period II buttress repair. Elsewhere, this Iron II wall had been constructed on *nârî* bedrock with a foundation trench of its own and was left standing to a height

of at least 1.80 m. The stones of this wall were smaller than the larger masonry blocks of the Fortress II tower and buttress.

A mid-wall with a lot of scree emerged just to the west (sec., plan 7; pl. 4c). Both walls were built on a fill which yielded pottery that consistently dated to Period II. Less than 2 m to the west the outer wall of the sloping revetment was uncovered. This wall, which had a step roughly halfway up its remaining 2-m height, was dismantled down to the step (pl. 3d). The pottery from this dismantled portion was clearly dated to Period III A (L. XIII-8; see above, p. 00). Albright's basic conclusions concerning the sloping revetment were completely confirmed with the slight modification that the III A pottery should be dated to the late 7th-early 6th century B.C. (Lapp 1965: 3).

In 1924 Albright called this Iron II revetted tower a *migdal* or watch tower and compared it to the fortresses of the Negeb then known, particularly Qasr er-Ruḥeibeh which had been examined by Woolley and Lawrence. Qasr er-Ruḥeibeh had no glacis, but from the "fine, ring-burnished, haematite, stained ware" (*TFL I*: 18; Woolley and Lawrence 1914-15: 41), Albright concluded that it may have been one of the *migdalim* built by Uzziah (2 Chr 26:10) and dated close to the time of Gibeah III. Albright attributed the greater strength of the Tell el-Fûl fortress to its greater importance and function as a protection for Jerusalem against surprise attacks. Other of the Negeb forts mentioned above can be compared, but in each instance the Tell el-Fûl tower is the stronger and the only one which was revetted. At Kadesh-barnea a glacis surrounded the whole fort, approximately 60 x 41 m (Dothan 1965: 138, fig. 2). Each of its four corner towers measured about 10 x 8 m.

Conclusions

Thus at Tell el-Fûl there were two defensive elements which were almost contradictory in purpose. The revetted tower is unique in its strength as a *migdal* or watchtower. The casemated walls to the north and on the east, which may have enclosed a village occupation, are thin and feeble, no stronger than the walls of some of the small Negeb forts.

It is possible to reconstruct the situation somewhat as follows. Albright's designation of the Iron II tower as a watchtower is substantially correct. The principal function of the tower was to serve as a lookout for Jerusalem against surprise attacks and, if necessary, to take the brunt of a surprise attack itself. The casemate walls provided limited protection against major attack although they did provide domestic space and storage for the families and supporters of those who manned the fort. This may explain why there was considerable evidence of destruction in the tower itself, which can be attributed to the Babylonians in 587 B. C. (cf. *TFL I*:

Fig. 22. Descriptions of the Tell el-Fûl silos.

Silo no.	Locus & Location	Above opening:	Description		Pottery & Artifacts	References
21	XXI-5 N. of Albright's excavations	sub-sf. debris above hard floor	in floor of Albright's Room 17; loose, fine, gray and brown fill	III II	pl. 68:13	**p. 43** plan 12 pls.9a,b,10a
22	XXI-4 N. of Albright's excavations	sub-sf. debris above hard floor	in floor, east in Room 17; fine loose brown fill	IV B III	pl. 75:20 very few sherds	**p. 68** plan 12 pl. 9a
23	sub XX-4e-c S. of H House	L. XX-4e-c fall & scree, stones blocked square cut entryway into scarp	possibly double silo; upper partly of rock scarp, partly built up with rock; groove for sliding lid in upper, cap recess for lower; plaster and sherds in cavity in lower	IV B III		**p. 68** plan 12 fig. 24 pl. 10a-c
24	XIX-3ext S. of NE III Building	sub-sf. stony debris and scree; large broken opening	brown gray fill; contents from lowest silt only	II I ?	no. 145	**p. 25** plan 11
25	XIX-7 S. of NE III Building	rubble and scree; tilted cap	very loose gray, white, and brown fill	IV B III	few most	**p. 68** plan 12 pl. 9c
26	XX-12 S. of H House	in balk; broken humped cap	in balk	IV B III		**p. 68** plan 12 pl. 9d
27	IX-4 W. of H House	compact sub-sf. debris; large stones at top of silo	soft brown fill, rocks at top, with ER ? body sherds	V IV B		**p. 68** plan 11 pl. 8b
	IX-10 (lower)		hard, wet yellow brown with charcoal; not totally cleared	IV B III II	few sherds	
28	IX-12	stones covering opening	yellow brown fill	IV B	pl. 76:7	**p. 43** plans 12; 8,
	IX-13		lower layer	III	pls. 64:17; 66:9, 10; 68:17; no. 60	sec. j-k pl. 8b-d
	IX-19 NE III Building		stones packed into natural cavity at bottom	III	insignificant sherds	
29	V-40 H House Room B	slabs not completely sealing silo; hard surface in room not over slabs	soft yellow brown fill to top	IV B III		**p. 68** plans 12; 8, sec. j-k pl. 20d
30	V-34 H House Room A	Early Phase Floor 32; rect. slab sealed with stone wedges	poor quality plaster patch over cavity; overlap with Silo 31; thin layer of earth wash and roof fall on their floors	IV B III	pls. 79:3, 20 nos. 22, 43, 167	**p. 65** plan 12 pl. 19a, b, d
31	V-33 H House Room A	Early Phase Floor 32 covered east side only	probably cut into Silo 30, overlap, with thin layer of earth wash and roof fall on their floors; with catchment pit	IV B III	most sherds in Silo 30	**p. 65** plan 12 pls. 19b, d, 20a, b

Silo no.	Locus & Location	Above opening:	Description	Pottery & Artifacts		References
32	V-65	Fill 54 for Early Phase Floor 32; coin nos. 17, 18 on lip	soft yellow brown earth layer over hard yellow brown	IV B III		**pp. 65, 68** plan 12 pl. 19b, c
	V-67 (floor) H House Room A		coins on Floor 67 of silo	IV B	nos. 15, 16	
33	V-57	sub Wall A/B-C; canal leading into silo	soft yellow brown fill	IV B III		**pp. 63, 65** plan 12 pl. 21c
	V-57L H House		lowest layer	IV A III	pl. 79:15-18	
34	V-92	stone basin (pl. 18b)		IV B III	few mostly	**p. 65** plan 12 pl. 18c
	East Casemate Room EC-1					
35	XVIII	surface	filled with stones	V IV B III	(top)	**p. 69** plan 11
	Mid-Field N. trench					
36	XVIII	sub-surface		II pre-III A	pl. 48:2, 3 pls. 49:1-6, 12, 18-22; 50:28-30, 33-34; 57:1-3, 21-22; 60:1-5, 7; 62:1-8, 10-13, 17-25, 27, 28; 64:1-4, 10-13; 66:1-3; 67:1-5, 7-9, 16-22; 71:1; no. 59	**p. 43** plan 11 pl. 10d
	Mid-Field					
37	XVIII	sub-surface		V IV B	pl. 81:5 pls. 72:31; 73:21, 22; 76:9; 78:9	**pp. 69, 78** plan 11 pl. 10d
	Mid-Field					
38	XVIII	sub-surface	connected with Silo 39	pre-III A	pls. 49:7, 13; 50:31, 32; 64:14; 67:6, 15; 70:1; nos. 80, 142, 264, 265	**p. 43** plan 11 pl. 10d
	Mid-Field					
39	XVIII	sub-surface	connected with Silo 38	pre-III A	pls. 49:8; 50:35, 36; 62:26, 30 no. 61	**p. 43** plan 11 pl. 10d
	Mid-Field					
40	XII-28	Wall K/J scree; mouth broken by wall	connection with settling basin ?	III B II	pls. 52:1-12; 68:18 few	**p. 40** plan 11 pl. 13d
	SW Rooms					
41	XIV-16	rockpile; L. 15 over mouth		IV C III	nos. 12, 46, 47	**p. 74** plan 11 pl. 16b
	NW, Area Z					
	XIV-17		sub stone fall in silo	IV C	pl. 74:1-8	
42	VI-24	lowest IV B Floor 15 and fall of Fill 22	constructed in clay and nari	IV B	pls. 72:20; 73:9; 75:1; 76:5, 13-14; 78:2, 6, 14; 79:4; no. 25	**p. 74** plan 11 pl. 16a
	NW, Area RE			III	few	
	VI-28	square cut opening	settling basin	IV III	pl. 77:8	
43	XXII-11	under Iron II wall but not sealed	some charcoal in fill	IV	pls. 73:23; 75:21; 76:1-3; 77:10; 78:11; 79:1; 80:1, 2; nos. 129, 133	**pp. 63, 74** plan 11 pl. 14c
	NW, Area Uw			III II	pls. 61:18; 68:14, 15	

Fig. 23. Dimensions of the Tell el-Fûl silos.

Silo	Location	Depth	Mouth Diameter	Floor Dia.	Cap	Notes
Group I (largest)						
24	East	2.89	0.99	1.72	—	recess for cap
27	East-NW	2.37	0.5 - 0.9	0.45-0.7?	—	
35	Mid-Field	2.2	0.5 - 0.95	1.75	—	
36	Mid-Field	2.26	1.1 - 2.15	1.6	—	
37	Mid-Field	2.66	0.82	1.78	—	
38	Mid-Field	2.02	0.6 - 1.15	1.4	—	
39	Mid-Field	1.7	0.6 - 1.0	1.6	—	
42	West-NE	1.97	1.15	1.7	—	recess for cap in settling basin, depth 1.35
Average:		2.26	0.78-1.14	1.59		
Group II (smaller)						
21	East	1.46	0.68	1 - 1.2	rectangular	recess for cap
22	East	1.89	0.51	1.4	round plug	
23	East	1.89	0.55	1.2	—	recess for cap
25	East	1.6	0.74	1.94	round	
26	East	1.51	0.68	1.3	round	
28	East-N	1.04	0.45	1.1+	—	
29	East-N	1.29	0.82	0.88	slabs	
30	East-N	1.66	0.5 - 0.8	1.3+	rectangular	
31	East-N	1.88	0.79	1.15	round	catchment pit depth: 0.45, floor dia. 0.5
32	East-N	1.6	0.52	1.1 - 1.4	round	
33	East-N	1.55	0.4 - 1.2	1.2	round	
34	East-N	2.07	0.67	1.86	round-plug	recess for cap
Average:		1.62	0.61	1.29		
Group III (others)						
40	West	2.32	0.88	1.55	—	recess for cap
41	West	2.22	0.6	1.72	—	
43	West	2.22	0.64	1.2 - 1.9	—	
Average:		2.25	0.71	1.49		
Average of all:		1.92	0.68	1.41		

20; above, p. 14), whereas there was little destruction evidence that could be due to the Babylonian conquest on the rest of the mound (cf. above, p. 39). The casemate walls were not defended; the tower was the only refuge and the enemy would be anxious to destroy any strategic advantage it gave. After it was destroyed peaceful occupation could be resumed in the village with little disruption of domestic life as long as the people submitted to the new overlords. The Babylonians were not even interested in these people as exiles once their one means of defense was out of commission. Occupation spread outside the walls in a relative period of prosperity until the town was abandoned for some reason about 538 B.C.

The Silos

The silos are described along with the other loci in the appropriate chapter according to their contents and their location. A brief discussion presenting their significance is supplemented by charts (figs. 22, 23) and the sections (plans 11, 12).

Grouped according to their contents, the silos cannot be typed in any way, nor is there any indication as to when they were originally hewn from bedrock. The contents would be deposited during the last use of the silo or during subsequent occupation either intentionally or incidentally. Most of the silos were probably hollowed out early in the occupational history of Tell el-Fûl and were used in succeeding periods.

The deepest and largest, Silo 24, did have Iron I sherds in its lowest silt layer and had not been cleaned out for later use. The next largest were generally those in the Mid-Field excavations, Silos 35-39 (pl. 10d), three of which were not used after 700 B.C., before the Period III A occupation. To this group of large silos may be added Silo 27, from the northwest corner of the eastern slope (pl. 8b), and Silo 42, on the eastern edge of the northwest, which had a deep, 1.35-m settling basin (pl. 16a). No caps for these silos were still *in situ* although Silo 24 (with the Iron I deposit) had a shelf recess for a cap, and Silo 42 had a cap recess at the top of its settling basin. These are the biggest silos (fig. 23), all but Silo 39 being over 2 m deep. They were probably dug in Iron I, but several were unsealed through the Hellenistic period, and Silo 37 contained sherds of the Roman period as well.

Concentrated on the eastern side of the mound were smaller silos (Silos 21-34, excepting Silos 24 and 27) with an average depth of 1.62 m (fig. 23). Perhaps it was harder to cut into the rock on the east, but more likely they were cut during another period of occupation according to the needs of the time. Usually the openings were smaller, averaging 61 cm as opposed to about 1 m for the deep silos. A number of them had

round or rectangular caps *in situ* (pls. 9b, 19d), but two of them, Silos 22 and 34, had the plug type (pl. 18c). Narrow necks were typical, and often there were recesses or splayed lips, either cut into the *nârī* (pl. 9a) or in the clay above, to receive the caps.

On the western side, where there were proportionally fewer silos, three of them may be grouped with the smaller silos on the east because of their narrow necks. Silo 40, with a recess for a cap, had a homogeneous III B deposit; the silo's top was broken by a Hellenistic wall which was constructed over it (pl. 13d). Silo 43 was beneath an Iron II wall but was unsealed (pl. 14c); besides some Period II sherds, it contained quantities of Period III pottery and some of the earliest Hellenistic (IV A). Silo 41 (pl. 16b) contained the latest Hellenistic pottery found on the mound (IV C).

These groups of silos with narrow necks and a smaller average capacity may have been hewn out in Iron II. Several are stratigraphically below Hellenistic constructions and contained significant Period III deposits. Silo 21 had a few Iron I and Iron II sherds in it, and Silo 28 had a homogeneous III B deposit in its lowest layer (pl. 8c). Silos 30-32 were below or in the earliest-phase Hellenistic floor of the north room of the Hellenistic House (cf. pl. 19b with pl. 20d), and Silo 33 was beneath its east-west inside wall (Wall A/B-C, pl. 21c). The Late Hellenistic sherds in them were deposited either by a pre-construction occupation or at the time of the Early Phase building period late in the 2nd century B.C. Silos 22, 25 and 34 contained principally Period III sherds but some IV B.

It is doubtful if any of the silos were original with the Hellenistic peoples (contrast Sinclair's conclusions from the second campaign, *TFL II*: 35); they probably made use of the earlier constructions.

Shallower cuttings were also uncovered in bedrock in many areas, and where these were in the floors they may have served some domestic or industrial use. In the Hellenistic House Room B there had obviously been a channel leading into Silo 33 (pl. 21c), and in Room A bedrock depressions may have formed a channel to Silo 32 (pl. 19b). A pit and channel of some sort was part of a Period IV A construction in the northwest (L. XIV-22, 24; pl. 16b). Pits in the western part of Room A and west of the Hellenistic house near Silo 27 (pls. 19b, 8b) and a peanut-shaped pit north of Albright's excavations, L. XX-6ext (pl. 10a), must have served functions at some time, but in most cases later floors were found over the rock cuttings and their original purposes cannot be determined.

Silo 23 may have been an unusual kind of double silo during some period of its use. Above the silo cut in bedrock was an opening that may have formed the west side of an upper silo cut into the rock scarp (fig. 24, pl.

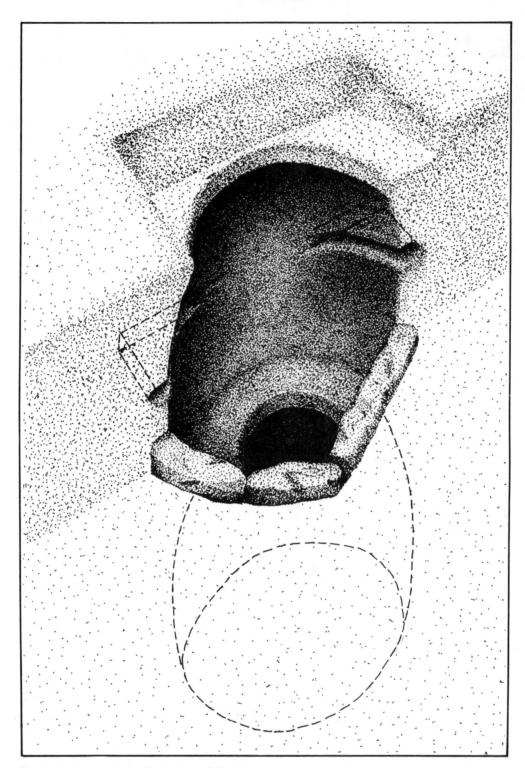

Fig. 24. Section and isometric drawing of Silo 23.

10a-c). The upper construction may have been built up with stone to form a complete silo. A groove midway in the upper structure would support a sliding cover. A cap recess was hollowed out for the lower silo, and plaster and sherds wedged a cavity in its wall. It is impossible to say what the upper portion was like or used for, but the cuttings indicate some elaborate industrial or domestic use.

Silos of the Previous Campaigns

"Numerous silos and cisterns" in the southeast building complex are mentioned from the second campaign at Tell el-Fûl and are located on the plan (*TFL II*: 35; "grain pits" in pl. 13; S 1-20 located on pl. 29). Sinclair dated them to the 4th-2nd centuries B.C. and the Roman period. No evidence for this dating is presented, so it may be assumed that they are similar to the silos of the third campaign in type and date, particularly those on the east side of the mound.

From the first campaign Albright mentions several "grain-pits excavated in the ḥuwar" around the edges of the glacis of the southwest Fortress (*TFL I*: 27). Pottery from them was Late Hellenistic or Early Roman, similar to the late constructions nearby. Most were small, "not exceeding a meter in diameter," although one was large — 4.75 x 3.6 and 1.7 m in average height. It had an arched doorway and stairs leading to it from the north as well as three capped holes in the top. Was this actually three silos cut into the *nârī* which overlapped and then were made into one large storage room, complete with stairs and entrance, in Roman times? Unfortunately no plan is given nor is it located on the site plan, and nothing similar was found in the third campaign.

Silos at Other Sites

Of sites with similar occupation and geological make-up as Tell el-Fûl, Tell en-Naṣbeh recorded a large number of silos and cisterns hollowed out of bedrock (*TN I*: 129). Cisterns differed from silos in their one or more layers of water-proofing material on the inside walls. Over 85 silos were excavated (*TN II*: 124-25), but only two are presented (*TN I*: 135-37). No plans or sections are published. Silo 295 was a complex of three silos with three separate openings, measuring 1.09 x 1.6, 1.78 x 1.6 and 2.32 x 2.40 m. The greatest depth of Silo 348, which was "roughly oval," was 2.05 m. Most probably these Tell en-Naṣbeh silos are quite comparable to those at Tell el-Fûl, though no typology can be presented. Most interesting is that at Tell en-Naṣbeh there was little occupation on the mound after the Persian period (*PCC*: 132), so that the construction of the silos and cisterns had to precede the Hellenistic period. Their contents come from Iron I, Iron II and Persian periods with occasionally earlier sherds.

Undoubtedly they were principally of Iron I and Iron II construction.

In a review of the El-Jîb "winery" publication soon after the 1964 campaign at Tell el-Fûl, P. W. Lapp came to the conclusion that the situation at El-Jîb was not much different than that at Tell el-Fûl (1968: 392). The data cited here from Tell el-Fûl is quite comparable to that from El-Jîb. Most of the El-Jîb "cellars" were larger than the Tell el-Fûl silos, but particularly those which may be Tell el-Fûl's earliest reached a comparable depth — 2.26 m at Tell el-Fûl, 2.2 m at El-Jîb (*Gibeon*: 2). The proportion of caps found *in situ* is similar at the two sites, and El-Jîb had rectangular and round types (*Gibeon*: 8-9). None of plug type are noted at El-Jîb, and the sections do not show any prominent cap recesses as were found at Tell el-Fûl. In form the El-Jîb holes seem to be closer to the first group at Tell el-Fûl which may be attributed to Iron I construction. The El-Jîb "cellars" contained pottery from Iron I to Byzantine times, with occasional earlier sherds. The contention that only Iron II pottery was "in the debris or on the floors of 43 cellars" (*Gibeon*: 16) cannot be accepted since much Hellenistic and Persian (or Tell el-Fûl Period III B perhaps) pottery has been published as Iron II (Lapp 1968: 391-92; see below, p. 85). Undoubtedly the situation is similar at El-Jîb and Tell el-Fûl: many silos contained mixed Iron II, 6th-century and Hellenistic pottery, sometimes with some Iron I; sometimes a silt layer or the lower debris of a silo may have a homogeneous deposit of Iron I or Iron II pottery although the published El-Jîb material does not testify to this. In any case, even where stratigraphy is carefully delineated at Tell el-Fûl, it is impossible to say when the silos were cut or to assign most of the silos to one period. At both sites some floors and walls were related to the silos; later constructions made use of the earlier silos and at other times covered them (although the latter situation was not distinguished by the excavator at El-Jîb).

The rock-cuttings at El-Jîb are assigned great importance and associated with the use of the "cellars." Much of it is conjecture, however, and numerous difficulties arise (*Gibeon*: 11). In some cuttings Iron I pottery was prominent, as in bedrock pockets at Tell el-Fûl (L. XXIII-12, 13; L. I-44). The situation is similar at the two sites: at one time some of the bedrock channels and depressions were related to the silos or had domestic and industrial use; later occupants no longer made use of them.

The Purpose of the Silos

A word should be said about the purpose of these silos. As has just been shown, the Tell el-Fûl silos are quite comparable to the bedrock pits and cuttings at El-Jîb which have been called a winery by the excavator. J. B. Pritchard (*Gibeon:* 25-26) assigns the plastered basins for the fermentation of the wine, the pits or "cellars" for the storage of the wine in large jars and the bedrock cuttings for treading and such; the wine is then transferred (by funnels, fragments having been found in the excavations) to the inscribed-handled jugs found so numerously in the El-Jîb cistern. R. de Vaux (1966: 132-33) has shown how unlikely this is for several reasons: first, in documented instances the construction of wine cellars was above ground in antiquity rather than below; second, fermentation would most likely be in the storage jars themselves rather than in a plastered basin; third, rather than the storage jars the excavator considered standard for the wine, which one would have expected in abundance, a variety of jar types and ceramic vessels are represented at El-Jîb; and fourth, the jugs with the inscribed

handles are absent in the "cellars." The cellars cannot be dated as readily as Pritchard suggests: the debris found in them is obviously subsequent to their use as a winery (de Vaux 1966: 134), and in any case, the material is quite mixed (Lapp 1968: 391-93) rather than consistently Iron II in their lower levels as the excavator maintains (*Gibeon:* 16). The conclusion must be drawn that their use at El-Jîb was similar to that at Tell el-Fûl and Tell en-Naṣbeh, where numerous similar pits hollowed in bedrock have been found. They were most probably silos, used for storage of grain or liquids in storage jars. Many were probably hollowed out in Iron I at all three sites; more were cut in Iron II, and some were used as long as the sites were occupied. Each domestic building or industrial installation probably needed such pits for storage.

NOTES

[1]If Saul's fortress had corner towers as Albright proposed, it has to be reconstructed along different lines than Albright's plan (Albright 1933: 7, fig. 1) because of the new segment of the Iron I wall found in 1964 (see above, p. 24). J. Graham has proposed an Iron I fortress of about 62 x 57 m if it had four towers (as seems unlikely since forts with corner towers of Iron Age date to late Iron II; see above, fig. 15, p. 30, and Aharoni 1967b: 5; Graham 1975: 90-93 and fig. 24). A similar reconstruction of a 62 x 57 m fortress could be proposed for Period III if there was sufficient evidence to suggest corner towers.

Chapter 7

The Late Hellenistic Occupation: Period IV

Nancy L. Lapp

Tell el-Fûl was abandoned after the Exilic period until the latter part of the 3rd century B.C. when there was perhaps some light occupation. The 1964 campaign indicated conclusively that the principal Hellenistic occupation belonged to the 2nd century B.C., to a certain extent in the second quarter, but mainly toward the end of the century. After the second campaign the Period IV occupation had been redated to principally the 3rd century B.C. from the Maccabean date suggested after the first campaign (*TFL I*: 26; Albright 1933: 10; and see the chronological table, p. xvii). Since then Persian and Hellenistic pottery chronology has been better defined (see especially *PCC*; the Beth-zur publication of the second campaign—*BZ II*: 70-79, especially p. 54, n. 4; see below, p. 101). It was on the basis of his early work at Beth-zur that Albright redated Tell el-Fûl in 1933, so with the refining of the Beth-zur chronology we can also firmly fix Tell el-Fûl. Sinclair's pottery study of the second campaign (see especially *TFL II*: 45) was published before the studies of the early 1960s.

There were Ptolemaic coins from the three campaigns, but many of these were probably from the 2nd-century occupation, and in any case they only provide a *terminus a quo*. A mortarium rim and a few jar and jug rims are all the ceramic remains pointing to a 3rd-century B.C. date. The postexilic handles which were originally assigned to the 3rd century B.C. (Lapp 1965: 7) can perhaps all be dated to the 2nd century (see below, pp. 112-13). It is difficult to determine the extent of the 3rd-century occupation since it is possible that the 2nd-century occupants swept away the evidence. However, since pockets of Iron I, Iron II and 6th-century occupation were left by the later operations, the lack of something comparable from the 3rd century suggests that occupation was slight (Lapp 1965: 7).

Toward the middle of the 2nd century B.C. the mound was reoccupied extensively, and the latter part of the 2nd century was one of the most flourishing periods of Tell el-Fûl's history. The early occupation, Period IV A, dated about 175 B.C. The most substantial occupation, Period IV B, came toward the end of the 2nd century. There remained from Period IV B two clearly distinct building phases on the northeast and a number of floors and installations on the west side. A number of coins (see below, p. 109), probably the stamped handles (cf. pp. 112-13) and an ostracon dated about 100 B.C. (pp. 113-15) provide chronological pegs for Period IV B. A slight occupation continued into the 1st century, Period IV C, as a couple of silo deposits, some late Hellenistic floors and occasional sherds on late Hellenistic floors indicate. Period IV C ended in the second quarter of the 1st century B.C., and the mound lay undisturbed until the small Roman occupation (see below, chap. VIII).

A few deposits yielded pottery slightly earlier than the bulk of the Late Hellenistic material, and they have been assigned to Period IV A (ca. 175-135 B.C.). These will be described fully as the various Late Hellenistic complexes are discussed below, but they may be noted briefly here. In the northeast, Silo 33 was covered by Wall A/B-C (pl. 21c) late in the 2nd century B.C., but the bottom layer of the silo contained cooking-pot fragments dating to Period IV A. On the other side of the mound, where Hellenistic operations disturbed debris to bedrock, the Period III Wall U/Z covering Silo 43 (pl. 14c) was disturbed in Period IV. Along with much Period III pottery, the earliest Hellenistic pottery recovered in 1964 came from this silo (see below, p. 74). In a trench about 2 m south of Wall U/Z a lower floor (L. XV-15) sealed IV A pottery beneath (in L. XV-16;

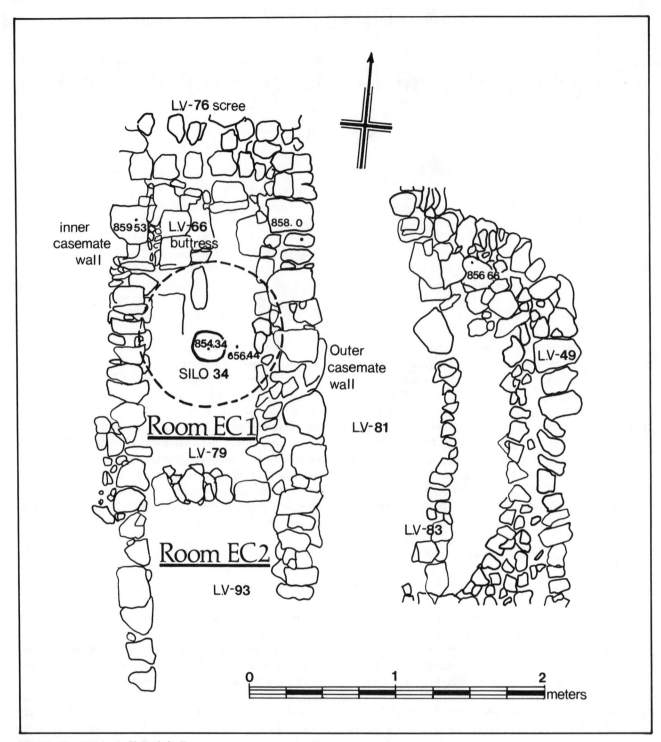

Fig. 25. The Northeast Hellenistic Tower.

plan 5, sec. n-s; see below, p. 73). Finally, to the north in Area Z the latest sherds from the bedrock installations (pl. 16b) — a basin and channel north of a door — were from Period IV A (L. XIV-21-24, 26; below p. 74). The rectangular blocks of soft limestone from the IV A installations were reused in late Hellenistic walls (Lapp 1965: 7).

The Period IV B occupation was very widespread, and the 2nd-century B.C. remains can now be described in detail. Mention will be made of the slight evidence for Period IV C in specific deposits.

Fortifications

A number of elements relating to Hellenistic defenses were uncovered in the third campaign although all evidence of the southwest Hellenistic tower had been removed in the earlier campaigns (see above, p. 14). Additional excavation did support Albright's indication that the lowest wall, to the west of the Iron I tower and the Iron II sloping revetment, was Hellenistic (L. XIII-6; plans 1, 7 [sec. e-f]; fig. 12, p. 15; pl. 4c). This wall helped support the glacis in Hellenistic times.

At the northeast corner of the mound a Hellenistic tower may have disturbed earlier fortifications (fig. 25; plans 8, 9 [sec. j-k, l-m]; pl. 18a; see above, p. 41). Excavation was not completed here but Hellenistic sherds as well as Early Roman were found in the debris (L. V-81, 83). In the early phase of Period IV B the Hellenistic occupants cleared out, repaired and added an interior buttress (L. V-66, with foundation trench, L. V-62; pl. 18b) to the Iron II casemate. A silo and stone basin indicate some domestic use of EC-1 (pl. 18b). This silo, Silo 34, was one of those with a plug-type cap which fit snugly into the silo mouth (pl. 18c; cf. p. 59 above). A few Hellenistic sherds were found in the silo (L. V-92) and in lower debris in EC-1 (L. V-79). In the later phase of Period IV B the casemate was filled with rubble (L. V-59, 76, 93), and a new wall line, over a meter to the west of the casemate, was constructed. Stones and fill between the new Hellenistic wall on the west and the inner casemate wall on the east (L. V-74, VIII-6) formed a kind of stepped revetment 1.8 m wide (pl. 18d). This could be traced over 20 m along the eastern edge of the excavations (plan 1). Abundant IV B pottery was discovered, sometimes down to bedrock, in deposits next to its foundations and when the west face was cleaned (L. VIII-8, XX-8, 9 and 5ext; XXI-3 [pl. 9a]; cf. the discussion of the Hellenistic House, below, and the deposits to the south, p. 66 below).

On the west side of the mound the 1.8-to-2-m wall (Wall H) must have originally served a defensive purpose, though as it was found by the excavators it had domestic floors on both sides (see below, p. 74). It may be presumed to have extended originally north from the southwest Hellenistic tower, but except for the 8-m segment it had been robbed by later builders.

Northeast Hellenistic House

In the excavations in the northeast a Hellenistic building complex, Rooms A, B and C (figs. 26, 27) produced evidence of two phases of construction as well as some preconstruction occupation, all near the end of the 2nd century B.C. (Period IV B). The Hellenistic "House" (probably more correctly "Building") yielded abundant pottery from about 100 B.C., with little or no distinguishable characteristics between Prebuilding and Early and Late Building Phase sherds.

The Early Phase builders of the Hellenistic House (fig. 26) used the inner wall of the Iron II casemate (pl. 18d) as their eastern wall but founded most of the other walls on bedrock (pl. 19a). A central east-west wall (Wall A/B-C, pl. 20d) divided the north and south parts of the house. It was built over Silo 33 (pl. 21c), which may have seen some Early Hellenistic use. Fragments of four Hellenistic cooking pots (pl. 79:15-18), dating to the second quarter of the 2nd century B.C. (Period IV A), were found in the bottom. A number of late 2nd-century B.C. sherds were found near the top of the silo, probably swept in by the builders as they constructed Wall A/B-C. A nārī bedrock channel led into the silo from the south.

In the northern room, Room A, the floor was shaped out of bedrock on the west, and in this process Silo 30 was cut off at the top (pl. 19a). The rectangular cut was covered by a slab and sealed with stone wedges, and the Early Phase floor, L. V-32, was laid over it. The floor did not cover Silo 31 except on the eastern edge of its large, round cap (pl. 20a; plan 12, cap sec.), and this silo was probably in use during most of the Early Phase. Silos 30 and 31 overlapped in bedrock (see plan 12, sec.), but it is difficult to determine which had been hewn out first. Silo 30 had a plaster patch on one side, plastered twice over a rock cavity which had first been blocked by a boulder and cemented. Silo 31 had a catchment pit (pl. 20b) for any drainage, but the silos would not have held liquid. A thin layer of earth wash and rockfall covered their floors. Most of the sherds and artifacts were in Silo 30 and probably had been swept in before the rectangular cap and Early Phase floor were laid. Among the artifacts was an Antiochus IV coin (no. 22), dated 175-164 B.C.

In the eastern part of Room A, fill (L. V-54) was imported and leveled, covering Silo 32 (pl. 19b-d). The Early Phase Floor V-32 was laid over Fill V-54; there were remains of plaster in places. A mortar or door socket was found in situ on Floor V-32, and the north door of the room was associated with it (pl. 20c). In Silo 32 (covered by Fill V-54 and Floor V-32) two silver Seleucid coins (nos. 15, 16) of Antiochus VII, dated 136/135 B.C. and 138-129 B.C., were found on the floor; they must have been deposited during pre-construction use or when the fill was leveled for the Early Phase floor.

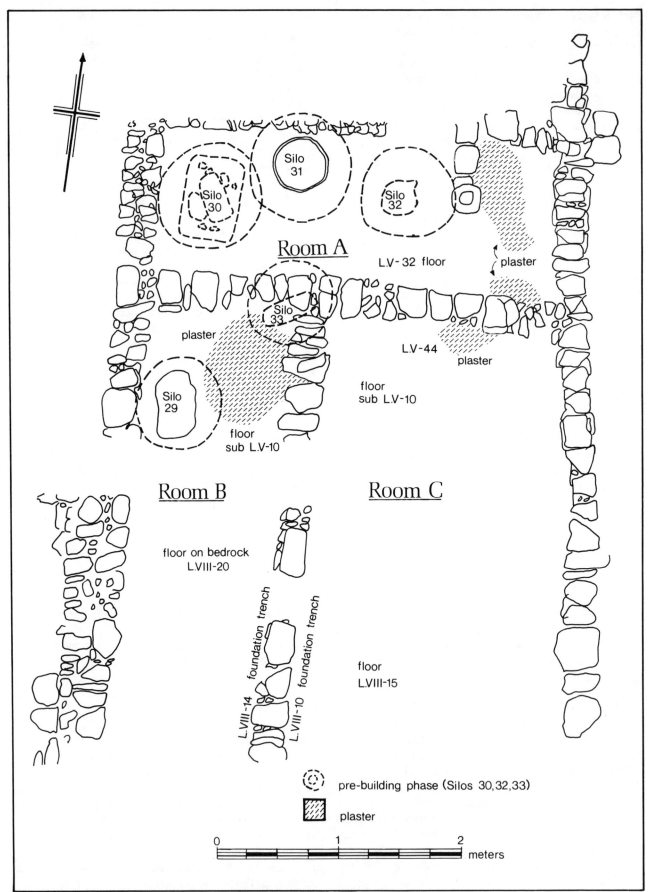

Fig. 26. The Northeast Hellenistic House, Period IV B Early Phase.

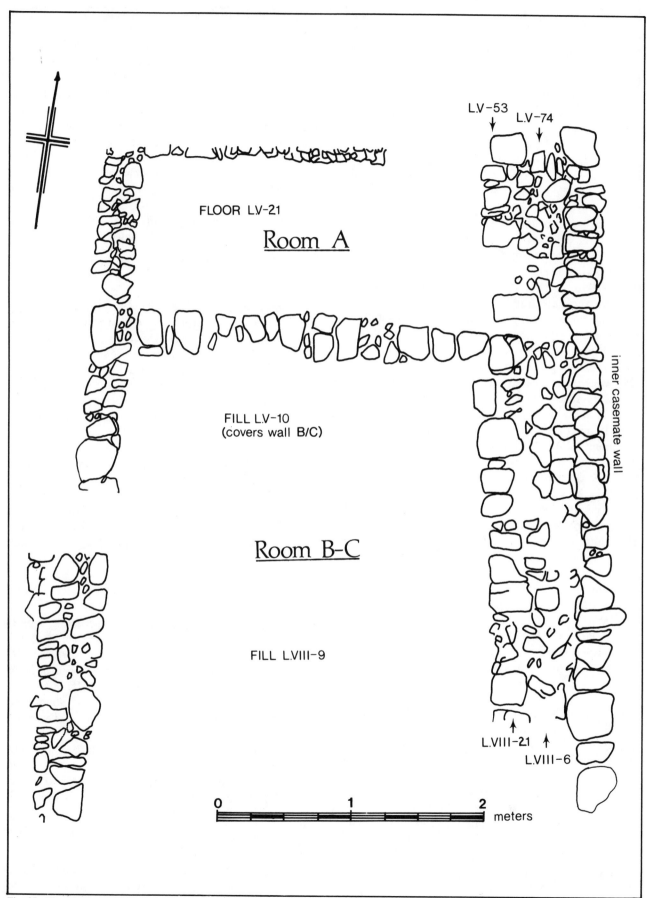

Fig. 27. The Northeast Hellenistic House, Period IV B Later Phase.

In Fill V-54 on the lip of the silo, underneath stones covering its top (cf. pl. 19c-b), were two more silver Seleucid coins (nos. 17, 18), also dated 136/135 B.C.

In Room B bedrock had not been cut or leveled (pl. 20d). Hard-packed earth on bedrock formed the floor (L. V sub-10, VIII-20) with evidence of plaster in a few places (pl. 21a). The hard surface did not cover Silo 29 in the southwest corner of the room. Stone slabs covered its mouth but did not completely seal it (cf. plan 8, sec. j-k). The soft, yellow-brown fill in the silo contained III and IV B sherds. Excavation revealed the foundation trenches for the dividing Wall B/C (L. VIII-14 on the west; L. VIII-10 on the east [pl. 21a]). The Room C floor was a hard surface showing touches of plaster (L. V sub-10, VIII-15 [pls. 20d, 21b]). Along Wall A/C in the north was a plaster trough (L. V-44). The floor covered a Period III wall (L. V-37 [pl. 21c]) and Period III debris (L. VIII-16, 18, 19 [pl. 21b; see above, p. 41]).

For the Late Building Phase in Room A a fill of small stones and tramped earth (L. V-29) was imported sealing all the silos, and new floor (L. V-21 [pl. 20d]) was laid. A new east wall (L. V-53) was set on top of this floor shortening the room by almost 2 m (cf. pl. 19d). This wall continued to the south to form the eastern boundary of Room C (L. VIII-21) in the Late Phase (pl. 21b). A stone fill between this Hellenistic wall and the Iron II inner casemate wall formed a kind of stepped revetment (L. V-74, VIII-6 [pl. 18d]; cf. p. 65 above). In the southern Rooms B and C, fill (L. V-10, VIII-9) was laid over the Early Phase floor; the dividing Wall B/C and Silo 29 were covered.

Subsurface debris (L. V-3, 8; VIII-5) consisted of a great deal of stone scree, containing quantities of III and IV B pottery. The latest pottery on and below the upper floors was similar to that of the lower floors and their fills, so only a few years could have separated the two building phases.

In the north, Silo 27, west of the Hellenistic House (pl. 8b), was uncovered below compact subsurface debris; large stones filled the silo at the top (L. IX-4). The hard and wet yellow-brown clay below (L. IX-10) yielded very few sherds and was not totally cleared.

To the South

South of the northeast Hellenistic building complex and west of the Iron II casemate was considerable evidence of Hellenistic occupation in stratified debris, often down to bedrock. As noted above (p. 65), the new eastern wall, constructed over a meter to the west of the Iron II casemate during the second IV B construction phase, was traced over 20 m south from the northeast excavations (plan 1). Excavation next to it produced IV B sherds to its foundations and bedrock (L. VIII-8; XX-8, 9 and 5ext, XXI-3 [pl. 9a]). In one area a disturbed floor was found, plastered on bedrock (L. XX-5ext), on which lay a complete Hellenistic lamp (pl. 80:10).

To the west of the Hellenistic wall, IV B occupants disturbed the evidence of earlier occupation and left no constructions standing, although Period III material was abundant. The debris included two stamped jar handles, nos. 55 and 57, of Period III. (There were some undisturbed Period III deposits, see above, p. 43.) Nor were any Hellenistic constructions uncovered, but there were stratified deposits with an abundance of Hellenistic pottery. Fill to the bedrock scarp in one area contained 1st-century B.C. Hellenistic material, Period IV C (L. XX-2ext, 4ext), which included numerous long-collared, storage-jar rims (pl. 72:1-14). This was in the area of the curious double silo, Silo 23 (see below, pl. 10a-c). Other stratigraphically sealed deposits with much late Hellenistic pottery included L. XIX-4, XX-3-7, 10, 11 and XXIII-7, 8.

Silos 22, 23, 25 and 26

There were a number of silos in this area. The little pottery recovered from them usually reflected the debris around them. Silo 22 (L. XXI-4, pl. 9a), north of Albright's excavations, contained a few small sherds, mainly Period IV B, including a jug base and a high cooking pot rim. The silo was cut into the hard floor of Period IV B. It had the plug-type cap and a cap recess cut in the bedrock into which the plug fit rather snugly (plan 12, sec.).

Silo 23 (sub L. XX-4e-c), uncovered beneath the 1st-century Hellenistic IV C fill, was beneath stone scree against the nârī scarp which rose toward the west (pl. 10a). Large stones blocked a square entryway cut into the scarp (pl. 10b). A kind of half-silo remained above a sunken silo (pl. 10c; see fig. 24, p. 60). About midway in the upper construction was a horizontal groove which could have held a sliding cover. Some kind of construction for domestic or industrial use is indicated though not enough evidence remains to describe it more fully (see above, pp. 59-61).

Silo 25 (L. XIX-7 [pl. 9c]) contained mainly Iron II sherds, but a few Hellenistic sherds had fallen in. It was perhaps in use the same time as the Northeast III Building just to the north. It may have been covered with the cap toward the end of period III, but it had been tilted (pl. 9c) so that later sherds had slipped in. The deposit to the north on bedrock (L. XIX-6; see above, p. 43) was from Period III A.

Silo 26 (L. XX-12), uncovered when the balk south of the Hellenistic House was removed, was partially covered by a broken cistern cap (pl. 9d). It contained III and IV B sherds, including several jar rims, similar to the pottery of the loci above and nearby (L. XX-5, 11).

Mid-Field

In the Mid-Field excavations, which attempted to relate the 1964 east and west areas, the debris was shallow and Hellenistic sherds were abundant. Constructions were few, but even in the small areas which were probed five silos were uncovered (pl. 10d). **Three had important Period III deposits (see above p. 43), but two were open and probably used during** the Hellenistic Period. Silo 35, to the north, was filled with stones and yielded only insignificant Period III and IV B sherds. Silo 37, just west of the three Period III Mid-Field silos, contained large quantities of Late Hellenistic sherds, some dating near the end of the Hellenistic occupation (IV C), and Roman sherds found near the top indicate that it was not closed until the final use of the mound. Several storage jars could be partially reconstructed including one from Period IV C (pl. 72:31).

West Casemate Rooms

The Period III West Casemate rooms were extensively reused in the Hellenistic Period. In the northwest the casemate walls had been cleared away and Hellenistic constructions replaced them, but toward the south the Hellenistic occupants used the casemate construction and evidence of Hellenistic occupation extended east of the casemate walls.

Area P

Area P, just north of the Iron II revetment and east of the casemate walls, preserved Hellenistic stratification (fig. 28; pl. 6c). The latest subsurface debris (L. II-9) cleared away down to a surface was from Period IV B. Pavement stones in the north (L. II-5) covered dark-brown soil with remnants of an oven and sherds, the latest belonging to Period IV B (L. II-41). Next to the revetment Area P was extended east. Surface debris covered a thin north-south wall (L. II-39) running parallel to the inner casemate wall 5 m to the east. There were Period IV B floors on either side. The floor on the west (L. II-40 [pl. 5a]) was the same level as the pavement stone surface (L. II-5). IV B sherds came from subsurface debris (L. II-42) down to the floor east of the wall.

Area Q

To the north in Area Q (pl. 4a), east of the casemate walls and south of the Period II wall (Wall S), two Hellenistic floors were distinguished. The late 2nd-century occupants had cleared to bedrock and left their debris in the fill (L. II-45) for the lowest floor (L. II-44). The lower part of a Hellenistic cooking pot (no. 163) was still intact (pl. 7a). Fill between the floors (L. II-43) had a good collection of IV B sherds. On the upper floor in the south (L. II-12=VII-16) were a door socket (pl. 4a) and a long collared rim (pl. 72:30), which dated to the 1st century B.C. (Period IV C), while

above the floor in the north (L. VII-15E) were found a Maccabean(?) coin (no. 14) and a typical small Hellenistic incurved-rim bowl (pls. 7b, 77:15).

Rooms L, N, and O

Within the inner and outer casemate walls (pl. 5b) there was a little Late Hellenistic pottery, in subsurface material above the floors in Room O (L. II-14, VII-14), Room N (L. II-19), and in debris over a floor in Room L (L. II-28) on which a small north-south wall (L. II-4) stood. Period III debris was used for fill beneath the floors, and all lower occupational levels in Rooms O, N, and L were from the Period III use of the casemate **(see above, p. 41).**

Room M

Room M, within the casemate walls, tied into the Hellenistic activity to the west. The latest subsurface debris (L. II-23) was from Period IV B. Two Hellenistic floors (L. II-24, 25) 10 cm apart, with thin ash layers over them, were below. The lower floor was plastered and had a drain in the northwest corner of the room connecting with the Hellenistic basin installation to the west in Room F (pl. 7c). These all were late 2nd century B.C., and the occupation covered a relatively short period of time.

Cistern 2

Cistern 2 (pl. 6b), to the north of Room O, was not **in use in Period IV (see above, p. 41), but the shaft** (L. VII-10a) contained large quantities of Hellenistic pottery. The subsurface debris (L. VII-8) among the stones above the cistern contained Hellenistic sherds.

North

The outer West Casemate wall extended about 2 m further north (fig. 29; plan 5, sec. n–s; pl. 6a). Stratigraphically sealed debris around the fallen stones from the wall (L. VII-6-8, 12, 13, 18a) and from the removal of the upper course (L. VII-5a, 9) gave evidence of Period IV B use and disturbance in this area.

East of the casemate the Hellenistic occupants must have made use of the Iron I wall, Wall S, which was exposed fairly close to the surface in 1964. At the north end (L. VII-3N, 17) the wall had been disturbed in Hellenistic times; the debris contained IV B sherds as did the subsurface material to the east (L. XVII-3, 5 [cf. pl. 2d where the Hellenistic debris has been removed]).

Southwest Rooms

The IV B period must have been relatively peaceful because there is evidence of considerable activity, both domestic and industrial, outside the defenses on the

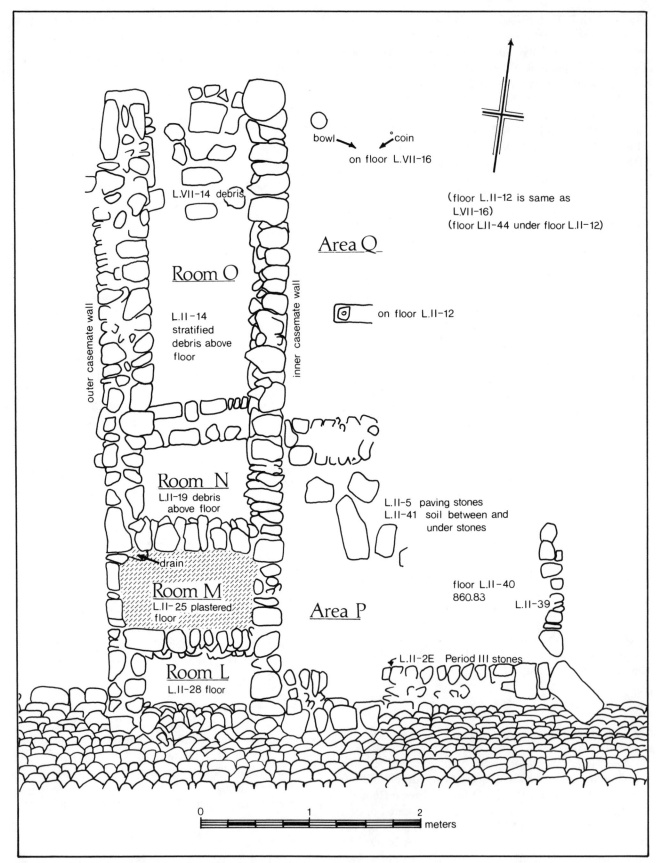

Fig. 28. The Hellenistic occupation of the West Casemate rooms.

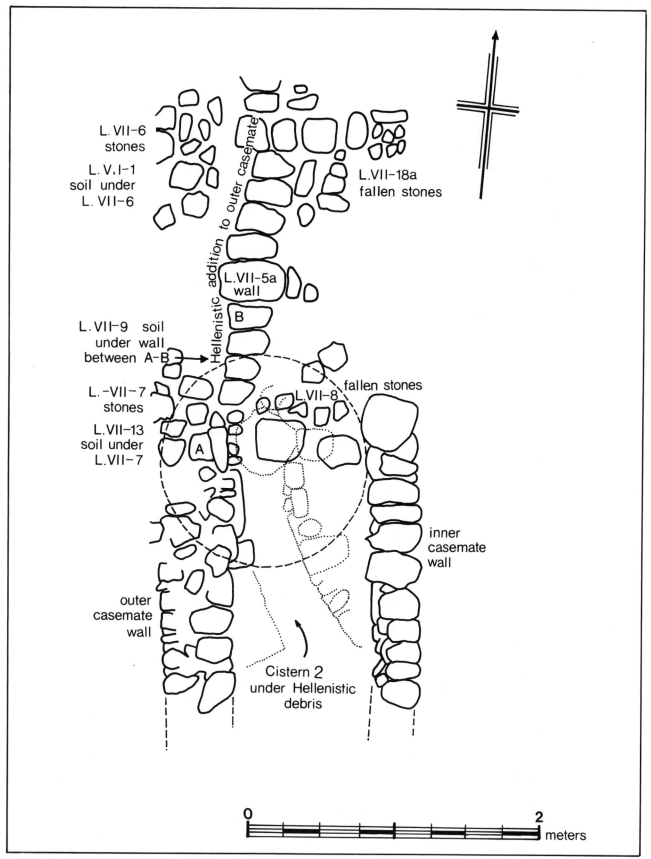

Fig. 29. Hellenistic occupation around the outer West Casemate wall in the north.

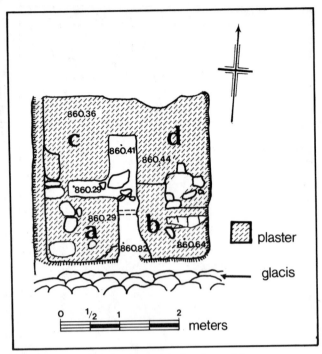

Fig. 30. The Hellenistic plastered basins, Locus I-8.

west. In the southwest, just north of the Iron II revetment, debris was of sufficient depth to show good Hellenistic stratification and some building activity (plan 1).

Room F-G

The late 2nd-century occupants made use of the revetment wall on the south, the outer casemate on the east, and the III B wall on the west to construct a unit of four plastered basins (L. I-8) in Room F (fig. 30; pl. 13a).[1] Stones were used to build up support for the basins over the bedrock pit (L. I-49 [see above, p. 44]). A rough wall of stones (L. 1-48 [plan 5, sec. n-s; pl. 12c]) supported the drain or channel of Basin *b*. In its removal Basin *d* was found to have had two layers of plaster: the top one, from 6-10 cm thick, was almost like modern concrete; the second layer was 5 cm thick. There were four basins in the 2.75 x 3 m area. A 30-cm-wide plastered wall, 30-50 cm high, separated Basins *a* and *b* on the south, but only partially separated Basins *c* and *d*. At places the plaster had disintegrated and stones showed through. A 9-cm channel ran through the wall from Basin *a* to Basin *b*, 77 cm from the glacis wall. The plaster ran up the east face of Wall E/F almost 5 cm, and there was evidence of at least three layers (cf. pl. 13a). The outer casemate was partially plastered on its western face above the basins (L. I-11), and it should be recalled that Room M, the casemate room to the east, was also plastered

during its Hellenistic use. A channel was found in the casemate wall connecting Room M with the basin installation in Room F (pl. 7c and above, p. 69). Also, as in Room M, there was some burned material around Basins *a* and *b*.

Upon removal of the basins the Period III wall, L. I-50 (see above, p. 44), which supported them was uncovered. In the debris beneath the Hellenistic basins (L. I-47) a few Period IV B sherds were found, similar to the pottery found around the basins, verifying their Late Hellenistic use.

During this occupation the area F-G was one room (pl. 13b). A surface above the debris around the Period III basins (L. I-35) and at the level of the Hellenistic basins formed the floor in the north of the room. Stratified layers of scree and soil were removed above this surface (L. I-9, 14, 20 [pl. 11d]).

Room J

From Room F-G at this time one stepped down into Room J (pl. 13b). The Late Hellenistic builders reconstructed the Period III entrances in Wall G/J, one on the east (L. I-32) and one on the west (L. I-34). Clearance of both doorways yielded a few Hellenistic sherds. In the southeastern area of Room J plaster appeared underneath the lower scree (L. I-22 [pl. 13c]), and an occupational level (L. I-29) continued to the west under the scree there (L. I-18 [pl. 11c-d]). Late Hellenistic pottery was found in the removal of L. I-29 debris down to the surface at its base (L. I-sub 29 = surface). This was probably the Period III floor (cf. p. 000, above). At one time in the late 2nd century B.C. a small wall (L. I-23), going north from Wall D/G, partitioned Room J (to the right in pl. 13b). Removal (L. I-28) revealed that it was poorly constructed, the stones all resting on soil with no evidence of preparation for construction. Excavation did not continue westward far enough to uncover the west wall of Room J, but as can be seen in the plan and photograph (plan 1, pl. 13d), it ran south just west of Silo 40 to meet the west wall of Room D.

The layers of scree and soil which had covered Room G also filled the south of Room J (L. I-9, 14). Beneath, in the southwest, the scree (L. I-18 [pl. 11c]) rested on the occupational layer (L. I-29). In the southeast the lower scree (L. I-19, 22) included stones fallen west from the outer casemate and stones from a poorly constructed Hellenistic wall (L. I-21) that had extended west 1.15 m from the outer casemate wall slightly north of Wall G/J (pl. 11d). It was standing on fine soil and removed with L. I-22 when the occupation level L. I-29 was reached. In the north of Room J, scree had fallen (L. XII-25 in L. XII-24) in regular patterns from Wall J/K, the IV B wall which covered Silo 40 (pl.

13d and see below). Beneath the scree just south of Wall J/K there appeared a sterile basin or depressed area (L. XII-26) without curb or plaster but with evidence of burning. Perhaps it was a fireplace in Period III B or Hellenistic times. The rectangular sill stone at the west end of Wall J/K indicated a doorway. Silo 40, which was covered by Wall J/K, contained a III B deposit (see above, p. 44).

Room D

The scree and very fine soil of Rooms G and J (L. I-9, 14) also covered the area west and south (Room D). The lower scree deposit of Room D (L. I-14) rested on an occupational level, and removal of the fill below (L. I-43) still yielded IV B sherds. There was evidence of a doorway at the junction of Walls D/E and D/G leading to Room G (pl. 11c-d).

Room E

The debris in Room E, the southeast room against the revetment, was largely from Period III (see above, p. 44). No Hellenistic constructions remained, and only one stratified deposit, L. I-25, was identified from Period IV B.

Area K

Area K, north of Room J, was perhaps another room although its west and north walls were not uncovered. It had several stratified Roman levels above the first layer of Hellenistic scree debris (L. XII-11 [cf. below, p. 77 and fig. 33]). Below, a circular area of scree and loose soil (L. XII-12) north of Wall J/K was enclosed by a low wall (L. XII-20 [fig. 31; pl. 14a]). A plastered settling basin (L. XII-13) was uncovered within the circular area against Wall J/K. A part of Wall J/K formed the south wall, and the curbstones around the sides were 41-44 cm above the bottom of the basin. A small channel was in the northwest side. The whole basin was plastered — floor, side of Wall J/K, and sides below the curbstones as well as part of the southeast curbstone. The soil of L. XII-12 above the basin was very plastic. Late Hellenistic Period IV B sherds exclusively were found in this area. The use of the basin could not be determined, but the siltlike plastic soil suggested clay for pottery making.

Outside the enclosed area an occupational level was reached (below the L. XII-11 scree and L. XII-14) and layers of Hellenistic fill and scree were beneath (L. XII-16-19, 21). Beneath L. XII-21 a floor level of packed nârī appeared. On removal of the L. XII-12 area (L. XII-22) some flat paving stones were uncovered. When wall XII-20 and the soil beneath were removed (L. XII-23) to the same level as L. XII-22, 21, more paving

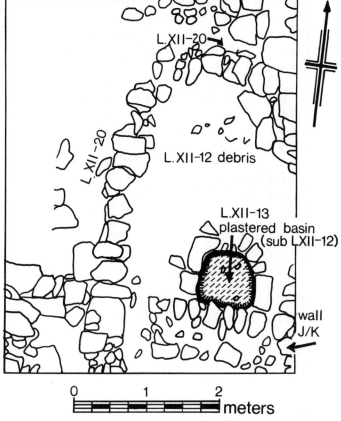

Fig. 31. The Area K basin.

stones were found. All debris down to the sub-L. XII-21-23 occupation level included Late Hellenistic pottery.

Northwest

Areas U, Uw and Zs

In the northwest excavations of the mound it was evident that the Hellenistic occupants had cleared out the earlier constructions and built theirs on bedrock or shallow debris. Period III sherds were mixed with almost all Hellenistic debris, but only one Iron II wall, Wall U/Z, was left standing (pl. 14b). During Period IV B the Hellenistic people made use of the wall with floors on either side, Floor XV-10 in Area Zs, Floor XV-8 in Area U (plan 5, sec. a-b [pl. 15b]). They were beneath Hellenistic debris (L. XV-6, 7, respectively) which was sealed below the debris (L. XV-3) covering Wall U/Z. In Area U the fill (L. XV-14) for Floor XV-8 was laid on top of an earlier floor (L. XV-15) with fill (L. XV-16) from the first half of the 2nd century B.C. below (plan 5, sec. a-b). To the west in Area Uw, IV B floors lay south of Wall U/Z (Floors XXII-7, 9), and the deposits beneath them (L. XXII-8, 10, respectively) contained Late Hellenistic pottery, dating to the third quarter of the 2nd century B.C. Fill (L. XXII-5) was laid in Roman times covering these floors and Wall U/Z for a floor (L. XXII-4) above. At the west end Wall U/Z went over Silo 43. The wall and silo, however, had been disturbed in Hellenistic times and were open in Period IV A (pl. 14c). The earliest Hellenistic pottery recovered in 1964 came from this silo, including an Early Hellenistic black-glazed lamp (pl. 80:1). Quantities of sherds were recovered which can be attributed to the first half of the 2nd century B.C.

A small section of the Period III Wall U/Z remained standing to the east of Wall H into Room T; the east-west Hellenistic Wall T/TV abutted but was not bound to it.

Area Z

Evidence for Period IV A was found on the bedrock installations of Area Z. There a basin (L. XIV-22) with a channel (L. XIV-24) was just north of what appeared to be a door set on bedrock (pl. 16b). The latest sherds of all bedrock deposits of this area appeared to be from the first half of the 2nd century (L. XIV-21-24, 26).

Above the IV A installations were a least three occupational layers, all with stratified Late Hellenistic debris in their fills and above (L. XIV-9 above floor, and fills L. XIV-14, 18, 20; floors are L. XIV-sub 9, sub 14, 19; cf. plan 5, sec. n-s). The large Wall H was associated with the latest floor (L. XIV-sub 9 [pl. 16b]). West of Wall H in subsurface fall from the wall (L. XIV-12) large fragments from a Late Hellenistic high-necked cooking pot were found (pl. 78:3). A IV B floor was uncovered in the debris below (L. XIV-13). North of Wall H, Silo 41 (pl. 16b) appeared beneath rockfall. This silo was open until the end of the Hellenistic occupation (Period IV C) and contained the latest deposit of Hellenistic pottery excavated in 1964 (pl. 74:1-8).

Walls

The remainder of the constructions in the northwest belonged to near the end of the 2nd century B.C., Period IV B. Except for the Iron II Wall U/Z, the walls are associated with these late floors. The large wide Wall H (pl. 15b), which must have served a defensive purpose at one time, was founded upon late Hellenistic floors, evident from excavation in Areas Z (Wall H on Floor XIV-sub 9 [pl. 16b]), U (Floor XV-8 [pl. 15c]) and Zs (Floor XV-10). Removal of some of the large stones toward the south end of Wall H (L. XV-11: A-D) and the debris immediately alongside of them yielded IV B sherds (pl. 15b-c).

Wall R/RE (pl. 14d) was on shallow debris just above bedrock and associated with the earliest of three IV B floors. Although set slightly higher, it was probably contemporary with the bedrock Walls T/R, T/TV, TV/V (pl. 14b) and the walls of Rooms CR and CRn (pl. 16c). Wall R/RE may at one time have extended over Cistern 1 and connected with Wall V/CR to the north. The 75-cm wall running north and south in Room T (pl. 14b) lay on clay just above bedrock and must have been a secondary construction.

Rooms R and RE

Contemporary floors on either side of Wall R/RE were surfaced three times; pure Late Hellenistic deposits came from the upper two floors, and late 2nd-century B.C. sherds were still found in the fill for the lowest (upper floor: L. VI-10, 11, 9 [pl. 14d]; second: VI-14-12; lower: VI-16, 15 [pl. 15a]; fill for lower: VI-22, 23). West of the floors in Room R there was considerable stone scree from the later "garden" wall (see below). From beneath the scree (L. VI-25) on a Hellenistic floor (pl. 14b) came a good collection of pottery including almost complete cooking pots and jugs (pls. 75:14, 79:6-14). This floor was probably contemporary with the earliest of the floors to the east. Beneath the floor (L. VI-30) Hellenistic sherds and artifacts continued to appear. Just to the north two small east-west walls formed a kind of channel (L. VI-27 [pl. 14b]). From their removal (L. VI-32) came Late Hellenistic pottery as well as earlier material including some Iron I sherds. North of the channel an occupational level (L. VI-sub 18) also was discerned above the lowest fill on bedrock (L. VI-29 [pl. 14b; plan 6, sec. a-b]).

Silo 42

Silo 42, in the southwest corner of Area RE, contained large quantities of IV B pottery, including a nearly whole cooking pot (pl. 78:2) and a Ptolemaic coin (no. 25). A rectangular opening in the bottom of the silo led to a settling basin (L. VI-28 [pl. 16a]) which also contained IV B sherds. The silo opening was below the Room RE floors but was either in use or filled just before the succession of floors was laid toward the end of the 2nd century B.C.

Rooms CR and CRn

To the north in Rooms CR and CRn debris was very shallow before bedrock was reached. In Room CRn a Late Hellenistic occupational level was discerned (L. III-8-9 [pl. 16c]). Subsurface rockfall over Cistern 1 (L. III-14 [pl. 16c]) was disturbed probably as late as Period IV C, and the debris that filled the upper layers of the cistern (L. III-19-22, 24, 27) contained much Late Hellenistic pottery. (For a description of Cistern 1, see above, pp. 44, 46.)

Area V, Rooms TV and T

In Area V blackened occupational earth (L. X-9a) contained some MB II and Iron II sherds as well as later material, but IV B sherds were in the debris to bedrock (L. X-14). In Room TV a IV B floor was discerned (L. X-sub 15 = XI-sub 7) above IV B debris on bedrock (L. X-16). A parallel floor was found in Room T (L. XI-sub 8) on Late Hellenistic bedrock debris (L. XI-19-20 [pl. 14b]). What remained of the thin north-south wall within Room T was apparently associated with this floor and 2nd-century sherds were found in the debris of its removal to bedrock (L. XI-21). To the west an upper floor (L. XI-13) was above Hellenistic debris (L. XI-18).

Garden Fence

Above the Hellenistic installations described in Areas V, TV, T, and R was a layer of fine sterile soil (L. XIV-3, X-4, XI-2) held back by a "garden fence" on the east side which ran from the northwest to the south through Rooms V and R (L. X-6, III-17, VI-18; fig. 32; pl. 15a). During the excavation the wind could be seen blowing the garden soil against the fence. This must have been constructed when the mound was used for cultivation after the site ceased to be occupied, but closer to Hellenistic than modern times since it lies directly over Hellenistic walls and debris, with surface and Hellenistic debris above (L. X-3, XI-2a, XIV-2). There was considerable stone scree from the fence in the debris of Areas V and R (L. III-15, VI-17).

NOTE

[1]The description of the Hellenistic basins and other southeast constructions is based on the careful field notes of the supervisor, H. K. Jamieson.

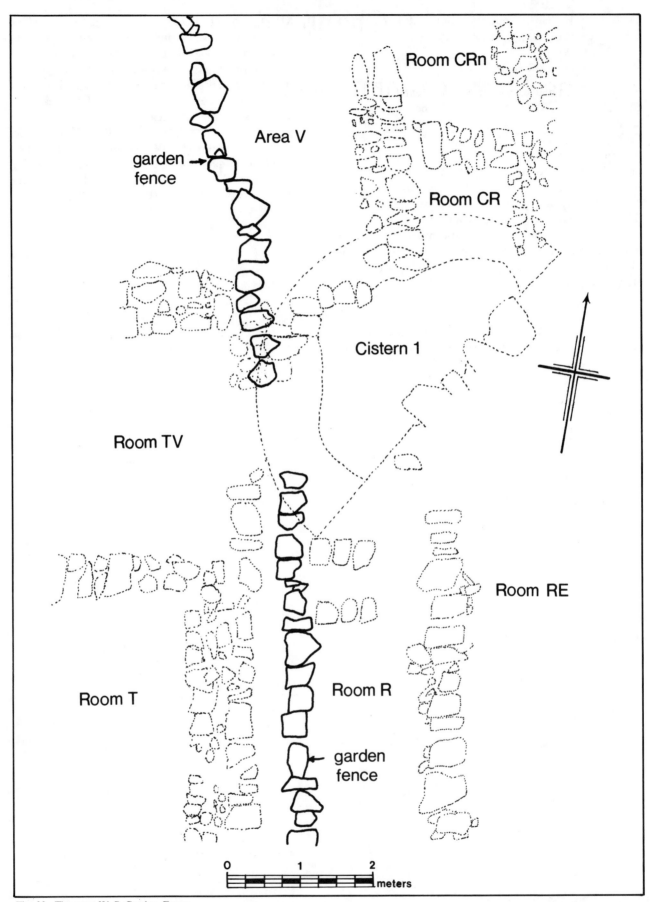

Room CRn

Area V

garden
fence

Room CR

Cistern 1

Room TV

Room RE

Room T

Room R

garden
fence

0   1   2

meters

Fig. 32. The post-IV B Garden Fence.

Chapter 8

The Early Roman Occupation: Period V

Nancy L. Lapp

Occasionally 1st-century A.D. sherds were found with the surface debris over all the mound in 1964, but only in the western excavations toward the north were there concentrated Roman remains. Nothing like the abundance of 1st-century B.C. through 1st-century A.D. pottery reported from the earlier campaigns was found. P. W. Lapp suggested that this was perhaps actually pottery from the 100 B.C. horizon (Period IV B), or that there may have been an Early Roman installation just north of the Iron II revetment on the west completely removed by the earlier excavations (1965: 8). Albright reported Roman occupation over the Hellenistic rooms in the southeast (1933: 10).

Above the Hellenistic floors in Area K of the Southwest Rooms were three Roman occupation levels (L. XII-5, 7, 9 [cf. above, p. 73]). **Early Roman sherds** were found in the stratified debris (L. XII-2) above Floor XII-5 and below in the fill (L. XII-6 [fig. 33]). In Room Uw, just to the north, fill (L. XII-5) was laid over Period III Wall U/Z and IV B floors on either side (see **above, p. 74) for a floor (L. XX-4) in Early Roman** times. The stratified layers (L. XXII-2-3) over Floor XXII-4 contained Roman material of the 1st century A.D., as did the subsurface debris in Room U (L. XV-3; plan 5, sec. n-s). A Herodian coin, no. 19, dated A.D. 42/43, came from L. XXII-3 and substantiates its Early Roman date.

A little to the south, subsurface Early Roman debris (L. VII-4) covered the northern end of the Period III outer West Casemate wall, which was still

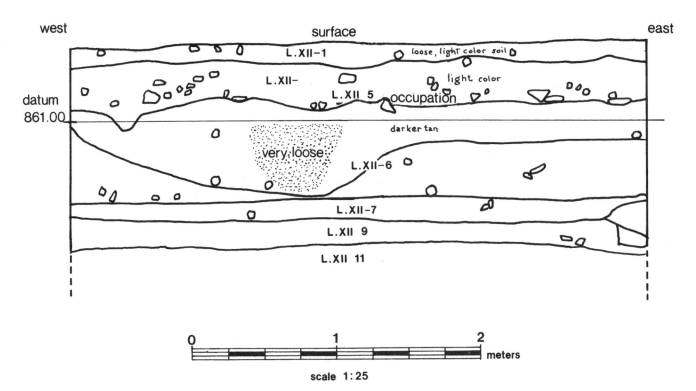

Fig. 33. West-east section north of Area K.

77

standing in 1964, as well as the Hellenistic debris in the **rockfall near the wall (see above, p. 69).**

There were Early Roman sherds in the upper debris of Mid-Field Silo 37, indicating that the silo had been filled in near the end or subsequent to the Roman **occupation (see above, p. 69).**

Although no Roman structures were found, the occupational levels and the amount of varied Roman material recorded from even the third campaign do suggest some Roman occupation. The final study of the material leads to the conclusion that it was probably from more than an overnight stand of Titus' army before he took Jerusalem in A.D. 70 (cf. Lapp 1965: 8). His camp alone hardly would have left occupational layers one above another, and Herodian and Early Roman pottery indicate there was a 1st-century A.D. occupation around A.D. 70 for several months or years. That it was a relatively limited occupation and nothing like the flourishing Periods III and IV settlements is indicated by the proportionally small number of Early Roman sherds recovered from all three campaigns. It is doubtful that all the structures mentioned by Sinclair (*TFL II*: 46) are strictly Early Roman. Only one Early Roman pot from the early campaigns is published (*TFL I*: 24b:3). As has been noted, Early Roman and Hellenistic pottery had not yet been sharply distinguished, and it is probable that much actually belonged **to the 100 B.C. horizon (cf. p. 63 and below, p. 105).**

Chapter 9

The Pottery from the 1964 Campaign

Nancy L. Lapp

The pottery from the 1964 campaign at Tell el-Fûl will be presented by period and type. Drawings are shown on pls. 47-81 with their provenience and ware descriptions listed on the page opposite. Some of the pottery is shown in photograph on pls. 33-46. In the discussion that follows particular attention is given to the stratified pottery which is important for pottery typology during the periods of Tell el-Fûl's occupation. For descriptions of the loci from which the pottery came, see chap. III (Periods I and II), chap. V (Period III), chap. VII (Period IV), chap. VIII (Period V) and Appendixes A and B where the loci are indexed and described.

There were only isolated sherds from periods predating Iron I (Lapp 1965: 8). One or two Early Bronze sherds were recovered in mixed debris, one a dark, heavily burnished body fragment with molding—probably Khirbet Kerak ware (from a vessel similar to Amiran 1969: pl. 19:9, 12, photo 68). Fragments of a MB IIA cooking pot (pl. 47:1) were found in shallow debris around a rocky outcrop at the northwest summit (plan 2, Area 4). It is of the well-known type with straight walls, flat bottom and punched holes below the rim with an applied rope border below (cf. Amiran 1969: pl. 30:1; for the MB IIA date of these cooking pots, see Dever 1974: 40-42).

Period I Pottery[1]
(ca. 1200 - 1150 B.C.)

The first two jar rims (pl. 47:2-3) are degenerate examples of the Late Bronze stepped-molded rim which appeared in the 12th century B.C. (Rast 1978: 9, and cf. Lapp 1967: 295). Good parallels come from Hazor Stratum XII (*Hazor III-IV*: pl. 168:1-13) and Shiloh "Iron I" (*Shiloh*: pl. 7:76). At Beth-zur "molded rims with slightly wavy profiles" were dated to the 11th century (*BZ II*: 46), but they could well date with the 12th-century material there. Rast maintains the stepped-jar rim became extinct in the 12th century (1978: 9).

Storage jars with "long-collared rims" have been firmly dated to the 12th century, while short-collared rims (jars with collars closer to the rim) also appear in the 12th century but continue into the late 10th century (Rast 1976: 9). The sherds shown in pl. 47:4-6 are of the long-collared type (the one in pl. 47:5 is broken off above the shoulder and collar, and pl. 47:6 shows a shoulder fragment with the collar). Twelfth-century contexts for these rims include Hazor XII (*Hazor III-IV*: pls. 167:5-6, 168:20), Tell Deir ʿAlla A (*TDA I*: pl. 47:1, 2), Tell Beit Mirsim B₁ (*TBM I*: pl. 26:18), ʿAfûla III B (*ʿAfûla*: fig. 16:4), Meggido VII B (*Meg. II*: pl. 64:8), and ʿAin Shems III (*AS IV*: pl. 61:1). This type of jar from Bethel (*Bethel*: pls. 56:1-21, 73:15), Shiloh (*Shiloh*: pls. 10:123, 15:186-89, 16:190-92),[2] and El-Jîb (*Gibeon*: pl. 36:16) can be dated to the 12th century by the comparative material. Period I and II pottery is not distinguished in the publication of the earlier Tell el-Fûl campaigns, and most of the sherds published are not of sufficient size to determine whether they had collars (*TFL I*: pl. 28; *TFL II*: pl. 20).

Rims, pl. 47:7-8, are from large storage jars which had handles attached to their rims. Parallels to these had collars on their shoulders, and it is possible that the Tell el-Fûl jars did also. Twelfth-century examples are published from Megiddo VII B-A (*Meg. II*: pl. 68:6), Taanach (Rast 1978: figs. 10:4, 88:1), and Hazor

79

(*Hazor I*: pl. 113:18, redated from LB II to 12th century by Rast, 1978: 9). A large jar from the late 12th-century phase at Taanach, Period I B (Rast 1978: fig. 10:1), has a rim very similar to pl. 47:8 but has no handles.

Knobbed LB II bases had about disappeared in the 12th century and are replaced by a base partially flattened, rounded, or slightly pointed (Rast 1978: 10). The base in pl. 47:9 is flattened but slightly rounded, similar to the bases from Taanach, Period I B (Rast 1978: fig. 10:17), Tell Beit Mirsim B₁ (*TBM I*: pl. 26:21), Hazor XII (*Hazor III-IV*: pl. 202:8), ᶜAfûla III B (*ᶜAfûla*: fig. 16:21), and Beth-zur, dated there to the 11th century (*BZ II*: fig. 10:3, 7).

The jug rim, pl. 47:10, has parallels to 12th-century rims at Taanach, especially those with simple rims, perhaps flattened on top, and long, ridged necks (Rast 1978: 10-11). A 12th-century, Early Phase parallel occurs (Rast 1978: fig. 6:13), but this type appears most prominently later (cf. especially Rast 1978: figs. 11:7, 15:6-7 of Period IB). Close parallels come from Tell Beit Mirsim B₁ (*TBM I*: pl. 26:2) and ᶜAfûla III B (*ᶜAfûla*: fig. 16:10).

Bowls of the 12th century are modifications of the Late Bronze bowl tradition (Rast 1978: 12). The sherd, pl. 47:11, has a shoulder and rim more incurved than the usual Late Bronze bowl. It sees little change through the 12th century and appears at Taanach both in Period I A (Rast 1978: figs. 1:14, 3:6-8, 8:1) and Period I B (figs. 13:1-4, 17:1-3), in Megiddo VII B (*Meg. II*: pl. 65:9), ᶜAin Shems III (*AS IV*: pl. 62:17), Tell Beit Mirsim B₁ (*TBM I*: pl. 26:8-9), and Hazor X-XII (*Hazor III-IV*: pl. 164:3). It also occurred at Bethel (*Bethel*: pl. 60:1-2, 6). Bowl sherd, pl. 47:12, is perhaps a variation of the rounded bowl with a cyma profile (Rast 1978: 12). Fair parallels to the Tell el-Fûl bowl come from ᶜAin Shems III (*AS IV*: pl. 61:10-11), Megiddo VII B (*Meg. II*: pl. 65:7), and ᶜAfûla III B (*ᶜAfûla*: fig. 17:30).

A surface sherd, pl. 47:13, is the rim fragment of a crater with painted design. It is a carry-over from the Late Bronze painted tradition where various painted bands and designs are employed. The vessel was probably quite similar to the painted crater from the Iron I Tomb 1101C at Megiddo (*MT*: pl. 9:2). Similar craters also came from Megiddo VII B and A (*Meg. II*: pls. 66:4, 69:14, 16).

The cooking pot rims, pl. 47:14-15, continue the Late Bronze tradition and have numerous 12th-century parallels; Taanach Period I A (Rast 1978: fig. 2:2-6), Period I B (pl. 14:11); Tell Deir ᶜAlla Phase A (*TDA I*: pl. 2:2-6); ᶜAin Shems III (*AS IV*: pl. 62:33); Tell Beit Mirsim B₁ (*TBM I*: pl. 26:12). Sherds from Bethel (*Bethel*: pls. 57:12-22, 58:1-16) and Shiloh (*Shiloh*: pl. 7:68-75) can probably be dated to the 12th century. For the dating of most of the Tell el-Fûl cooking pots of

the earlier campaigns (*TFL I*: pl. 25; *TFL II*: pl. 21), see the following discussion of the continuation of the type.

Period II Pottery
(ca. 1025 - 950 B.C.)

The rims of the large, heavy storage jars or pithoi, pl. 48:1-3, are typical of Tell el-Fûl Period II (cf. *TFL I*: pl. 27; *TFL II*: pl. 20). The rims are thickened and rounded, sloping to the shoulder with little or no neck. Similar 11th-century rims of large, heavy jars are published from ᶜAfûla III A (*ᶜAfûla*: fig. 11:25) and Hazor XI (*Hazor III-IV*: pl. 203:13), but these, as well as an early 10th-century pithos from Taanach (unpublished), may have had necks. From 10th-century Samaria (Pottery Period I) comes one with no neck (*SS III*: pl. 10:13). It is possible that these large pithoi are the antecedents of the large, heavy "neckless" jars of late Iron II (cf. below, pl. 49:18-28; *BZ II*: fig. 15:9-15), but they are too different in form in Iron I to classify with the later type (cf. Rast 1978: 18).

Handle sections (pl. 48:5-8) are smooth and oval; some are more flattened, but none are ridged yet. Period II handles from the first campaign were similar (*TFL I*: pl. 30:1-10). Bases are flattened (pl. 48:9) similar to early Iron I bases (cf. above, pl. 47:9), and the type continues through Iron I (cf. Rast 1978: fig. 30:3). Plate 48:10 is similar to one from Taanach and may also be the base of a jug (cf. Rast 1978: 18; fig. 24:2).

The rims on pl. 48:11-14 are from jugs or small jars. The rounded, thickened, and slightly everted rim (pl. 48:11) is similar to the early 10th-century jar rim at Taanach (Rast 1978: fig. 24:3) which Rast thought belonged to a heart-shaped storage jar (Rast 1978: 18). Plate 48:12 is a profiled-type jug rim which begins toward the latter part of the 11th century and is very common through the 10th (Rast 1978: 19). Note especially the early 10th-century jug at Taanach (fig. 26:2), the many Stratum III A examples from ᶜAfûla (*ᶜAfûla*: fig. 11:6-15), over 40 examples from Samaria Period I (*SS III*: fig. 2:4, p. 104), and the numerous sherds from the early Tell el-Fûl campaigns (*TFL I*: pl. 28:1-26; *TFL II*: pl. 25:3, wrongly dated Hellenistic). Jug rims (pl. 48:13-14) are of the high-neck, plain or wavy type with late 11th- and early 10th-century parallels from Taanach (Rast 1978: fig. 20:2, and unpublished examples). From the first campaign at Tell el-Fûl (*TFL I*: pl. 28:5, 15) came similar rims, and a good parallel is published from ᶜAin Shems II A (Iron IC, *AS IV*: pl. 62:40). Two unstratified jugs from Beth-zur with plain rims are dated to the 11th-10th centuries B.C. (*BZ II*: 47, fig. 8:1-2). To be noted are the high, nearly vertical necks of these jugs.

Bowl fragments, pl. 48:15-18, are from good Stratum II loci. They are too small to characterize sufficiently, but they are of common late Iron I types with red or pinkish ware and sometimes hand burnished like similar sherds from Tell Beit Mirsim (*TBM I*: pl. 25). Several fragments with knob and bar handles were found (pl. 48:19-22). Plate 48:19 is from a stratified Period II context while the others are from mixed or later loci where Period II material occurred. Knob handles were common at ʿAin Shems in Stratum II A and the early part of II B (*AS IV*: pl. 63:14-22) and Tell Beit Mirsim B (*TBM I*: pl. 25:11, 17, 36). Bar handles also were found in Tell Beit Mirsim B (*TBM I*: pl. 25:1, 7, 16), and fragments very similar to the 1964 Tell el-Fûl sherds came from the 1924 campaign (*TFL I*: pl. 30:15-16). Plate 48:22 is probably similar to an example from Taanach (Rast 1978: fig. 47:1) which has vertical knob handles at the ends of a bar handle attached to about a third of the exterior rim of the bowl. Rast points out that bar handles have a long history from the 12th century well into Iron II times (1978: 32). One must turn to other features to date the bowls more closely, as the bar handle was adapted to the bowl form of the period.

Bowl-base forms (pl. 48:23-26) were concave, disc and low-ring, similar to the variety from Tell Beit Mirsim B (*TBM I*: pl. 30:46, 48-53), ʿAin Shems II A (*AS IV*: pl. 63:1-10), and the first campaign at Tell el-Fûl (*TFL I*: pl. 29:1-14).

One chalice stem (pl. 48:27) was found in a Period III A locus not far from "Saul's Wall." It is too fragmentary to date closely, but chalices are popular throughout Iron I. The plain stem can be compared to one from the early 10th century at Taanach (Rast 1978: fig. 27:2) and several from ʿAin Shems III (*AS IV*: pl. 61:48-50).

A number of stratified sherds contribute to the typology of Iron I cooking pots. The sherds (pl. 48:28-32) are close to those of Period I (pl. 47:14-15) and the Late Bronze tradition in rim form and stance. The triangular shape with a rounded or flattened exterior face continues. Plate 48:33-36 differs little in the triangular rim form, but the rim stance has changed; the top tip of the rim is vertical rather than everted as in the former. Similar forms come from Tell Beit Mirsim B (*TBM I*: pl. 30:39-43, "LB II-EI I type," p. 66), ʿAin Shems II A or B (*AS IV*: pl. 63:31-32), Bethel Iron I (not stratified: *Bethel*: pls. 37:12-22, 58:2-20), and the earlier Tell el-Fûl campaigns (*TFL I*: pl. 25:1-21; *TFL II*: pl. 21:1-13).

From the study of the Taanach material, Rast came to the conclusion that an elongated, concave, cooking-pot rim began to replace the Late Bronze triangular rim by the end of the 12th century. By the late 11th and early 10th centuries this development was virtually complete, and this is the most common type

of cooking-pot rim in the late 10th century (1978: 13-14). He points to similar evidence from Deir ʿAlla and Hazor, and Dothan thought the "concave" rims at ʿAfûla were later, whereas the "slanting" and "rounded" continued the Late Bronze tradition (*ʿAfûla*: 36-37).

From the study of the Tell el-Fûl material and consideration of other southern sites, it seems that while the more elongated, usually concave (or "grooved") cooking-pot rim virtually replaced the triangular, Late Bronze-type rim in the north, in the south the triangular (rounded, flat, or sometimes concave) rim persisted as the most common form through the end of Iron I. The rims with the more vertical stance (pl. 48:33-36) may indicate development or a relation to the lengthened and/or grooved rim.[3]

A small lamp sherd (pl. 48:37) is probably from a typical Iron I lamp (cf. Amiran 1969: pl. 100).

Two small sherds with wide lines of black paint (pl. 48:38-39) were found with later material, but they are probably pieces of Iron I painted ware (cf. *TFL I*: pl. 31).

Period III Pottery
(ca 640 - 538 B.C.)

Late Iron II Stratified Pottery of Palestine

Tell el-Fûl was located in the tribal territory of Benjamin (hence it was known as Gibeah of Benjamin as well as Gibeah of Saul). At the time of Solomon's death and the breakup of his kingdom, the border between Judah and Israel lay north of Benjamin. The exact border varied with the periodic wars, but from the 8th century on the border lay south of Bethel, ca. 8 km north of Tell el-Fûl. D. Lance (1971: 331) points out that the lack of royal, stamped jar handles at Bethel, as at other northern sites, is a definite indicator that the border was south of Bethel during late Iron II. In the 8th through 6th centuries one therefore expects to find the closest pottery parallels to Tell el-Fûl in the southern kingdom and the excavated sites of Judah (cf. Amiran 1969: 191, and the references cited there).[4] It is the sites with occupation in late Iron II (Wright's Iron IIB, Amiran's Iron III or IIC; see Amiran 1969: 191) which are the most helpful for Tell el-Fûl III A and pre-III A comparative material. Some important stratified material will first be cited, and then other late Iron II pottery will be mentioned for comparative purposes.

The ceramic chronology of Iron II was first delineated with some accuracy by Albright's stratigraphical excavations at Tell Beit Mirsim, and his work has been basic for all succeeding studies. Stratum A_1

was dated to the 9th-8th centuries after the fourth campaign, and Stratum A₂ to the 7th and early 6th (*TBM III*: 40, 66). Although Albright dated most of his Stratum A pottery to period A₂ (*TBM III*: 145), stratification now known from other sites (Ramat Raḥel, En-gedi, and Beth-zur, in addition to Tell el-Fûl, see below) indicates that there are many 8th-century forms among the Stratum A pottery. As M. and Y. Aharoni (1976: 73-74) have pointed out, Albright himself realized that all the constructions of Stratum A₂ did not survive to the end of Iron II, and there were at least two phases of his "Western Tower" which must be dated after the A₂ destruction (*TBM III*: 40-44). Now that the Eliakim handle from Stratum A₂ should no longer be dated to the exile of King Jehoiachin (597-587 B.C.), it is probable that the widespread destruction of Stratum A₂ should be attributed to Sennacherib (701 B.C.). Tell Beit Mirsim A₁ is thus perhaps 9th century B.C., A₂ is 8th, and A₃ lasts down to the end of the Judean kingdom (cf. M. and Y. Aharoni 1976: 73).[5] Pottery forms comparable to those of Tell Beit Mirsim A₂ were in the Tell el-Fûl Mid-Field silos.

At ᶜAin Shems, Stratum II C was dated to the 8th-6th centuries B.C. (*AS IV*: 134). Correlation with the revised Tell Beit Mirsim chronology and Lachish Level III (see below) favors ending Stratum II C at the end of the 7th century (cf. M. and Y. Aharoni 1976: 74; fig. 5; Holladay 1976: 265, 271). Tombs 2-8 and Cistern 25 have been singled out as dating more specifically to the 7th and early 6th centuries B.C. (*AS IV*: 77, 136). There are parallels to these groups from Tell el-Fûl III A, and the span of ᶜAin Shems II C includes the period of the earlier Mid-Field silos.

Ussishkin's recent excavations convincingly have dated Lachish III to the 8th century, attributing its widespread destruction to Sennacherib in 701 B.C. (Ussishkin 1977). It is necessary therefore to adjust the stratification dates of a number of late Iron II sites, but the excellent quality of the present excavations at Lachish would win the support of a number of the late excavators (Albright, Wright, and Lapp) and undoubtedly cause adjustments to be made by others (Kenyon, Cross, and Lance). There is a marked comparison between the pottery of Lachish III and the Tell el-Fûl Mid-Field silos on one hand and Lachish II and the Tell el-Fûl III A deposits on the other. Beside the loci of Level II, some constructions in the Bastion and Tomb 105 are primary late 7th-early 6th century loci.

Beth-zur Stratum III is dated 640-587 B.C. (*BZ II*: 28-29). The similarity of Beth-zur III pottery to Tell el-Fûl Iron II pottery already had been noted before the 1964 campaign at Tell el-Fûl took place (*BZ II*: 54, n. 4). Tell el-Fûl III A and Beth-zur III are without doubt contemporary. Furthermore, the Mid-Field silos at Tell el-Fûl have their complement in the Beth-zur "Pottery Cache." The latter consisted of a large group of homogeneous pottery associated with Stratum III in Field II, Area 6 (*BZ II*: 56). In the Pottery Cache are forms which were placed early in Beth-zur III. The pottery is similar to that from the Mid-Field silos, but includes perhaps slightly later pieces. Due to the parallels in these two groups to Lachish III, it is necessary now to extend their dates back at least to the early 7th century.[6]

Gezer Stratum V is dated 7th through early 6th centuries, and pottery from Field II (Stratum 4) has been published (*Gezer II*: 4-5, 75-82). The number of *lmlk* handles from Gezer indicated to Lance (1971: 330) that Gezer was a part of the southern kingdom during Josiah's reign. If the *lmlk* handles are dated to Hezekiah's reign (Ussishkin 1977: 54-57), serious difficulties are not presented since the recent Gezer excavators believed Stratum V "lasted well over a century, i. e., from the late 8th cen. B.C. into the 6th cen. B.C." (*Gezer II*: 75). The end of Stratum VI is attributed to the Assyrian campaigns of 733-721 B.C., and some of its features were reused in Stratum V (p. 73). The destruction levels of Stratum V are dated to the Babylonian campaigns of 698-586 B.C. (p. 83). The small published repertoire of pottery from Gezer V has some similarities to that of Tell el-Fûl III A and the Mid-Field silos.[7]

Beersheba II is dated by Aharoni to the 8th century B.C. with its destruction in 701 B.C. (*Beersheba I*: 5-8). Its pottery types are "virtually identical with those of Level III at Lachish" (p. 5). Aharoni always has adhered to the 701 date for the destruction of Lachish III, and Beersheba II must be dated with it. There are many pottery parallels between the Tell el-Fûl Mid-Field silos and Beersheba II. As noted by Aharoni (*Beersheba I*: 5), Beersheba III should be dated very close to Stratum II. Beersheba I follows Stratum II, but no pottery evidence is published.

En-gedi Stratum V was dated from Josiah's reign to the Babylonian exile, 630-582/1 B.C. (the third deportation), by the excavators (*ᶜAtiqot V*: 16, 18). It was noted by them that their material paralleled the Tell el-Fûl finds from the end of the 7th century and the beginning of the 6th century B.C. (*ᶜAtiqot V*: 38). The short occupation at En-gedi (p. 21) and its close association with Period III A at Tell el-Fûl confirms the occupational history of the two sites. Furthermore, some of the slightly earlier forms in the Mid-Field silos are not present in En-gedi V.[8]

In the last season of excavation at Ramat Raḥel, Stratum V was divided into Stratum V B, 9th-8th centuries B.C., and Stratum V A, ca. 608-597 (587?) B.C. (*RR II*: 38). There is a very small amount of pottery published from Stratum V B, and it differs little from the pottery of V A on the floors of the V A citadel (cf. *RR II*: 31; and especially Lance 1971: 320, n. 26). In fact, there is virtually no evidence cited for an 8th/9th- or even early 7th-century occupation (*RR II*: 58, 119). Only the heavy-grooved cooking pot (*RR II*: fig. 35:16) found in Stratum V B, but absent in V A, does not fit into the latter part of the 7th century B.C.

As will be seen in the detailed pottery study below, Tell el-Fûl III A has a very similar repertoire to the pottery of Beth-zur III, En-gedi V, and Ramat Raḥel V (A), all dated approximately from the last third of the 7th century B.C. to the fall of Judah. Many parallels also are found at Lachish II, Tell Beit Mirsim A₃, and some loci of ᶜAin Shems II C. The Tell el-Fûl Mid-Field silos have some forms not found in the closely dated En-gedi V and Ramat Raḥel V A strata, but which are present in the Beth-zur III "Pottery Cache," Tell Beit Mirsim A₂, ᶜAin Shems II C, Lachish III, and Beersheba II. Based upon the absolute dates suggested for these sites, the following groups are suggested:

8th century to 701 B.C. destruction:
   Lachish III
   Beersheba II
   Tell Beit Mirsim A₂
   ᶜAin Shems II C
ca. 700 B.C.
   Ramat Raḥel V B
   Tell el-Fûl Mid-Field silos
   Beth-zur Pottery Cache
ca. 640-587 B.C.
   Tell el-Fûl III A
   Beth-zur III
   Lachish II
   Tell Beit Mirsim A₃
   ᶜAin Shems Tombs 2-8, Cistern 25
   Ramat Raḥel V A
   En-gedi V (to 582 B.C.)

Beside this stratified material, the final publication of Kenyon's Jerusalem excavations will present more closely dated pottery from this period. This will be significant because of Tell el-Fûl's location close to Jerusalem and close historical relations with that city. M. and Y. Aharoni (1976) have recently published pottery from Arad VIII-VI and Tell Masos which dates to the 8th and 7th centuries. Since final reports describing their stratification have not yet appeared, the material is difficult to interpret critically. Where possible, reference will be made to Arad VIII as of the 700 B.C. horizon and Arad VII and VI and Tell Masos parallels to Tell el-Fûl III A.[9] The Meṣad Ḥashavyahu material is evaluated elsewhere (cf. n. 23 below).

A number of other sites have produced late Iron II pottery, but their stratification is unclear and must be dated on a comparative basis. The large corpus of pottery from Tell en-Naṣbeh, only 6 km to the north of Tell el-Fûl, has much material contemporary with Tell el-Fûl III A. El-Jîb (Gibeon) probably had a similar history to Tell el-Fûl during late Iron II and the 6th century (see especially the similarities in the silos, chap. VI above), and its published pottery must be considered. Bethel, though a part of the northern kingdom during late Iron II, was located near Tell el-Fûl and was occupied at the same time. It, too, has some similar material. Ashdod Strata VII-VI (Area D Strata 3-2) have been dated by Dothan from the second half of the 7th century to Nebuchadnezzar's destruction of the city (*Ashdod II-III*: 21), but by Bachi from the 8th century to Nebuchadnezzar's conquest (*Ashdod II-III*: 113-15). The Ashdod pottery repertoire does differ in many respects from Judean sites (p. 113), and if the pottery is stratified as described in Ashdod II-III, there is difficulty correlating it with the stratified material of the southern kingdom (cf. for example, the cooking pots in fig. 55 designated from Strata 2-1 with the **discussion below, pp. 95-96). The Ashdod material is** not very helpful until further stratified material is published and correlated by the excavators. (Dothan's dates for Ashdod Iron II are accepted in *Gezer II*: 79-80, yet the "perceptive analysis of G. Bachi" is praised, n. 156, although her dates are almost a century higher.) Tell el-Fûl parallels at Ashdod occasionally will be noted, but they do not contribute to the understanding of the pottery.

Far north, Stratum III at Hazor and some of the Stratum I pottery at Megiddo date from this time, but variations in the northern forms minimize the importance of these sites for Tell el-Fûl.[10] Samaria Period VIII has some forms comparable to Tell el-Fûl III A and B. Finally, the published pottery from earlier excavations at Tell el-Fûl has to be reexamined to place the Period III A material within that period as determined by the 1964 campaign.

A word must be said about the published contemporary pottery from Heshbon and other Transjordanian sites. As Sauer noted in his study of the 7th-6th-century pottery from Heshbon (1972: 64), the pottery there shares very few basic types with the West Bank. Typical western forms are missing at Heshbon; dominant types at Heshbon are only represented on the West Bank in occasional instances. The Heshbon repertoire shares the basic tradition of the Amman tombs, Baluᶜah, and Deir ᶜAlla, but differs essentially from the southern Transjordanian tradition (which in turn differs from the West Bank). Even Syrian parallels with the Heshbon material are rare (Sauer 1972: 31). Parallels between the Tell el-Fûl and Transjordanian pottery will be noted infrequently, but the traditions are distinctly different.

Comparative Exilic Pottery of Palestine

Published mid- and late-6th-century pottery groups from Palestine are still few. A first step was taken when five groups from the "Persian" period were published by P. W. Lapp in 1970 in the Galling Festschrift. The first group he used was the lowest layer of Cistern 1 from Tell el-Fûl, dated near the middle of the 6th century B.C., and the second was selected pottery from Stratum V at Balâṭah, dated about 500 B.C. (Lapp 1970: 179-80). No further stratified groups of the post-587-6th century B.C. have yet been published.

There are several known groups of pottery and some sites where occupation continued past 587 B.C. that are important for comparative purposes. Since this period is relatively unknown in Palestinian ceramic chronology, these groups will be presented. Consideration first will be given to some groups and sites where occupation continued into the Exilic period, 587-538 B.C., the period of Tell el-Fûl III B. Several other deposits and strata will then be mentioned which date to the end of the 6th century and the beginning of the 5th, the period of Balâṭah Stratum V, to help delineate a *terminus ante quem* for Tell el-Fûl III B.

Bethel. Locus sub-104 at Bethel, which represents the latest 6th-century pottery at the site, has been dated about 570 B.C. (Lapp 1970: 181, n. 13). Some definite Iron II B characteristics are lacking and slight developments can be seen; yet some of the later 6th-century features of Tell el-Fûl III B do not appear. This would favor the destruction of Bethel, as a result of rebellion, at the hands of Nabonidus in conjunction with the Syrian revolts of 553 B.C. (cf. Albright 1953: 173, and his discussion of Bethel in the 6th century, pp. 171-73). Sub-104 is the locus beneath a plaster floor in Room 104 of the 1934 campaign (*Bethel*: pl. 8, lower plan). Other Bethel 6th-century pottery must be dated typologically since there are no other published homogeneous groups.[11]

Some of the characteristics that fit the Bethel pottery into the Exilic period may be examined. In the sub-104 group, as well as on a number of other vessels, ring burnishing no longer seems to be in use. This is true of Tell el-Fûl III B, and the end of spiral burnishing on open bowls can probably be placed at the beginning of the Exile (Lapp 1970: 184; *Bethel*: 71). The Bethel sherds (pl. 64:1-2) should be dated preexilic because of the burnishing (pl. 64:1), as well as the inturned profiles, so characteristic of Iron II.

Most of the jars (*Bethel*: pls. 66-67), should be dated pre-587 B.C. although a few later sherds may be noted. There is no evidence that hole-mouth jars, plain or rilled-rim (pl. 66:3-6, 9-12), continued into the Exilic period (cf. below, p. 89). Profiled rims with inside groove (pls. 66:15; 67:14, 19) are certainly Iron II, and those sharply ridged (pls. 66:14; 67:1, 4-6, 11-13, 15-17) are most probably pre-587 B.C. Plate 67:10 and 18 are closer to the degenerate type which appears in the Persian period. (Note published examples from Balâṭah, ca. 500 B.C., and Taanach, ca. 450 B.C.; Lapp 1970: figs. 3:1; 4:1.) No grooved rims appear for this jar type at Bethel or Tell el-Fûl, as they do later at Balâṭah and Taanach (Lapp 1970: figs. 3:2; 4:2-3). Plate 80:10 and 12 are typical Iron II storage jars.

The cooking pots in pls. 65:4 and 66:1 (called a "jar," but undoubtedly a cooking pot from form and ware description; *Bethel*: 74, 106) are quite possibly Exilic forms similar to some from Period III at Tell el-Fûl. Plate 66:1 may be the first appearance of a high-necked type which is found in Tell el-Fûl III B, and pl. 65:4 is the angular type which is known from late 7th **through the 6th century B.C. (below, p. 96). The lamp** from sub-104 is an Iron II type which continues at least through Tell el-Fûl III B (*Bethel*: pl. 65:21; below, pl. 71. especially nos. 2-3).

No chevron ware is published from Bethel, and there is only one small fragment of what may be a crater among the sherds from Bethel in the Pittsburgh Theological Seminary collection. The period of popularity for the chevron impressed design was the latter half of the 6th century and the first half of the 5th century B.C. (Lapp 1970: 185).

In concluding the discussion of exilic material, it should be mentioned that the jugs from Locus 145 (pl. 64:17, 19) are Early Roman, and there is no post-587 B.C. evidence for the highly burnished red-jug type (pl. 78:8 [cf. *TN II*: 12-13]). The vertically burnished dipper juglets (pl. 78:1-2) are not clearly post-587 B.C.

ᶜAin Shems (Beth-shemesh). Long recognized as a post-587 B.C. tomb group is Tomb 14 from ᶜAin Shems (*AS V*: 144-45; see *AS IV*: pls. 48, 68 for the pottery). The pottery is not homogeneous, but most of it seems contemporary with the Bethel group sub-104 (Lapp 1960: 184, n. 24).

Looking briefly at the ᶜAin Shems pottery, the vessels on pl. 68:1 and 5 are similar to Tell el-Fûl flasks. There are also rims at Tell el-Fûl which may be from decanters similar to pl. 68:2, 6, 13-14. The elongated juglet (pl. 68:3) apparently was not burnished; it perhaps postdates Iron II. The elongated bottle (pl. 68:10) has been dated 6th-4th centuries and appears in Tell el-Fûl III B deposits. Plate 68:11 recalls the ubiquitous Tell el-Fûl Cistern 1 jug which dates throughout Tell el-Fûl III. Plate 68:12 is unburnished so perhaps it is a degenerate Iron II orange-red globular juglet. The lamps (pl. 48:7-8, 12) have parallels throughout Tell el-Fûl III, but the flat Persian lamp (pl. 48:9) and the Mesopotamian lamp (pl. 48:10) date into the 5th and 4th centuries. It is probable also that some of the fragments at the bottom of pl. 68 date down into the Hellenistic Period. In summary, all the vessels (pl. 68:1-14) plus the lamps (pl. 48:7, 8, 12) could date to the Exilic period contemporary with **Bethel sub-104 although the unburnished Iron II forms** may predate Tell el-Fûl III B.

Khirbet esh-Sheikh Ibrahim. A deposit of pottery thrown into a collapsed cave at Khirbet esh-Sheikh Ibrahim, 15 km southeast of Jerusalem (Aharoni 1963: 337), belongs to the period of Tell el-Fûl III B. The pottery has not been published, but it is said to be similar to that of this period (Stern 1971: 26, n. 2; Weinberg 1969: 83; P. Lapp, unpublished notes). This will be an important group especially considering its proximity to Tell el-Fûl and other northern Judean sites.

El-Jîb. Tell en-Naṣbeh and El-Jîb, both within 4 km of Tell el-Fûl toward the northwest and in the territory of Benjamin, had occupation after the fall of the southern kingdom in 587 B.C., but their stratification is not clear. However, from the study of the Tell el-Fûl pottery and the material which is published from the two sites, some observations can be made.

The excavator, James B. Pritchard, thought the final use of his "winery" at El-Jîb was in or at the end of the Iron II period because of what he considered Iron II pottery on the floors and lower levels of his "cellars" (*Gibeon*: 16). However, it has been shown that a large percentage of the pottery dates past the Iron II period (Lapp 1968: 391-92; Wright 1963: 211, n. 1). Wright dates "the wine jars from which the inscribed handles derive not much before the middle and probably in the second half of the sixth century." The ceramic and paleographical evidence assign the inscribed handles a post-Iron II date in the second half of the 6th century B.C. (Cross 1962: 23).

The excavator gives special attention to Loci 135 and 153 in determining a terminus in Iron II for use of the cellars (*Gibeon*: 19-20). A closer examination of the pottery discussed shows that the large storage jars (fig. 32:2, 8-11) probably date later in the 6th century. Rounded rims of large oval or bulbous jars were recovered from the Tell el-Fûl III B loci, as well as III A loci (below, pls. 50-51). They have been compared to Stratum V storage jars at Balâṭah, dating about 500 B.C. (Wright 1963: 211). Figure 33:14, also designated a storage jar, is compared to a Tell Beit Mirsim one-handled jug, but by form it is closest to a new type of Exilic cooking pot distinguished at Tell el-Fûl (pl. 20:16-22). Figure 33:18 is said to date to the Iron Age, but it is more typical of Hellenistic rims. The cooking pots (fig. 34:1, 4-5) are Hellenistic (cf. below, pl. 29:1-7, and many others); fig. 34:2 is the late Iron II-Early

Persian type common throughout Tell el-Fûl III (pl. 68:1-11; p. 96 above).

Although the lower meter of Locus 141 is described as having exclusively Iron II pieces of pottery, those published best fit into post-587 B.C. periods. Figure 33:15 is similar to the storage jar discussed above (fig. 32:2). Figure 32:4 is most likely Hellenistic. The jug (fig. 32:6 [not jar, *Gibeon*: 20 and as reconstructed]) could be Exilic as are some of those from Tell el-Fûl (pl. 58), but it is probably Hellenistic as fig. 32:1 certainly is. The cooking pot (fig. 34:3) is Hellenistic, and the juglet (fig. 34:12) is comparable to some from Tell el-Fûl III B (pl. 61:1-8). The published material of Locus 141 is a mixture of Exilic and Hellenistic pieces.

Other published pottery from the El-Jîb "cellars" is post-587 B.C. Chevron ware (figs. 32:7, 33:13) appeared first in the mid-6th century as indicated by its absence from Bethel but presence at Tell el-Fûl (see **below, pp. 94-95**). The lamps (fig. 33:7-10) all continue past the Iron II period, and a similar variety is found in Tell el-Fûl III B. The juglet (fig. 34:14) can be compared to the Persian-dated juglet at Tell en-Naṣbeh, but not to the Lachish Stratum II (Iron II) vessel (*TN II*: pl. 75: 1730; *Lachish III*: pl. 87:277). The cooking pots and jugs (fig. 34:6-11) can be specifically dated to the 1st century B.C. (*PCC*: Corpus 71.1.K-N, 21.1.M, Q, 32.1.A).

As has been observed (Lapp 1968: 392; and above, chap. VI), a detailed study of the pottery as well as the construction and probable stratification of the El-Jîb "winery" calls to mind the houses, floors, and silos in the shallower layer of debris at Tell el-Fûl. Most silos contained a similar mixture of Iron II, Exilic, Hellenistic, and Early Roman pottery, and undoubtedly, carefully observed stratification at El-Jîb would have indicated use of some of the silos or cellars in more than a single period.

Some of the pottery from the houses of Area 17 should be noted (*Gibeon*: 51). In fig. 47, stand no. 2, lamps nos. 4-7, globular juglet no. 10, jug no. 11, elongated juglet no. 12, and cooking pot no. 14 could be dated down to the mid-6th century B.C.—into the Exilic period—as they are at Tell el-Fûl. From unstratified debris came some more sherds of chevron ware (fig. 48:17, 22) which should be dated to the latter half of the 6th century.

In summarizing the pre-Hellenistic pottery from El-Jîb, it is evident that occupation continued at the site past Iron II into the Exilic period. The history seems to parallel that at Tell el-Fûl: occupation continued to the middle of the 6th century, with abandonment sometime in the third quarter of the 6th century until Hellenistic times.[12]

Tell en-Naṣbeh. The stratification of Tell en-Naṣbeh is quite uncertain, and dating the finds has been dependent upon comparative study and a limited number of objects of chronological significance (*TN I*: 179). A few pieces of imported ware date to the later 6th century B.C., and postexilic seals and stamps were fairly numerous (*TN I*: 164-67, 176-77). If Tell en-Naṣbeh is identified with Mizpah, its importance in the Exilic period is certain (*TN I*: 46-49). However, the pottery must be dated by comparative material since no true stratification was ascertained. Beside scattered material on the mound, a number of cisterns are dated to the middle and late 6th century B.C. (*TN I*: 129-47).

Cistern 166 has a few forms perhaps as late as 570 B.C. and much late material dating from the 7th-early 6th century (Tell el-Fûl III A). (Parallels to ᶜAin Shems Tomb 14, dating ca. 570 B.C., are seen in *TN I*: fig. 20:D 5-7.) Cistern 183 represents at least three periods: pre-587 B.C., middle-to-late 6th century, and Hellenistic. The conclusion that there are two major groups (*TN I*: 133) needs revision in light of refined typologies of the post-587 periods. (Dated middle-to-late 6th century are the impressed ware and fig. 25:C 8-9, 12, 18-20, 23.) Cisterns 191, 325, 363, and 368 do not necessarily continue into the Exilic period. Cistern 304 is mixed and may span the 625-450 B.C. period suggested (Wampler 1941: 36; *TN I*: 135). However, there are few characteristic Exilic or Persian period sherds except for the imported ware and the triangular impressed fragment, and many sherds can not be closely identified (Wampler 1941: 31-32, 34-35). It is preferable to place a lower limit of the cistern's use to the early 5th century, with the fragment of an imported cup or kylix having been deposited shortly before its final closing. Cistern 361 is dated mainly 5th and 4th century, but there is some important 6th-century pottery (note especially *TN I*: fig. 28:B 1, 3, 6; and the burnished ware mentioned, Wampler 1941: 42).

Lachish. The Persian occupation at Lachish does not begin before the middle of the 5th century B.C., but some tombs may have been in use past the destruction of 587 B.C.

Tomb 109 was disturbed (*Lachish III*: 188-89), but the pottery recovered may span the first half of the 6th century. The burnished bowls, juglets, and decanters (Types 69, 274, 276, 292, 312, 318, 326) are late Iron II, but the unburnished bowls, low-footed lamp, and the Tell el-Fûl Cistern 1-type jugs extend into the Exilic period.

Tomb 114 has similar pottery (*Lachish III*: 190), except that the jugs are missing, the lamps have rounded bottoms, and the two bowls are burnished. One or two juglets, Types 278 and 292, may date beyond 587 B.C., but use of the tomb most probably ended about that time. It is even less likely that the first period use of

Tomb 106 continued past Iron II (*Lachish III*: 179-87). The only forms represented which may be common to Tell el-Fûl A and B are cooking-pot Types 443 and 445 and some indistinguishable unburnished bowls.

Samaria. A word should be said about Samaria Period VIII. Some of the pottery belongs to the 7th-century levels of the Period VIII makeup while the rest is thought to belong to the 6th and 5th centuries B.C. (*SS III*: 129, 132; fig. 12:1-12, 7th century; fig. 12: 13-32, later). To the last half of the 6th century may be assigned the chevron ware (figs. 12:17; 32:9-10), the degenerate profile jar rims (fig. 12:22, 29; cf. *Bethel*: pl. 67:10; Lapp 1970: 181-82), and the crater rims (*SS III*: fig. 12:30-32; cf. fig. 16:8-12). The mortaria cannot be dated to the 6th century (they are absent from 6th-century deposits; cf. Lapp 1970: 184-85), and probably most of the remainder of the pottery should be dated later. Cistern 7, Strip I, to which much of the Period VIII pottery is compared, dates to the late 5th and 4th centuries B.C. (*SS III*: 132).

Comparative Early Persian Pottery of Palestine

Beth-zur Reservoir 44 and the other sites discussed below date after Tell el-Fûl III B. Typical Iron II forms have disappeared, especially bowl forms. Some Exilic ceramic characteristics, such as chevron ware, continue for a while, and the small, shallow cooking pot with angular rim continues through the 6th century. Soon typical Persian characteristics appear: flat Persian lamps, chalky orange ware; later, there are basket handles and mortaria. Greek imported wares become more frequent and serve to establish absolute dates.

Beth-zur Reservoir 44 falls within the last quarter of the 6th century when the Persians were in control of Palestine and a few Israelites had returned after the captivity. The "Exilic" period was over and the Early Persian period was underway. By this time Tell el-Fûl and El-Jîb, as well as Bethel, had been abandoned.

Beth-zur Reservoir 44 will be discussed, and Balâṭah Stratum V described. Following that, some sites and tombs for which late 6th-century occupation has been suggested will be mentioned, but the published pottery from them is more characteristic of the 5th-century corpus.

Beth-zur. A cistern deposit, Reservoir 44, from Beth-zur has been assigned a date in the last quarter of the 6th century B.C. (Lapp 1970: 185). Some of the Reservoir 44 pottery was published in the excavation report from the 1931 Beth-zur campaign, and it was reexamined after the 1957 excavation.

Two small bottles belong to the late 6th century, and the small squat one has parallels from Tell el-Fûl III B and ᶜAin Shems Tomb 14 (*CBZ*: pls. 7:15, 10:15; cf. Lapp 1970: fig. 1:4; *AS IV*: pl. 68:7-9). A bowl with horizontal handles can be compared with some from the III B deposit of Cistern 1 at Tell el-Fûl (cf. pl. 65:11 with *CBZ*: pl. 11:6; the handles should be described as horizontal handles rather than unpierced lug handles as the plate caption indicates). At least three chevron-impressed sherds are from Reservoir 44 (*BZ II*: pl. 32b:12-14 are from Reservoir 44; cf. *CBZ*: fig. 38). They fit well into the latter part of the 6th century. The absence of unburnished, Iron II bowl forms, found still in Bethel sub-104 and Tell el-Fûl III B, place Beth-zur Reservoir 44 after them, but before the appearance of chalky orange ware in the 5th century B.C. (Lapp 1970: 183; cf. *BZ II*: 70). Isolated sherds of chalky orange ware did turn up at Beth-zur, but none were found in Reservoir 44, and they must represent a slight occupation into the 5th century.

Balâṭah (Shechem). By the time of Balâṭah V, about 500 B.C., the Early Persian period was well under way. Most Iron II forms have disappeared, and some later forms have come on the horizon (for example, "Persian" lamps, Lapp 1970: 186). However, some more typical 5th-century forms have not yet appeared (for example, high, looped "basket" jar handles, Lapp 1970: 183 and n. 21; and mortaria, Lapp 1970: 185).

Balâṭah V represents a period of occupation for which only one architectural feature has been isolated (Wright 1964: 167). It has been defined by separating out a pottery horizon from mixed fills. Their absolute date has been determined by a study of sherds of imported Greek vases, all of which date between 525 and 475 B.C. (N. Lapp 1964a: 238-41). Only a little Balâṭah pottery has been published (N. Lapp 1964a: fig. 113; Lapp 1970: fig. 3), but what is known is important in characterizing the pottery that follows the Exilic period.

Coastal sites. It has been contended that marked differences occur in the various geographical regions of Palestine during the Persian period. E. Stern distinguishes between the pottery of the Judean hills and that of the Samaria and Benjamin regions, and then between those and the pottery of Galilee and the coastal plain (1971: 26, n. 2). From the pottery known, the distinction cannot be made in the Exilic period (587-538 B.C.); parallel material to that from Tell el-Fûl is found not only nearby in the territory of Benjamin (Bethel, El-Jîb, and Tell en-Naṣbeh) but in Judah (ʿAin Shems and Lachish) and even Samaria. Later in the 6th century, that is the Early Persian period, similar characteristics can still be found in the pottery of southern Palestine and at least as far north as Samaria. Whether regional differences can be distinguished between these sites of northern and southern Palestine and the coastal plain is not clear.

Tell Abu Hawam Stratum II A was dated 569-525 B.C., and II B, 525-early 4th century B.C. by R. W. Hamilton, the excavator (1934: 2, 66). Stern convincingly lowers these dates. On the basis of the imported wares and coins, he places Phase II A from 538, or a little later, to 385/3 B.C. and Phase II B shortly after until 332 B.C. (1968: 218-19; see also Lapp 1970: 185, n. 35). Considering what is known, the characteristic locally made vessels from Tell Abu Hawam should be placed in the 5th century B.C., at least as late as Balâṭah V (about 500 B.C.). Of the pottery published (Hamilton 1934: 4), compare to fig. 3, Lapp 1970: 182-83 and the "orange" ware predominant in 5th-century groups. For fig. 4, compare Lapp 1970: 184-85, "introduced after the beginning of the fifth century." For fig. 5, see Lapp 1970: 186; the "Persian" lamp first appears in Balâṭah V and is frequent in the 5th century. Figure 6 is probably Hellenistic (cf. *PCC*: Corpus 71.B). To fig. 7, compare *Hazor I*: pl. 80:1 (Stratum II), *Lachish III*: pl. 87:255 (Level I and late graves), *Meg. I*: pl. 1:2-6 (Stratum I), and from the Athlît tombs, Johns 1933: 51, fig. 4h (5th- and 4th-century strata and loci).

The settlement of Tell Abu Hawam in the Persian period was a part of the Phoenician expansion to the south which perhaps included the occupation of Tell el-Fukkar, Shiqmona, and Gilʿam (Stern 1968: 217, n. 19). Little of the pottery from these sites has been published however, so it is difficult to relate them to the rest of Palestine. It is most probable that Tell Abu Hawam and other northern coastal sites flourished only toward the very end of the 6th century and later. (Stern himself leaves this possibility open, 1968: 217 and n. 19. Compare Weinberg 1969: 87, where he notes "the abandonment of a number of coastal sites in the tenth, ninth, and eighth centuries, all reoccupied by Phoenicians in the late sixth and fifth centuries.") It also seems likely that when more pottery is known from stratified contexts of the 5th and 4th centuries B.C., many parallels will be found between the coastal sites and those of northern and southern Palestine, and regional differences will be difficult to distinguish. Weinberg's remarks concerning imported wares should be noted: "One can as yet see little difference between coastal sites and inland sites; if there is material from the last quarter of the sixth century at ʿAtlit, there is also some at Shekhem" (1969: 89).

Ramat Raḥel. After the fifth campaign at Ramat Raḥel Stratum IV B was dated 5th-3rd centuries B.C. (*RR II*: 38). Most of the pottery is dated too broadly and too late to be of interest here, but some sherds from one deposit, Refuse Pit 484, are significant. This was a large accumulated heap of sherds more than a meter high against a wall which the excavators thought dated to the end of the Persian period (*RR II*: 18). Besides a little pottery from the Iron Age and Persian bowls they dated to the 6th century, Aharoni thought almost all types were from a transitional phase between the Persian and Hellenistic periods (*RR II*: 18-19). The "Persian bowls" (mortaria), fig. 12:17-22, cannot be dated before the middle of the 5th century (Lapp 1970: 184), but this form most probably belongs to the 4th or 3rd century B.C. (cf. N. Lapp 1964b: 17-18). The triangular incised ware (figs. 13:9, 14:37) and horizontal-handled craters (fig. 13:4-10) date to the latter half of the 6th century or early 5th century (cf. below, pp. **94-95 or the sherds from the Beth-zur Reservoir 44, above, pp. 86-87; Lapp 1970: 185). One cooking pot** (fig. 13:14) is of the new type described from Tell el-Fûl **III B (below, p. 96). Juglets (fig. 14:8-10) could be** from as early as Tell el-Fûl III B, but they probably continue through most of the Persian period. Elongated painted bottles and globular bottles (fig. 14:40-41, 43) also appear in the Exilic period, but they may continue for a considerable time and no *terminus a quo* has yet been determined for them. It is sufficient to say that there are some late 6th- or first half of the 5th-century forms as well as 4th- and 3rd-century sherds in Refuse Pit 484. The mixed pottery does not add significantly to the Exilic and Early Persian pottery corpus.

En-gedi. Not much of the Stratum IV pottery from En-gedi has been published, but the excavators date the stratum from the second quarter of the 5th century through the first half of the 4th century B.C. by means of the Attic ware (Mazar and Dunayevsky 1967: 137-38). A sherd of East Greek ware dating to the end of the 6th or early 5th century suggests some earlier occupation. The large amount of chevron ware (Mazar and Dunayevsky 1964: pl. 28) points to occupation contemporary with Balâṭah V. Especially to be noted is the impressed design on the crater with crude lug handle (second row left), a form known from Balâṭah V (Lapp 1970: fig. 3:8). Published evidence does not suggest occupation quite as early as Weinberg suggests (1969: 83), and Stern pushes Locus 254 of Building 234 earlier in the 5th century than the excavators maintain (1971: 28; cf. Mazar and Dunayevsky 1967: 138). On the basis of what is published, reoccupation took place around 500 B.C.

ᶜ*Ain ᶜArrub.* Among several tomb caves discovered 2 km west of Beit Fajjar, near Hebron, there was one of the Persian period. E. Stern published the finds, including some pottery of interest (1971: 25-30).

The flasks (1971: fig. 2) are dated by Stern to the end of the 6th century and the 5th century B.C. They display a number of differences from the Tell el-Fûl and ᶜAin Shems flask: short necks, "ear handles," and depressed or doubled-ridged handles in section. Stern compares them to flasks from the southern sites of En-gedi, Khirbet esh-Sheikh Ibrahim, Gezer, Lachish, Tell Jemmeh, and Tell el-Farᶜah (South). From the

parallels he presents, it is necessary to date these flasks in the 5th century, probably the latter half (see below, **p. 91). Further, the juglets (fig. 3:1-3) found in the tomb also should be dated late in the 5th century. The parallel** juglet and the characteristic "peculiar, raised handle in the form of a triangle" are found in contexts of the **second half of the 5th century B.C. (see below, n. 13).** The body form of the "jug" (juglet) Stern published, (1971: fig. 3:9) is similar to that of Early Hellenistic juglets from Balâṭah Stratum IV and Bethany.[13] The cups from the tomb (fig. 3:4-7) are without parallels in Palestine (Stern 1971: 29). But from the present state of knowledge, the pottery in the tomb must be dated late in the 5th century B.C.

Tell Jemmeh. Buildings A and B at Tell Jemmeh cannot be dated as early as the end of the 6th century, but rather in the 5th century with possible extension into the 4th century B.C. Stern (1971: 28) misinterpets Sinclair, who makes no mention of a 6th-century date for Building A but points out the typical 5th- and 4th-century pottery forms (cf. *TFL II*: 42, n. 34). Persian pottery from the granary in the new excavations has not yet been published, but the excavator is inclined to date it late in the Persian period, with construction of the granary in the 4th or even early in the 3rd century (Van Beek 1972: 245).

Period III Pottery
(pre-III A ca.   700 B.C.
 III A ca. 640-587 B.C.
 III B ca. 587-538 B.C.)

Jars

Typical of late Iron II sites are "hole-mouth" jars—rather small jars with no shoulders, usually with a sharp angle where the wide rim meets its cylindrical body (pl. 49:1-11). Examples were numerous at Tell el-Fûl in the Iron II loci, but they were absent from homogeneous Exilic contexts. Evidence seems to limit them to late Iron II at Tell el-Fûl as elsewhere. The evidence for hole-mouth jars was summarized after the 1957 campaign at Beth-zur (*BZ II*: 57-58, and references cited there). To be added now is the evidence from Ramat Raḥel Stratum V A, En-gedi V, Gezer V (general stratum), Beersheba II, and Ashdod VI (Area D, Stratum 2).

The thicker, heavier rim form with remnants of a slight exterior projection are from Silos 36 and 38 (pl. 49:1-7), the earliest Iron II deposits of Stratum III. These have parallels from the Beth-zur III Pottery Cache (a homogeneous group of pottery, probably representing the earliest Stratum III pottery at Beth-zur; *BZ II*: 55; fig. 15:1-2) and the similar rims cited there (58, n. 34) from Tell Beit Mirsim A, ͨAin Shems II C, and Tell en-Naṣbeh. To these may be added the hole-mouth jars from Beersheba II (*Beersheba I*: pls. 58:17-28; 70:2-3). From Tell el-Fûl only pl. 49:4 shows incipient ribbing, and the ribbed rim does not seem to be characteristic of Tell el-Fûl. Plate 49:6 is perhaps an early ancestral form for these hole-mouths similar to a Gezer V rim (*Gezer II*: pl. 35:15). The other four hole-mouth rims (pl. 49:8-11) are less heavy ware and flatter, thus giving the appearance of a wider rim. Plate 49:10 came from above the III A burn in the Northeast III Building, and pl. 49:9 and 11 are from III A-B loci. The Tell el-Fûl sherds thus support other evidence indicating that the longer and flatter rims are the latest development of the true hole-mouth jar (cf. *Gezer II*: 81 and n. 163). Similar rims came from Ramat Raḥel V (*RR I*: figs. 12:6, 26:5-8, 29:8-11; *RR II*: figs. 19:13, 21:1-12, 35:5), En-gedi V (ͨ*Atiqot V*: fig. 21:1-2), Beth-zur III (*BZ II*: fig. 15:5-7), and parallels cited to the Beth-zur rims (*BZ II*: 58, n. 36) from ͨAin Shems II C, Megiddo IV-I, and Lachish II (cf. also *Lachish III*: pl. 96:498, the Stratum II jar of Ostraca II, VI, VII, VIII, XVIII). From the second campaign at Tell el-Fûl came several rims of this type (*TFL II*: pl. 23:8, 11, 13-14).

No hole-mouth rims came from the homogeneous III B loci, and there is no evidence for them at Tell el-Fûl or other sites after 587 B.C. The Tell en-Naṣbeh jars of this type are represented in cisterns dated 700-550 B.C. and probably belong with the early 6th- and 7th-century material (cf. *TN II*: 12 and *BZ II*: 57-58, nn. 35-36). Hole-mouth jars at Bethel have been dated to the 6th century (*Bethel*: 73-74), but the material there was not stratified and must be dated by comparative pottery.[14]

A larger jar with hole-mouth-type rims but a rounded shoulder had two or four handles and a ring base (pl. 49:12-17). The whole form is that of Lachish III (*Lachish III*: pl. 96:499), Beersheba III (*Beersheba I*: pl. 56:18), Beersheba II (58:29-36; 65:1-4, 7; 73:6-8), En-gedi V (ͨ*Atiqot V*: pls. 9:15, 21:7-8), and Tell Beit Mirsim A (*TBM III*: pl. 13:1-2, 4). At Gezer they are called "krater-storejars" (*Gezer II*: 81). The flat or rounded rim was typical of the 8th century, especially at Samaria (*SS III*: fig. 6:20-24, Period IV; see also *Beersheba I*: pl. 55:20, Stratum IV; *BZ II*: fig. 15:8, mixed context), and this seems true in Tell Beit Mirsim A, Lachish III, Beersheba III and II (references above), and the Tell el-Fûl Mid-Silo (pl. 49:12); it continues to the end of Iron II at Ramat Raḥel (*RR I*: fig. 25:11) and En-gedi V (ͨ*Atiqot V*: figs. 9:15, 21:7). A slightly grooved modification of the rim (pl. 49:14-17) seems to be characteristic of the end of Iron II at Tell el-Fûl (see also *TFL II*: pl. 23:9-10, 12—wrongly dated Hellenistic, p. 37; cf. *BZ II*: 58, and n. 37), Ramat Raḥel (*RR I*: fig. 12:8), and En-gedi (ͨ*Atiqot V*: fig. 21:3, 8). The

evidence indicates that this type of "hole-mouth" existed side by side with the smaller jar with angular shoulders and nearly vertical sides and was not replaced by it (contrast *SS III*: 107, 116; *BZ II*: 58 and n. 57).

The evidence concerning the large, heavy, "neck-less" jars with rounded base and two relatively small handles (pl. 49:18-28) is similar to that of the hole-mouth. Many rim sherds came from the pre-III A Silo 36 (pl. 49:18-22) and more from other III loci, but none from the III B homogeneous groups. All the Mid-silo rims were heavily thickened and grooved. The evidence parallels that from Beth-zur III (*BZ II*:58-59).[15] It is a common form at both sites, with similar thickened, unthickened, and down-turned variations (cf. *BZ II*: fig. 15:9-16). Parallels from other sites are still not plentiful, but a rim from Ramat Raḥel V (*RR I*: fig. 12:5) may be added to the ͨAin Shems (*AS IV*: pl. 65:4-12), Lachish (*Lachish III*: pl. 94:466), and Tell en-Naṣbeh examples (*TN II*: pls. 4:56, 59-61; 5:6; 7:94). There are no certain stratified examples before the end of the 8th century B.C. The two published rims from the second campaign at Tell el-Fûl (*TFL II*: pl. 23:15-16) should be dated with the 1964 Stratum III material (*TFL II*: 37; cf. *BZ II*: 59 and n. 43).

On pl. 50 are a variety of Period III jar fragments. Most of them belong to a rounded-rim and rather high-necked, oval- to bag-shaped jar.[16] Similar storage jars came from En-gedi V (ͨ*Atiqot V*: figs. 9:14; 11; 22:3-5), Ramat Raḥel V (*RR I*: figs. 12:2, 29:1-3; *RR II*: fig. 11:14, and cf. p. 18 tracing the development of fig. 11:14), and Beth-zur III (*BZ II*: fig. 16:2). A similar type rim is a rather popular form at Heshbon (Sauer 1972: 54, Jar Type 9, and pl. 8). Tell el-Fûl rims (pl. 50:20-25) were all from burnt debris near bedrock in the west of Room E from which a *lmlk* handle also came (no. 205). Several of the rims could be from the high-necked *lmlk* jars (especially pl. 50:16, 20-21). This type jar continued to be in use after 701 B.C. without the stamp even at Lachish (Ussishkin 1977: 56), and the same type handles had rosette stamps at En-gedi (ͨ*Atiqot V*: 33-34; see below, pp. 111-12).

The handles shown on pl. 50 are from a variety of jar types, some from heavy neckless jars (pl. 49:18-28). Handle sections are oval and usually double ridged. Punched impressions on handles (pl. 50:33-35) are not **uncommon from Late Iron I on (cf. Rast 1978: fig. 75:4, 7th century; *Meg. I*: pl. 42, Stratum V; *Hazor I*: pl. 84:6-10, Strata III-V). The two huge pithoi handles (pl. 50:26-27) were found in the debris around the Period III plastered basin complex in Room G.

The sherds shown in pl. 50:28-36 are from the pre-III A silos. The rims (pl. 50:28-32) are plain on short necks with sloping shoulders. They are perhaps from amphora similar to some from Tell Beit Mirsim A and

Beersheba II (*TBM I*: pls. 52:10, 14; 53:2, 4-5; *Beersheba I*: pl. 57:6, 11, 15). Some similar rims from Gezer VII-VI (*Gezer II*: pl. 33:13-18) are probably from these ovoid jars rather than "sausage jars" to which they are compared (p. 71).

The homogeneous III B deposits show that in the Exilic period a definite rim form emerges (pls. 51:1-6; 33:2, 4). It is thickened and out-turned with the folded-over appearance of Hellenistic rims. The elongated, thickened rims (pl. 51:7-11) are perhaps related. At the bottom of Silo 40 were a large number of jar fragments (pl. 52:1-12) with a number having rims of this type. Although this deposit did not have a great variety of pottery forms, the rims indicate this was also a III B deposit. Other Period III B rims (pl. 51:12-16) display the variety of Period III (cf. pl. 50:1-23). In the III A-B layer of Cistern 1 were several large fragments of rounded-rim, high-necked jars (pl. 52:13-16) similar to other Period III A and B rims (cf. especially III A rims, pl. 50:1, 7, 10 and III B rims, pl. 51:13-15). Since high-necked bag-shaped jars have not been pointed out as particularly characteristic of late Iron II (cf. *BZ II*: 59-60), perhaps they started very late in the period and became more characteristic from the Exilic times onward. Significantly, they are missing from the pre-III A Mid-Field silos (Silo 36 and Silo 38) and the early Stratum III Pottery Cache at Beth-zur. Parallels to the Tell el-Fûl jars came from Ramat Raḥel V, En-gedi V, and Beth-zur III, the latest stratified Iron II material.

The small handleless (?) jar from Cistern 1 (pls. 51:18-19; 33:1) shows the probable oval to bag shape of all the III B and III A-B jars represented on pls. 51 and 52. Contrary to previous conclusions (Lapp 1970: 182), "sausage" jars with flat or rounded tops do not seem to be present at Tell el-Fûl. Their absence from Tell Beit Mirsim, ʿAin Shems, Beth-zur, Tell en-Naṣbeh, and Tell el-Fûl seems to sustain this as mainly a northern form during Iron II. There are some published from Stratum VI (Iron II) at Ashdod (*Ashdod II-III*: fig. 57:8-9) and Stratum III and later at Lachish (*Lachish III*: 313, 314, pls. 95:488-89; 96:530), but at least some of these are Persian types of orange chalky ware and probably do not appear until about 500 B.C. (cf. Lapp 1970: 182-83).

A body sherd with a potter's mark is shown on pl. 51:17 (pl. 33:5), but the scratches on the fragment, pl. 52:12 (pl. 33:6) are illegible.

Jugs

Fragments of many water jugs were imbedded in the lowest silt layer of the large, plastered cistern, Cistern 1, the very important deposit of homogeneous **III B pottery (cf. above, p. 46, and Lapp 1970: 179).** These jugs (pls. 34, 53-56) were of the wide-mouthed

type with a ridge around the neck and are indistinguishable from some appearing at the end of Iron II (Lapp 1970: 183, and reference to *TBM III*: pl. 14:1, 4; see also *TBM I*: pl. 58:4-5, 7-9 [TBM A]; *AS V*: pl. 67:10 [Stratum IIC, Cistern 25]; *Lachish III*: pl. 86: 238, 248-50 [Stratum II]; ʿ*Atiqot* V: figs. 9:11, 20:7 [En-gedi V]; *RR I*: fig. 11:25 [Stratum V]; *TN II*: pl. 33:584-88 and p. 17 [dating these jugs 700-500 B.C.]; cf. also Meṣad Hashavyahu, Naveh 1962: fig. 5:6). At Tell el-Fûl the same jug appeared in stratified III A (late Iron II) deposits (pl. 57:1-5, 12-14) including the pre-III A Mid-Field Silos 36 and 38 (pl. 57:1-3), as well as loci with both phases of Stratum III pottery (pl. 57:6-11). P. W. Lapp thought the form continued through the late 5th century (1970: 183), but the Taanach rim (Lapp 1970: fig. 6:6) is fragmentary and dissimilar to the 6th-century type at Tell el-Fûl, Tell Beit Mirsim, and Tell en-Naṣbeh. More evidence is needed to be certain that this same form continued past 500 B.C.

The jugs which had incised marks on their shoulders (pls. 55:9, 11, 13; 34:4-6) should be noted, as well as the jug (pl. 55:10; photo pl. 34:2) which had holes pierced on either side of two breaks made in antiquity. The holes could be laced with a cord to mend the jug, but then it would hardly hold liquid. The smallest jug (pls. 55:12; 34:3) should be contrasted to the larger vessels of the same form.

There was one fragment of the type of Iron II jug which had a ridge near the rim (pl. 57:15; cf. *TBM III*: pl. 14:3, 5-6; *TBM I*: pl. 58:3; *TN II*: pl. 32:563-64; *Beersheba I*: pl. 68:18). There is no evidence that this form continued into the Persian period, and it is possible that the cistern-type jug gradually replaced it.[17]

In Period III B a wide-mouthed jug with a plain neck and thickened out-turned (folded-over?) rim appears (pls. 58:1-5; 33:3; 35:1-2, 5). It differs considerably from the smoothly rounded rim of the late 5th and 4th centuries (Lapp 1970: figs. 6:4-5, 7; 9:3-4; cf. pp. 183-84), and yet there is no evidence for similar forms until Hellenistic times when the jugs are much more delicate and lighter in weight (see below, Hellenistic jugs pl. 75).

The very large wide-mouthed jugs represented by three lip fragments (pls. 58:6, 7; 35:3, 4, 6) are quite interesting. The rims are plain and unthickened, the mouth is trefoil, and the necks are rather short. A large jug with a trefoil rim belonging to the "Red Coarse Ware" class (*Hazor I*: 60, pl. 81:7) is published from Stratum II at Hazor (probably Late Persian).

There were only a few fragments of narrow-necked jugs or decanters (pl. 57:16-19), and a similar situation was seen at Beth-zur (cf. *BZ II*: 61-62, with references and parallels cited there). Albright suggested (*TBM III*: 148) that the decanter with conical body and ring base flourished at the end of the 8th century B.C., but this date should now be pushed back into the 8th century. That the form continued to the end of Iron II is evident from the Beth-zur III decanter sherds as well as representation in Ramat Raḥel V (*RR I*: figs. 11:26; 25:4; 28:41, 43; *RR II*: figs. 20:12, 35:4) and En-gedi (*ᶜAtiqot* V: figs. 9:6-10; 20:1-5).[18] The fragmentary Tell el-Fûl sherds could be from narrow-necked jugs such as *TBM I*: pl. 16:1-9 and *RR II*: fig. 20:16-17. Since the Tell el-Fûl sherds were from Period III A-B loci, it is also possible that they were from a post-587 B.C. type of decanter like those from Tomb 14 at ᶜAin Shems (*AS IV*: pl. 68:2, 6, 13-14). Plate 57:16 could be from the "Gibeon" type jug (Pritchard 1959: fig. 6), but conclusions cannot be drawn from the fragments.

Plate 57:20-22 shows spouts and a rim fragment from three-handled jugs (or jars) which appear in Iron II (cf. *TBM III*: 146; *TBM I*: 80 and pls. 34, 53:1, 3, 54:1-3 [Stratum A]; *Meg. I*: pl. 12:2-3 [Strata IV-I]; *Beersheba I*: pls. 58:30-32, 65:8 [Stratum II]; *AS IV*: pl. 66:41 [Stratum II], 67:12 [Stratum II C, Cistern 25]; *SS III*: pl. 31:1-3, p. 192; M. and Y. Aharoni 1976: figs. 2:10, 3:10 [Lachish III and Arad VIII]; *ᶜAtiqot* V: fig. 9:13 [En-gedi V]). As the variety of parallels indicates, they had a fairly long and widespread history. The two Tell el-Fûl spouts were from the pre-III A Silo 36 deposit, but that the type persisted until late in the 7th century is demonstrated by the Stratum III A and En-gedi examples.[19]

Plate 57:23-25 shows sections of depressed handles such as those found on Iron II decanters, but the same type of handle was used for other jugs (cf. *BZ II*: 61, and references cited there). A number of such handles were found in Period III contexts.

Flasks

It is fortunate to be able to assign the tops of three flasks to Period III B. Two are from the III B deposit at the bottom of Cistern 1, the other from the III B Pottery Cache (pls. 59:1-3; 35:7-9). In addition, parts of two other flasks (pl. 59:4-5) from the cistern in all probability can be assigned to this period. Outsplayed rounded rims and smooth, oval-sectioned handles give a pleasant finished appearance, not typical of the Hellenistic flasks (see pl. 76). The upper handle attachment is about midway up the neck which is not shorter than the Hellenistic flask neck, as some thought (cf. *TFL II*: 42). The Tell el-Fûl examples have close parallels from Tomb 14 at ᶜAin Shems which has some nearly contemporary pottery (*AS IV*: pl. 68:1, 5; cf. **above, pp. 84-85). The similar flask from En-gedi is** thought to date toward the end of the 5th century (Mazar and Dunayevsky 1967: pl. 33:7; p. 138; cf. also *ᶜAtiqot* V: fig. 32:1 from the Clark collection). The flasks published by E. Stern from near ᶜAin ᶜArrub are dated by him to the end of the 6th century and the 5th

century B.C. (1971: 25-30), but they must be redated to late in the 5th century. They display several characteristics different from the Tell el-Fûl and ᶜAin Shems flasks: short necks, "ear handles" with depressed or double-ridged sections and rather poor firing. The reconstructed flask from Tell el-Fûl (pl. 59:5) did have a similar flattish ridge running around the body lengthwise where the two parts were joined together.

Stern compares the ᶜAin ᶜArrub vessels to flasks from En-gedi, Khirbet esh-Sheikh Ibrahim, Gezer, Lachish, Tell Jemmeh, and Tell el-Farᶜah (S)—"all in the southern part of the country" (1971: 28). It seems necessary, from the parallels he presents, to put these flasks within the 5th century B.C., probably the latter half. The En-gedi flask is dated to the end of the 5th century by the excavators (Mazar and Dunayevsky 1967: pl. 33:7; p. 138), but Stern dates the flask broadly from the beginning of the 5th to the first quarter of the 4th century B.C. (1971: 28). The Gezer "Philistine Tomb" which contained a flask should be dated to the 5th century according to Iliffe (1935: 185) and Woolley (1914-16: 127-29). Stern misinterprets these references and dates the tombs to the end of the 6th and 5th centuries B.C. (1971: 28 and n. 14). Although he speaks of two flasks from the Philistine tombs (26, n. 9; 28), there is only one (*Ex. Gezer I*: 296, fig. 157:1; cf. *Ex. Gezer II*: 199). In any case, those to which Stern refers (*Ex. Gezer III*: pls. 170:1, 107:5), are doubtful parallels. The Lachish flask, *Lachish III*: pl. 92:436, parallels the ᶜAin ᶜArrub vessel, but the context is not as certain as Stern suggests (1971: 28). Tufnell (*Lachish III*: 240) prefers to put the flask with the 10th-century material of L. 4005. The flask fragments, *Lachish III*: pl. 103:679, are from the postexilic houses and residency and date to the last half of the 5th century B.C. during the Persian occupation at Lachish. The Tell Jemmeh flasks are difficult to compare, but they date within the 5th century rather than to the end of the 6th century. Sinclair even dated them to the early 4th century B.C. (*TFL II*: 42, n. 34), but Stern overlooks this (1971: 28 and n. 16). The Tell el-Farᶜah (S) flasks are from Tombs 707 and 800 (*CPP*: 87 S, 87 L; not 860, cf. Stern 1971: 28) which included typical late 5th-century storage jars (*CPP*: types 47 T, U 5, also 47 H and H 4 from the 700 and 800 cemeteries; cf. Lapp 1970: figs. 4:4-6, 6:1-2). No pottery has been published from Khirbet esh-Sheikh Ibrahim so the flasks there are not helpful.

Considering the evidence of the 6th-century Tell el-Fûl and ᶜAin Shems flasks and the parallels Stern himself presents, it is necessary to date the flasks from the ᶜAin ᶜArrub burial to the 5th century B.C., more exactly, to the second half. Further, the other pottery in the tomb also demands a late 5th-century date for the deposit (cf. n. 13).

Juglets

Plate 60:1-5 is of typical late Iron II vertically burnished, elongated juglets (cf. *TBM I*: pls. 68, 69) from pre-III A Silo 36. Plate 60:6, a juglet from a mixed layer of Cistern 1, most probably dates to Period III A. At ᶜAin Shems (*AS V*: 78, 144) and Bethel (*Bethel*: 72-73) this form was called degenerate and dated late in the 6th century. The ᶜAin Shems vessel, *AS V*: pl. 48:52, is unburnished so it easily could date later. The post-587 B.C. date of the Bethel vessels **is not certain (see above, p. 84). The Tell el-Fûl** vessel is close to some of the Tell Beit Mirsim specimens, but the form may have continued through the 7th century. Plate 60:7 shows the lower part of a two-handled juglet similar to the elongated type but with the two handles on mid-body rather than one at the rim. It has typical vertical burnishing.

In the III B deposit of Cistern 1 is found the first closely dated example of a more elongated juglet (pl. 60:8), probably a descendant of the common Iron II type (Lapp 1970: 184). There were parts of two others (pl. 60:9-10) in the mixed layers of the cistern. These juglets appeared at En-gedi and Ramat Raḥel in broadly dated Persian and Iron II contexts (Mazar and Dunayevsky 1967: pl. 32:2 [En-gedi]; Aharoni 1956: fig. 8:4 [Ramat Raḥel Stratum IV]; *RR II*: fig. 20:15 [Stratum Va]). At Tell en-Naṣbeh they are believed to be 6th-5th century and perhaps somewhat later (*TN II*: 24, pls. 38:679, 41:788). Also in the cistern was the lower part of a heavy, flat-bottomed cylindrical juglet (pl. 60:11). Parts of similar heavy-ware juglets are published from Gibeon (*Gibeon*: fig. 47:12), Jerusalem (Bliss and Dickie 1898: pl. 25:8), and a mid-5th-century cistern at Taanach (Lapp 1970: fig. 5:9). *Lachish III*, pl. 87:277 and 278, may be of this type. Tomb 114, from which two of them came, may extend slightly into the **Exilic period (see above, p. 86), and they also are** present in Stratum II (one of Type 277 and *Lachish V*, pl. 48:13). One comes from Arad VII-VI (possibly post-587 B.C.), and M. and Y. Aharoni (1976: 86) consider them degenerate water decanters. As yet there is no evidence of them before the 6th century.

Only three small fragments of the typical Iron II black burnished juglets were recorded (pl. 60:12-13), one from Period III A and the other two unstratified. Their scarcity at other sites is noted (*BZ II*: 63, and references, n. 76)—they had passed their height of popularity by the end of the 7th century. They are completely absent from some late Iron II sites (Aharoni and Aharoni 1976: 84).

The globular juglets (pl. 61:1-7) are all from mixed deposits in Cistern 1, but typologically they precede the common Hellenistic globular juglet (pl. 76). The ware is heavier, the rim thicker and more profiled. In the two specimens with their lower portion preserved, there is a

slight flat base. A parallel came from the Persian Building 234 at En-gedi in a deposit in Room 254 which the excavators believe to date from the end of the 5th century (Mazar and Dunayevsky 1967: 138 and pl. 33:2). In Tomb 8 at ᶜAin Shems (Mackenzie 1912: pls. 56:15, 57:20) two of these jugs appeared. The tomb **dates to the very end of Iron II (above, pp. 82-83).** and "the type is certainly a late comer, just appearing as these tombs were closed for the last time" (Mackenzie 1912: 89). The globular juglet from the end of the Persian period at Wadi ed-Dâliyeh has a rounded base and plain rim (Lapp 1970: fig. 10:3). The Tell el-Fûl juglets should be dated with the III B material of Cistern 1. Plate 61:8 is the top of a similar juglet from within the West Casemate walls. Plate 61:9 shows part of a wider-necked globular juglet from Cistern 1.

Bottles

Pointed bottles (pl. 61:10-14) have been found throughout Palestine. This form with painted horizontal stripes was found in Amman tombs and dated to Iron II (Henschel-Simon 1945: 75-80); it is thought to be Assyrian in origin (Amiran 1969: 296). In coarser ware, rougher workmanship, and without painted bands, it is considered later and dated to the 6th through 4th centuries B.C. (*AS V*: 145 and n. 46; *Hazor I*: 58-59; ᶜ*Atiqot* V: 31; *RR II*: fig. 14:41, from the Refuse Pit 484 with quantities of Persian sherds; Holladay [1976: 289-90] does not point out any unpainted examples that have to be dated before the 6th century). The similar fragment from the 1933 Tell el-Fûl campaign was thought to be Hellenistic because of its "collar at the point where the neck joins the shoulder" (*TFL II*: 42, pl. 26:4). The 1964 specimens also show the join where the neck meets the body, but there is little doubt that they come from Period III. Plate 61:10 is from a stratified-III deposit at bedrock in Southwest Room E; pl. 61:11 and 12 are from mixed deposits of Cistern 1; 61:13 is from the basin area in the southwest which contained Period III and IV pottery. Plate 11:14 was from the surface. Most likely all specimens belong with the III B pottery corpus, and the 1933 bottle fragment can be dated with them.

Small globular bottles also appeared in Period III-IV deposits and date to the Exilic period (pl. 61:15-21). Similar vessels have been found in Reservoir 44 at Beth-zur which dates slightly after Tell el-Fûl III B (Lapp 1970: 185; see above, pp. 86-87) and Ain Shems Tomb 14, dating about 570 B.C. (Lapp 1970: 184, n. 24; **see above, p. 84). From Ramat Raḥel a globular** bottle comes from Refuse Pit 484 and another from Stratum IV of the 1954 excavations (Aharoni 1956: fig. 8:lower 3, p. 139; *RR II*: fig. 14:43).

Bowls

The sherds of ring-burnished bowls were plentiful as has been true at most southern Palestinian late Iron II sites (cf. Amiran 1969: 200-6; *BZ II*: 63-65; Aharoni and Aharoni 1976: 76; contrast Holladay 1976: 287). The most usual Tell el-Fûl form, with a thickened, slightly inverted rim, appears in quite large bowls (pls. 62:1-9, 63:1-8), more medium sizes (pls. 62:10-16, 63:9-18) [20] and quite small, delicate bowls (pls. 62:29, 63:19-22). They were burnished on the interior and rim, and two or four handles were common on the large and medium-sized bowls. Many were present in the pre-III A Mid-silos (pl. 62), but they are also common in III A and III B loci (not homogeneous III B loci, but loci that also contained earlier material, pl. 63). Similar bowls came from 8th- through early 6th-century contexts at Lachish, Tell Beit Mirsim, Beth-zur, Ramat Raḥel, En-gedi, and one-period settlements in the Buqeʾah (cf. *BZ II*: fig. 17:1-14, pp. 63-65 and parallels there cited; *RR I*: figs. 11:12-14, 17-19, 21; 28:22-34; *RR II*: figs. 16:35-60; 17:1-49; ʿ*Atiqot* V: figs. 14:1-11; 16:3-6; *TFL I*: pl. 27; *TFL II*: pl. 22; Stager 1975: esp. pls. 1, 3, 9).[21] All stratified Tell el-Fûl burnished bowls are from loci which contained Iron II material, and there is no evidence that the typical late Iron II burnishing continued into the Exilic period. On the other hand, the bowl form continued for a while longer, as several unburnished bowls from the homogeneous III B deposit of Cistern 1 indicate (pl. 65: 1-2). A few unburnished forms from III A-B loci also may be Exilic (pl. 64:17-20), but the form apparently disappeared fairly rapidly after the mid-6th century (Lapp 1970: 184-85 and n. 31).

Medium-sized bowls which are thickened slightly on the interior (pl. 62:17-22) appeared only in Iron II deposits, most of them from the pre-III A Silo 36, although several sherds not illustrated came from III A loci. The tendency toward inner thickening was disappearing late in Iron II (cf. *Gezer II*: 82, n. 167), and it is generally missing from Beth-zur III (where some sherds from the early Pottery Cache have a slight inner thickening, cf. *BZ II*: fig. 17), Ramat Raḥel V (cf. *RR II*: fig. 17), and En-gedi V (cf. ʿ*Atiqot* V: fig. 14, but note bowls with handles, fig. 16).

A medium-sized bowl form with an everted or flared rim and rounded body was popular both with and without burnishing. It appears in both finishes in pre-III A and III A loci (pls. 62:23-26, burnished; 64:1-8, unburnished) and stratified later deposits (pls. 63: 23-29, burnished; 64:21-27, unburnished), but it is absent from homogeneous III B groups. At Beth-zur this everted-rim bowl appeared without burnishing in Stratum III (late Iron II), and up to that time it had usually been considered a 9th-to-8th-century form (*BZ II*: fig. 18:1-4, and references). In addition to the Beth-zur and Tell el-Fûl sherds, it has now appeared in En-gedi V (ʿ*Atiqot* V: figs. 8:6; 15:1-2) and Ramat Raḥel V (*RR I*: figs. 11:1, 4, 25:1, 28:11-15; *RR II*: fig. 16:29-31, and see p. 30). Some of the Tell Beit Mirsim bowls may be from late in Iron II as Albright originally thought (cf. *TBM I*: 86; *TBM III*: 152-53). At Bethel the unburnished form was called a 6th-century continuation of the Iron II burnished form (*Bethel*: pl. 64:3, 5, 9; p. 71). However, Tell el-Fûl deposits indicate that unburnished everted-rim bowls were common in late Iron II, and since the form did not appear in homogeneous III B deposits, continuation in the Exilic period is not likely.

Plain flat plates were not common, but a few specimens were among the Iron II stratified material. From the Silo 36 pre-III A deposit came a burnished saucer, pl. 62:27 (cf. *BZ II*: fig. 17:15 which has brown paint and is from the Pottery Cache; *TBM I*: pl. 65:28, 30; *Lachish III*: pl. 80:63; *RR I*: figs. 11:3, 28:2-6; *RR II*: fig. 16:1-12; ʿ*Atiqot* V: fig. 15:3-4; Sauer 1972: pl. 9A:505-15), and a very flat unburnished plate (pl. 64:10).

Ring, disc, and flat bowl bases were among the stratified material, but there were few complete profiles so that it was impossible to characterize the bases of most vessels. However, from comparative material, it is known that the thickened-rim burnished-bowl form had a ring base such as pls. 62:30, 63:30-31, and 64:16, or a disc base such as pls. 63:32-34 and 64:20. Note the complete profile, pl. 63:22, and compare the large number of whole vessels, *TBM III*: pls. 20-23. Some of the flat bases (as pl. 63:29) are probably from bowls with everted rims, as exemplified by pls. 63:23 and 64: 6, 9, 21-23.

A few thin-walled, plain rounded-rim, deep bowls should be noted. Some are very delicate and of fine ware. The specimens in pl. 64:12-13 from pre-III A deposits are unburnished, while those from later fills are burnished (pls. 63:35-37) and unburnished (64:29). The small flat and disc bases (pls. 63:38 [III A-B, burnished], 64:14-15 [III A unburnished], and 64:31-32 [III A-B, unburnished]) may come from these plain rounded bowls. A variety of delicate, attractive, small bowls came from Tell Beit Mirsim (*TBM I*: pls. 64:13-20, 67:15-19; *TBM III*: pls. 24-25), Lachish (*Lachish III*: pl. 98:569-76), Beersheba (*Beersheba I*: pls. 59:45, 69:10-12), and Ramat Raḥel (*RR I*: fig. 11:5-9). To the unburnished bowls compare especially the delicate bowls from Ramat Raḥel V (*RR II*: 30, fig. 17:53-56; *RR I*: fig. 28:21) and En-gedi V (ʿ*Atiqot* V: fig. 15:6-7). Many of these bowls are cited by Holladay (1976: 84) in his "rice bowl" classification. The only specimens cited from northern Palestine are some doubtful Hazor sherds (*Hazor II*, pl. 98:7-8) and unpublished Shechem examples. The bowl can be designated a southern type that spanned the 8th and 7th centuries B.C.[22] The rounded bowls from Bethel Locus sub-104 (*Bethel*: pl. 64:4, 6-7, 12-14) were of heavier ware and considered **degenerate Iron II forms (*Bethel*: 70-71). They were dated** about 570 B.C. by Lapp (1970: 181, n. 4).

There were a variety of small sherds in III deposits from deep bowls of thicker ware with "vertical" necks or curved sides which were burnished on the interior in the Iron II manner (pl. 63:40-48; cf. generally *Bethel*: pl. 63:1, 18; *TFL II*: pl. 22:24). These were very fragmentary, excepting the base and body fragment shown in pl. 63:39 which might be classed with these, and no comparable sherds were found in either pure III A or III B deposits. Since there is no evidence that interior burnishing continued down to mid-6th century, it is probable that they are III A bowls even though their complete form may be comparable to Exilic and Persian deep bowls and craters. Burnished sherds, pl. 63:40-43, are too fragmentary to consider how closely they may compare to the unburnished III B craters, pl. 65:9-12, discussed below.

Two unburnished rounded bowl sherds of medium-heavy ware came from the III B deposit of Cistern 1 (pl. 65:3-4). Several more came from its mixed deposits (pl. 64:33-39). All were unburnished, and the latter group could also be of the III B horizon, especially since one had a horizontal handle (pl. 64:38), a common Exilic and postexilic feature (cf. pl. 65:11). The closest parallels to these fairly heavy deep bowls came from post-587 B.C. deposits. The simple rounded bowls (*Bethel*: pl. 64:12-13) were from the sub-104 locus, dated 570 B.C. (Lapp 1970: 181, n. 14; see above, **p. 84). The deep bowl with handle from Taanach** (Lapp 1970: fig. 5:10) dates to the mid-5th century. None of the Tell el-Fûl bowls seem to have vertical handles like that from Taanach. From the Ramat Raḥel Refuse Pit 484, which contained some late 6th-century pottery as well as late Persian, came part of a comparable bowl (*RR II*: fig. 12:2).

Deep bowls or craters with "vertical" necks are characteristic of Persian typology (Lapp 1970: 185), and Tell el-Fûl evidence points to their presence in the Exilic period (pl. 65:5-12). Plate 65:9-12 is from the homogeneous deposit of III B in Cistern 1, whereas pl. 65:5-8 (and pl. 33:1-4) with the chevron design are from the III A-B layer (overlooked by Lapp 1970: 185, n. 30).

Attention should first be directed to pl. 65:7 (and pl. 39:3) with its delicate chevron design, thin walls, light red exterior surface with half-centimeter-wide, horizontal, ring burnishing and lack of handles. It is of much finer quality than the craters (pl. 65:5-6 [cf. pl. 39:1-2, 4 with 39:3]), and it could be an import. Two of the Tell en-Naṣbeh craters, also handleless, were burnished: *TN II*: pl. 67:1511 on the top of the rim, and pl. 67:1514 (drawn with a handle stub but cf. the

photograph in pl. 89 and description, p. 175) both on the top of the rim and below the band on the exterior. One from Ramat Raḥel has traces of horizontal burnishing (Aharoni 1956: 143). Most likely the burnish on the rim of a 1933 Tell el-Fûl triangular-impressed crater was not accidental (*TFL II*: fig. 26:16; contrast Lapp 1970: 184, n. 26). In addition, high-necked craters with continuous wheel burnishing have come from En-gedi V (*ʿAtiqot* V, fig. 15, esp. no. 12), Ramat Raḥel V (*RR I*: fig. 12:3), Lachish Tomb 106 (*Lachish III*: pl. 90:388), and Tell el-Farʿah (N), unpublished but cited by Holladay (1976: 288—his "handleless necked jars"). One En-gedi bowl (fig. 12:13) and the Lachish burnished vessel are similar in form but are smaller. Holladay relates these to "miniature jars" which he compares to Assyrian forms from Fort Shalmanezer (cf. Tell el-Fûl small pots, **below, p. 95); similarly, he designates a "triangular-**rimmed, necked" bowl from Gezer as an Assyrian import (*Gezer II*: fig. 36:13, pp. 80, 82 and references cited). This is interesting because the chevron impressed wares have been associated with the wedged-shape, cuneiform writing (Wampler 1940: 15) though Albright preferred placing their origin in Syria (p. 16, n. 6). However, no similar forms to the high-necked (and footed?, cf. *ʿAtiqot* V, pl. 15:12, 14), burnished craters are included with the Nimrud and Fort Shalmaneser repertory (Lines 1954; Oates 1959).

Whether or not these burnished craters were imports or fine Palestinian wares, perhaps something may be proposed chronologically. The Ramat Raḥel rim (*RR I*: fig. 12:3) is from late Iron II Stratum V, and the En-gedi vessels are from Stratum V (which extends slightly past 587 B.C.). The Lachish vessel from Tomb 106 probably dates to the end of Iron II (above, **p. 86); the Tell en-Naṣbeh craters are not closely dated.** The Tell el-Fûl burnished crater with chevron design is from the level of Cistern I which contained both III A and B pottery. It seems probable that these finely burnished pots (burnished on the exterior, not the interior like the common late Iron II bowls) were imported into Palestine in a small quantity at the very end of Iron II.

On the other hand, no examples of the rougher, locally made chevron-designed wares have to be dated before the Exilic period (Lapp 1970 and references cited there). The Ramat Raḥel evidence (Aharoni 1956: 143, cited *BZ II*: 68) must now be interpeted to indicate that the triangular-impressed ware should be dated post-Stratum V since it was found *on* Stratum V floors (cf. *RR II*: 34, where Aharoni considers royal jar handles found on the Stratum V floors the same as in mixed debris). No chevron ware is published from Stratum V from the later campaigns, but only from Refuse Pit 484 (*RR II*: figs. 13:9, 14:37). It may also be noted that no chevron-designed sherds are published from Bethel where the latest 6th-century horizon seems to be about 570 B.C. (Lapp 1970: 181, n. 14).

The Tell el-Fûl craters with triangular impressions should therefore be placed in the III B period along with the crater rims of similar form (pl. 65:5-8). The high vertically-necked crater from Balâṭah Stratum V, about 500 B.C. (Lapp 1970: fig. 3:9), is just one of the numerous sherds of that type from that stratum. From a mid-5th-century pit at Taanach comes a similar form (Rast 1978: 49 and fig. 77:6), and there is another from a late 5th-century context (Rast 1978: fig. 86:2). From Megiddo Stratum I came a nearly whole vessel (*Meg. I*: pl. 13:66), and a sherd came from Samaria VIII (*SS III*: pl. 12:32). At Tell en-Naṣbeh necked craters with a flanging or thickened rim (*TN II*: pls. 66-67:1508-25) were thought to be "subsequent to 600 B.C." (*TN II*: 40). From the second campaign at Tell el-Fûl note *TFL II*: pl. 23:2. From the Ramat Raḥel Refuse Pit 484 came several sherds (*RR II*: fig. 12:25-30 [especially fig. 12:26 parallel to Tell el-Fûl pl. 65:5; 12:30 parallel to 65:6, 8]). On the other hand, no high-necked, unburnished craters are published from En-gedi Stratum V or Ramat Raḥel Stratum V.

High-necked craters with triangular impressions are known from other sites. A quite similar vessel from Lachish came from a late 6th- or early 5th-century house (*Lachish III*: pl. 9:405 and p. 146). An El-Jîb crater is similar although the sherd was probably not complete enough to indicate whether there were any handles (*Gibeon*: fig. 48:22). The 1933 Tell el-Fûl high-necked craters with triangular impressions (*TFL II*: pl. 26:15-16) should be redated to Tell el-Fûl Period III B (cf. *TFL II*: 43; Lapp 1970: 185, n. 30). There were a number of the high-necked craters with the chevron impressions at Tell en-Naṣbeh in addition to the burnished specimen (*TN II*: pl. 67:1515, 1520-21, pl. 89). A fragment from Samaria is of an unusual red ware (*SS III*: fig. 32:10 and p. 195). None of these are from closely stratified contexts but all could fit into the second half of the 6th century B.C.

The sherd with circle impressions (pl. 65:13) is from a mixed layer of Cistern 1 so it does not aid in dating this pattern. The form is that of the Iron II neckless jars, so it may date to Period III A along with the circular impressed sherds from Beth-zur III (*BZ II*: fig. 20:1-2).

One crater from the 1933 Tell el-Fûl campaign should be noted (*TFL II*: pl. 23:17). It is very similar to crater fragments from Stratum V at Balâṭah, one of which has been published (Lapp 1970: fig. 3:8). Those from Balâṭah often had small, vertical lug handles right at the rim, whereas the Tell el-Fûl specimen has a more conventional, though ugly and poorly-made, handle. Unfortunately no sherds from these craters were

identified in the 1964 campaign, but the 1933 vessel can be assigned to the III B horizon, marking this type's first appearance in the mid-6th century (rather than Hellenistic, as dated by Sinclair, *TFL II*: 38; the Tell en-Naṣbeh vessel cited as a parallel is quite different from this type with its distinctive rim).

In concluding the discussion of bowls, it should be pointed out that in addition to the number of bowls and craters found in the homogeneous III B layer and the III A-B layer of Cistern 1, a large number and variety of these III bowl fragments (including some large pieces) were in the upper mixed layers (see loci descriptions opposite the pottery drawings). The Period III pottery has been distinguished by ware, finish, and form, and the Hellenistic pottery is considered below, pp. 101-5. The forms discussed here belong with the Period III pottery corpus and sometimes contribute to the ceramic chronological framework of the 7th and 6th centuries B.C.[23]

The little pots, pl. 66:1-3, come from III A Silo 36, and pl. 66:4 (pl. 40:4) comes from the III A lower deposit of Cistern 2. They are not especially common, but similar small vessels are published from Tell Beit Mirsim A and ʿAin Shems II (*TBM I*: pl. 67:20-28; *AS IV*: pl. 66:45-46). These are the "miniature pots" which Holladay relates to Assyrian bowls found in the 612 B.C. destruction at Fort Shalmaneser (Holladay 1976: 288; Oates 1959: pl. 37:72-77). Plate 66:5-7 (pl. 40:1-3) are parts of rather crude pots from Cistern 1; pl. 66:5-6 are from the III B deposit.

Stands

The jar stands, pl. 66:8-10 (pl. 40:5-6), are typical of Iron II, and there is not yet clear enough evidence to know how long they continued into the Exilic and postexilic periods. Plate 66:9-10 may be from Period III B. Some similar stands from Gibeon (*Gibeon*: fig. 47:2), Tell en-Naṣbeh (*TN II*: pl. 77:1764-65, 1767; p. 51), Ashdod (*Ashdod II-III*: fig. 79:4) and Ramat Raḥel (*RR II*: fig. 14:46) may also be post-587 B.C. Parallel stands from late Iron II were found at Tell Beit Mirsim (*TBM I*: pl. 71:7, 11), Ramat Raḥel (*RR I*: figs. 11:40, 26:4), and Hazor (*Hazor III-IV*: pl. 232:17).

Cooking Pots

The familiar Iron II shallow cooking pot with grooved rim (pl. 67:1-10) was found at Tell el-Fûl almost exclusively in the Mid-Field silos; only two were found in later contexts (pl. 67:10 and one not shown). Throughout Palestine there is abundant evidence for this type from the 10th century through the 8th century B.C. (cf., for example, *TN II*: 29-31 and the parallels cited in Appendix A; cf. perhaps Sauer 1972: 49 and pl. 5:312-13). This heavy, grooved type of pot does not appear in Ramat Raḥel V or En-gedi V, and since its appearance at Tell el-Fûl is principally in the Mid-Field pre-III A silos, there is evidence that the form disappeared early in the 7th century (cf. now Aharoni and Aharoni 1976: 76). Noteworthy are the handles with incised *taw* on this type of pot (pls. 67:7-8; 41:2, 9). This was a common marking on the globular cooking pots with rilled rims (see below). One handle (pls. 67:9, 41:7) had a small impressed circle where the *taw* is usually found.

By the second half of the 7th century this heavy, grooved type had been replaced by a type which persisted through the Exilic period and into the Early Persian period (pls. 67:11-13, 68:1-11).[24] It is in the wide-mouthed, shallow cooking-pot tradition, but it is more globular and approaches the deep globular shape which becomes the usual form from the Persian period onward. The ware is thinner, metallic, and the overall proportions tend to be smaller than those of the usual Iron II pot (cf. the whole pots from En-gedi, *Atiqot* V: fig. 18). There is usually a groove or ridge in the rim, but the most characteristic feature is a sharp angle on the inner side of the rim about 1.5 cm from the top edge. The shelf formed by the angle may have held a lid. Plates 67:11 and 68:1-2 are perhaps transitional from the heavy Iron II rim form to the fully developed late Iron II and Exilic ridged rim (pls. 67:12-13, 68:6-11). At least seven Tell el-Fûl rims are from Stratum III A deposits (pls. 67:11-13, 68:6-7, and two other registered sherds), but none are from the early Mid-Field silos. Many more are from III A-B contexts (pl. 68:1-5, 8-11).

The popularity of this type with an interior angle below the rim probably spanned the 6th century; it developed in the 7th century and continued into the early 5th. One rim (*BZ II*: fig. 19:3) is published from the Beth-zur Pottery Cache (ca. 700 B.C.), which may mean that that group is slightly later than the Tell el-Fûl Mid-Field silos. Its absence from Beersheba II was one of the main reasons Aharoni dated Stratum II's destruction to 701 B.C. (*Beersheba I*: 5). Several pots may be transitional to the later type (such as *Beersheba I*: pls. 60:83; 74:10-11). Three pots of this type are published from Meṣad Ḥashavyahu (Naveh 1962: fig. 5:1-3). The fortress at Meṣad Ḥashavyahu was dated to the last third of the 7th century, and there is evidence of some Persian occupation (Lapp 1970: 184, n. 28). The pot, fig. 5:3, approaches a cooking-pot form dated about 500 B.C. from Balâṭah evidence (Lapp 1970: 186, fig. 3:16-17; contrast *Atiqot* V: 28 and n. 56), but the ware appears thin and light compared to the large and heavy Balâṭah pots.

A number of this cooking-pot type have been published from En-gedi Stratum V (*Atiqot* V: figs. 8: 14-15; 18:1-8). They were common in Ramat Raḥel V (*RR I*: figs. 11:21, 24, 28:35-37; *RR II*: figs. 18:9-12,

20:8-10), and Aharoni thought they replaced the grooved-neck deep pots in the 7th century (*RR II*: 30 and n. 10). At Lachish they appeared in Stratum II (*Lachish III*: pl. 93:460; *Lachish V*: pl. 47:19) and Tomb 106 (*Lachish III*: pl. 93:443, 445). M. and Y. Aharoni have recently published select pots from Arad VII-VI and Tell Masos (1976: figs. 7:3, 8:3). Two specimens from Tell en-Naṣbeh are shown, and it is said that the "major phase probably begins in late Middle Iron" (*TN II*: 160; pl. 18:1020-21). The example from Tell el-Fûl published by Sinclair (*TFL II*: pl. 23:3) was dated Hellenistic (p. 38), but it is undoubtedly from the III A-B occupation. The Bethel parallels he mentions are 6th-century rather than Hellenistic; strata there were not distinguished. Only one rim of this type is published from Bethel (*Bethel*: pl. 65:4), but the writer has seen several more in the Pittsburgh Theological Seminary Bethel pottery collection (PTS museum nos. 2-9, 2-234, 2-235, 2-236). One (no. 2-9) has an unusual incised mark on its handle.

This type is common from the Early Persian period at Balâṭah in Stratum V (ca. 500 B.C.; Lapp 1970: fig. 3:13-15). Because of a rim found in one of the late 5th-century pits at Taanach, Lapp thought the same type might have persisted through most of the Persian period (1970: 186; fig. 8:19). However, this is a narrow-necked pot and the characteristic interior angle is not present; more probably it belongs with the globular, high-necked pots described below. The evidence seems to indicate that the Tell el-Fûl angular type of cooking pot developed late in Iron II and continued into the Early Persian period but not much beyond 500 B.C.

Deep, globular cooking pots with high necks make their appearance in the latter part of Iron II. This form has included rim and neck types variously identified as rilled (cf. Tell el-Fûl pl. 67:14), plain (cf. pl. 69:16), and ridged (at Lachish, but which at En-gedi is described as having "a carinated ridge surrounding the high neck" with a plain rim [cf. Tell el-Fûl pl. 67:25] or grooved rim [cf. pl. 67:24]). Actually both the rilled and ridged type have the characteristic ridge around the base of the neck (Tell el-Fûl pl. 67:14-27) and to a certain extent the rilling is mere variation. At Tell el-Fûl both the ridged (pl. 67:18-19) and rilled (pl. 67:15, 17) appeared in the Mid-Field silos as well as later (pl. 67: 14, 24-27). At Beth-zur they were grouped together, but the rilled necks appeared in Stratum III (*BZ II*: pl. 19:8 and another stratified sherd) and the plain with ridge around the neck in the Pottery Cache (pl. 19:7). At En-gedi the excavators did not think they had the rilled type ("with ridges or grooves round the neck," *Atiqot* V: 28), but some specimens are not too distant (cf. fig. 17:2, 5). From Ramat Raḥel V (*RR I*: pl. 11:22) comes a rim which is distinctly rilled. At Beersheba and Tell

Beit Mirsim most are heavily rilled, but compare *Beersheba I*: pls. 61:98, 66:3, and 67:9 to Tell el-Fûl pl. 67:16, 22. At Lachish most of the rilled type (*Lachish III*: pl. 93:451-56) are from Level III, but the ridged (pl. 93:458, 462) apparently appeared in Level III loci also (Tomb 1002, Loci 1012, 1013, 1087, 1092).

At Tell el-Fûl most sherds of these types came from the Mid-Field silos; they had both rilled and plain necks (pl. 67:15-22). The rims that came from other loci had a pronounced ridge at the base of the neck, were of better fired, thinner ware, and were well levigated (pl. 67:14, 24-27). They were not found in homogeneous III B loci, and there is no evidence that they continued into the Exilic period. To be noted is that most of the handles with the incised *taw* on them (cf. *BZ II*: 67; *TBM I*: 81) came from the Mid-Field silos (pls. 67:18-22, 41:3, 6, 8, 10-11) as did those from shallow, groove-type cooking pots. At Beersheba the mark also appeared on both type cooking pots in Stratum II (*Beersheba I*: pls. 61:96-97, 66:13, 67:8, 11, 68:4, 16, 70:11, 71:14).

The stratified evidence seems to indicate that the rilled neck was the popular form in the 8th century, although some were ridged at the neck without elaborate rilling. In the 7th century the rilling deteriorated or disappeared, but the ware tended to be thinner and better fired. Without doubt the rilled- and ridged-neck types were southern Palestinian forms. A few deep cooking pots were published from northern sites, but they were from the plain-rim classes below. Holladay claims a number came from Shechem Stratum VI (Holladay 1976: 288), but they were rare (*BZ II*: 66, n. 10) and are not yet published.

Two hitherto undistinguished cooking-pot types are characteristic of the Tell el-Fûl Period III B groups. The first (pl. 69:1-8) comes from a short-necked cooking pot, most likely globular and squat in shape. The short neck curves slightly outward and the rim is thickened and shaved or rounded on the exterior, usually showing an "overhang." Three of the Tell el-Fûl rims are from homogeneous III B deposits, and probably the others from Cistern 1 can be dated with them. Published parallels are few thus far, particularly because anything like this form has usually been called Hellenistic or even Roman. Of the cooking pots Lapp published (1970), fig. 8:18 from Taanach is probably of this type, but being an isolated example and not as typical as the Tell el-Fûl series, it was not recognized as such. "Good" Roman parallels are cited (Lapp 1970: 186), but those in *PCC* Corpus 71.1.N₁ are obviously not of the Persian type which has a characteristic short, slightly flaring neck and thickened rim.

Another rim from Taanach, from a pit with a homogeneous mid-5th-century B.C. deposit, may be of this new type (Rast 1978: fig. 79:6). At Tell en-Naṣbeh

two examples are dated generally late Middle Iron to Hellenistic (*TN II*: pl. 50:1053-54; pp. 30, 161). A good parallel was found at En-gedi in the Persian building destroyed near the end of the 5th century B.C. (Mazar and Dunayevsky 1967: pl. 33:4). Evidence thus far indicates that this type of cooking pot is typical of the Exilic and early Persian periods to about the end of the 5th century B.C.

A second characteristic type of globular cooking pot appeared in the Exilic period. It has a plain, unthickened rim on a very high, vertical neck (pl. 69:9-15). The unusual height is striking. Other necks are not quite as high but are very straight (pls. 69:16-22, 41:13-14). Unlike the usual Hellenistic, plain, high rim, they are hardly outsplayed (cf., for example, the high, plain, Hellenistic rims at Beth-zur [*BZ II*: fig. 27:1-3] which have everted necks that are quite typical, and the Hellenistic cooking pots below, pl. 78:1-9). Some of the Tell el-Fûl rims are from Stratum III B, and those from Cistern 1 most probably belong with the lower III B deposit.

Parallels to this newly distinguished form are few. A cooking pot published from Taanach has the tall, straight neck with plain rim, but the rim diameter is much larger so the pot shape is uncertain (Rast 1978: fig. 82:4; Lapp 1970: fig. 5:12, p. 186 where it is called a deep bowl). A large cooking pot from Tell en-Naṣbeh has the high, vertical neck, but no close dating is possible; it is from a cistern with Iron II remains and some possibly later material (*TN II*: pl. 50:1059; *TN I*: 134). Samaria has two examples of this type (*SS III*: fig. 12:11-12) which Kenyon assigns to the 7th-century group of Period VIII, but they could just as well belong with the 6th-century material. Kenyon bases her dating to the 7th century on comparisons with Tell Beit Mirsim Stratum A material. However, once the tall, straight-neck, cooking-pot type is recognized, it must be distinguished from the globular, rilled-rim pots (*TBM I*: pls. 55-56) which Kenyon uses for 7th-century dating (*SS III*: 131). From Refuse Pit 454 at Ramat Raḥel came one very high-necked cooking pot and another not quite as high but with a vertical neck (*RR II*: fig. 13:34-35).

The type probably developed into the typical Hellenistic cooking pot with high and slightly everted neck and plain rim, like the many 2nd-century B.C. pots at Tell el-Fûl (pl. 78). A step in this transition is evident in the Late Persian cooking pots from Wâdī ed-Dâliyeh which are high, plain, slightly everted, but obviously of thicker ware than in the 2nd century B.C. (N. Lapp 1974: pl. 23:2-3).

Plates 68:12-18 and 41:12 display a variety of rims from globular cooking pots of the 6th century B.C., Period III A or B. The rims, pl. 68:12-16, may be varieties of the high-neck type with slight thickening at the rims.

The rarity of all types of deep cooking pots in northern Palestine still exists, as Kenyon emphasized in 1957 (*SS III*: 131). Besides some of those cited above, Holladay (1976: 288), in his efforts to show the homogeneity of pottery throughout all Palestine in late Iron II, can only cite an additional form from Hazor (*Hazor III-IV*: pl. 184:11, but identification as a cooking pot is questionable).

Lamps

Iron Age-type lamps continue down to the end of Iron II and at least until the middle of the 6th century—Period III A and B at Tell el-Fûl. Plate 70:1-4 is in the Iron I tradition and is hardly distinguishable when viewed from the top but has a flatter bottom than the usual, quite rounded Iron I lamp (pl. 70:1-4; cf. *TBM I*: 86 and pl. 70:1-3). Plate 70:1 is from one of the pre-III A Mid-Field silos, while pl. 70:2 (pl. 42:10) is from the homogeneous III B deposit of Cistern 1. Plate 70:3-4 and 42:1-2 are from levels of the cistern with pottery of Periods III and IV. Late Iron II lamps of this kind were found in En-gedi Stratum V (*ᶜAtiqot* V: figs. 8:17-18; 23:1-2).

The Iron II form therefore continues into the Exilic period, but while the rounded but flattened base continues, the lamp tends to get smaller (pls. 70:5-10, 42:3, 4). The tendency may have started as early as late Iron II as two smaller forms published from Ramat Raḥel Stratum V indicate (*RR I*: figs. 11:35, 28:51). They are missing from clearly stratified later Persian groups (Lapp 1970: 186) even though they have been dated through the Persian period down into Hellenistic times. Often-cited parallels, which are probably 6th-century, come from ᶜAin Shems Tomb 14 (*AS IV*: pl. 48:7), the second campaign at Tell el-Fûl (*TFL II*: pl. 17:4-5), Tell en-Naṣbeh (*TN II*: pl. 71:1632), Ramat Raḥel Stratum IV (Aharoni 1956: fig. 8:2), Bethany (*Bethany*: fig. 33:2), and the Tyropoeon Valley excavations at Jerusalem (Crowfoot and Fitzgerald 1929: pl. 17:1). The lamp from Jerusalem is published as Type 81.1, "Small Folded Lamps," by P. Lapp and dated from its context and another lamp from Bethany to the 1st century B.C. (*PCC*: 192). However, the Jerusalem lamp was from the "lower level," Room 44, which contained much Iron II as well as later pottery (Crowfoot and Fitzgerald 1929: pls. 11-12; pp. 66-71, 89, cf. p. 90). The lamp from Bethany (*Bethany*: 161, no. 18) from Cistern 61 is not shown, but it is compared to a number of open lamps for which Saller prefers a 6th-century or Early Persian date (p. 162). Of the other sites listed in the *PCC* corpus which have parallel lamps (*PCC*: 192), the Tell Sandahannah specimen is a ring of folded lamps of somewhat different form (probably

later), and the others are from sites with 6th-century occupation.

The same form appeared in even smaller specimens (pl. 70:11-13). Unfortunately, none of these are from stratified Period III deposits, so it is impossible to say from the Tell el-Fûl evidence whether these very small lamps also come from the Exilic period or whether they belong with the small Hellenistic folded lamps having sides that meet or overlap and usually a flat base (see below, pl. 80:11; *CBZ*: fig. 41; *PCC*: Corpus 81.2). The Hellenistic type appeared in the 2nd century (cf. *PCC*: Corpus 81.2 and p. 101), but it is doubtful that it appeared before then since folded lamps are completely lacking from Early Hellenistic deposits at Balâṭah (cf. N. Lapp 1964b: 14-26) and Samaria (cf. Zayadin 1966: 53-54, pls. 27-31). Early excavators did not always make distinctions between Persian and Hellenistic pottery (*CBZ*: p. 41) so that Hellenistic folded lamps frequently were dated too early (cf. *TBM I*: 87; *TN II*: 46, pl. 71:1643-44). The very small Tell el-Fûl lamps (pl. 70:11-13) could date with the Period III lamps according to their form, or, if they belong with some of the Hellenistic material with which they were found, they could be related to the small Hellenistic folded lamp and belong to Stratum IV B (late 2nd century B.C.).

Similar to the open saucer lamps (pl. 70:1-4) are the pl. 71:1-3 lamps except that they follow the Iron II tradition in which a disc base develops (*TBM I*: 86). As Albright pointed out at Tell Beit Mirsim, these broad-lipped lamps with either rounded bottoms or disc bases were made simultaneously from the 8th century through the end of Iron II (*TBM I*: 86-87), and that they continued into the Exilic period is demonstrated at Tell el-Fûl. Plate 71:1 is from pre-III A Mid-Silo 36; pl. 71:2 is from a Stratum III A deposit; but pl. 71:3 (and pl. 42:8) is from the homogeneous III B Cistern 1 deposit. (Compare *ᶜAtiqot* V: fig. 23:3-4, and contrast p. 35 where it is stated that they disappeared at the end of the 7th century B.C.).

Heavy, thick-based, high-footed lamps (pls. 71:4-13; 42:6, 7, 11-12) were abundant in Period III contexts. None were from the pre-III A silos, nor are there any published from the Beth-zur Pottery Cache, Tell Beit Mirsim, Beersheba (cf. *Beersheba I*: 5), or Gezer V. They appeared late in the 7th century and continued for more than a century. Although none of the Tell el-Fûl specimens were from Stratum III A, some from later deposits undoubtedly came from this period since these heavy-based lamps are popular at other late Iron II sites (Lachish II [*Lachish III*: pl. 83:153, p. 326], Beth-zur III [*BZ II*: fig. 19:13, 15], En-gedi V [*ᶜAtiqot* V: fig. 23:8-9], Ramat Raḥel V [*RR I*: figs. 11:36-38, 27:7-8, 28:50]). It was a common III B lamp type (pl. 71:8-10). Many were found chipped off at their bases, and they were probably used either whole or broken as stoppers (cf. *Atiqot* V: 32-33, fig. 11). The form continued in use until the middle of the 5th century (Lapp 1970: 186 and fig. 5:17).[25]

The fragments of a sharply folded lamp with a wide, flat rim and flat base (pl. 71:14) are from the only example of this type found at Tell el-Fûl, and it is from a mixed layer of Cistern 1. Present evidence indicates that this form, usually known as the "Persian lamp," probably did not appear in Palestine until the 5th century B.C. and disappeared by the Hellenistic period (Lapp 1970: 186). A fragment of one was also found at Heshbon in an otherwise 7th-6th-century context (Sauer 1972: 59).

The types of lamps in use during Period III B are illustrated on the lower part of pl. 42. Plate 42:10 is the open, saucer type with rounded base. Plate 42:9 is a smaller variety of the same type. To the left in pl. 42:8, the saucer type with disc base is illustrated. Plate 42:11-12 is of high-footed lamps.

Summary

Some significant conclusions have been drawn concerning pottery of late Iron II and the Exilic period from the well-stratified Period III material at Tell el-Fûl. They will be briefly summarized, and they are shown in chart form in fig. 34.

Plain-rimmed, short-necked, jar fragments with sloping shoulders (pl. 50:28-32) appeared in the Mid-Field silos but not in the Period III A and B deposits. Parallel forms occurred in Tell Beit Mirsim A and Gezer VII-VI, but the Mid-Silo use must have been the tail-end of their existence. In the Mid-Silos the heavy, thicker, hole-mouth rim with a slight exterior projection (pl. 49:1-7) was still found, as in Tell Beit Mirsim A, ʿAin Shems II C, Beersheba II, the Beth-zur Pottery Cache, Gezer V, and Tell en-Naṣbeh. In the III A deposits the rims are longer and flatter (pl. 49:9-11) like those from Ramat Raḥel V, En-gedi V, Beth-zur III, Lachish II, some from ʿAin Shems II C, Megiddo IV-I, and the second campaign from Tell el-Fûl. Larger hole-mouth jars with a rounded shoulder, two or four handles, and ring base were represented by the flat or rounded rim which appeared in the Mid-Silo (pl. 49:12). The rounded rim continued at other sites to the end of Iron II, but at Tell el-Fûl a grooved type was typical in Period III A deposits (pl. 49:14-17), and it appeared in Ramat Raḥel V, En-gedi V, and the Tell el-Fûl second campaign. Neckless jar rims from large pithoi with two small handles and rounded bases came from both the Mid-Silos and other III A deposits (pl. 49:18-28), and although evidence for these heavy jars is still not extensive, parallels have been found at Beth-zur III, ʿAin Shems II C, Lachish, Tell en-Naṣbeh, Ramat Raḥel V, and in the second Tell el-Fûl

campaign. None of these hole-mouth or neckless types continue into Period III B and there is no stratified evidence for them after 587 B.C.

On the other hand, rounded rims on high necks, belonging to oval or bag-shaped jars, did not appear in the Mid-Field silos nor the Beth-zur Pottery Cache but made their first appearance in III A (pls. 50:1-10, 51:12-16, 18-19). There are none published from Tell Beit Mirsim or ʿAin Shems although two whole jars are shown from Beersheba II. They do come from En-gedi V, Ramat Raḥel V, and Beth-zur III, and the form continues at Tell el-Fûl into Period III B. A jar, probably with a similar shape, which had an out-turned, thickened or folded-over rim (pls. 51:1-6, 52:1-5), and variations (pl. 51:7-11), appeared in Period III B and is thus far without parallel.

Sherds of characteristic Iron II three-handled jars or jugs appeared in the Mid-Silos and III A deposits (pl. 57:20-22), but none in Period III B. The "cistern" type of jug—wide-mouthed and ridged-neck—appeared in all the Period III deposits (pls. 53-57:14) and must have been popular throughout the period. Similar jugs have been published from Tell Beit Mirsim A, ʿAin Shems II C, Lachish II, En-gedi V, and Ramat Raḥel V. Only one sherd of a jug with a high ridge (pl. 57:15) was found in a Period III deposit, so the jug popular at Tell Beit Mirsim and Tell en-Naṣbeh must have been replaced by the cistern type at Tell el-Fûl. In Period III B a wide-mouth jug with a thickened, out-turned rim (pl. 58:1-5) and a short-necked jug with a unique, plain rim and trefoil lip first appeared (pl. 58:6-7). A flask type also has developed by Period III B (pl. 59:1-5) which has parallels in ʿAin Shems Tomb 14 and En-gedi IV.

The typical, elongated, vertically burnished juglet appears through III A (pl. 60:1-6), but there is no evidence for it, burnished or unburnished, after 587 B.C. A more elongated form does appear in III B (pl. 60:8-10) which has parallels in En-gedi IV, Ramat Raḥel IV and V A, and Tell en-Naṣbeh. A heavy flat-bottomed form, similar to juglets from Gibeon, Jerusalem, Taanach, and Lachish, may appear in III B also (pl. 60:11). Black-burnished juglets were few (pl. 60:12-13) with evidence only in Period III A. Post-Iron II globular juglets (pl. 61:1-7), like some from En-gedi IV and ʿAin Shems Tombs 7 and 8, are of an early form, and they probably date to the Exilic period. The small globular bottles (pl. 61:15-21) probably belong with the Period III B material in the loci in which they were found. They have been found in Beth-zur Reservoir 44, ʿAin Shems Tomb 14, Ramat Raḥel Refuse Pit 484, and the second campaign at Tell el-Fûl. There were none of the painted, pointed, Iron II bottles, but some rough, crudely made examples (pl. 61:9-14) probably belong with the Exilic material.

Fig. 34. Summary of significant Period III pottery forms.

	Mid-Silos ca. 700 B.C.	III A 640-587 B.C.	III A-B 640-538 B.C.	III B 587-538 B.C.

Jars

   plain, short-necked
   hole-mouth
   rounded-shoulder hole-mouth
   neckless
   rounded rim, high neck
   out-turned, folded rim; elongated rim

Jugs

   false-spouted, 3-handled
   cistern type
   wide-mouthed, out-turned rim
   wide-mouthed, plain rim, trefoil lip

Flasks

Juglets

   elongated
   more elongated
   globular
   pointed bottles
   globular bottles

Bowls

   burnished, thickened int.
   burnished, thickened ext., everted
   unburnished, thickened ext., everted
   flared everted
   delicate rounded
   deep rounded
   crater, vertical neck
   crater/chevron
   horizontal handle

Cooking pots

   shallow grooved
   rilled
   interior angle
   short neck, ext. overhang
   high straight neck

Lamps

   saucer/flat-bottomed
     smaller
     very small
   saucer/disc base
     high foot

Key: ———————— stratified evidence

— — — — — probable

- - - - - - - possible, but doubtful

The burnished bowl, thickened on the interior, still appears in the Mid-Field silos (pl. 62:17-22), but probably not later at Tell el-Fûl. Besides in the Beth-zur Pottery Cache and Beersheba II, the form appears in Beth-zur III, En-gedi V, and Ramat Raḥel V, but it is not common and is apparently disappearing. The common type at all the sites has the rim thickened on the exterior in large, medium and small sizes (pls. 62:1-16, 63:1-22). Burnishing disappears after 587 B.C., but this form continues awhile unburnished (pl. 65:1-2). A medium-sized, rounded bowl with flare rim appeared in the Mid-Field silos and Period III A, both burnished (pls. 62:23-26, 63:23-29) and unburnished (pl. 64:1-9, 21-27), but the form probably ceased about 587 B.C. Similar evidence is reflected at Tell Beit Mirsim A, Beth-zur III, En-gedi V, Ramat Raḥel V, and Bethel. There is also a deep, thin-walled vessel, often very delicate, which appears burnished (pl. 63:35-37) and unburnished (pl. 64:12-13, 29) in Period III. Parallels come from Tell Beit Mirsim, Lachish, Ramat Raḥel V, and En-gedi V.

Some other types of unburnished bowls and craters do not seem to appear at Tell el-Fûl before Period III B. A rather deep, rounded, medium-sized bowl (pls. 64:33-39, 65:3) probably does not appear until the Exilic period as do somewhat similar bowls from Bethel Locus sub-104, a Taanach Persian period pit, and Ramat Raḥel Refuse Pit 484. More typical are the vertical-necked craters (pl. 65:5-12). Notable are the chevron impressed design (pl. 65:5-7) and horizontal handles (pls. 64:38, 65:11) often found on these craters. The finely made, high-necked craters with ring burnishing on the exterior and sometimes with chevron impressions (pl. 65:7) may have been sparingly imported into Palestine late in the 7th century. It may have been the stimulus for the locally made, high-necked Exilic crater. Examples with some of these characteristics from other sites appeared in Balâṭah V, Taanach Persian pits, Tell en-Naṣbeh, Ramat Raḥel V and Refuse Pit 484, En-gedi V, Samaria, Lachish I, El-Jîb, and the second Tell el-Fûl campaign.

The heavy, shallow, Iron II cooking pot with grooved rim appeared almost exclusively in the Mid-Field silos (pl. 67:1-10). These were common Tell Beit Mirsim, Beersheba, Tell en-Naṣbeh, and Beth-zur Pottery Cache forms, but they do not appear in En-gedi V or Ramat Raḥel V A. The globular, narrow-necked cooking pot with a ridge at the base of the rilled or plain neck is popular in the Mid-Silos and III A deposits (pl. 67:14-27) but has disappeared by Period III B. This type appears in Beth-zur III and En-gedi V. But beginning in Period III A, first in transitional form from the heavy, shallow pot (pls. 67:11, 68:1-2), is a thinner ware, ridged-rim cooking pot with a characteristic inner angle (pls. 67:12-13, 68:3-11). This is now

well-documented as a 7th- and 6th-century form from En-gedi V, Beth-zur III, Ramat Raḥel V, Lachish, Balâṭah V, Meṣad Ḥashavyahu, and the second campaign from Tell el-Fûl.

Two new cooking-pot forms were recognized beginning in Period III B. One is a short-necked, probably squat, globular pot with an overhanging rim (pl. 69:1-8). Similar forms can be recognized from Taanach Persian period pits, En-gedi IV, and Tell en-Naṣbeh. A high-necked, vertical, plain-rimmed, globular pot was also typical of III B (pl. 69:12-22). Possible parallels come from Taanach, Tell en-Naṣbeh, and Samaria VIII.

Iron II saucer lamps with rounded but flattened bottoms continue through Period III B (pl. 70:1-4). Smaller lamps, but of the same form, appear in Period III B (pl. 70:6-10) and now can be recognized as Exilic or Early Persian where they have been found in ʿAin Shems Tomb 14, Ramat Raḥel IV, Bethany, Tell en-Naṣbeh, the Tyropoeon Valley of Jerusalem, and the Tell el-Fûl second campaign. Very small lamps of the same form appeared at Tell el-Fûl (pl. 70:11-13) in contexts which had Hellenistic material as well as Period III, so it cannot be said with certainty whether they are a III B development or belong with the overlapping or closed Hellenistic lamps of similar size with flat bottoms.

Iron II saucer lamps with disc bases also appeared through Period III B (pl. 71:1-3). No high-footed, heavy lamps (pl. 71:4-13) appeared in the Mid-Silos, but they are very popular by Period III B. That they developed late in Iron II seems substantiated by their absence from Tell Beit Mirsim A, Beersheba II, and Gezer V and their presence in Lachish II, En-gedi V, and Ramat Raḥel V. They still appear at Taanach in the mid-5th century B.C.

Period IV Pottery
(IV A ca. 175-135 B.C.
 IV B ca. 135-100 B.C.
 IV C ca. 100-75 B.C.)

Late Hellenistic pottery was systemized in the early 1960s with the publication of P. W. Lapp's *Palestinian Ceramic Chronology, 200 B.C.-A.D. 70* (*PCC*). Since that time much more Hellenistic pottery has been published, but *PCC* is still basic and adequate for presenting most Late Hellenistic forms. In the following discussion *PCC* will be supplemented when necessary and will be presented in detail when Tell el-Fûl offers new information. Otherwise, *PCC* will be referred to frequently and no attempt will be made to give additional parallels when the form is well known.

Jars

Storage jars were of the typical 2nd-century, Hellenistic types (*PCC*: Corpus 11.2, 11.3). All of the Tell el-Fûl jars were probably cylindrical-to-bag-shaped with rounded bases, relatively short necks, and two handles on the shoulders (see the whole forms, pls. 43, 72:19, 31, 73:19-20; 74:1-2). There were many "collared" rims—folded over and forming a long narrow profile, usually slightly concave on the exterior (pl. 72). Also there were numerous thicker, more square rims (pl. 73:1-21) and a variety of more rounded rims (pl. 73:22-38). It was noted that over half of the Hellenistic rims collected at Bethel, Beth-zur, and Balâṭah were jar rims (*Bethel*: 78), and the same seems to be true of Tell el-Fûl. All three of the Tell el-Fûl jar rim types were found in stratified IV B loci, both fills and floors, and it is doubtful that any chronological distinctions can be made between them. At Bethel (*Bethel*: 78-79) the three types are placed in different phases. But those distinctions were not made stratigraphically, and the evidence from Tell el-Fûl seems to indicate that all three rim forms were in use at the same time. Note that in *PCC*: Corpus 11.2 the squared as well as the lengthened rims appear to the end of the 2nd century B.C. A similar assortment of rims was uncovered at Tell el-Fûl during the second campaign (*TFL II*: 24).

The narrow-profiled collared rims ranged from approximately 2 to 4 cm long. The longest, pl. 72:30, is from the latest Hellenistic floor east of the West Casemate in Area Q (L. II-12) and dates into the 1st century B.C., Period IV C (cf. *PCC*: Corpus 11.2.E). The bedrock Hellenistic fill to the west of the East Casemate (L. XX-4ext) contained the shortest but also very long collars (pl. 72:1-7). The reconstructed vessel, pl. 72:31 (and pl. 43:3), is from the Mid-Field silo which had a Hellenistic deposit that dated into the 1st century B.C. (Period IV C). The longer Roman rim has a slight ridge at the bottom of the collar and is from a "bell-shaped" jar (cf. pl. 80:12-19 and *PCC*: Corpus 12 [p. 152]).

The "squared" profiles were even more uniform (pl. 73:1-21). These appeared consistently in the same deposits as the longer, collared rims, including the Silo 42 deposit beneath the three IV B floors in Room RE (p. 74 above). Although the general trend, as the Hellenistic period progressed, was toward longer collars (*PCC*: Corpus 11.2, Observation 1), squared or shorter collars persisted to the end of the period (cf. *PCC*: Corpus 11.3; although classed there as "round," they belong with the Tell el-Fûl "squared" types—cf. Corpus 11.2.B). Some rims are hard to classify, and a "square" rim such as pl. 73:19 could be considered a "collar" rim. Likewise some "square" rims are closely related to the more rounded rims (pl. 73:23-28). Almost all squared and rounded rims are out-turned, a 2nd-

century B.C. characteristic which had begun in the 3rd century (N. Lapp 1964b: 19). Lacking are some of the quite plain 3rd-century rims (N. Lapp 1964b: fig. 1a:3-4 and p. 19) and the rounded rims with an undercut, a 4th-century and Early Hellenistic rim characteristic (N. Lapp 1964b: fig. 1a:1-2 and p. 17; P. Lapp 1970: fig. 10:2). Evidence for the rounded rim after 100 B.C. is lacking, and the Tell el-Fûl rims are either closely related to the squared rims or are a varied assortment of dying forms.

Storage jars and rims from the bottom of Silo 41 are shown on pl. 74. This deposit dates to the end of the 2nd century and the first quarter of the 1st century B.C. (Period IV C). Collared (pl. 74:1-3), squared (pl. 74:4-5), and round (pl. 74:6) rims are present. Almost all Tell el-Fûl Hellenistic handle sections are irregularly **oval with a single ridge on the top and nearly pointed edges** typical of the sloppily made handles of the period (pls. 74:1, 2, 7, 8, 72:19, 31, 74:19, 20, 39). To be noted also is a body sherd with a potter's mark on it (pls. 73:40, 33:7) from near the top of Cistern 2.

In summary, narrow-profiled collared rims of varying length are the most popular storage-jar rims of Period IV B and C at Tell el-Fûl. Fairly uniform, squared, collared rims and more varied, rounded rims are contemporary. The longest collars probably date into the 1st century B.C., but the rounded rims are disappearing about the turn of the century. Absent are Early Hellenistic and 3rd-century B.C. characteristics: rounded rims, plain and unthickened, not out-turned; rounded rims with an undercut; or extremely concave collar rims.

Jugs

The Tell el-Fûl jug rims are typical of the 2nd century B.C. All tend to flare; some are rounded (pl. 75:1-7), some more flattened and elongated (pl. 75:8-13), and others are more squared (pl. 75:14-21). Parallels are illustrated in *PCC*: Corpus 21.1.A-H. These jug sherds are all from the IV B occupation except pl. 75:21. At Tell el-Fûl near the end of the 2nd century B.C., a flared, rounded rim was the most popular jug form, not a squared type with a groove in the top as at Balâṭah (*PCC*: Corpus 21.1.E; N. Lapp 1964b: 21-22). No Hellenistic, grooved, jug rims were distinguished at Tell el-Fûl (see also Sinclair's observation, *TFL II*: 41). Most bases were concave (pl. 75:20-21). The reconstructed vessel in pls. 75:21 and 44:1 is a comparatively small and heavy jug from the Silo 43 IV A deposit.

A few smaller jugs of thin ware (pl. 75:22-26) may date to the beginning of the 1st century B.C. (Period IV C) although none had developed the inside rim shelf (cf. *PCC*: Corpus 21.1.K-M). The jug and base sherds (pl. 75:22-24) are from the same fills which had the many collared jar rims (L. XX-2ext, 4ext). A unique jug (pl. 75:27) probably had two handles. It is from a mixed layer of Cistern 1 and cannot be closely dated.

Flasks

The Hellenistic flasks from Tell el-Fûl (pl. 76:1-12) fit easily into the 2nd-century B.C. repertoire (*PCC*: Corpus 29.A-D). Those published from the second campaign at Tell el-Fûl (*TFL II*: pl. 26:1-3) must be redated to the 2nd century B.C. There is still no evidence for development in the flask within the Hellenistic period (*PCC*: 16); they become rougher and less pleasing in appearance when compared to the Tell el-Fûl III B forms from several centuries earlier. Note, for example, the interior neck ridging of pl. 76:1, 5-6 and the irregular neck sections of most of the others, in contrast to the smooth interior finish of the earlier flasks (pl. 59:1-7). The square-cut lip of pl. 76:5 (from the IV B deposit in Silo 42) is unusual but is perhaps a simple variation. A smaller type of flask is represented by pl. 76:8-12. Plate 76:8 is from the Late Hellenistic fill inside the East Casemate (L. XX-2ext, Period IV C); pl. 76:9 is from Mid-Silo 37 which has IV B and C pottery; pl. 76:10 is from sub-surface rock scree which filled the Southwest Rooms J, G and D (L. I-9); and pl. 76:11-12 is unstratified. The smaller size may indicate a trend at the turn of the century. Tell el-Fûl examples are not late enough to show the trend toward a longer neck above the upper handle attachment (*PCC*: 16) if this observation is valid. The unstratified fragment (pl. 76:12) seems to be from a flask, but the vessel has only one handle.

Juglets

The Hellenistic globular juglets are typical of the 2nd century B.C. (*PCC*: Corpus 31.1.C). The fragments, pls. 76:13-18, 44:2, are from IV B loci and date from about 100 B.C. Note the typical cup-shape mouth. The more collared rim (pl. 76:19) is from the rock fall over Cistern 1 which was disturbed in Period IV C and is typical of the first centuries B.C. and A.D. (*PCC*: Corpus 31.1.E; *ᶜAlâyiq*: pl. 24:A 137, A 74, and others).

Unguentaria

No whole or nearly complete unguentaria were found, and the 15 or so pieces were fragmentary as is frequently the case in tell rather than tomb clearances. All fragments except one are from the heavy-ware type. The pl. 77:1-6 fragments are from tall and slender vessels, while pl. 77:7-10 is of the more squat form (*PCC*: Corpus 91.A-S*, 91.B-S*). Most of the sherds are from IV B deposits; this is stratified evidence that the heavy-ware types continued until the end of the 2nd century. Plate 77:11, a unique fragment of thin ware, is of a form similar to pl. 77:8. The former is from debris on a IV B occupational level in Southwest Room J (L. I-18) and is perhaps a transitional form from the 2nd-century, heavy-ware type to the 1st-century, slender unguentaria of thin ware (cf. *PCC*: Corpus 91-92).

Miniature Vase

Very small miniature vases like pl. 77:12 (and pl. 44:3) have been found at a number of sites. The Tell el-Fûl vessel has a poorly preserved reddish brown paint on both exterior and interior surfaces. From Samaria came several similar Hellenistic "minute jars" (*HE I*: fig. 181:17a-b, f). One is published from Ramat Raḥel Stratum IV, dated from the 5th century B.C. through A.D. 70 (Aharoni 1956: fig. 7:6). There are a number of these tiny vases from the excavations at Bethel which have not been published (PTS museum nos. 2-20, 2-44, 2-45). Two of these latter also have poorly preserved paint.

The Tell el-Fûl specimen is from a stratified Hellenistic fill west of the East Casemate (L. XX-5), and these miniature vases can be added to the late 2nd-century B.C. corpus.

Spouts or Nipples

Three little spouts or nipples were found, and two are shown (pls. 77:13-14, 44:4-5). They are small, cone-shaped knobs which were probably attached to the side walls of a vessel. They had very small holes through their centers. One (pl. 77:13) was from stratified Hellenistic fill in the Southwest (L. XII-19), another from stratified fill west of the East Casemate (L. XX-9), and the third from surface debris. No parallels are known. They are quite different from spouts from Megiddo Strata V-III (cf. *Meg. I*: pl. 19: 106, 111) or **10th-century Taanach (Rast 1978: figs. 26:1, 36:1-2, 57:1). Nor can they be compared to hollow legs like** those from Ashdod on an imported, glazed and painted Amphora-rhyton (*Ashdod II-III*: fig. 24:12). The Tell el-Fûl specimens do not show any evidence of use as legs.

Bowls

Small, deep bowls with incurved rims and hemispherical shapes (pls. 77:15-18, 44:6) are typically Hellenistic (*PCC*: Corpus 51.1, 51.2). The thin ware of most of the small bowl sherds is a late 2nd-century B.C. characteristic. All these bowls are of plain kitchen ware without the slightest evidence of slip or paint.

Plate 77:19 is also from a rather deep bowl, but its straight sides give it a shallower appearance like the flat plates (77:20-24). These plates, with thickened or slightly inverted rims, are also locally made of plain ware and are derived from earlier "fish plates" (*PCC*: Corpus 53.A-G; cf. *SS III*: fig. 37:8-10 and p. 222, fig. 51:5-8 and p. 253, and especially fig. 56:4 of "household ware"). The unpainted form did not appear at Balâṭah before the 2nd century B.C. (N. Lapp 1964b: 22; cf. also Kee's typological discussion of fish plates, *Ashdod II-III*: 51-53), and those from Tell el-Fûl belong to the late 2nd-century Stratum IV B.

An unstratified sherd (pl. 77:25) is from the base of a small bowl with a black glaze or well-preserved paint. It was one of the few pieces of Hellenistic Decorated Ware (for the designation see *PCC*: 21, n. 136) and was the best specimen from the 1964 Tell el-Fûl campaign. It is probably from the Early Hellenistic occupation, and the ring base and deep shape may indicate a 3rd-century B.C. date (cf. *SS III*: 225). At Ashdod a similar base which has similar, painted concentric circles on the bottom is dated in the "fourth-third century range" (*Ashdod II-III*: fig. 14:15, pp. 52-53).

Cooking Pots

The Tell el-Fûl Stratum IV cooking pots are typical of 2nd-century B.C. globular pots throughout Palestine. Most common is the pot with a high neck which is slightly everted and topped by a plain rim (pls. 78:1-10, 45:1-2, 5-6). Those illustrated, and many other fragments, were from stratified IV B loci, pl. 78:9-10 possibly extending into the 1st century. At all Palestinian Hellenistic sites these are common in the 2nd century B.C., especially in the latter half (*PCC*: Corpus 71.1.A, C). Two similar pots from previous Tell el-Fûl campaigns should be noted (*TFL I*: pl. 24b:3; *TFL II*: pl. 25:7).

There are a number of high-necked cooking pots with rims which are variants of the plain type. Those in plate 78:11-13 have grooves in their tops. The first (pl. 78:11) came from the IV A deposit in Silo 43, and its handle is heavier than most of the Hellenistic cooking-pot handles from Tell el-Fûl. A few cooking pots have everted rim tips, pl. 78:14-15 (cf. *PCC*: Corpus 71.1.B). Plate 78:15 is of very thin ware and comes from beneath the latest floor in the Northeast Hellenistic House (L. V-29).

The second common, cooking-pot type has a short, somewhat-everted neck with concave interior (pls. 79:1-5, 45:3, 7). These pots are often smaller than the high-necked type. It is another typical 2nd-century B.C. form (*PCC*: Corpus 71.1.F-J; N. Lapp 1964b: fig. 3: 19). The whole pot (pls. 79:1, 45:3) is from the IV A deposit of Silo 43. Several rims of this kind also came

from the second quarter of the 2nd century B.C. at Beth-zur (*PCC*: Corpus 71.1.F-G; cf. *BZ II*: fig. 24: 1-2 with other examples listed), and there the form also continued to the end of the century (*PCC*: Corpus 71.1.J).

Two loci which had caches of cooking pots should be mentioned. The first was on a floor in the west part of Room R (pl. 79:6-14 from L. VI-25). The pots are all small and delicate; those which are not too fragmentary to characterize represent the concave, short-necked type (pls. 79:6-8, 46:4-5). This is a homogeneous, late 2nd-century group dating near 100 B.C. The second cache (pls. 79:15-18, 46:1-3) comes from Silo 33 in the Northeast Hellenistic House. The southern wall of Room A, constructed in the Early Phase of Period IV B, ran over the mouth of the silo (pl. 21c). In the silo, near the top, were IV B sherds, but the cooking-pot deposit in the lower level dates to Period IV A. One (pl. 79:15) is high-necked with a grooved rim like the variants (pl. 78:10-12). The concave, interior neck, similar to pl. 79:1-8 above, is represented by pl. 79:16-17, but the pots are larger. The only Tell el-Fûl fragment from a 2nd-century casserole came from this IV A deposit (pl. 79:18). The casserole was most popular in the first half of the century (*PCC*: Corpus 72).

It is interesting to note that in Silo 42, which contained a good selection of late 2nd-century pottery, three common neck-rim types of cooking pots were present: the high-necked (pl. 78:2, 6), the everted-rim variant (pl. 78:14), and the shorter, concave-necked (pl. 79:4).

Two cooking-pot lid fragments from IV B loci are illustrated (pl. 79:19-20). The second, pl. 79:20 (cf. *PCC*: Corpus 61.1.A), was found in Silo 30 along with the cooking-pot rim and handle sherd (pl. 79:3) and was probably used as a lid for that vessel.

Finally, the squat cooking pot (pls. 78:16, 45:4) has an unusual, rounded, thickened rim. It came from a mixed layer of Cistern 1 which had pottery dating down to the 1st century B.C. The squat form, short neck, and strap handle show development toward Early Roman forms.

Lamps

The best-made and earliest Hellenistic lamp (pls. 80:1, 46:6) came from Silo 43, whose III A deposit represented the first significant Hellenistic occupation at Tell el-Fûl during the second quarter of the 2nd century B.C. It is the finest piece of pottery recovered from the Hellenistic period and probably was not made locally. The pink clay is well levigated and is covered with a reddish brown paint. The body has an angular profile; the ring base is raised in the middle; and there is a deep groove near the oil hole. On its left side is the typical, pierced knob so that the lamp could be held by a string (cf. Broneer 1930: Type IX; *SS III*: fig. 85:6 and p. 367, with references given there). A 3rd-century date is possible, but the lamp probably belongs with the 2nd-century debris of the silo.

There are fragments of two lamps with poorly preserved paint. These (pl. 80:2 also from Silo 43, and another, too fragmentary to reconstruct, from Hellenistic fill L. I-29) have ring bases and, together with pl. 80:1, are the only Tell el-Fûl Hellenistic lamps to have finished bases. The rest are flat-based, and often they have not been smoothed off and their wheel marks remain.

The remainder of the Hellenistic closed lamps (pl. 80:3-10) are typical of the late 2nd century B.C. and the heavy, Late Hellenistic occupation at Tell el-Fûl. They have a plain, round body, rather short, pointed nozzle, flat, roughly finished base, and little or no groove or built-up rim (*PCC*: Corpus 83.1). They belong to Broneer (1930) Type X. Sinclair (*TFL II*: 44) classified the same type of lamp (*TFL II*: pl. 17:1) as Broneer Type VII (one of his Greek types) and places it in the 4th century B.C. Close examination puts it without question into Type X (second half 3rd-2nd century B.C.). Broneer's Greek types are characteristically glazed on the exterior; the Tell el-Fûl lamps are not. The Tell el-Fûl lamps were mass produced locally.

Only one tiny fragment of a molded lamp with the ray or ribbed motif (cf. *PCC*: Corpus 83.2) was found in the third campaign, and it is too small to illustrate. There was poorly preserved, black paint near the rim on the exterior, with red paint extending slightly over the rim. Molded lamps first appeared in the 2nd century B.C. and became popular in the 1st century (Broneer 1930: Type XVIII, middle 2nd-middle 1st century B.C.).

The fragments of Hellenistic folded lamps were very small, and only three came from stratified deposits, two from removing the second Late Hellenistic floor in the northwest (L. VI-13-14), and one from Mid-Silo 37. The reconstructed Hellenistic lamp (pl. 80:11), with its nearly touching edges (which often overlap) and flat base (cf. *CBZ*: fig. 41, and *BZ II*: fig. 29:4 and pl. 32b:3), should be contrasted with the **Period III B lamps (pl. 70:11-13 and p. 98 above).**

Period V Pottery
(ca. A.D. 70)

Nothing like the abundance of 1st-century B.C.-1st-century A.D. pottery was found in the 1964 campaign as had been reported in the earlier campaigns (cf. chap. VIII above). There were Roman sherds from the surface and sub-surface layers (West Casemate, L. VII-4; Southwest Rooms, L. XII-4, 6; and Northwest Rooms, L. XV-3, L. XXII-2-3). A Herodian coin (no. 19), dated A.D. 42/43, came from a sub-surface level above the Hellenistic floors in Room U (L. XXII-3). There were Early Roman occupational levels in the southwest (above Hellenistic Rooms J and K, L. XII-7, 9), and the evidence points to a 1st-century settlement around A.D. 70 for a few months or years.

Jars

The Roman jar-rim sherds (pl. 81:1-7) have the typical ridge at the base of the neck, which appeared around the beginning of the 1st century A.D. (*PCC*: 15 and Corpus 12.C-G). Thickened, everted-rim tips are not as characteristic at Tell el-Fûl as in Bethel Phase 3 (4 B.C.-A.D. 69, *Bethel*: 79 and pl. 70:2-23). Note, however, that those in pl. 81:2-3 exhibit characteristic **shaving** of the rim. Plate 81:5, from the top of Silo 37, is a late example of the lengthened-collar rim (cf. *Bethel*: pl. 70:2-3 and p. 78). The typical poorly made handle (pl. 81:8) is from the shoulder of a ribbed, Early Roman storage jar (cf. *PCC*: Corpus 12.D from Qumran II, A.D. 50-68).

Jugs

Jug rims (pl. 81:9-11) date to the Early Roman occupation. Note the suggestion of an inside shelf (pl. 81:9), often found on late jugs (cf. *PCC*: Corpus 21.R). Thin ware and grooved rims are characteristic of pl. 81:10-11.

Lamps

Several Herodian lamp spouts (pls. 81:12-14, 44:7-9) witness to the Roman occupation. These are very common in Palestine from about 50 B.C.-A.D. 70 (*PCC*: Corpus 82.1). The incised line across the spout (pl. 81:12, 14) is often found.

NOTES

[1]The writer wishes to thank Walter Rast for the help he has given in the study of the Iron I pottery. He kindly examined the sherds in Jerusalem with the writer in 1972; he furnished her with a copy of the Taanach Iron Age pottery manuscript while it was in preparation; and he checked the writer's conclusions. The final conclusions are, however, in every case, those of the writer.

[2]Dating these jars to the 12th century B.C. brings into question the attribution of the destruction in which they were found to the

Philistines in 1050 B.C. Cf. Albright 1960: 118; *Shiloh*: 31, 105; Kjaer 1930: 105.

[3]It might be argued that the Tell el-Fûl cooking-pot rims from the Period II deposits (pl. 48:28-36) really belong with a few Period I sherds in these deposits. This is hard to accept since most of the Iron I pottery was from Period II and it would be very unlikely that *all* the stratified cooking pots, pl. 48:28-36 (as well as the cooking pots from the earlier campaigns where no distinction was made between most of the pottery from Periods I and II), would be from Period I with none representing Period II. There were *no* examples of the elongated, grooved rim from the 1964 campaign.

[4]Holladay (1976) argues strongly against regional and for chronological differences in pottery in late Iron II. His methodology is not convincing (for example, p. 273), and much revision must be made in his data if a 7th-century date is accepted for Lachish Level III. See below.

[5]Holladay recognised earlier elements in Tell Beit Mirsim A₂, but dated most of the material with Lachish III (thus down to 597 B.C. according to his chronology [1976: 265, 271]).

[6]Consideration of Beth-zur III would have added strong support to M. and Y. Aharoni's discussion (1976) of Judahite sites in the 8th and 7th centuries B.C.

[7]Holladay (1976: 270) places Gezer V only in the early 6th century, but he may not have had the final report, *Gezer II*, to consider.

[8]M. and Y. Aharoni (1976: 73-74) do not recognise, as the excavators did, that En-gedi V extended past 587 B.C. For their dating of the mortarium (fig. 6:2) see note 23 below.

[9]It is unfortunate that a distinction is not made between Arad VII and VI, because it is possible Arad VI continued slightly past 587 B.C. and has comparable material to Tell el-Fûl III B. When the final publications and pottery corpus are published (Aharoni and Amiran 1964: 14, 144; Aharoni 1976: 244), there should be much parallel material to Tell el-Fûl.

[10]As noted above (n. 4), Holladay (1976) argues for chronological differences rather than regional. But notice that as the individual pottery forms are discussed, in almost every case Holladay has few and often atypical, northern parallels. When one considers much of his late 7th-century pottery from southern sites as belonging to the 8th century (Lachish III, *TBM A₂*, etc.), it becomes necessary to attribute differences to geographic and political factors. Regional differences in late Iron II must be considered. Note the following discussion of the very dissimilar pottery from Heshbon. The Heshbon Transjordanian tradition is different from that of the southern Transjordanian tradition.

[11]Contrary to what Sinclair says (*Bethel*: 71), Loci 129 and 136 cannot be considered homogeneous unless all the pottery is pre-587 B.C. From Locus 129, pl. 64:1-2 should be dated Iron II (probably pl. 67:2-3 as well). From the Iron II pottery of pl. 65, nos. 17 and 22 must certainly be dated that way. Plates 64:3, 9 and 65:18 may be post-587 B.C. with the sub-104 group. From Locus 136, pl. 67:4 must be dated pre-587 B.C.; pl. 64:5, 10-11 could be later. It is interesting to note that pls. 64:2, 9 and 62:2 from Locus 129 and pl. 64:10-11 are "smoked," evidence which indicates their use up to the final 6th-century destruction.

[12]Wright (1963: 211, n. 1) dates the purposeful filling of the large stairwell at El-Jîb to the second half of the 6th century and thinks Gibeon has pottery equivalent to Balâṭah Stratum V. The pottery from the stairwell has never been published, but from the El-Jîb pottery the writer would prefer to date the end of the occupation at El-Jîb to the time of Tell el-Fûl III B, slightly before Balâṭah V.

[13]The juglets from the burial (Stern 1971: fig. 3) are compared to the En-gedi juglet from the same 5th-century locus as the flask (Mazar and Dunayevsky 1967: pl. 33:3). The "peculiar raised handle in the form of a triangle" is a Late Persian period characteristic. The juglets, *Meg. I*: pl. 1:6-7 (Stern 1971: 29, n. 18) are from Stratum I, which should be dated to the 4th century B.C., and the Hazor juglets

are from Stratum II (late 5th and first half of the 4th centuries B.C.). The juglets Stern cites, *Hazor I*: pl. 154:15-19 (pl. 80:1, 5, 7-9) are not good illustrations of the triangular handle. Plate 80:5-6, also from Stratum II, are better examples. The lower portion of the jug (juglet) cited by Stern (1971: fig. 3:9) is similar to some unpublished Early Hellenistic juglets from Balâṭah (Stratum IV, 325-250 B.C.) and the Bethany juglet, *Bethany*: 293, fig. 58:745 (and pl. 125:1), with the bulge well below the center of the vessel. The latter is dated Persian-Hellenistic, compared to a similar Tell en-Naṣbeh juglet (*TN II*: pl. 38:683), dated Late Iron to Hellenistic (*TN II*: 21).

[14]See Holladay's summary of the hole-mouth jar evidence (1976: 288-89).

[15]Holladay (1976: 289) uses this type of jar to support his chronologically, rather than regionally, based typology. However, his northern parallels are not close. No whole vessels are represented, and it is doubtful that the rims come from the "neckless" jar type described in *BZ II*: 58-59. *Hazor I*: pl. 72:31, is not a good parallel to *BZ II*: fig. 15:10-11. It comes closer to Tell el-Fûl pl. 49:27, which is rather atypical and may belong with pl. 49:12. The Samaria examples are quite distant, if related at all. The published Shechem example is the closest, although still atypical. Other parallels are unpublished, and from my own experience at Shechem, I do not recall "many" rims that could be classified as belonging to this type of jar.

[16]Holladay (1976: 289) calls them "pre-Hellenistic bag-shaped." Some of his four-handled craters/store jars can best be compared to Tell el-Fûl pl. 50:28-32. For the *lmlk*-type jars, Lachish Type 484, cf. M. and Y. Aharoni 1976: type 6, from their earlier assemblages and Ussishkin 1976: figs. 1, 3. Note, although the rims and necks of the various jar types may at first glance seem similar, the *lmlk* jars have a slight slope outward, whereas the bag-shaped jar necks are usually somewhat inverted with a turned-out rim. Interesting also is that few of the specimens Holladay cites are from northern Palestine.

[17]The "one-handled" jug with wide mouth and rounded bottom (Holladay 1976: 290-91) so common at Tell Beit Mirsim, Lachish III, Beth-shemesh, and other southern sites does not appear at Tell el-Fûl. As M. and Y. Aharoni (1976: 84) have noted, it does not appear in closely dated late assemblages. Holladay cites a few northern examples, some atypical, but considering their popularity in the south in the 8th century, we must continue to think of it as mainly a southern form.

[18]M. and Y. Aharoni do not comment on the Ramat Raḥel and En-gedi evidence (1976: 84, type 13; 86, type 8). Many parallels are given by Holladay (1976: 291-92), but as he states, typological progression is difficult to demonstrate.

[19]M. and Y. Aharoni (1976: 83, type 10) have overlooked the En-gedi V specimen, ʿAtiqot V, fig. 9:13 pictured pl. 24:9, probably because the drawing is misleading. The photograph shows that the fragment consisted of most of the spout with only a piece of the rim attached. Undoubtedly the vessel had three handles attached to the rim like other vessels of this type. The Tell el-Fûl sherd alone does not demonstrate that the form lasted into the latter part of the 7th century (it could belong with the pre-III A material), but an 8th-century form is unusual at En-gedi.

[20]M. and Y. Aharoni have separated out this medium-size bowl as the "standard type, which points to mass production" appearing "only in the 7th-century assemblages" (1976: 86, type 1). Their appearance in the Mid-Field silos at Tell el-Fûl (pl. 62:12-13), Tell Beit Mirsim (*TBM III*: pls. 22-23), Beth-zur Pottery Cache (*BZ II*: fig. 17:1-14), and other earlier assemblages, along with the continuation of the other forms of burnished bowls into the 7th century, make the designation "standard type" rather tenuous.

[21]The bowls cited by Holladay (1976: 286) from northern sites do create an "overall impression" of differing vessel ware-form modes which is "marked and unmistakable" as he says. Again, he credits the difference to chronology (the northern forms are 8th-century, the southern are 7th), but when the southern forms have to be placed back in the 8th century, we are compelled to see regional differences.

[22]On the other hand, Holladay's "Assyrian" bowls and beakers are mainly a northern type; parallels cited from southern sites are few and not close (1976: 284). None have been found at Tell el-Fûl.

[23]Again the attempt has been made to place the heavy mortaria in the late Iron II period (Aharoni and Aharoni 1976: 86). The unreliability of the Meṣad Ḥashavyahu evidence is still valid (Lapp 1970: 184, n. 28; cf. Holladay 1976: 281, n. 33, where he fails to recognize the nonhomogeneous nature of the material published). Unfortunately, the stratification of Arad has not yet been published, and Strata VII-VI are not separated (see above, note 10). The presence of a mortarium in that group is not yet convincing. At Engedi, dating the only mortaria (ᶜAtiqot V: fig. 16:1-2) found in supposed Stratum V contexts to Stratum V has been questioned by the excavators in light of Persian material found nearby (ᶜAtiqot V: 27). The introduction of mortaria before the beginning of the 5th century B.C. has not yet been demonstrated (cf. Lapp 1970: 185).

[24]Contrary to Holladay (1976: 288), the form was recognized in TN II: 30 and Lapp 1970: 186.

[25]The lamp evidence for northern Palestine in late Iron II is still very sparse. To be added to the specimens mentioned in BZ II: 67-68 are a couple from Hazor (Hazor III-IV: pl. 232:9-10) and one from Balâṭah (Toombs and Wright 1963: 52-53, fig. 22:14). Note that Holladay (1976: 293) has no "low-based" forms from northern sites. His Tell el-Farᶜah example of "high-based" lamps is from the surface (de Vaux 1951: 419, fig. 12:17), and only his Balâṭah reference is very helpful for his stratigraphic purposes.

Chapter 10

Other Finds from the 1964 Campaign

Nancy L. Lapp

Coins[1]

There were a number of Ptolemaic coins (pl. 22:1-6), and except for the tetradrachma, they were all from the surface or very late mixed deposits. The silver tetradrachma of Ptolemy II, dated 253/252 B.C. (pl. 22:1, no. 113), was from the bedrock Period IV A channel of Area Z. The Ptolemaic coins do not alter the late date for Stratum IV since they only provide a *terminus post quem*, and the large coins had lasting value in antiquity. Plate 22:1-3 dates to Ptolemy II, pl. 22:4-6 to Ptolemy III.

The Seleucid coins (pl. 23) are more helpful for dating. The coins of Antiochus VII (pl. 23:1-4, nos. 15-18), including three tetradrachmas dating 136/135 B.C., were found on the floor and lip of Silo 32, which was covered for the Early Phase construction of the Hellenistic House. The two building phases of the Hellenistic House must therefore postdate 135 B.C., the beginning date indicated for Tell el-Fûl Period IV B. The small Seleucid coins (pl. 23:5-6, 9, nos. 13, 4, 10) are from surface material and date to Antiochus III or IV. Antiochus IV coins come from Silo 30 of the Hellenistic House (pl. 23:8, no. 22) and from beneath a floor in Area Uw (pl. 23:10, no. 70). Again, they only provide a *terminus post quem* for these constructions.

One clear Maccabean coin of John Hyrcanus II (pl. 22:7, fig. 5) came from sub-surface, unstratified debris. A Herodian coin of Herod Agrippa II, dated A.D. 42/43 (pl. 22:8, no. 19), came from Stratum V and is contemporary with the 1st-century A.D. material there.

The identifications of the coins and their descriptions are given in the chart, plan 15, p. 312-13.

Fig. 35. Inscription on Maccabean coin, no. 5.

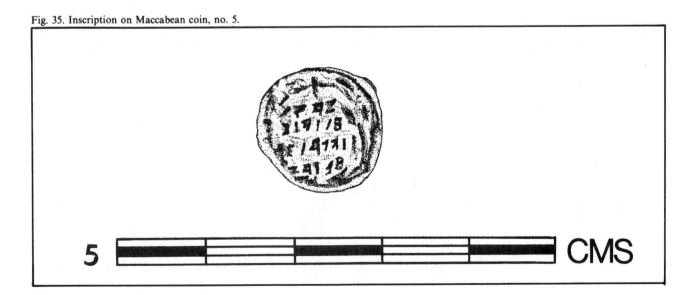

Artifacts[2]

Stone

Two interesting stone tools should be noted (pl. 24:1-2). Although such tools were hand worked from prehistoric times, both were from Late Hellenistic loci (L. I-29, V-8) and were probably used during most of the occupation of Tell el-Fûl. The first has a pierced hole and was probably an axehead; a handle would be mortised through the hole. The second was shaped to the hand for use as a scraper.

A crudely made small cup (pls. 24:12, 27:1) was found on the upper Hellenistic floor in Room RE in the northwest (L. VI-9, pl. 14d). Part of a large basalt bowl with a ring base (pls. 24:13, 27:2) came from the Period III/IV debris of Cistern 1. Such bowls were common throughout the Iron Age (cf. for example, *Meg. I*: pl. 113:2, 6-7 [Strata I-V]; *Lachish III*: pl. 65:8 [Level III-II]), and similar bowls came from the second campaign at Tell el-Fûl (*TFL II*: pl. 26:8, 9). The rim of a limestone bowl, perhaps alabaster (pl. 27:3), came from the surface in Mid-Field. Somewhat similar bowls came from the second campaign (*TFL II*: pl. 26:10) and the Harvard excavations at Samaria (*HE I*: fig. 206:7c, p. 334); a marble one was found in the Lachish Residency (*Lachish III*: pl. 64:5).

An alabaster cylinder (pl. 27:12) from the Exilic deposit in Cistern 1 may have been used as a weight. An elongated pellet (pl. 24:4) of calcite limestone[3] from Period II Silo 24 was perhaps a weight also (cf. *Meg. I*: pl. 104), or it may have been part of some ornamentation.

A number of well-preserved polishing stones or pounders were found, especially in the Cistern 1 deposit. Some are shown on pl. 24:5-11. Plate 24:11 is pitted lava (scoria). A grinding stone of fossilized limestone has been worked with a pick (pl. 24:3). These stone implements are well known from other sites and are without particular significance chronologically (cf. *TBM II*: pl. 44; *TBM III*: 84; *Meg. I*: pl. 106).

Loom Weights

A variety of loom weights (pl. 25:1-8), found throughout the excavations in Period III A and B and Period IV deposits, witness to the domestic activity carried on at the site. Both the pyramidal and doughnut shapes are found. Iron Age cone and pyramidal loom weights were found at Samaria (*SS III*: fig. 92a:23-26), but Albright considered the pyramidal weights as MB II and doughnut shapes as Iron II at Tell Beit Mirsim (*TBM II*: 56, pl. 45:1-16).

Spindle Whorls

A typical Iron II pottery disc spindle whorl (pl. 25:9) came from pre-III A Silo 38 (cf. *Meg. I*: pl. 93:6, 23, 32, 54, 62; *Lachish III*: pl. 65:11; *TBM II*: 55-56; *TFL I*: pl. 33:1-2). Small, stone spindle whorls had a long period of use (cf. *Meg. I*: pls. 93-94; *SS III*: fig. 92a; *Gerar*: pl. 44). The specimen from a Period IV B locus (pls. 25:10, 27:13) is of serpentinized gabbro imported from Cyprus or Turkey.[4]

Beads

Cylindrical and round beads (pl. 27:14-20) were quite irregular in shape. They were formed from shell or bone (14), glass (15, 17-18), bronze (16), soft stone (19), and possibly a seed (20). None were particularly significant as imports or important chronologically.

Bone

Cistern 1 and other deposits yielded the assortment of bone spatulas and picks common at Iron Age and Hellenistic sites. Some of them are shown in pls. 25:11-23 and 27:5-6, 8. Flat on one side, rounded at one end and sharply pointed at the other, they seem particularly suited for weaving. They also are thought to have cosmetic use. Most of the Israelite and Hellenistic spatulas at Samaria were wider than those at Tell el-Fûl (cf. *SS III*: 461, fig. 115:4-6; *HE I*: 271, fig. 241), and one as small as pl. 25:23 is unusual (cf. also *Meg. I*: pls. 95:39-62, 96:1-9; *Lachish III*: pl. 63:22-27; *Gerar*: pl. 34).

An elaborately carved knife handle (pls. 25:24, 27:4) came from the III B deposit in Cistern 1. A similar one is published from Samaria (*HE I*: fig. 240:1c and p. 370) although the size and design differ slightly. Plain, hollow bone handles are fairly common at Iron Age sites (cf. *Meg. I*: pl. 96:24-30; *Meg. II*: pl. 196:2-6), but elaborately carved handles are found infrequently (*Hazor III-IV*: pls. 345:20, 191:24; *Gerar*: pl. 33:24).

One isolated piece of ivory inlay was found (pls. 25:25, 27:7). It is a border-design fragment, consisting of circles containing schematically represented eight-petalled flowers. Such border fragments, from wall panels or furniture, were found at Samaria (*SS II*: pl. 21, fig. 11, pp. 39-40). The Samaria ivories are dated to the 9th or 8th century (Albright 1960: 137); they show Egyptian influence but were manufactured in Phoenicia and have affinities with the ivory collections from Arslan Tash and Nimrud. The Tell el-Fûl fragment came from the III A deposit in Cistern 2 and was probably brought to the site during the late Iron II occupation.

Metal

The most interesting metal artifact was an iron compass, pl. 26:9 (and pl. 27:9), found beneath the early phase IV B floor of the Hellenistic House (L. V-32). Such an instrument could have been used to make bone inlay designs.

Only a few copper or bronze rings and bracelets were found (pl. 26:10, 12, 13, 15). A bronze disc (pl. 26:14) was perhaps used for a mirror (cf. *Lachish III*: pl. 57:33) or a cover (*Meg. I*: pl. 57:33). The bronze base of a small vessel (pls. 26:11, 27:11), came from Silo 41. There was a small assortment of pins and needles (pl. 26:1-7); pl. 26:7 is part of a fibula (cf. *Meg. I*: pl. 79). The lowest fill on bedrock (L. II-45) just south of Wall S ("Saul's Wall") contained many pieces of iron (no. 144), but they were too fragmentary to know whether they were part of iron knives, sickles, or plow tips (cf. *TFL II*: pl. 19; *Meg. I*: pls. 82-83). An iron arrowhead (pl. 26:8) from the III B deposit in Cistern 1 was smaller than the usual arrowhead cast in iron. Most small arrowheads are of bronze (cf. *Meg. I*: pl. 80; *Lachish III*: pl. 60; *TN I*: 263, fig. 71). A small iron one from Samaria has more rounded shoulders (*SS III*: fig. 111:14).

Skeletal Material[5]

No burials or complete skeletons were found. There was one deposit of cranial and mandible bones which, upon study, was shown to be from one individual, a female, between the ages of 15 and 20. There was no evidence of disease.

Stamped Handles

Royal Stamped Handles

Three royal stamped handles of the *lmlk* type were found in the 1964 campaign. To these three should be added the five from the *migdal* area in the two earlier campaigns (*TFL II* refers only to these) plus seven more, from the top of the hill in the second campaign, stamped with the *lmlk* stamp or rosette (Albright 1933: 10).

On one handle, no. 205 (pls. 28:1-2, 29:1), two *mem*'s are very clear on the lower right-hand portion of the seal, but the remainder of the stamp completely missed the raised rib of the handle and made no impression. This handle had the concentric-circle impression to the left of the seal. The seal was undoubtedly a class 3 *mmšt* impression, nearest to Lapp's third stamp of that class (1960: 15; Pritchard 1959: fig. 9:499, 486-87; note that the Gibeon impression [fig. 9:499] has the concentric-circle stamp to its left). A second Tell el-Fûl *lmlk* handle, no. 57 (pls. 28:3, 29:3), had no visible letters, but the type-3

winged impression was perhaps from the same stamp as the first *mmšt* seal (cf. Pritchard 1959: fig. 9:486-87). It will be recalled that the 1922 *lmlk* handle was of the unusual *mmšt* type with the place name at the top of the seal (cf. *TFL I*: 23, pl. 30:14; *Ex. Gezer II*: 211, fig. 361:1). The name is very clear although there was some confusion in writing or impressing the two *mem*'s; it is virtually impossible to determine what the rest of the seal is like. A new photograph of the handle is reproduced on pl. 28:8-9.

The other *lmlk* handle, no. 55 (pls. 28:4, 29:2), was read by Lapp (Pottery Book, p. 39) as having the *hbrn* impression. Parts of the *reš* and *nun* are discernible in the left-hand corner (cf. Lapp 1960: 15, *hbrn* class 3; *Lachish III*: pl. 46B:4-6; Pritchard 1959: fig. 9:521).

Of the *lmlk* handles of the second campaign at Tell el-Fûl, no letters were distinguished in the final publication except *lamed* and *mem* of pl. 16:6 (*TFL II*: 32). The evidence is not conclusive, but it should be noted that of the handles from Tell el-Fûl in which a place name can be distinguished, three of the four have *mmšt*. Albright concluded after the second campaign that *mmšt* was the most frequent place mentioned at Jerusalem, Gezer, and Tell el-Fûl (*TBM III*: 75), and this parallels the situation at other sites in northern Judah where the *mmšt* seals are most common (Tell en-Naṣbeh, El-Jîb, and others; see Lemaire 1975: 17-19). *Mmšt* is the only unknown site of the four towns mentioned, but because of its predominance in northern Judah attempts to locate it are usually in this area. The most recent suggestion is made by A. Lemaire (1975: 15-23), identifying Amwas with *mmšt*.

The *lmlk* handles from the 1964 campaign were all unstratified. Major studies of these jar handles in the last few years have dated them to the 8th or 7th centuries B.C. (Lapp 1960: 11-22; Cross 1969: 20-27; Lance 1971: 315-22). Lance clearly demonstrated that the handles from Starkey's excavations at Lachish came from Stratum III. Those from the new excavations directed by Ussishkin are also from Stratum III (Ussishkin 1977: 55-56). Furthermore, Ussishkin (pp. 50-54) has convincingly shown that the destruction of Stratum III must be attributed to Sennacherib in 701 B.C.

Whether all royal stamped handles must be dated in the late 8th century during Hezekiah's reign is, of course, not proven (Ussishkin 1977: 56), but Lachish at present provides the best stratigraphic evidence available. They were probably made until at least the end of Hezekiah's reign, and their use could have continued for some time. In the Buqeʿah, two-winged stamped handles were found at briefly occupied late Iron II settlements (Stager 1975: 250). The pre-III A pottery from the Mid-Field silos (Silos 36, 38-39) has been shown to have parallels from Lachish III (above,

p. 82, chap 9 *passim*), and Albright's first phase of Fortress III also may date late in the 8th century (above, p. xvii). As noted above, at least five royal stamped handles came from the *migdal* area in the two early campaigns. It is thus possible that the *lmlk* handles should be dated with the pre-III A pottery and constructions, about 700 B.C.; conversely, if the late 8th-century date for the royal jar handles is born out, the Tell el-Fûl handles may help date the earliest Period III pottery at Tell el-Fûl.

One more rosette handle, no. 58 (pls. 28:5, 29:4), was found in the 1964 campaign (see the discussion of those from the second campaign, *TFL II*: 32-33). Unfortunately, it was from mixed debris. Besides the concentric-circle impression with the winged-disc seal noted above, no. 205, two other handles with the circle impresion were found in 1964, nos. 267 and 268 (pls. 28:7-8; 29:5-6). One was from the lower Period III A deposit in Cistern 2. Several were found in 1933 (*TFL II*: 32).

The rosette-stamped handles, as Cross has suggested (1969: 22), may have replaced the *lmlk* handles toward the end of the southern kingdom. Those from Tell el-Fûl are not clearly stratified, but they could belong with the Period III A material. No *lmlk* handles have come from En-gedi V, but there are some with rosette stamps and a private-seal stamp on the standard two-ridged type of handle (*ᶜAtiqot* V: 33-34).

Hellenistic Stamped Handles

The five-pointed star, *yrslm* seal impressions and the *yhd*-plus-symbol seals have been considered contemporary for some time. Cross and P. Lapp considered their paleo-Hebrew script the latest in the series of postexilic stamps (Lapp 1963: 26, n. 20). At Ramat Raḥel many of both kinds were found in a Stratum IV B dump (*RR II*: 19, 43, pl. 18:4-6, fig. 11-15). One stamped handle of each type was recovered in the 1964 Tell el-Fûl campaign (pl. 30), but unfortunately they were both from surface debris. Yet because of the extensive Late Hellenistic occupation at Tell el-Fûl, they can make a contribution to fixing a date for these handles.

The dating of archaizing script is only possible within broad time spans (Cross 1961: 192, n. 28; Avigad 1974: 55), so that closer dating for these handles has to depend upon archeological context. The Ramat Raḥel evidence has been helpful; the pottery from the Stratum IV B dump has been dated to the late 4th century by the excavator and the 3rd-2nd century by G. Garbini (*RR I*: 29-30, 68). Analyzing by the form, ware, paleography, and archeological context,

Lapp (1963: 31) favored a third quarter of the 3rd-century B.C. date for the two groups of handles. A cooking-pot handle of Hellenistic date with the *yrslm* impression was found by Richardson (1968: 12-16), concurring with the 3rd- or 2nd-century dates.

The most important archeological evidence for the dating of these handles comes from the recent excavations in the Jewish Quarter of the Old City of Jerusalem where several handles of the *yrslm* and *yhd*-plus-symbol types were found underneath an Early Herodian floor in Area C, together with quantities of Late Hellenistic pottery (Avigad 1974: 55). One *yrslm* handle was found attached to the rim and shoulder of a jug similar to other jugs which can be dated closely to the second half of the 2nd century B.C. (Avigad 1974: 56-57). Avigad notes that this does not necessarily indicate a *terminus post quem* for the seal impressions and that it is still possible that they go back to the 3rd century B.C. (1974: 58). However, the second half of the 2nd century B.C. is a very satisfactory time in which to place the Tell el-Fûl handles since that is when the site experienced heavy occupation (there was little occupation before then during the Hellenistic period; see above, p. 63, Lapp 1965: 7). Thus Tell el-Fûl evidence supports the date established by the Jerusalem dig for these handles.

The Tell el-Fûl *yrslm* handle is of a dark gray ware with reddish surface and small, medium, and large white inclusions. The handle section is smooth and oval. The shape and ware seem quite similar to those discussed by Lapp (1963: 29-30). None of the letters between the points of the star can be clearly distinguished, but there is evidence that they were present on the seal. The handle came from surface debris on the east side of the mound.

The *yhd*-plus-symbol handle is interesting and unique. The *he* and *dalet* are the archaizing, paleo-Hebrew forms, with the three strokes hanging from the stem of the *he* and the closed head of the *dalet*. Above, to the left, the *yod* is less clear, but the paleo-Hebrew form can be distinguished. At the top, the *ṭet* is also less clear, but a single horizontal line can be distinguished within a circle. This is the characteristic lapidary form of the *ṭet*, and it is interesting that the symbol remained the same while the other letters shifted to the paleo-Hebrew (cf. Cross 1969: 21, and nn. 16-17). The appearance of the standard Hebrew *ṭet* with two crossed lines on one of the *yhd* handles from the Jerusalem excavations indicated to Avigad that the single-line symbol was indeed meant to be a *ṭet* (1974: 53). Unfortunately, the meaning for this symbol is still unknown.

It is very interesting that the Tell el-Fûl seal impression is on a jug handle (pl. 30:3-4), not a jar handle as is the case in other published *yhd*-plus-symbol impressions. Unfortunately, the rim is broken off at both sides of the handle so that the rim shape cannot be ascertained. However, what is there is very similar to the *yrslm* handle that Avigad published (1974: 56, fig. 1) and the other late 2nd-century B.C. jugs (pp. 56-57), and it is very possibly the same type of jug that is well represented in the Jerusalem excavations. The handle section is oval with irregular edges; the handle rises slightly above the rim with a smooth interior line. The diameter is 10 (?) cm. The ware can be described in the same terms: light brown, slightly darkened at the core, fairly well levigated, with fine white inclusions. The pottery from Locus 745 at Jerusalem which had a whole jug like the *yrslm* stamped jug (Avigad, 1974: fig. 2) can be compared to the Tell el-Fûl pottery (pls. 27:14-16, 20, 32:3-11). It should be noted also that Lapp (1963: 31, n. 44) found good 2nd- and 1st-century B.C. parallels for the Ramat Raḥel dump deposit with many *yrslm* and *yhd*-plus-symbol handles.

Although they are surface sherds, the Tell el-Fûl *yrslm* and *yhd*-plus-symbol handles can be dated to Tell el-Fûl Period IV B (135-100 B.C.) and lend support to a late 2nd-century B.C. date for these stamped impressions.

Figurines

The clay figurines from the 1964 campaign, some from good Stratum III contexts, are the usual types found at late Iron II sites. Fragments (pl. 32:1-3) are of the common pillar or "snowman" type with faces which were impressed in a mold and then set on hand-formed pedestals. The type is especially common in southern Palestine (*TBM III*: pls. 30; 55:6-11; 56, pp. 69-70; *TN II*: pl. 85; *AS IV*: pl. 51:21-24, 29-34; *AS V*: 155-56; *Lachish III*: pls. 27:4, 8, 28:10-11, 13, 31:1-15). The head of a crude, hand-made, "beaked face" or "pinched face" figurine (pl. 32:4) was found with abundant Period III surface material (L. I-41). The type is well known from Tell Beit Mirsim (*TBM III*: pls. 31:7, 54:9), ʿAin Shems (*AS IV*: pl. 51:36; *AS V*: 156), Lachish (*Lachish III*: pls. 27:1, 3, 28:14), and Tell en-Naṣbeh (*TN I*: pls. 86, 87:2).

The pillar (pl. 32:5) is probably a pedestal for a lamp or bird figurine (cf. *TBM III*: pls. 32:1-3, 57B:2-4, 57C:4-5; *Lachish III*: pl. 28:12).

The animal heads (pl. 32:6-7) are hollow and their noses form spouts for animal-shaped vases. Parallels are known from other sites (*TBM III*: pl. 58:1; *Lachish III*: pls. 27:7, 30:23-24, 26-27; *TN I*: pl. 89). The animal figurines or toys (pl. 32:8-12) were molded as solid pieces. They are usually considered horses (*TBM III*: 81-82) although P. Lapp thought they might represent

domesticated dogs. They are frequently found at late Iron II sites (*Lachish III*: pls. 27:5, 29:17-18, 32:5; *AS IV*: pl. 51:1-2; *TBM III*: pl. 58; *TN I*: pl. 88).

An Ostracon

Walter E. Rast

An inscribed sherd was discovered at Tell el-Fûl during the 1964 excavations in a locus consisting of surface soil (L. II-11) in Room Q. Below the surface layer were two Hellenistic floor levels (L. II-12, 44) separated from each other by a fill (L. II-43). The provenience of the ostracon was thus an open locus with mixed contents. Pottery remains from L. II-11 dated to late Iron II (Period III at Tell el-Fûl) as well as to ca. 100 B.C. (Period IV B). Other objects from the same locus included two coins, one (no. 3) from the reign of Ptolemy III (246-221 B.C.) and a second (no. 4) from the time of Antiochus IV (175-164 B.C.). A fragment of a brass pin and a small piece of glass came from the same locus.

The inscription was written between 5 and 6 cm below the lower handle attachment on a body sherd (pl. 31). The sherd was apparently a fragment of a large cylindrical jar of the Late Hellenistic or Hasmonean period. Lapp's Corpus Type 11.2 may be cited for comparison (*PCC*: 147). Clay color (Munsell) is 10R 6/6 (light red), while a wash on the exterior is 5R 7/4 (pink), the latter providing a light surface for the inscription. The writing was in black ink. Letters are heavily made, suggesting an instrument with a pliable tip. At several places the initial point of contact is thicker, narrowing toward the end of the stroke.

The Script

The inscription consists of a proper name plus a patronymic: *ḥnnyh br ḥwr*, "Ḥananiah, son of Ḥur." The following features may be noted in the letter forms.

1. *Ḥet*. There are two examples of *ḥet*, the first and the third from the last letters. The first *ḥet* was made in three bold strokes—a downstroke on the right, a crossbar from upper left to the middle of the right downstroke, and the left downstroke. Slight blotching, probably caused by the roughness of the sherd surface, occurred where the crossbar terminated at the right downstroke. The *ḥet* in the third to the last letter is more dimly preserved, but it is clear that it was made also with three strokes. Both forms are close to examples in 4QDanᶜ, the sloping crossbar being a cursive feature (Cross 1961: 149, fig. 4:2; pp. 184-85).

2. *Nun*. Two *nun*'s follow as the second and third letters, the first a medial, the second a final form. The medial *nun* is slim and slightly oblique in the downstroke. At the lower right it bends to the left where it terminates against the long downstroke of the neighboring final *nun*. The medial *nun* is without a head. The form is similar to one in 4QXII[a] (Cross 1961: 149, fig. 4:1; cf. Birnbaum 1971: pl. 85). The final *nun* is ticked at the top and is a straight vertical form which breaks through the baseline (Cross 1961: 186). It is heavier in the upper half than the lower. Parallels are found in 4QDan[c] (Cross 1961: 149, fig. 4:2). The usage of final *nun* to terminate the first element in the theophoric name results in the distinction of the medial and final forms (Cross 1961: 143, 155). This is noteworthy over against earlier custom which could employ final *nun* in the medial position (Geraty 1975: 57; Naveh 1970: 46). The forms here also are interesting to compare with Murabba‘ât Ostracon 72 in which the name *yhwḥnn* has both medial and final *nun*'s consisting of a long vertical stroke. In line 3 of the Murabba‘ât Ostracon the medial *nun* has a tick, while in line 6 the same form is bent to the left at the base and the final *nun* is a long vertical stroke (Benoit, Milik, and de Vaux 1960: pl. 52).

3. *Yod*. This is a heavily made letter. It is distinguished by its upper curve which tapers to a point below. The flexible end of the writing instrument was employed to its full capacity in making this form. The same tendencies are seen in Murabba‘ât Ostracon 72 (Benoit, Milik, and de Vaux 1960: pl. 52, line 2; Cross 1961: 148, fig. 3:2).

4. *He*. This letter was executed by means of two strokes, a right vertical and a curved-v set on its side which was begun at the left, meeting the right downstroke midway before bending back to the lower left. The type is sometimes referred to as the reversed-k form (Cross 1961: 184; Naveh 1970: 47), and its features are those of the cursive script. Again Murabba‘ât Ostracon 72 has examples of this type (Benoit, Milik, and de Vaux 1960: pl. 52, line 6).

5. *Bet*. This form was made in two noncontinuous strokes, a further cursive tendency in the script of this ostracon (Cross 1961: 183). Beginning with a pronounced head on the upper left, the form bends horizontally before rounding into the vertical downstroke on the right. The base is a strong, independent stroke from left to right, beginning beneath the neighboring *reš*. The tilted form of the letter is distinctive. Note that Murabba‘ât Ostracon 72 still has the older *bet*, made with one continuous movement, including a base formed from right to left (Cross 1961: 175, 148, fig. 3:2; Naveh 1970: 46).

6. *Reš*. The letter *reš* occurs twice in the inscription, in the fourth and last positions. Both examples have a pronounced head on the upper left, the last letter being slightly more exaggerated in this regard. The round-shouldered form is related stylistically to the Hasmonean semiformal script, but eventually this type evolves into the s-curved *reš* (Cross 1961: 187). The forms here are slightly tilted and are closer to examples in 4QDan[c] than to Murabba‘ât Ostracon 72 (Cross 1961: 148, fig. 3:2; 149, fig. 4:2).

7. *Waw*. The shape of *waw* is an inverted-v form. It was begun on the left side, coming to a point at the top before being completed with a vertical stroke on the right. This form of *waw* is characteristic of scripts in the formal hand such as 4QDeut[c] (Cross 1961: 138, fig. 2:2). Cross notes that the development of the *waw* in the semicursive script follows the pattern of the formal hand (Cross 1961: 184). The identical feature is found in 4QXII[a] (Cross 1961: 149, fig. 4:1).

Summary

The script of the Tell el-Fûl Ostracon may be fitted into the series described by Cross as semicursive (Cross 1961: 181). The designation "semicursive" is preferable to "cursive" for this inscription since features deriving from the formal script, such as *waw* and *reš*, are still present. *Waw*, *nun*, *yod*, and *he* place the inscription closer to Murabba‘ât Ostracon 72 and 4QXII[a], while *ḥet*, *bet*, and *reš* have features similar to 4QDan[c]. On this basis the Tell el-Fûl Ostracon would fall between the Murabba‘ât Ostracon and 4QXII[a] on the one hand, and 4QDan[c] on the other. If Cross' chronology is followed, this would mean that the first two may be slightly earlier than 100 B.C.; the Tell el-Fûl inscription may be dated just about exactly 100 B.C., and the Daniel fragment to shortly after 100 B.C. It should be noted that Lapp's original call in the field assigned this ostracon to +/- 100 B.C. The inscription thus belongs to the main Hellenistic occupation (Period IV B) at Tell el-Fûl.

Interpretation

The names Ḥananiah and Ḥur were both common names in the Old Testament, the latter possibly of non-Israelite origin. Among other places, a Ḥananiah is found in Jer 28:1, 37:13, and Dan 1:6, while Ḥur was an important contemporary of Moses (Ex 17:10, 12). Both names were employed during the postexilic period, and in Neh 3:8-9 the two are found in proximity. Outside the Old Testament the name Ḥananiah occurs in the Aramaic onomasticon of Elephantine, being found twice in the Passover papyrus (Cowley 1923: 21:2, 11). At the same site a "Ḥor, servant of Ḥananiah" is attested (Cowley 1923: 38:7; Porten 1968: 280, cf. 149, n. 133), while Ḥor is also found in a 5th-century B.C. epitaph from Saqqara (Lipínski 1975: 193; Donner-Röllig 1973: 267:1). The usage of the name Hananiah continued during the Christian era as witnessed in the Greek form Ananias in Acts 5:1 and 9:10. We also find "Yehonathan, son of Hananiah" in Murabbaᶜât Papyrus 30 which is closely dated to A.D. 134 (Benoit, Milik, and de Vaux 1961: 145, line 10).

The association of the name Hananiah with the Benjaminites in 1 Chr 8:24 has special significance. Given the likelihood that Tell el-Fûl is to be identified with biblical Gibeah as a prominent city of Benjamin (Josh 18:24, Judg 19:14), the appearance of this name on an ostracon from this site is as striking as it is expected. The name Hur, on the other hand, was also at home in nearby territory, being found in the Judahite list of 1 Chr 2:19-20 (Dahlberg 1962).

The Tell el-Fûl Ostracon provides no clear assistance in deciding whether its inscriber was at home in the Aramaic or Hebrew tongue (Fitzmyer 1970: 520). The presence of *br* instead of *bn* would not necessarily prove that the writer was Aramaic-speaking since these terms became interchangeable in Hebrew and Aramaic (Fitzmyer 1970: 529; Geraty 1975: 57, n. 8). Nevertheless, although little can be concluded concerning the language of the writer, the ostracon makes an important contribution to the late 2nd- and early 1st-century B.C. onomasticon of Palestine, and its semicursive hand fits nicely in the typologies of the later Jewish scripts and their developments.

NOTES

[1]Thanks are due to the late Father A. Spijkerman who assisted with the identification of the coins.

[2]Grateful thanks are due to Mrs. Jean Boling who supervised the photography of the artifacts in Jerusalem in the winter of 1975-76 and otherwise assisted in describing these artifacts.

[3]This identification was made by Mira Bar Matthews of the Israel Geological Survey, Alan Matthews, Department of Geology, Hebrew University, and Dina Grauer.

[4]The geologists (see n. 3) reported that serpentinized gabbro is not found in Palestine. A little is found in Sinai, but that is almost definitely not the source of this piece. Cyprus has an abundance, and it is also found in Turkey.

[5]Thanks are due Jeffrey Schwartz for the identification of these bones in August, 1971.

Appendix A
Index to Loci

See plan 1 (excavated remains) and plan 2 (areas of excavation).

Locus	Period	Location	Appendix B p.	Discussion p.
AREA I (Southwest)				
8	IV B	Room F	137	72
9	IV B	Rooms G, J, D	138	72, 73
11	IV B	Room F	137	72
14	IV B	Rooms G, J, D	138	72, 73
16	III B	Room D	130	44
18	IV B	Room J	138	72
19	IV B	Room J	138	72
20	IV B	Room G	138	72
21	IV B	Room J	138	72
22	IV B	Room J	138	72
23	IV B	Room J	138	72
25	IV B	Room E	138	45, 73
26	III A	Revetment-N; Room E	126, 129	40, 44
27	III A	Room E	129	44
28	IV B	Room J	138	72
29	IV B	Room J	138	44, 72
32	IV B	Room J	138	44, 72
34	IV B	Room J	138	44, 72
35	III B	Room G	129	44, 72
41	—	Room E	129	44
42	—	Room E	130	44
43	IV B	Room D	138	73
44	I	Room E	125	25, 44
45	III B	Room E	130	44
46	sub-III A	Room E	130	44
47	IV B	Room F	137	72
48	IV B	Room F	137	72
49	III A	Revetment-N; Room F	126, 130	40, 44, 72
50	III A	Room F	130	44, 72
AREA II (West Casemate)				
2E	III A	Revetment-N	126	40
4	—	Room L	136	69
5	IV B	Area P	135	69
9	IV B	Area P	135	69
12	IV C	Area Q	136	69
14	IV B	Room O	136	69
15	III A	Room O	127	41
17	III A	Room O	127	41
18	III A	Walls	127	41
19	IV B/III A	Room N	127, 136	41, 69
22	III A	Revetment-N	126	40
23	IV B	Room M	136	69
24	IV B	Room M	136	69
25	IV B	Room M	136	69

27	III A	Room N	127	41
28	IV B	Room L	136	69
29	III B	Room L	127	41
30	III B	Room L	127	41
31	III B	Room L	127	41
32	III B	Room L	127	41
34	III A	Room N	127	41
35	III B	Room L	127	41
36	sub-III B	Room L	127	41
37	III A	Room L	127	41
39	IV B	Area P	135	69
40	IV B	Area P	135	69
41	IV B	Area P	135	69
42	IV B	Area P	135	69
43	IV B	Area Q	136	69
44	IV B	Area Q	136	69
45	IV B	Area Q	136	69
46	II	Fortress-N	126	24, 25

AREA III (Northwest)

8	IV B	Room CRn	141	74
9	IV B	Room CRn	141	74
14	IV C	Room CR	142	74
15	post-IV B	"Garden Fence & Soil"	143	75
17	post-IV B	"Garden Fence & Soil"	143	75
19	IV	Room CR	142	74
20	IV	Cistern 1	142	74
21	IV	Cistern 1	142	74
22	IV	Cistern 1	142	74
24	IV	Cistern 1	142	74
27	IV	Cistern 1	142	74
28	III A-B	Cistern 1	130	
29	III A-B	Cistern 1	130	
30	III B	Cistern 1	130	46
31	III B	Cistern 1	130	46
32	III B	Cistern 1	130	46
33	III B	Cistern 1	130	46
34	III B	Cistern 1	130	

AREA IV (none)

AREA V (Northeast)

3	IV B	H House, Late Phase	133	68
8	IV B	H House, Late Phase	133	68
10	IV B	H House, Late Phase	133	68
21	IV B	H House, Late Phase	133	68
22 (=10)				
23 (=10)				
28 (=21)				
29	IV B	H House, Late Phase	133	68
30 (=29)				
31 (=29)				
32	IV B	**H House, Early Phase**	132	65
33	IV B	H House, Early Phase, S-31	132	59, 65
34	IV B	H House, Pre-Bldg., S-30	132	59, 65

35 (=10)				
36 (=10)				
37	III A	Room C	126	41, 68
39 (=10)				
40	IV B	H House, Early Phase, S-29	132	59, 65
44	IV B	H House, Early Phase	132	68
45	III A	Room C	126	41
46 (=81)				
48 (=91)				
49	IV B	Fortifications	131	41
50	III A	Room C	127	41
51 (=10)				
53	IV B	H House, Late Phase	133	68
54	IV B	H House, Early Phase	132	65, 68
55 (=54)				
56 (=54)				
57	IV B	H House, Pre-Bldg., S-33	132	59, 63, 65
57L	IV A	H House, Pre-Bldg., S-33	132	59, 63, 65
59	IV B	Fortifications, EC-1	131	65
61 (=59)				
62	IV B	Fortifications	131	65
63 (=62)				
64 (=59)				
65	IV B	H House, Pre-Bldg., S-32	132	59, 65
66	IV B	Fortifications	131	65
67	IV B	H House, Pre-Bldg., S-32	132	59, 65
68 (=59)				
69 (=59)				
70 (=54)				
73 (=29)				
74	IV B	Fortifications; H House, Late Phase	131, 133	65, 68
75 (=29)				
76	IV B	Fortifications	131	65
77 (=81)				
79	IV B	Fortifications, EC-1	131	65
81	IV B	Fortifications	131	65
82 (=81)				
83	IV B	Fortifications	131	65
86 (=81)				
87 (=59)				
88 (=59)				
89	III A	Room EC-2	126	41
90	III A	Room EC-2	126	41
91	IV B	Fortifications	131	41
92	IV B	Fortifications, S-34	131	59, 65
93	IV B	Fortifications, EC-2	132	65

AREA VI (Northwest)

9	IV B	Room RE	141	74
10	IV B	Room R	141	74
11	IV B	Room R	141	74
12	IV B	Room RE	141	74
13	IV B	Room R	141	74
14	IV B	Room R	141	74
15	IV B	Room RE	141	74

16	IV B	Room R	141	74
17	post-IV B	"Garden Fence and Wall"	143	75
18	post-IV B	"Garden Fence and Wall"	143	75
18n	IV B	Room R	141	74
22	IV B	Room RE	141	74
23	IV B	Room R	141	74
24	IV B	S-42	141	59, 74
25	IV B	Room R	141	74
27	IV B	Room R	141	74
28	IV B	S-42	141	59, 74
29	IV B	Room R	141	74
30	IV B	Room R	141	74
32	IV B	Room R	141	74

AREA VII (West Casemate and Wall S)

3b	II	Wall S	126	24
3N	IV B	WCas-North	137	69
4	V	WCas-North	144	77
5a	IV B	WCas, to North	137	69
5b	III B	WCas Walls	128	41
6	IV B	WCas-North	137	69
7	IV B	WCas-North	137	69
8	IV B	C-2; WCas-North	136, 137	69
9	IV B	WCas-North	137	69
10a	IV B	C-2	136	41, 69
10b	III A	C-2	128	41
12	IV B	WCas-North	137	69
13	IV B	WCas-North	137	69
14	IV B	Room O	136	69
15E	IV B	Area Q	136	69
15W	III A	C-2	128	41
16	IV B	Area Q	136	69
17	IV B	WCas-North	137	69
18a	IV B	WCas-North	137	69
20	I	Wall S	125	25
21	II	Wall S	126	24
22	I	Wall S	125	

AREA VIII (Northeast)

5	IV B	H House, Late Phase	133	68
6	IV B	Fortifications; H House, Late Phase	132, 133	65, 68
8	IV B	Fortifications; W of H wall	132, 134	65, 68
9	IV B	H House, Late Phase	133	68
10	IV B	H House, Early Phase	133	68
11 (=9)				
12 (=9)				
13 (=9)				
14	IV B	H House, Early Phase	133	68
15	IV B	H House, Early Phase	133	68
16	III A	Room C	127	41, 68
17 (=15)				
18	III A	Room C	127	41, 68
19	III A	Room C	127	41, 68
20	IV B	H House, Early Phase	133	68
21	IV B	Fortifications; H House, Late Phase	132, 133	68

AREA IX (Northeast)

4	V	S-27	133	59, 68
5 (=4)				
7	III B	Room NE	128	43
10	IV	S-27	133	68
12	IV B	S-28	133	43, 59
13	III B	S-28	128	43, 59
14	III B	Room NE	128	41-43
19	III B	S-28	128	43, 59

AREA X (Northwest)

3	post-IV B	"Garden Fence and Soil"	143	75
4	post-IV B	"Garden Fence and Soil"	143	75
6	post-IV B	"Garden Fence and Soil"	143	75
8	III B	Pottery Cache	131	46
9a	IV	Area V	142	75
9b	III B	Pottery Cache	131	
14	IV B	Area V	142	75
15	IV B	Room TV	142	75
16	IV B	Room TV	142	75

AREA XI (Northwest)

2	post-IV B	"Garden Fence and Soil"	143	75
2a	post-IV B	"Garden Fence and Soil"	143	75
7	IV B	Room TV	142	75
8	IV B	Room T	142	75
13	IV B	Room T	142	75
18	IV B	Room T	143	75
19	IV B	Room T	143	75
20	IV B	Room T	143	75
21	IV B	Room T	143	75

AREA XII (Southwest)

2	V	Area K	143	77
3 (=6)				
4 (=6)				
5	V	Area K	144	77
6	V	Area K	144	77
7	V	Area K	144	77
9	V	Area K	144	77
11	IV B	Area K	139	73
12	IV B	Area K	139	73
13	IV B	Area K	139	73
14	IV B	Area K	139	73
16	IV B	Area K	139	73
17	IV B	Area K	139	73
18	IV B	Area K	139	73
19	IV B	Area K	139	73
20	IV B	Area K	139	73
21	IV B	Area K	139	73
22	IV B	Area K	139	73
23	IV B	Area K	139	73
24	IV B	Room J	138	72
25	IV B	Room J	138	72
26	IV B	Room J	138	73
28	III B	S-40	130	44, 59, 73

AREA XIII (Southwest Fortifications)

2	II	Fortress-W	125	23, 40
6	IV B	Fortress-W	131	65
8	III A	Revetment-NW	126	40
10	II	Fortress-NW	125	23
11	II	Fortress-NW	125	23
12	II	Fortress-NW	125	23
15	II	Fortress-NW	125	23

AREA XIV (Northwest)

2	post-IV B	"Garden Fence and Soil"	143	77
3	post-IV B	"Garden Fence and Soil"	143	77
9	IV B	Area Z	140	74
12	IV B	Area Z	140	74
13	IV B	Area Z	140	74
14	IV B	Area Z	140	74
16	IV B	Area Z, S-41	140	59, 74
17	IV C	Area Z, S-41	140	59, 74
18	IV B	Area Z	140	74
19	IV B	Area Z	140	74
20	IV B	Area Z	140	74
21	IV A	Area Z	140	65, 74
22	IV A	Area Z	140	65, 74
23	IV A	Area Z	140	65, 74
24	IV A	Area Z	140	65, 74
26	IV A	Area Z	140	65, 74

AREA XV (Northwest)

3	V	Area U	144	77
6	IV B	Area Zs	139	73
7	IV B	Area U	139	73
8	IV B	Area U	139	73
10	IV B	Area Zs	139	73
11	IV B	Area U	139	
14	IV B	Area U	139	73
15	IV B	Area U	139	63, 73
16	IV A	Area U	139	63, 73
17	III A	Area U	130	44

AREA XVI (Northeast)

4	III B	Room NE	128	43
5	III B	Area W	128	43
6	III B	Area Y	128	43
7	III A	Area Y	128	43
9	III B	Room NE	128	43
10	III A	Room NE	128	41
11	III A	Room NE	128	43
12	III A	Room NE	128	43
14	III A	Room NE	128	41

AREA XVII (West Fortifications)

3	IV B	WCas-to North	137	69
4	II	Wall S	126	
5	IV B	WCas-to North	137	69

8	I	Wall S	125	25
11	(=3)			
12	II	Wall S	126	24
14	I	Wall S	125	25

AREA XVIII (Mid-Field)

	IV B	S-35	135	59, 69
	pre-III A	S-36	129	43, 59
	V	S-37 top	144	59, 69, 78
	IV C	S-37	135	59, 69
	pre-III A	S-38	129	43, 59
	pre-III A	S-39	129	43, 59
	III B	Gray Ash	129	43

AREA XIX (South of Northeast III Building)

2ext	III A	Stratified debris	129	43
3ext	II	S-24	126	25, 59
4	IV B	Stratified debris	134	68
6	III A	Stratified debris	129	43, 68
7	IV B	S-25	135	43, 59, 68

AREA XX (South of Hellenistic House)

3	IV B	Stratified debris	134	68
4	IV B	Stratified debris	134	
5	IV B	Stratified debris	134	68
6	IV B	Stratified debris	134	
7	IV B	Stratified debris	134	68
8	IV B	Fortifications; W of H wall	132, 134	65, 68
9	IV B	Fortifications; W of H wall	132, 134	65, 68
10	IV B	Stratified debris	134	68
11	IV B	Stratified debris	134	68
12	IV B	S-26	135	59, 68
2ext	IV C	Stratified debris	134	68
4ext	IV C	Stratified debris	134	68
4e-c	IV B	over S-23	135	59-61, 68
5ext	IV B	Fortifications; W of H wall	132, 134	65, 68

AREA XXI (North of Albright's Excavations on East)

3	IV B	Fortifications; W of H wall	132, 134	65, 68
4	IV B	S-22	135	59, 68
5	III	S-21	129	43, 59

AREA XXII (Northwest)

2	V	Area Uw	144	77
3	V	Area Uw	144	77
4	V	Area Uw	144	74, 77
5	V	Area Uw	144	77
7	IV B	Area Uw	139	73
8	IV B	Area Uw	140	73
9	IV B	Area Uw	140	73
10	IV B	Area Uw	140	73
11	IV A	Area Uw, S-43	140	59, 63, 74

AREA XXIII (North of Albright's Excavations on East)

7	IV B	Stratified debris	135	68
8	IV B	Stratified debris	135	68
12	I	Bedrock Cavity	125	25
13	I	Bedrock Cavity	125	25

AREA XXIV (East Casemate)

8	III A	Room EC-3	127	41
9	III A	Room EC-3	127	41
10	III A	Room EC-3	127	41
11	III A	Room EC-3	127	41
12	III A	Room EC-3	127	41

Appendix B
Loci Descriptions

See plan 1 (excavated remains) and plan 2 (areas of excavation).

PERIOD I

Locus		Description	Pottery Period	Published pl.	Other registered artifacts
FORTIFICATIONS (Plan 13)					
Wall S (pp. 24-26; plan 6, sec. c-d; pls. 2d, 3a-c)					
XVII	8	floor, sub L. 4, E of Wall S	few I	47:9	27
	14	sub L. 8 to bedrock	Iron I	47:14	
VII	20	sub L. 5 & 18 on bedrock & sub Wall S level	I few II	47:15	
	22	sub chalky layer, L. 21	I prob. II ?		
North of Revetment (p. 25; pl. 11a)					
I	44	inside diagonal wall in Room E	Iron I		
NORTH OF ALBRIGHT'S EXCAVATIONS ON THE EAST					
Bedrock Cavity (p. 25)					
XXIII	12	dark brown, sub L. 11	I		
	13	sub L. 12, compact clay in cavity in bedrock	I	47:2, 8, 10, 11	

PERIOD II

Locus		Description	Pottery Period	Published pl.	Other registered artifacts
FORTIFICATIONS (Plan 13)					
Fortress-NW (pp. 23-24; fig. 13; plan 7, sec. g-h; pl. 2a-c)					
XIII	10	hard debris; N end of tower	II	48:9, 24, 25, 31, 32	
	11	sub L. 10	II	48:33, 34	
	12	sub L. 11 to bedrock	II		
	15	sub L. 14 rubble around buttress at NW corner of tower	II	48:19, 35	
Fortress-W (p. 23; plan 7, sec. e-f; pl. 4c)					
XIII	2	sub-sf. between III tower facing and III sloping revetment	II	48:1, 6, 7, 10, 12, 13, 14, 15, 16, 23, 28, 30, 36	
			I	47:5, 7	

125

Fortress-N (p. 24; pl. 5a)

II	46	base of revetment, sub L. 2E, in line with Fortress and Wall S	II	

Wall S (pp. 24-26; plan 6, sec. c-d; pls. 2d, 3a-c, 4a)

VII	3b	on, alongside, and removal of Wall S (except N end where contaminated)	II I	48:8, 11 47:6
	21	sub Wall S in Trench T	few II	
XVII	4	sub L. 3 fallen stones to Floor 8, E of Wall S	II	48:5, 17, 18, 26, 29
	12	Floor, sub L. 11 vs. E side of Wall S	II	

SOUTH OF NORTHEAST III BUILDING

Silo 24 (pp. 25, 59; figs. 22, 23; plan 11)

XIX	3ext	silt layer in silo	II I ?	145

PERIOD III
(plan 14)

Locus		Description	Pottery		Other registered artifacts
			Period	Published pl.	
REVETMENT					

Trench at NW Corner of Period II Tower (p. 40, plan 7, sec. e-f; pls. 3d, 4c)

XIII′	8	dismantling outer III wall of sloping revetment	III A few II	57:5, 12; 67:13	

North of revetment (p. 40; pls. 5a-b, 11b, 12c)

II	2E	vs. N face (in Area P) (fig. 28)	III A II		
	22	vs. N face (in Area P)	III A		
I	26	deposit between 5 large stones and revetment, Room E	III A II		62
	49	pit N of revetment in bedrock, Room F	III A	50:1, 62:9; 64:5-7, 9, 15	

CASEMATE WALLS

East Casemate (pp. 40-41)

Room EC-2 (pl. 18b)

V	89	vs. W wall of EC-2	III A	
	90	sub L. 89	III A	49:14, 28; 57:4; 68:6, 7

Room C (plan 8, sec. j-k; pl. 21b-d)

V	37	wall in Room C	III A	
	45	pit in NE corner	III	

	50	occ. debris by Wall 37	III A II		
VIII	16	in S, E along terrace wall	III A II	50:2	30, 31, 39
	18	lower debris in S	III A one II		
	19,	stone pile removal in S	III	50:3	

Room EC-3 (pl. 4b)

XXIV	8	in & on top of E wall	III A	49:24; 62:14-16, 29; 66:8; 67:12
	9	sub L. 8, E of E wall	III A	
	10	cleaning top of E wall	few III A	
	11	sub L. 9, to floor	III A	50:5, 6
	12	sub L. 11, below floor	III A	49:23; 50:4

West Casemate (p. 41; plan 5, sec. n-s; pl. 5b)

Room L   (pl. 5c)

II	29	deposit, sub Floor 28	III	49:15; 50:13; 63:19; 64:16
	30	on floor, sub L. 29	III	57:10
	31	deposit E & below L. 30 level	III	50:14; 63:20; 64:28
	35	sub L. 30	III	49:9; 50:12; 27:9; 63:7, 17, 18; 68:9, 11; 69:14; 71:4-6
	36	Floor, sub L. 31	—	
	37	soil W of L. 36	III A II	

Room N   (pl. 5d)

II	19	on floor (IV B pottery to floor)	III A	
	27	E and sub L. 19 level	III A II	
	34	sub L. 27 to bedrock	III A II	

Room O

II	15	removing large stones	III A	50:9-11; 67:10
	17	broken floor, sub L. 15	III A II	60:12; 71:2

Walls

II	18	removing crosswall N/O	III A II	
	32	40 cm wall W side of Room L on L. 30 (pl. 5c)	III A	57:7; 63:6, 27; 71:7

VII	5b	northern section of outer casemate, lower course (plan 6, sec. c-d; pl. 6a)	III II	48:4, 27, 37	

Cistern 2 (pp. 41, 69, plan 10, pl. 6b)

VII	10b	lower levels	III A few II	57:23; 66:4; 67:11, 14	111, 112 155, 159, 267
	15W	above and in channel to C-2	III A II		138

NORTHEAST III BUILDING   (pp. 41-43; fig. 18)

Room NE   (pl. 8a-b)

XVI	4	stone scree to black	III	49:10; 50:15; 57:18; 63:3, 11, 34, 46, 48; 68:10	
	9	sub L. 4 in burn	III IV B		150
	10	sub L. 9, E Foundation Trench of Wall NE/W	III A		
	11	sub L. 9	III A		42, 44, 95
	12	sub 11	III A		
	13	stone removal in south	III A		
	14	sub L. 9, deepening & widening Foundation Trench 10	III A		
IX	7	in NW between W wall and angular wall	III	50:19; 57:8; 63:44, 45; 64:20	
	14	in NW sub L. 7	III	50:16, 18; 63:30	

Area Y

XVI	6	sub-surface	III	63:10, 28; 69:13	
	7	cleaning floor, sub L. 6	III A		

Area W

XVI	5	sub-surface, around rocky outcrop	III few II few I	49:16; 50:17; 57:6, 12, 15, 16, 24; 63:1, 2, 4, 5, 9, 42, 47; 64:29; 68:3 47:4	

Silo 28   (pp. 43, 59; figs. 22, 23; plans 8, sec. j-k, 11; pl. 8b-d)

IX	13	lowest level	III	64:17; 66:9, 10; 68:17	60
	19	blocking in L. 13	III		

SOUTH OF NORTHEAST III BUILDING   (p. 43)

Stratified Debris

XIX	2ext	NW of Albright's excavations	III A	49:26, 27; 50:7, 8; 57:12, 14, 19, 20, 25; 64:8	
			II	48:21	
			I	47:3, 12	
	6	S of Room NE	III A		
			II		

Silo 21   (p. 59; figs. 22, 23; plan 12; pl. 9a-b, 10a)

XXI	5	in Albright's Room 17	III	68:13	
			II		

MID-FIELD   (p. 43; pl. 10d)

Gray Ash Deposit

XVIII		E of center N-S wall in E extension	III	69:15	
			II		

Silo 36   (p. 59; figs. 22-23; plan 11)

XVIII		center area of S extension	pre-III A	49:1-6, 12, 18-22; 50:28-30, 33, 34; 57:1-3, 21, 22; 60:1-5, 7; 62:1-8, 10-13, 17-25, 27, 28; 64:1-4, 10-13; 66:1-3; 67:1-5, 7-9, 16-22; 71:1	59
			II	48:2, 3	

Silo 38   (p. 59; figs. 22-23; plan 11)

XVIII		center area of S extension	pre-III A	49:7, 13; 50:31, 32; 64:14; 67:6, 15; 70:1	80, 142, 264, 265
			II		

Silo 39   (p. 59; figs. 22-23; plan 11)

XVIII		center area of S extension	pre-III A	49:8; 50:35, 36; 62:26, 30	61

SOUTHWEST ROOMS   (p. 44).

Room E   (pl. 11b)

I	26	scree in E next to revetment	III A		62
			II		
	27	scree in E, N of L. 26 and 5 stones	III A		
			II		
	41	surface in W (not stratified but early material)	III A	71:13	122
			II		

	42	surface in W (not stratified but early material)	III A II		
	45	burnt deposit, sub L. 41 and 42 to bedrock	III	49:25; 50:20-25; 57: 17; 61:10; 63:8, 12, 13, 15, 16, 43; 67:23, 24; 68:2, 8; 69:19	58
	46	sub L. 27	—		

Room D (pl. 11c-d)

I	16	N of Wall D/E	few III		

Room F (fig. 19; pl. 12b-c)

I	49	pit N of revetment	III A	50:1; 62:9; 64:5-7, 9, 15	
	50	Wall F/G supporting channel	few III A		

Room G (fig. 19; pl. 12a-b)

I	35	removal of debris around plastered basin complex	III	50:26, 27; 63:14, 21, 26; 64:27; 69:12	

Room J (pl. 12b)

I		sub-29 floor level below L. 29	—		

Silo 40 (pp. 44, 59; figs. 22, 23; plan 11; pl. 13d)

XII	28	S-40, below Wall K/J	III B II	52:1-12; 68:18	

NORTHWEST (pp. 44-46)

Area U (plan 5, sec. n-s; pl. 15c)

XV	17	pit	III A II		

Cistern 1 (pp. 44-46; plan 10; pls. 16c-d, 17a-c)

III	28	in cistern: sub L. 24	III A-B	52:13-16; 59:5; 64:19; 65:7; 70:6, 7	97, 98 99, 104, 107
	29	in cistern: sub L. 28	III A-B	63:23; 64:34; 65:5, 6, 8	152
	30	in cistern: sub L. 29	III B	35:4; 51:5-11, 13-19; 53:1-4; 54:5-8; 55:9-13;	74, 75, 76, 77, 78, 81,
	31	in clay, sub L. 30	III B	56:14-27; 58:2, 3, 5-7; 59:1, 2; 60:8;	83, 96, 101, 106,
	32	= L. 31 in passageway	III B	65:1-4, 9-12; 66:5, 6; 67:25-27; 68:4,	108, 109, 110, 156,
	33	= L. 30 over clay beyond passageway	III B	5, 12; 69:2-8, 10, 11, 16-18; 70:2, 5; 71:3, 8-11	157
	34	= L. 31 clay, beyond passage	III B		

Pottery Cache   (pl. 16c)

Locus		Description	Pottery Period	Published pl.
X	8	in Room V beneath "Garden Fence" W of C-1	III B	51:1-4, 12; 58:1; 59:3; 69:1, 9
	9b	black earth W of C-1	III B II MB II	

PERIOD IV

Locus		Description	Pottery Period	Published pl.	Other registered artifacts

FORTIFICATIONS

Southwest   (p. 65; plan 7, sec. e-f; pl. 4b)

XIII	6	W of lowest wall	IV B III A II		

Northeast   (p. 65; fig. 25; plan 8, sec. j-k, 9, sec. l-m; pl. 18a-d)

V	49	wide wall, perhaps forming outer wall of H tower	—		
	59	dirt & scree in Room EC-1	IV B III		
	62	foundation trench for buttress, L. 66	IV B III		
	66	buttress, NW corner of EC-1	—		
	74	large stones between inner casemate & H wall	—		
	76	sub L. 24 scree, N of EC-1	IV III		
	79	debris S in EC-1	IV B III II		
	81	sub L. 24, E of outer casemate wall	V IV B III II EB ?		
	83	within "tower" walls	IV B III		
	91	large stones, sub L. 81 between outer casemate and Wall 49	IV B III		
	92	*Silo 34,* sub stone basin (p. 59; figs. 22, 23; plan 12)	IV B III		

	93	sub L. 24 in EC-2	IV B III I		
VIII	6	large stones between inner casemate & H wall; cleaning	IV B III		
	8	cleaning and clearing west of H wall	IV B III	72:18, 73:18	
	21	E wall of Room C	—		
XX	8	vs. W face of H wall	IV B III		
	9	sub L. 8 to bedrock	IV B III II		79
	5ext	near H wall to bedrock, plaster floor	IV III	70:10, 11; 75:13, 17; 76:4; 80:10	
XXI	3	sub-sf. near H wall (pl. 9c)	IV B III	78:13	

NORTHEAST HELLENISTIC HOUSE (pp. 65-68; figs. 26, 27; plan 8, sec. j-k)

Pre-Building Phase (pls. 19a-d, 21c; silos: p. 59; figs. 22, 23; plan 12)

V	34	*Silo 30*, Room A	IV B III	79:3, 20	22 (coin) 43
	57	*Silo 33*, sub Wall A/B-C	IV B III		
	57L	*Silo 33*, lower level	IV A III	79:15-18	
	65	*Silo 32*, Room A, sub Early Phase floor	IV B III		
	67	*Silo 32*, on floor of silo	IV B III		15 (coin) 16 (coin)

Early Phase (fig. 26; pls. 18d, 19d, 20a-d, 21a-b)

V	32	floor, Room A, plastered in part	IV B III		37, 134
	33	*Silo 31*, Room A (p. 59; figs. 22, 23; plan 12)	IV B III		
	40	*Silo 29*, Room B (p. 59; figs. 22, 23; plan 12)	IV B III		
	44	plaster trough along N wall of Room C	IV B III		
	54	Fill for Floor 32	IV B III	73:17; 77:16, 21; 79:19	17 (coin) 18 (coin) 50

VIII	10	foundation trench for Wall B/C on E	IV B III		
	14	foundation trench for Wall B/C on W	IV B III	75:11	
	15	hard-packed floor in Room C	IV B III		
	20	hard-packed floor on bedrock in Room B	—		

Late Phase (fig. 27; pl. 20d)

V	3	stone scree above Room A in W, Room B-C in W	IV B III		
	8	stone scree above Room B-C in E	IV B III	78:4	149, 171
	10	fill in Room B-C	IV B III		
	21	upper floor in Room A	IV B III	78:1, 5	
	29	fill for Floor 21	IV B III	72:19; 77:17; 78:15	
	53	E wall of Room A	—		
	74	large stones between wall 53 and inner casemate	—		
VIII	5	around stone scree in Room B-C	IV B III II		8 (coin)
	6	large stones between east wall (21) & inner casemate	IV B III		
	9	fill covering Wall B/C	IV B III		
	21	E wall of Room C (pl. 21b)	—		

Silo 27 (p. 59; figs. 22, 23; plan 11; pl. 3b)

IX	4	top	V IV B	
	10	lower	IV B III II	

Silo 28 (p. 59; figs. 22, 23; plan 11; pl. 8b)

IX	12	upper layer	IV B III	76:7

SOUTH OF HELLENISTIC HOUSE & NORTH OF ALBRIGHT'S EXCAVATIONS (p. 68)

West side of Hellenistic Wall

VIII	8	vs. wall, sub-sf. debris	IV B	72:18; 73:18	
			III		
XX	8	vs. wall, sub scree, L. 7	IV B		
			III		
	9	sub L. 8 to bedrock	IV B		79
			III		
			II		
	5ext	near wall to bedrock	IV B	70:10, 11; 75:13, 17; 76:4; 80:10	
			III		
XXI	3	sub-sf. near H wall (pl. 9c)	IV B	78:13	
			III		

Stratified debris

XIX	4	sub-sf., scree & soil across square	IV B		
			III		
			II		
XX	3	sub-sf., whole square	IV B		57
			III		
			II		
	4	sub L. 3	IV B		
			III		
			II		
	5	sub L. 4, W side of scree	IV B	72:15; 75:7; 77:1, 12, 18	
			III		
	6	sub L. 4, E side of scree	IV B	72:16, 17	55
			III		
	7	sub L. 6	IV B		
			III	70:12	
			II	48:38, 39	
	10	sub L. 9, S side of square on bedrock	IV B		
			III		
	11	in NW of square, as L. 3 & 4	IV B		
			III		
	2ext	sub-sf. to south	IV B, C	72:8-14; 73:4-7; 75:24; 76:8; 78:10	
			III		
			II		
	4ext	sub L. 2ext, W side over S-23 & to bedrock	IV B, C	72:1-7; 73:1-3, 24; 75:22, 23; 76:4	
			III		

XXIII	7	sub-surface	IV B			
			III			
			II			
	8	sub-surface	IV B			
			III			
			II	48:22		

Silo 22   (p. 59; figs. 22-23; plan 12; pl. 9a)

| XXI | 4 | N of Albright's excavations | IV B | 75:20 | | |
| | | | III | | | |

Silo 23   (pp. 59-61; fig. 22-24; plan 12; pl. 10a-c)

| XX | 4e-c | over S-23 opening | IV B | | | |
| | | | III | | | |

Silo 25   (p. 59; figs. 22, 23; plan 12; pl. 9c)

| XIX | 7 | S of NE III Building | IV B | | | |
| | | | III | | | |

Silo 26   (p. 59; figs. 22, 23; plan 12; pl. 9d)

| XX | 12 | S of H House, Room B | IV B | | | |
| | | | III | | | |

MID-FIELD   (pp. 68-70; pl. 10d)

Silo 35   (p. 59; figs. 22, 23; plan 11)

| XVIII | | in N trench | IV B | | | |
| | | | III | | | |

Silo 37   (p. 59; figs. 22, 23; plan 11)

| XVIII | | in S extension, center | IV C | 43:2; 72:31; 73:21, 22; 76:9; 78:9 | | 223 |
| | | | III | | | 224, 225 |

WEST CASEMATE ROOMS   (p. 69; fig. 28; pl. 5b)

Area P   (pl. 6c)

II	5	paving stone floor in N	—			
	9	sub-sf. debris down to surface	IV B			
			III			
	39	N-S wall 5m E of inner casemate	—			
	40	floor W of Wall 39, E of inner casemate (pl. 5a)	—			
	41	sub Floor 5	IV B			
			III			
			II			
	42	floor E of Wall 39	IV B			
			III			

Area Q   (pls. 4a, 7a-b)

II	12	upper floor = L. VII-16	IV C III	72:30; 79:2		door socket
	43	fill for Floor 12	IV B III II			
	44	lower floor, sub L. 43	—			
	45	lowest fill on bedrock, sub Floor 44	IV B III			144, 163
VII	15E	sub-sf. stratified debris, above Floor 16	IV B III	77:15		14 (coin) 177
	16	floor = L. II-12	IV B			

Room O

II	14	sub-sf. stratified debris, = L. VII-14	IV B III			
VII	14	sub-sf. stratified debris, = L. II-14	IV B III II			

Room N

II	19	sub-sf. down to floor	IV B III			

Room L

II	4	N-S wall on west	IV B III II			
	28	floor below sf. & IV B debris	—			

Room M   (pl. 7c)

II	23	sub-sf. debris	IV B III		61:8	
	24	floor sub L. 23	IV B III	75:18		
	25	plastered floor sub L. 24	IV B III			

Cistern 2   (pp. 41, 69; plan 10; pl. 6a-b)

VII	8	debris above C-2	IV B III			27
	10a	shaft of C-2	IV B III	73:40		26, 71

North (fig. 29; plans 5, sec. n-s, 6, sec. c-d; pls. 6a, 2d)

VII	3N	H disturbance N end of Wall S	IV B III II		9
	5a	removing loose stones & upper course of outer casemate	IV B III II	76:18	
	6	rockfall W of outer casemate	IV B III II		
	7	rockfall W of outer casemate, S of L. 6	IV B III		
	8	rockfall E of outer casemate and above C-2	IV B III		
	9	soil below L. 5a toward S (below stones A-D)	IV B III II		
	12	soil sub L. 6	IV B III	72:22	
	13	soil sub L. 7	IV B III	72:21	
	17	sub L. 3N	IV B III II I		
	18a	rockfall E of outer casemate	IV B III II		
XVII	3	sub-sf. debris above floors, whole area inc. L. 11 in balk	IV B	72:25	
	5	sub L. 3 in S	IV B III II	72:23, 24; 73:39; 77:20; 78:8	

SOUTHWEST ROOMS (pp. 69-73)

Room F (fig. 30; pls. 12b-c, 13a-b)

I	8	debris around plastered basins	IV B III	73:16, 29, 30
	11	cleaning face of outer casemate	IV B III	73:31-33; 77:3
	47	below plastered basins	IV B III	 61:13
	48	wall sub L. 8 supporting Basin b (plan 5, sec. n-s)	—	

Room G   (pls. 11d, 13b)

I	9	sub-sf. stone scree in Rooms G, J, & D	IV B III	73:34; 75:5, 15; 76:10
	14	sub-L. 9, fine soil, some scree	IV B III	61:20
	20	scree & soil above Period III basins, down to surface	IV B III	

Room J   (pls. 11c-d, 12b, 13b-d)

I	9	as in Room G			
	14	as in Room G			
	18	sub L. 14, scree in SW Room J on occupational level L. 29	IV B III II	77:11	
	19	sub L. 14, SE Room J	IV B III	75:3, 4; 77:23	
	21	poor wall in Room J	—		
	22	lower scree, sub L. 19 & Wall 21 removal	IV B III		
	23	poor wall N to S from Wall D/G	—		
	28	removal Wall 23	IV B III		
	29	sub L. 22, occupational level & below to surface	IV B III	78:12	147
	32	E doorway in Wall G/J (plan 5, sec. n-s)	IV B III		
	34	W doorway in Wall G/J	IV B III		
XII	24	sub-sf. N in Room J	IV B III	73:37 68:16	139
	25	scree in L. 24	IV B III II		125
	26	depression N in Room J	—		

Room D   (pl. 11c)

I	9	as in Room G		
	14	as in Room G		
	43	sub L. 14	IV B III	

Room E

I	25	sub-sf. L. 24	IV B III II	

Area K   (fig. 31; pls. 13d, 14a)

XII	11	scree below Roman levels	IV B III	73:38; 80:9
	12	circular area of scree & loose soil	IV B	72:28, 29; 73:14; 76:17; 78:7
	13	plastered basin sub L. 12	IV B	
	14	sub L. 11, outside L. 12	IV B III	
	16	sub L. 14	IV B	73:13
	17	sub L. 16	IV B III	73:15
	18	scree from L. 17	IV B III	73:12; 75:9, 25; 77:2
	19	sub L. 17 & 18	IV B III	77:13
	20	low wall enclosing L. 12	—	
	21	sub L. 19 & scree removal to floor	IV B III	
	22	sub L. 12 to paving stones	IV B III	
	23	removal Wall 20	IV B III	73:35, 36; 75:19

NORTHWEST   (pp. 73-75)

Area U   (plan 5, sec. n-s; pls. 14b, 15b-c)

XV	7	sub-sf., sub L. 3	IV B III	72:26
	8	floor, sub L. 7	—	
	11	beside Wall H and removal of stones A, B, C, D	IV B III	72:27; 73:11
	14	fill for Floor 8	IV B III	
	15	floor, sub L. 14	—	
	16	sub-Floor 15	IV A III	73:26

Area Zs   (plan 5, sec. n-s; 6, sec. a-b; pl. 15b)

XV	6	sub-sf., sub L. 3, parallel L. XV-7	IV B III II	
	10	floor, sub L. 6, parallel L. XV-8	—	

Area Uw   (pl. 14c)

XXII	7	floor, sub L. 5	—	

	8	fill for Floor 7	IV B III		
	9	floor, sub L. 8 in center	—		
	10	fill for Floor 9	IV B III		

Silo 43   (p. 59; figs. 22, 23; plan 11; pl. 14c)

XXII	11	from silo	IV A III II	73:23; 75:21; 76:1-3; 77:10; 78:11; 79:1; 80:1, 2 61:18; 68:14, 15	129, 133

Area Z   (plan 5, sec. n-s; pl. 16b)

XIV	9	sub-rockfall to floor	IV B III II		
	12	sub-sf. removal	IV B III	78:3	
	13	sub L. 12 with floor	IV B III II		
	14	sub L. 9 to floor	IV B III		
	18	sub L. 14 to Floor 19	IV B III		
	19	floor, sub L. 18	IV B III		
	20	fill for Floor 19	IV B III II		
	21	on basin and channel	IV A III		
	22	in bedrock basin	IV A III		
	23	N of basin	IV A III		
	24	bedrock channel	IV A III		
	26	N end of channel	IV A III II		113 (coin)

Silo 41   (p. 59; figs. 22, 23; plan 11; pl. 16b)

XIV	16	top of silo	IV B III		12 (coin) 46, 47
	17	sub L. 16 in silo	IV C	74:1-8	

Room R   (plan 6, sec. a-b; pls. 14b, d, 15a)

VI	10	upper floor in N	IV B		
	11	upper floor in S	IV B		
	13	second floor in S	IV B	72:21; 80:11	
	14	second floor in N	IV B III	75:26; 76:16	
	16	lower floor	IV B III		
	18n	N of channel to occupation level	IV B III		
	23	fill for lower Floor 16	IV B III		
	25	sub scree on floor W of above	IV B III	75:14; 79:6-14 61:19	
	27	channel	IV B III		
	29	sub L. 18n on bedrock	IV B III		
	30	sub L. 25	IV B III I		130, 132
	32	removing channel	IV B III I	73:8, 25; 75:2	

Room RE   (pls. 14d, 15a)

VI	9	upper floor	IV B		148
	12	second floor	IV B	72:22; 76:15	
	15	lower floor	IV B III	77:9	
	22	fill for Floor 15	IV B III II		

Silo 42   (p. 59; figs. 22, 23; plan 11; pl. 16a)

VI	24	in silo	IV B III	72:20; 73:9; 75:1; 76:5, 13, 14; 78:2, 6, 14; 79:4	25 (coin)
	28	settling basin in silo	IV B III	77:8	

Room CRn   (pl. 16c)

III	8	floor to E, = L. 9	IV B III		
	9	floor to W, = L. 8	IV B III		

Room CR (pls. 14d, 16c-d)

III	14	sub-sf. rockfall over C-1	IV III II	73:19; 76:19	21 (coin)

Cistern 1 (plan 10; pls. 16d, 17)

III	19	top layer	IV III		
	20	sub L. 19, black dirt	IV III	77:19, 22; 80:4 61:4	40, 52, 153
	21	sub L. 20	IV III	80:3 64:38; 69:21; 70:8	41, 45, 53 54
	22	sub L. 21	IV III	80:5, 6 60:10; 61:12, 15-17; 63:22, 24, 25, 29, 31-33, 35-41; 64:18, 21-26, 30-33, 35-37, 39; 69:22	29, 33
	24	sub L. 22	IV III	75:27; 77:7; 80:7 49:11, 17; 52:17; 58:4; 59:4; 60:6, 9, 11; 61:1-3, 5-7, 9, 11; 65:13; 66:7; 69:20; 70:3, 4, 9; 71:14	32, 34, 35, 36, 48, 100, 102, 103, 105, 158
	27	parallel L. 22 in balk	IV	73:20; 78:16; 80:8	28

Area V (pl. 16c)

X	9a	blackened occupational debris	IV B III II MB II		
	14	W end of Wall V/TV to bedrock	IV B III		

Room TV (pls. 14b, 15c)

X	15	sub-sf. to floor	IV B		
	16	sub L. 15, removing floor to bedrock	IV B III		
XI	7	sub-sf. to floor = L. X-15 (plan 6, sec. a-b)	IV B III		

Room T (pls. 14b, 15a)

XI	8	sub-sf. to floor, parallels L. XI-7	IV B III		
	13	floor E of Wall H, W of Wall 21	—		

	18	sub Floor 13	IV B	73:10, 27; 75:6, 16; 77:24	131 (coin)
			III		
	19	sub L. 8 & L. 18, in W to bedrock	IV B		
	20	sub L. 8, in E to bedrock	IV B		
			III		
	21	removal of thin N-S wall in center, sub L. 18	IV B	73:28	
			III		

POST IV B IN NORTHWEST

"Garden Fence and Soil"   (p. 75; fig. 32; plan 6, sec. a-b; pl. 15a)

III	15	stone scree from fence	IV B		
			III		
			II		
			EB		
	17	garden fence removal	IV B		
			III		
VI	17	stone scree from fence	IV B		
			III		
			II		
	18	garden fence removal	IV B		
			III		
X	3	debris above sterile soil	IV B		
			III		
	4	fine sterile soil	—		
	6	garden fence	IV B		
			III		
XI	2	fine sterile soil	—		
	2a	debris above sterile soil	IV B		
			III		
XIV	2	debris above sterile soil	IV B		
			III		
	3	fine sterile soil	—		

PERIOD V

| | | | Pottery | | Other registered |
| Locus | | Description | Period | Published pl. | artifacts |

SOUTHWEST ROOMS   (p. 77)

Area K

XII	2	sub-sf. debris	V	81:10, 11	
			IV B		
			III		
			II		
			MB		

	5	occupational level, sub L. 2	—		
	6	sub L. 5	V		glass
			IV B		
			III		
			II		
	7	occupation level, sub L. 6	V	81:1, 8, 12	glass
			IV B		lead
			III		
	9	occupation level, sub L. 7	V	81:2, 9	
			IV B		
			III		
			II		

NORTHWEST (p. 77)

Area Uw

XXII	2	sub-sf. layer over floor	V	81:13	glass
			IV		90 (coin)
			III		
			II		
	3	sub-sf. layer over floor	Turkish		
			V	81:4	glass
			IV		19 (coin)
			III		
			II		
	4	floor, sub L. 3 and 4	—		
	5	fill for Floor 4	IV		glass
			III		

Area U (plan 5, sec. a-b)

XV	3	sub-sf. layer	V		
			IV		
			III		

WEST CASEMATE (pp. 77-78)

To north

VII	4	sub-sf. debris over	V	81:3	glass
		outer casemate & H debris	IV B		
			III		

MID-FIELD (p. 78)

Silo 37

XVIII		top of silo	V	81:5	
		(figs. 22, 23; plan 11)	IV		
			III		

Appendix C
List of Registered Artifacts

No.	Artifact	Locus	Stratum	Photo pl.	Drawing pl.	Discussion p.
1	ostracon	II-sf.	—	31:1	31:2	113-15
2	rubbing stone	II-sf.	—	24:5		110
3	coin	II-sf.	—	22:4		109
4	coin	II-sf.	—	23:6		109
5	coin	VI-4	—	22:7	Fig. 35	109
6	ring	VII-3b	II	26:10		111
7	loom weight	IX-2	—			110
8	coin	VIII-5	IV B	22:2		109
9	spindle whorl	VII-5a	IV B	25:10	27:13	110
10	coin	XIV-5	—	23:9		109
11	coin	XXIII-sf.	—			109
12	coin	XIV-16 S-41	IV C	22:3		109
13	coin	XIV-15	—	23:5		109
14	coin	VII-15E	IV B			69, 109
15	coin	V-67 S-32	IV B	23:1		65, 109
16	coin	V-67 S-32	IV B	23:2		65, 109
17	coin	V-54	IV B	23:3		68, 109
18	coin	V-54	IV B	23:4		68, 109
19	coin	XXII-3	V	22:8		109
20	coin	XVIII-sf.	—			109
21	coin	III-14	IV C	23:7		109
22	coin	V-34 S-30	IV B	23:8		65, 109
23	coin	XVIII-sf.	—			109
24	coin	XVIII-sf.	—	22:5		109
25	coin	VI-24 S-42	IV B	22:6		74, 109
26	loom weight	VII-10a C-2	IV B	25:5		110
27	loom weight	VII-8	IV B	25:3		110
28	loom weight	III-27 C-1	IV	25:4		110
29	loom weight	III-22 C-1	IV			110
30	bone spatula	VIII-16	III A	25:11	27:5	110
31	bone spatula	VIII-16	III A	25:12		110
32	bone spatula	III-24 C-1	IV	25:13		110
33	bone spatula	III-22 C-1	IV	25:14		110
34	shell	III-24 C-1	IV			
35	bead	III-24 C-1	IV		27:14	110
36	bronze pin pieces	III-24 C-1	IV	26:6		111
37	compass	V-42	IV B	26:9	27:9	111
38	bead	XXI-sf.	—		27:15	110
39	bone spatula	VIII-16	III A	25:15		110
40	bronze bracelet	III-20 C-1	IV	26:13		111
41	bone spatula	III-21 C-1	IV	25:16		110
42	bronze disc	XVI-11	III A	26:14		111
43	bronze pin	V-34 S-30	IV B	26:1	27:10	111
44	bone spatula	XVI-11	III A	25:17		110
45	bone spatula	III-21 C-1	IV	25:18	27:6	110
46	bronze bead	XIV-16 S-41	IV C		27:16	110
47	bronze base of vessel	XIV-16 S-41	IV C	26:11	27:11	111
48	bone spatula	III-24 C-1	IV			110

No.	Artifact	Locus	Stratum	Photo pl.	Drawing pl.	Discussion p.
49	glass bead	XIV-11	—		27:17	110
50	iron spatula	V-54	IV B			111
51	bronze pin	VII-10a C-2	IV B	26:2		111
52	bone spatula	III-20 C-1	IV			110
53	glass bead	III-21 C-1	IV		27:18	110
54	marked sherd	VII-10a C-2	IV B	33:7	73:40	102
55	stamped handle	XX-6	IV B	28:4	29:2	111-12
56	miniature vase	XX-5	IV B	44:3	77:12	103
57	stamped handle	XX-3	IV B	28:3	29:3	111-12
58	stamped handle	XIX-3	—	28:5	29:4	112
59	figurine fragment	XVIII S-36	pre-III A	32:22	32:10	113
60	figurine fragment	IX-13 S-28	III B	32:19	32:7	113
61	figurine fragment	XVIII S-39	pre-III A	32:13	32:1	113
62	figurine fragment	I-26	III A	32:21	32:9	113
63	lamp	III-21	IV B	46:8	80:3	105
64	lamp	III-20	IV B	46:12	80:4	105
65	lamp	III-22	IV B	46:11	80:5	105
66	lamp	III-22	IV B	46:7	80:6	105
67	lamp	III-24	IV B	46:9	80:7	105
68	lamp	XII-11	IV B	46:13	80:9	105
69	bowl	IX-13 S-28	III B	38:69 8c	64:17	43, 93
70	coin	XXII-5	V	23:10		109
71	juglet	III-24 C-1	IV	37:5	61:11	92
72	lamp	III-24 C-1	IV	42:4	70:9	98
73	bowl	VII-15E	IV B	44:6 7b	77:15	69, 103
74	bronze fibula	III-31 C-1	III B	26:7		111
75	loom weight	III-31 C-1	III B			110
76	loom weight	III-31 C-1	III B			110
77	bone knife handle	III-30 C-1	III B	25:24	27:4	110
78	arrowhead	III-31 C-1	III B	26:8		111
79	knife blade	XX-9	IV B			111
80	spindle whorl	XVIII S-38	pre-III A	25:9		110
81	alabaster cylinder	III-31 C-1	III B		27:12	110
82	alabaster bowl rim	XVIII-sf.	—		27:3	110
83	loom weight	III-30 C-1	III B	25:6		110
84	lamp	III-22 C-1	IV	42:2	70:4	98
85	lamp	III-30 C-1	III B	42:9	70:5	98
86	lamp	III-24 C-1	IV		70:6	98
87	lamp	III-24 C-1	IV	42:1	70:13	98
88	cooking-pot	VII-10b C-2	III A	41:11	67:14	96
89	cooking-pot	II-12	IV B	45:7	79:2	104
90	stand	IX-13 S-28	III B	40:6	66:9	43, 95
91	stand	IX-13 S-28	III B	40:5 8c	66:10	43, 95
92	cooking-pot	VI-24 S-42	IV B	45:2	78:2	74, 104
93	lamp	III-31 C-1	III B	42:8	71:3	98
94	lamp	III-31 C-1	III B		71:8	98
95	loom weight	XVI-11	III A	25:1		110
96	shell	III-31 C-1	III B			
97	bronze needle	III-28 C-1	III A-B	26:3		111
98	bead	III-28 C-1	III A-B		27:19	110

No.	Artifact	Locus	Stratum	Photo pl.	Drawing pl.	Discussion p.
99	bronze ring	III-28 C-1	III A-B	26:12		111
100	bronze toggle pin	III-24 C-1	IV	26:4		111
101	bronze bracelet frag.	III-30 C-1	III B	26:15		111
102	bone spatula	III-24 C-1	IV			110
103	bone spatula	III-24 C-1	IV			110
104	bone pick	III-28 C-1	III A-B	25:19		110
105	bone spatula	III-24 C-1	IV	25:20		110
106	bone spatula	III-30 C-1	III B	25:21		110
107	bone spatula	III-28 C-1	III A-B	25:22		110
108	bone spatula	III-31 C-1	III B			110
109	bone spatula frag.	III-31 C-1	III B			110
110	bone spatula frag.	III-31 C-1	III B			110
111	loom weight	VII-10b C-2	III A	25:7		110
112	loom weight	VII-10b C-2	III A	25:8		110
113	coin	XIV-26	IV A	22:1		109
114	lamp	XX-8	IV B			
115	jug	III-31 C-1	III B			90
116	cooking-pot	XXII-11 S-43	IV A	45:3	79:1	104
117	pot	III-31 C-1	III B	40:1	66:5	95
118	lamp	XXII-11 S-43	IV A	46:6	80:1	104-5
119	lamp	III-31 C-1	III B	42:11	71:9	98
120	lamp	III-31 C-1	III B	42:12	71:10	98
121	lamp	I-41	III B	42:7	71:13	98
122	figurine head	I-41	III B	32:16	32:4	113
123	jug	III-31 C-1	III B			90
124	jug	III-31 C-1	III B			90
125	flask	III-22 C-1	IV		59:4	91
126	juglet	III-24 C-1	IV	37:3	61:3	92
127	bone spatula	XII-25	IV B	25:23	27:8	110
128	coin	XXIV-sf.	—			109
129	bone spatula	XXII-11 S-43	IV A			110
130	coin	VI-30	IV B			109
131	coin	XI-18	IV B			109
132	bead	VI-30	IV B		27:20	110
133	bronze pin	XXII-11 S-43	IV A	26:5		111
134	loom weight	V-67 S-32	IV B	25:2		110
135	figurine fragment	XIX-sf.	—	32:24	32:12	113
136	lamp	XX-5ext	IV B	46:10	80:10	105
137	juglet	XXII-11 S-43	IV A	37:12	61:18	92
138	animal vase fragment	VII-15W	III A	32:18	32:6	113
139	figurine fragment	XII-24	IV B	32:20	32:8	113
140	lamp	II-17	III A		71:2	98
141	juglet	VI-25	IV B	37:11	61:19	92
142	figurine fragment	XVIII S-38	pre-III A	32:14	32:2	113
143	bowl	III-30 C-1	III B	38:1	64:19	93
144	iron fragments	II-45	IV B			111
145	stone pellet	XIX-3ext S-24	II	24:4		110
146	cooking-pot	VI-25	IV B	46:4	79:6	74, 104
147	stone	I-29	IV B	24:1		110
148	stone cup	VI-9	IV B	24:12 14d	27:1	110
149	flint	V-8	IV B	24:2		110
150	grinding stone	XVI-9	III B	24:3		110

No.	Artifact	Locus	Stratum	Photo pl.	Drawing pl.	Discussion p.
151	rubbing stone	I-sf.	—	24:11		110
152	stone pounder	III-29 C-1	III A-B	24:8		110
153	stone pounder	III-20 C-1	IV	24:6		110
154	stone pounder	III-21 C-1	IV	24:7		110
155	stone weight ?	VII-10b C-2	III A			110
156	stone pounder	III-31 C-1	III B	24:9		110
157	stone pounder	III-31 C-1	III B	24:10		110
158	stone bowl fragment	III-24 C-1	IV	24:13	27:2	110
159	bone inlay	VII-10b C-2	III A	25:25	27:7	110
160	cooking-pot	IX-13 S-28	III B	41:12	68:17	43, 97
161	jug top	VI-25	IV B		75:14	74, 102
162	cooking-pot	V-21	IV B	45:1	78:1	104
163	cooking-pot fragment	II-45	IV B	7a		69
164	cooking-pot	VI-25	IV B	46:5	79:7	74, 104
165	lamp	III-11	—		71:11	98
166	lamp	XXIV-7	—	42:6	71:12	98
167	cooking-pot fragment	V-34 S-30	IV B			104
168	cooking-pot top	V-34 S-30	IV B		79:3	104
169	cooking-pot	XIV-12	IV B	45:5	78:3	104
170	cooking-pot	V-8	IV B	45:6	78:4	104
171	jug rim	V-8	IV B			
172	juglet	III-14 C-1	IV C	37:9	61:17	92
173	juglet	III-14 C-1	IV C	37:13	61:15	92
174	cooking-pot top	XII-24	IV B		68:16	97
175	cooking-pot fragments	VI-25	IV B		79:8	74, 104
176	cooking-pot fragment	VI-25	IV B		79:9	74, 104
177	juglet fragments	VII-15E	IV B			
178	lid fragment	V-34 S-30	IV B		79:20	104
179	juglet	VI-24 S-42	IV B	44:2	76:13, 14	103
180	cooking-pot fragment	XII-24	IV B		68:18	97
181	jar	V-29	IV B		72:19	102
182	jar	XIV-17 S-41	IV C		74:1	102
183	jar	XIV-17 S-41	IV C		74:2	102
184	jar rim	XIV-17 S-41	IV C		74:5	102
185	jar rim	XIV-17 S-41	IV C		74:6	102
186	jar rim	XIV-17 S-41	IV C		74:3	102
187	jar rim	XIV-17 S-41	IV C		74:4	102
188	jar handle	XIV-17 S-41	IV C		74:7	102
189	jar handle	XIV-17 S-41	IV C		74:8	102
190	jar rim	XIV-17 S-41	IV C			102
191	lamp	III-30 C-1	III B	42:10	70:2	98
192	lamp	III-21 C-1	IV	42:3	70:8	98
193	lamp	III-24 C-1	IV		71:14	99
194	lamp	III-28 C-1	III A-B		70:1	98
195	lamp	XVIII S-36	pre-III A	42:5	71:1	98
196	lamp	XX-6ext.	—		70:10	98
197	lamp	III-27 C-1	IV	46:14	80:8	105
198	jar	III-27 C-1	IV	43:1	73:20	102
199	jar top	III-28 C-1	III A-B		52:14	90
200	jar top	III-22 C-1	IV		52:15	90
201	jar top	III-28 C-1	III A-B		52:13	90
202	jar top	III-28 C-1	III A-B		52:16	90
203	jar handle	XXI-sf.	—	30:1	30:2	112-13

No.	Artifact	Locus	Stratum	Photo pl.	Drawing pl.	Discussion p.
204	jug handle	I-sf.	—	30:3	30:4	112-13
205	jar handle	I-45	III B	28:1, 2	29:1	111-12
206	jar	III-30 C-1	III B	33:1	51:18,19	90
207	jug	XXII-11 C-43	IV A	44:1	75:21	102
208	flask top	VI-24 S-42	IV B		76:5	103
209	juglet	III-24 C-1	IV	36:4	60:9	92
210	juglet	III-30 C-1	III B	36:3	60:8	92
211	juglet	III-24 C-1	IV	36:1	60:6	92
212	juglet	III-24 C-1	IV	37:10	61:16	92
213	juglet	III-22 C-1	IV	37:6	61:12	92
214	juglet	III-24 C-1	IV	36:5	60:11	92
215	juglet	I-47	IV B	37:11	61:13	92
216	juglet top	I-45	III B	37:7	61:10	92
217	crater	I-30 C-1	III B	38:4	65:1	93
218	pot	III-24 C-1	IV	40:3	66:7	95
219	pot	III-30 C-1	III B	40:2	66:6	95
220	cooking-pot	III-27 C-1	IV	45:4	78:16	104
221	pot	VII-10b C-2	III A	40:4	66:4	95
222	cooking-pot top	III-24 C-1	IV		69:20	97
223	jar	XVIII S-37	IV			
224	jar top	XVIII S-37	IV			
225	jar	XVIII S-37	IV			
226	jar	XVIII S-37	IV	43:2		102
227	jar	XVIII S-37	IV	43:3	72:31	102
228	crater	III-30 C-1	III B	38:3	65:2	93
229	jug top	III-24 C-1	IV		75:27	103
230	jug top	I-9	IV B		75:15	102
231	jug	III-30 C-1	III B		53:1	90
232	jug	III-30 C-1	III B		56:14	90
233	jug	III-30 C-1	III B	34:1	53:2	90
234	jug	III-30 C-1	III B		53:3	90
235	jug	III-30 C-1	III B		56:15	90
236	jug	III-30 C-1	III B		56:16	90
237	jug	III-30 C-1	III B		53:4	90
238	jug	III-30 C-1	III B		54:5	90
239	jug	III-30 C-1	III B		56:17	90
240	jug	III-30 C-1	III B		54:6	90
241	jug	III-30 C-1	III B		54:7	90
242	jug	III-30 C-1	III B		56:18	90
243	jug	III-30 C-1	III B		56:19	90
244	jug	III-30 C-1	III B		54:8	90
245	jug top	III-30 C-1	III B		56:20	90
246	jug	III-30 C-1	III B	34:4	55:9	90
247	jug top	III-30 C-1	III B		56:21	90
248	jug top	III-30 C-1	III B		56:22	90
249	jug top	III-30 C-1	III B		56:23	90
250	jug top	III-30 C-1	III B		56:24	90
251	jug top	III-30 C-1	III B		56:25	90
252	jug	III-30 C-1	III B		56:26	90
253	jug	III-30 C-1	III B	34:2	55:10	90
254	jug	III-30 C-1	III B	34:6	55:11	90
255	jug	III-30 C-1	III B	34:3	55:12	90
256	jug fragment	III-30 C-1	III B	34:5	55:13	90

257	jug	III-30 C-1	III B		56:27	90
258	crater	III-28 C-1	III A-B	39:3	65:7	94-95
259	crater	III-29 C-1	III A-B	39:1	65:5	94-95
260	crater	III-29 C-1	III A-B	39:2	65:6	94-95
261	crater	III-29 C-1	III A-B	39:4	65:8	94-95
262	bowl	III-22 C-1	IV		64:33	94
263	bowl	III-22 C-1	IV		64:21	93
264	figurine fragment	XVIII S-38	pre-III A	32:23	32:11	113
265	figurine fragment	XVIII S-38	pre-III A	32:17	32:5	113
266	figurine fragment	I-2	—	32:15	32:3	113
267	jar handle	VII-10b C-2	III A	28:6	29:5	112
268	jar handle	XVIII-sf.	—	28:7	29:6	112
269	jar rim	X-8	III B	33:2	51:3	90
270	jug rim	X-8	III B	33:3	58:1	90
271	jar rim	X-8	III B	33:4	51:1	90
272	marked sherd	III-30 C-1	III B	33:5	51:17	90
273	marked sherd	XII-28 S-40	III B	33:6	52:12	90
274	jug top	III-30 C-1	III B	35:1	58:3	90
275	jug top	III-30 C-1	III B	35:2	58:2	90
276	jug top	III-30 C-1	III B	35:3	58:7	90
277	jug lip	III-30 C-1	III B	35:4		90
278	jug top	III-30 C-1	III B	35:5	58:5	90
279	jug lip	III-30 C-1	III B	35:6	58:6	90
280	flask top	III-30 C-1	III B	35:7	59:1	91
281	flask top	III-30 C-1	III B	35:8	59:2	91
282	flask top	X-8	III B	35:9	59:3	91
283	cooking-pot top	V-57 S-33	IV B	46:3	79:17	104
284	juglet	XVIII S-36	pre-III A	36:2	60:7	92
285	juglet	III-24 C-1	IV	37:1	61:2	92
286	juglet	III-20 C-1	IV	37:2	61:4	92
287	juglet	III-24 C-1	IV	37:4	61:6	92
288	cooking-pot top	III-24 C-1	IV	41:13	69:16	97
289	cooking-pot top	III-30 C-1	III B	41:14	69:18	97
290	nipple ?	I-sf.	—	44:4	77:14	103
291	nipple ?	XII-19	IV B	44:5	77:13	103
292	cooking-pot top	V-57 S-33	IV B	46:2	79:16	104
293	lamp spout	XII-7	V	44:7	81:12	105
294	lamp spout	XXII-2	V	44:9	81:13	105
295	lamp spout	V-2	—	44:8	81:14	105
296	cooking-pot top	V-57 S-33	IV B	46:1	79:15	104

Bibliography

ᶜAfûla M. Dothan. The Excavations at ᶜAfula. *ᶜAtiqot* 1 (1955): 19-70.

Aharoni, M., and Aharoni, Y.
1976 The Stratification of Judahite Sites in the 8th and 7th Centuries B.C.E. *Bulletin of the American Schools of Oriental Research* 224: 73-90.

Aharoni, Y.
1956 Excavations at Ramat Raḥel, 1954; Preliminary Report. *Israel Exploration Journal* 6: 137-57.

1958 The Negeb of Judah. *Israel Exploration Journal* 8: 26-38.

1959 The Date of the Casemate Walls in Judah and Israel and Their Purpose. *Bulletin of the American Schools of Oriental Research* 154: 35-39.

1963 Notes and News: Ḥorvat Dorban (Khirbet esh-Sheikh Ibrahim). *Israel Exploration Journal* 13: 337.

1967a Excavations at Tell Arad: Preliminary Report on the Second Season, 1963. *Israel Exploration Journal* 17: 233-49.

1967b Forerunners of the Limes: Iron Age Fortresses in the Negev. *Israel Exploration Journal* 17: 1-17.

1967c *The Land of the Bible.* Philadephia: Westminster.

1967d Notes and News: Arad. *Israel Exploration Journal* 17: 270-72.

1972 The Stratification of Israelite Megiddo. *Journal of Near Eastern Studies* 31: 302-11.

1973 See *Beersheba I.*

1974a The Building Activities of David and Solomon. *Israel Exploration Journal* 24: 13-16.

1974b Excavations at Tel Beer-sheba. *Tel Aviv* 1: 34-42.

1975 See *Lachish V.*

Aharoni, Y., et al.
1960 The Ancient Desert Agriculture of the Negev, V: An Israelite Agricultural Settlement at Ramat Maṭred. *Israel Exploration Journal* 10: 23-36, 97-111.

1962 See *RR I.*

1964 See *RR II.*

Aharoni, Y., and Amiran, R.
1958 A New Scheme for the Sub-Division of the Iron Age in Palestine. *Israel Exploration Journal* 8:171-84.

1964 Excavations at Tel Arad; Preliminary Report on the First Season, 1962. *Israel Exploration Journal* 14: 131-47.

ᶜAlâyiq J. B. Pritchard. *The Excavation of Herodian Jericho.* Annual of the American Schools of Oriental Research 32-33. New Haven, CT: American Schools of Oriental Research, 1958.

Albright, W. F.
1924 See *TFL I.*

1932a An Anthropoid Clay Coffin from Sahab in Transjordan. *American Journal of Archaeology* 36: 295-306.

1932b The Seal of Eliakim and the Latest Pre-exilic History of Judah, with some Observations on Ezekiel. *Journal of Biblical Literature* 51: 77-106.

1932c See *TBM I.*

1933 A New Campaign of Excavation at Gibeah of Saul. *Bulletin of the American Schools of Oriental Research* 52: 6-12.

1938 See *TBM II.*

1943 See *TBM III.*

1953 *Archaeology and the Religion of Israel.* Baltimore: Johns Hopkins.

1960 *The Archaeology of Palestine.* Baltimore: Penguin.

1966 Syria, The Philistines, and Phoenicia. Pp. 507-36 in vol. II, chap. 33 of *Cambridge Ancient History,* 3rd ed., eds. I. E. S. Edwards, et. al. Cambridge: Cambridge University.

Alt, A.
1953 Die Staatenbildung der Israeliten in Palästina. Pp. 1-65 in vol. II of *Kleine Schriften zur Geschichte des Volkes Israel.* Munich: Beck.

1959 Der Stadtstaat Samaria. Pp. 258-302 in vol. III of *Kleine Schriften zur Geschichte des Volkes Israel.* Munich: Beck.

Amiran, R.
1969 *Ancient Pottery of the Holy Land.* Jerusalem: Masada.

AS IV E. Grant and G. E. Wright. *Ain Shems Excavations, IV (Pottery).* Haverford, CT: Haverford College, 1938.

AS V E. Grant and G. E. Wright. *Ain Shems Excavations, V (Text).* Haverford, CT: Haverford College, 1939.

Ashdod II-III M. Dothan. *Ashdod II-III: The Second and Third Seasons of Excavations, 1963, 1965* (Text and Plates). ᶜAtiqot 9-10 (1971).

ᶜAtiqot V B. Mazar, T. Dothan, and I. Dunayevsky. *En-Gedi: The First and Second Seasons of Excavations, 1961-1962.* ᶜAtiqot 5 (1966).

Avigad, N.
1974 More Evidence on the Judean Post-Exilic Stamps. *Israel Exploration Journal* 24: 52-58.

Avi-Yonah, M., ed.
1969 *The History of the Holy Land.* Jerusalem: Jerusalem Publishing House.

Babelon, E.
1901 *Traité des Monnaies Grecques et Romaines,* vol. I. Paris.

Barag, D.
1966 The Effects of the Tennes Rebellion on Palestine. *Bulletin of the American Schools of Oriental Research* 183: 6-12.

Bar-Deroma, H.
1970 Ye Mountains of Gilboa (Last Battle of Saul). *Palestine Exploration Quarterly* 1970: 116-36.

Barnett, R. D.
1969 The Sea Peoples. Pp. 359-78 in vol. II, chap. 28 of *Cambridge Ancient History.* 3rd ed., eds. I. E. S. Edwards, et al. Cambridge: Cambridge University.

Beersheba I Y. Aharoni. *Beer-sheba I: Excavations at Tel Beer-sheba, 1969-1971 Seasons.* Jerusalem: Tel Aviv University Institute of Archaeology, 1973.

Bennett, C. M.
1974 Buseira. Chronique archéologique. *Revue biblique* 81: 73-76.

Benoit, P.; Milik, J. T.; and Vaux, R. de
1961 *Les Grottes de Murabbaᶜat.* Discoveries in the Judean Desert 2. Oxford: Clarendon.

Bethany S. J. Saller. *Excavations at Bethany (1949-53).* Jerusalem: Franciscan, 1957.

Bethel J. L. Kelso. *The Excavation of Bethel (1934-60).* Annual of the American Schools of Oriental Research 39. Cambridge, MA: American Schools of Oriental Research, 1968.

Birch, W. F.
1877 Note on Nob. *Palestine Exploration Fund Quarterly Statement* 1877: 204-5.

1911 Gibeah of Saul and Zela, the Site of Jonathan's Home and Tomb. *Palestine Exploration Fund Quarterly Statement* 1911: 101-9.

1913 Gibeah at ᶜAdaseh. *Palestine Exploration Fund Quarterly Statement* 1913: 38-40.

1914 The Site of Gibeah. *Palestine Exploration Fund Quarterly Statement* 1914: 42-44.

Birnbaum, S. A.
1971 *The Hebrew Scripts.* Leiden: Brill.

Bliss, F. J., and Dickie, A. C.
1898 *Excavations at Jerusalem, 1894-1897.* London: Palestine Exploration Fund.

Bliss, F. J., and Macalister, R. A. S.
 1902 *Excavations in Palestine*. London: Palestine Exploration
        Fund.
BMC   *British Museum Catalogue*.
Bright, J.
 1959 *A History of Israel*. Philadelphia: Westminster.
Broneer, O.
 1930 Terracotta Lamps. Vol. IV, part 2 of *Corinth*. Cambridge,
        MA: Harvard University.
Bull, M-L., and Holm-Nielsen, S.
 1969 See *Shiloh*.
BZ II O. R. Sellers, et al. *The 1957 Excavation at Beth-zur*.
        Annual of the American Schools of Oriental Research 38.
        Cambridge, MA: American Schools of Oriental Research,
        1968.
Caird, G. B.
 1953 Exegesis of I Samuel. Pp. 876-1040 in vol. II of *The
        Interpreter's Bible*, ed. G. Buttrick. Nashville: Abingdon.
Callaway, J.
 1976 Excavating Ai (et-Tell): 1964-1972. *Biblical Archaeologist*
        39: 18-30.
CBZ   O. R. Sellers. *The Citadel of Beth-zur*. Philadelphia:
        Westminster, 1933.
Conder, C. R.
 1877 Gibeah of Saul. *Palestine Exploration Fund Quarterly
        Statement* 1877: 104-5.
Conder, C. R., and Kitchener, H. H.
 1883 *The Survey of Western Palestine, Memoirs of the
        Topography, Orography, Hydrography and Archaeology*,
        vol. III. London: Palestine Exploration Fund.
Cowley, A.
 1923 *Aramaic Papyri of the Fifth Century B.C.* Oxford:
        Clarendon.
CPP   J. G. Duncan. *Corpus of Palestinian Pottery*. London:
        British School of Archaeology in Egypt, 1930.
Cross, F. M.
 1961 The Development of the Jewish Scripts. Pp. 133-202 in *The
        Bible and the Ancient Near East*, ed. G. E. Wright. Garden
        City, NY: Doubleday.
 1962 Epigraphical Notes on Hebrew Documents of the Eighth-
        Sixth Centuries B.C.: III. The Inscribed Jar Handles from
        Gibeon. *Bulletin of the American Schools of Oriental
        Research* 168: 18-23.
 1969 Judean Stamps. Pp. 20-27 in *Eretz-Israel* 5 (Albright
        Volume). Jerusalem: Israel Exploration Society.
Crowfoot, J. W., and Crowfoot, G. M.
 1938 See *SS II*.
Crowfoot, J. W.; Crowfoot, G. M.; and Kenyon, K. M.
 1957 See *SS III*.
Crowfoot, J. W., and Fitzgerald, G. M.
 1929 *Excavations in the Tyropoeon Valley, Jerusalem, 1927*.
        Palestine Exploration Fund Annual 5. London: Palestine
        Exploration Fund, 1927.
Crowfoot, J. W.; Kenyon, K. M.; and Sukenik, E. L.
 1942 See *SS I*.
Dahlberg, B. T.
 1962 Hur. P. 664 in vol. II of *The Interpreter's Dictionary of the
        Bible*, ed. G. Buttrick. Nashville: Abingdon.
Demsky, A.
 1973 Geba, Gibeah, and Gibeon—An Historico-Geographic
        Riddle. *Bulletin of the American Schools of Oriental
        Research* 212: 26-31.
Dever, W. G.
 1973 Notes and News: Shechem (Balata). *Israel Exploration
        Journal* 23: 243-45.
 1974a The MB IIC Stratification in the Northwest Gate Area at

Shechem. *Bulletin of the American Schools of Oriental
        Research* 216: 31-52.
 1974b The Middle Bronze Occupation and Pottery of ʿArâq en-
        Nâʿsânah (Cave II). Pp. 33-48 in *Discoveries in the Wâdī
        ed-Dâliyeh*, ed. P. W. Lapp and N. L. Lapp. Annual of the
        American Schools of Oriental Research 41. Cambridge,
        MA: American Schools of Oriental Research.
Dever, W. G.; Lance H. D.; and Wright, G. E.
 1970 See *Gezer I*.
Dever, W. G., et al.
 1975 See *Gezer II*.
Donner, H., and Röllig, W.
 1973 *Kanaanäische und aramäische Inschriften*. Vol. II,
        Kommentar. Wiesbaden: Harrassowitz.
Dothan, M.
 1955 See ʿAfûla.
 1965 The Fortress at Kadesh-Barnea. *Israel Exploration
        Journal* 15: 134-51.
 1968 Notes and News: Tel Ashdod. *Israel Exploration Journal*
        18: 253-54.
 1971 See *Ashdod II-III*.
Dothan, T.
 1957 Archaeological Reflections on the Philistine Problem.
        Antiquity and Survival 2: 151-64.
 1967 *The Philistines and Their Material Culture*. Jerusalem:
        Bialik Institute and Israel Exploration Society.
 1973 Anthropoid Clay Coffins from a Late Bronze Age
        Cemetery near Deir el-Balah (Preliminary Report II).
        Israel Exploration Journal 23: 129-46.
Duncan, J. G.
 1930 See *CPP*.
Elgavish, J.
 1969 Notes and News: Shiqmona. *Israel Exploration Journal*
        19: 247-48.
 1970 Notes and News: Shiqmona. *Israel Exploration Journal*
        20: 229-30.
 1972 Notes and News: Shiqmona. *Israel Exploration Journal*
        22: 167.
Eloni, N.
 1958 Hananiah. Cols. 218-19 in vol. III of *Encyclopaedia
        Biblica*. Jerusalem: Bialik (Hebrew).
Evenari, M., et al.
 1958 The Ancient Desert Agriculture of the Negev, III: Early
        Beginnings. *Israel Exploration Journal* 8: 231-39.
Ex. Gezer I-III   R. A. S. Macalister. *The Excavations of Gezer:
        1902-1905 and 1907-1909*, 3 vols. London: Murray, 1912.
Feldman, J.
 1959 *Mibifnim* 21: 102-4 (Hebrew).
Fitzmeyer, J. A.
 1970 The Languages of Palestine in the First Century A.D.
        Catholic Biblical Quarterly 32: 501-31.
Franken, H. J.
 1969 See *TDA I*.
Franken, H. J., and Franken-Battershill, C. A.
 1963 *A Primer of Old Testament Archaeology*. Leiden: Brill.
Gerar W. M. F. Petrie. *Gerar*. London: British School of
        Archaeology in Egypt, 1928.
Geraty, L. T.
 1975 The Khirbet el-Kôm Bilingual Ostracon. *Bulletin of the
        American Schools of Oriental Research* 220: 55-61.
Gezer I W. G. Dever, H. D. Lance, and G. E. Wright. *Gezer I:
        Preliminary Report of the 1964-66 Seasons*. Annual of the
        Hebrew Union College Biblical and Archaeological School
        in Jerusalem. Jerusalem: Keter, 1970.
Gezer II W. G. Dever, et al. *Gezer II: Report of the 1967-70 Seasons in
        Fields I and II*. Annual of the Hebrew Union College/

Nelson Glueck School of Biblical Archaeology. Jerusalem: Keter, 1975.

Gibeon   J. B. Pritchard. *Winery, Defenses, and Soundings at Gibeon*. Philadelphia: University Museum, 1964.

Glueck, N.

1956   A Fourth Season of Exploration in the Negeb. *Bulletin of the American Schools of Oriental Research* 142: 17-35.

1957   A Fifth Season of Exploration in the Negeb. *Bulletin of the American Schools of Oriental Research* 145: 11-25.

1959   *Rivers in the Desert*. New York: Farrar, Straus and Cudahy.

1965   Ezion-geber. *Biblical Archaeologist* 28: 70-87.

Graham, J.

1975   Saul's Fortress at Tell el-Fûl. Unpublished Th.M. dissertation. Pittsburgh Theological Seminary.

Grant, E., and Wright, G. E.

1938   See *AS IV*.

1939   See *AS V*.

Gray, J.

1963   Gibeah. Pp. 327-28 in *Dictionary of the Bible*, ed. Hastings, rev. F. C. Grant and H. H. Rowley. New York: Scribners.

Gross, —

1843   Review of E. Robinson, *Biblical Researches. Theologische Studien und Kritiken* 1843: 1082.

Guy, P. L. O.

1938   See *MT*.

Hallo, W. W., and Simpson, W. K.

1971   *The Ancient Near East: A History*. New York: Harcourt Brace.

Hamilton, R. W.

1934   Excavations at Tell Abu Hawām. *Quarterly of the Department of Antiquities in Palestine* 4: 1-69.

Hazor I, II, III-IV   Y. Yadin et al. *Hazor I, II, III-IV*, 3 vols. Jerusalem: James A. de Rothschild Expedition at Hazor, 1958, 1960, 1961.

HE I, II   G. A. Reisner, C. S. Fischer, and D. G. Lyon. *Harvard Excavations at Samaria, 1908-1910*, 2 vols. Cambridge, MA: Harvard University, 1924.

Henschel-Simon, E.

1945   Note on the Pottery of the Amman Tombs. *Quarterly of the Department of Antiquities in Palestine* 11: 75-80.

Hindson, E. E.

1971   *The Philistines and the Old Testament*. Grand Rapids, MI: Baker.

Holladay, J. S.

1971   Notes and News: Khirbet el-Qôm. *Israel Exploration Journal* 21: 175-77.

1976   Of Sherds and Strata: Contributions toward an Understanding of the Archaeology of the Divided Monarchy. Pp. 253-93 in *Magnalia Dei: The Mighty Acts of God*, eds. F. M. Cross, W. E. Lemke, and P. D. Miller. Garden City, NY: Doubleday.

Ibrahim, M.; Sauer, J.; and Yassine, K.

1976   The East Jordan Valley Survey, 1975. *Bulletin of the American Schools of Oriental Research* 222: 41-66.

Iliffe, J. H.

1935   A Tell Fārᶜa Tomb Group Reconsidered. Silver Vessels of the Persian Period. *Quarterly of the Department of Antiquities in Palestine* 4: 182-86.

James, F. W.

1966   *The Iron Age at Beth Shan: A Study of Levels VI-IV*. Philadelphia: University Museum.

Johns, C. N.

1933   The South Eastern Cemetery. *Quarterly of the Department of Antiquities in Palestine* 2: 41-104.

JW   F. Josephus. *The Jewish War*. Trans. J. St. J. Thackeray.

Cambridge, MA: Harvard University, 1957.

Kelso, J. L., et. al.

1968   See *Bethel*.

Kenyon, K. M.

1970   *Archaeology in the Holy Land*. 3rd ed. New York: Praeger.

1976   The Date of the Destruction of Iron Age Beer-sheba. *Palestine Exploration Quarterly* 108: 63-64.

Kjaer, H.

1930   The Excavation of Shiloh 1929. *Journal of the Palestine Oriental Society* 10: 87-174.

Lachish III   O. Tufnell. *Lachish III: The Iron Age*. London: Oxford University, 1953.

Lachish V   Y. Aharoni. *Investigations at Lachish: The Sanctuary and the Residency*. Tel Aviv: Gateway, 1975.

Lamon, R. S., and Shipton, G. M.

1939   See *Meg. I*.

Lance, H. D.

1971   The Royal Stamps and the Kingdom of Josiah. *Harvard Theological Review* 64: 315-32.

Lapp, N. L.

1964a   Black- and Red-Figured Fragments from Stratum V. Pp. 238-41 in Wright 1964.

1964b   Pottery from Some Hellenistic Loci at Balâtah (Shechem). *Bulletin of the American Schools of Oriental Research* 175: 14-26.

1974   The Late Persian Pottery. Pp. 30-32 in *Discoveries in the Wâdī ed-Dâliyeh*, ed. P. W. Lapp and N. L. Lapp. Annual of the American Schools of Oriental Research 41. Cambridge, MA: American Schools of Oriental Research.

1976   Casemate Walls in Palestine and the Late Iron II Casemate at Tell el-Fûl. *Bulletin of the American Schools of Oriental Research* 223: 25-42.

Lapp, P. W.

1960   Late Royal Seals from Judah. *Bulletin of the American Schools of Oriental Research* 158: 11-22.

1961   See *PCC*.

1963   Ptolemaic Stamped Handles from Judah. *Bulletin of the American Schools of Oriental Research* 172: 22-35.

1963-64   American Schools of Oriental Research *Archaeological Newsletter* 1963-64, no. 6: 1-7.

1964   Tell el-Fûl Diary (Unpublished). Tell el-Fûl Pottery Book (Unpublished).

1965   Tell el-Fûl. *Biblical Archaeologist* 28: 2-10.

1967   The Conquest of Palestine in the Light of Archaeology. *Concordia Theological Monthly* 38: 283-300.

1968   Review of *Gibeon. American Journal of Archaeology* 72: 391-93.

1969a   *Biblical Archaeology and History*. New York: World.

1969b   The 1968 Excavations at Tell Taᶜannek. *Bulletin of the American Schools of Oriental Research* 195: 2-49.

1970   The Pottery of Palestine in the Persian Period. Pp. 179-97 in *Archäologie und Altes Testament; Festschrift für Kurt Galling*, ed. A. Kuschke and E. Kutsch. Tübingen: Mohr.

Lemaire, A.

1975   MMŠT—Amwas, vers la solution d'une énigme de l'épigraphie hébraïque. *Revue biblique*. 82: 15-23.

Lines, J.

1964   Late Assyrian Pottery from Nimrud. *Iraq* 16: 164-67.

Lipínsky, E.

1975   *Studies in Aramaic Inscriptions and Onomastics I*. Orientalia Lovaniensia Analecta 1. Louvain: Leuven University.

Loud, G.

1948   See *Meg. II*.

Lugenbeal, E. N., and Sauer, J. A.

1972   Seventh-Sixth Century B.C. Pottery from Area B at

Hesbon. *Andrews University Seminary Studies* 10: 21-69.

Macalister, R. A. S.
1912 See *Ex. Gezer I-III.*
1912 The Topography of Rachel's Tomb. *Palestine Exploration Fund Quarterly Statement* 1912: 74-82.

Mackenzie, D.
1911 Report from Dr. Mackenzie of ᶜAdaseh. *Palestine Exploration Fund Quarterly Statement* 1911: 97-100.
1912-1913 *Excavations at Ain Shems.* Palestine Exploration Fund Annual 2 (1912-1913). London: Palestine Exploration Fund.

Maisler, B. (Mazar)
1950-51 The Excavations at Tell Qasile: Preliminary Reports I, II, and III. *Israel Exploration Journal* 1: 61-76, 125-40, 194-218.

Masterman, E. W. G.
1914 An address with lantern slides. *Palestine Exploration Fund Quarterly Statement* 1914: 118.
1924 Review of *TFL I. Palestine Exploration Fund Quarterly Statement* 1924: 46-47.

Mazar, B.
1964 The Philistines and the Rise of Israel. *Proceedings of the Israel Academy of Sciences and Humanities* 1.7: 1-22.

Mazar, B.; Dothan, T.; and Dunayevsky, I.
1966 See *ᶜAtiqot V.*

Mazar, B., and Dunayevsky, I.
1964 En-Gedi: The Third Season of Excavations (Preliminary Report). *Israel Exploration Journal* 14: 121-30.
1967 En-Gedi: The Fourth and Fifth Seasons of Excavations (Preliminary Report). *Israel Exploration Journal* 17: 133-43.

McCown, C. C.
1947 See *TN I.*

Meg. I R. S. Lamon and G. M. Shipton. *Megiddo I.* Oriental Institute Publications 42. Chicago: University of Chicago, 1939.

Meg. II G. Loud. *Megiddo II.* Oriental Institute Publications 62. Chicago: University of Chicago, 1948.

Meshel, Z., and Sass, B.
1974 Notes and News: Yotvata. *Israel Exploration Journal* 24: 273-74.

Miller, J. M.
1974 Saul's Rise to Power: Some Observations concerning 1 Sam 9:1-10:36, 10:26-11:15 and 13:2-14:46. *Catholic Biblical Quarterly* 36: 157-74.
1975 Geba/Gibeah of Benjamin. *Vetus Testamentum* 25: 145-66.

Mitchell, T. C.
1962 Gibeah. Pp. 466-67 in *The New Bible Dictionary*, ed. J. D. Douglas. London: Inter-Varsity Fellowship.
1967 Philistia. Pp. 405-27 in *Archaeology and Old Testament Study*, ed. D. W. Thomas. Oxford: Clarendon.

MT P. L. O. Guy. *Megiddo Tombs.* Oriental Institute Publications 33. Chicago: University of Chicago, 1938.

Munsell
1971 *Munsell Soil Color Charts.* Baltimore: Munsell Color Company.

Myers, J. M.
1962 Saul, Son of Kish. Pp. 228-33 in vol. IV of *The Interpreter's Dictionary of the Bible*, ed. G. A. Buttrick. Nashville: Abingdon.

Naveh, J.
1962 The Excavations at Meṣad Ḥashavyahu; Preliminary Report. *Israel Exploration Journal* 12: 89-113.
1970 *The Development of the Aramaic Script.* Proceedings of the Israel Academy of Sciences and Humanities 5.1. Jeru-

salem: Israel Academy of Sciences and Humanities.

Noth, M.
1928 *Die israelitischen Personennamen in Rahmen der gemeinsemitischen Namengebung.* Beitrage zur Wissenschaft vom Alten und Neuen Testament III, 10. Stuttgart: Kohlhammer.
1958 *History of Israel.* New York: Harper and Row.

Oates, J.
1959 Late Assyrian Pottery from Fort Shalmanezer. *Iraq* 21: 130-46.

Oren, E. D.
1973 *The Northern Cemetery of Beth Shan.* Leiden: Brill.

PCC P. W. Lapp. *Palestinian Ceramic Chronology, 200 B.C.–A.D. 70.* New Haven, CT: American Schools of Oriental Research, 1961.

Petrie, W. F.
1928 See *Gerar.*

Porten, B.
1968 *Archives from Elephantine.* Berkeley: University of California.

Pritchard, J. B.
1955 *Ancient Near Eastern Texts.* 2nd ed., ed. J. B. Pritchard. Princeton: Princeton University.
1958 See *ᶜAlâyiq.*
1959 *Hebrew Inscriptions and Stamps from Gibeon.* Philadelphia: University Museum.
1964 See *Gibeon.*

Rachmani, L.
1964 A Partial Survey of the Adulam Area. *Yediot* 28: 209-31 (Hebrew).

Rast, W. E.
1978 *Taanach I: Studies in the Iron Age Pottery.* Cambridge, MA: American Schools of Oriental Research.

Reisner, G. A.; Fischer, C. S.; and Lyon, D. G.
1924 See *HE I, II.*

Revue Numism. Revue Numismatique.

Richardson, H. N.
1968 A Stamped Handle from Khirbet Yarmuk. *Bulletin of the American Schools of Oriental Research* 192: 12-16.

Robinson, Edward
1844 Notes on Biblical Geography. *Bibliotheca Sacra* 1: 598-604.
1856 *Biblical Researches in Palestine*, vol. 1, 2nd ed. Boston: Crocker and Brewster.
1874 *Biblical Researches in Palestine*, vol. 1, 11th ed. Boston: Crocker and Brewster.

Rothenberg, B.
1961 *God's Wilderness: Discoveries in Sinai.* London: Thames and Hudson.

RR I Y. Aharoni, et al. *Excavations at Ramat Raḥel I: Seasons 1959 and 1960.* Rome: Centro di studi semitici, 1962.

RR II Y. Aharoni, et al. *Excavations at Ramat Raḥel II: Seasons of 1961 and 1962.* Rome: Centro di studi semitici, 1964.

Saller, S. J.
1957 See *Bethany.*

Sellers, O. R.
1933 See *CBZ.*

Sellers, O. R., et. al.
1968 See *BZ II.*

Shiloh M-L. Buhl and S. Holm-Nielson, *Shiloh: The Danish Excavations at Tall Sailūn, Palestine, in 1926, 1929, 1932 and 1963.* Copenhagen: National Museum of Denmark, 1969.

Sinclair, L.
1960 See *TFL II.*
1964 An Archaeological Study of Gibeah (Tell el-Fûl). *Biblical Archaeologist* 27: 52-64.

1976 Gibeah. Pp. 444-46 in vol. II of *Encyclopedia of Archaeological Excavations in the Holy Land*, English edition, ed. M. Avi-Yonah. Jerusalem: Israel Exploration Society and Masada.

SS I   J. W. Crowfoot; K. M. Kenyon; and E. L. Sukenik. *The Buildings at Samaria*. Vol. I in *Samaria-Sebaste. Reports of the Joint Expedition in 1931-1933 and of the British Expedition in 1935*. London: Palestine Exploration Fund, 1942.

SS II   J. W. Crowfoot, and G. M. Crowfoot. *Early Ivories from Samaria*. Vol. II in *Samaria-Sebaste. Reports of the Joint Expedition in 1931-1933 and of the British Expedition in 1935*. London: Palestine Exploration Fund, 1938.

SS III   J. W. Crowfoot; K. M. Kenyon; and G. M. Crowfoot. *The Objects from Samaria*. Vol. III in *Samaria Sebaste. Reports of the Joint Expedition in 1931-1933 and of the British Expedition in 1935*. London: Palestine Exploration Fund, 1957.

Stager, L. E.
1975 Ancient Agriculture in the Judean Desert: A Case Study of the Buqêᵓah Valley in the Iron Age. Unpublished Ph.D. dissertation. Harvard University.

Stern, E.
1968 The Dating of Stratum II at Tell Abu Hawam. *Israel Exploration Journal* 18: 213-19.

1971 A Burial of the Persian Period near Hebron. *Israel Exploration Journal* 21: 25-30.

1973 Notes and News: Tel Meborach. *Israel Exploration Journal* 23: 256-57.

1974 Notes and News: Tel Mevorakh (Tel Meborach). *Israel Exploration Journal* 24: 266-68.

1975 Israel at the Close of the Period of the Monarchy: An Archaeological Survey. *Biblical Archaeologist* 38: 26-54.

Swauger, J. L.
1969-70 The Fifth Season at Ashdod. American Schools of Oriental Research *Archaeological Newsletter* 1969-70, no. 5: 1-4.

TBM I   W. F. Albright. *The Excavation of Tell Beit Mirsim, I.* Annual of the American Schools of Oriental Research 12. New Haven, CT: American Schools of Oriental Research, 1932.

TBM II   W. F. Albright. *The Excavation of Tell Beit Mirsim, II.* Annual of the American Schools of Oriental Research 17. New Haven, CT: American Schools of Oriental Research, 1938.

TBM III   W. F. Albright. *The Excavation of Tell Beit Mirsim, III.* Annual of the American Schools of Oriental Research 21-22. New Haven, CT: American Schools of Oriental Research, 1943.

TDA I   H. J. Franken. *Excavations at Tell Deir ᶜAllā: I, A Stratigraphical and Analytical Study of the Early Iron Age Pottery*. Leiden: Brill, 1969.

TFL I   W. F. Albright. *Excavations and Results at Tell el-Fûl (Gibeah of Saul)*. Annual of the American Schools of Oriental Research 4. New Haven, CT: American Schools of Oriental Research, 1924.

TFL II   L. A. Sinclair. *An Archaeological Study of Gibeah (Tell el-Fûl)*. Annual of the American Schools of Oriental Research 34-35, part 1. New Haven, CT: American Schools of Oriental Research, 1960.

TN I   C. C. McCown. *Tell en-Nasbeh, I: Archaeological and Historical Results*. Berkeley: Palestine Institute of Pacific School of Religion, 1947.

TN II   J. C. Wampler. *Tell en-Nasbeh II: The Pottery*. Berkeley: Palestine Institute of Pacific School of Religion, 1947.

Toombs, L. E., and Wright, G. E.
1963 The Fourth Campaign at Balâṭah (Shechem). *Bulletin of the American Schools of Oriental Research* 169: 1-60.

Tufnell, O.
1953 See *Lachish III*.

Ussishkin, D.
1976 Royal Judean Storage Jars and Private Seal Impressions. *Bulletin of the American Schools of Oriental Research* 223: 1-14.

1977 The Destruction of Lachish by Sennacherib and the Dating of the Royal Judean Storage Jars. *Tel Aviv* 4: 28-60.

Van Beek, G. W.
1972 Notes and News: Tel Gamma. *Israel Exploration Journal* 22: 245-46.

1974 Notes and News: Tel Gamma. *Israel Exploration Journal* 24: 138-39.

Vaux, R. de
1951 La troisième campagne de fouilles à Tell el-Fâᶜrah, près Naplouse. *Revue Biblique* 58: 393-430.

1965 *Ancient Israel: Its Life and Institutions*. Paperback ed. New York: McGraw-Hill.

1966 Review of *Gibeon. Revue biblique* 73: 130-35.

Waldbaum, J.
1966 Philistine Tombs at Tell Fara and Their Aegean Prototypes. *American Journal of Archaeology* 70: 331-40.

Warren, C.
1869-70 *Supplement: The Warren Reports I-XLVII, 1867-1870*. Palestine Exploration Fund Quarterly Statement 1869-1870. London: Palestine Exploration Fund.

Wampler, J. C.
1940 Triangular Impressed Design in Palestinian Pottery. *Bulletin of the American Schools of Oriental Research* 80: 13-16.

1941 Three Cistern Groups from Tell en-Naṣbeh. *Bulletin of the American Schools of Oriental Research* 82: 25-43.

1947 See *TN II*.

Weinberg, S. S.
1969 Post-Exilic Palestine; An Archaeological Report. *Proceedings of the Israel Academy of Sciences and Humanities* 4.5: 78-97.

Woolley, C. L.
1914-16 A North Syrian Cemetery of the Persian Period. *Annals of Archaeology and Anthropology* 7: 115-29.

Woolley, L., and Lawrence, T. E.
1914 The Wilderness of Zin. *Palestine Exploration Fund Annual* 3: 39-51.

Wright, G. E.
1955 Review of *Lachish III. Vetus Testamentum* 5: 97-105.

1959 Philistine Coffins and Mercenaries. *Biblical Archaeologist* 29: 54-66.

1961 The Archaeology of Palestine. Pp. 73-112 in *The Bible and the Ancient Near East*, ed. G. E. Wright. Garden City, NY: Doubleday.

1963 Review of Pritchard, *The Water System of Gibeon. Journal of Near Eastern Studies* 22: 210-11.

1964 *Shechem: The Biography of a Biblical City*. New York: McGraw-Hill.

1966 Fresh Evidence for the Philistine Story. *Biblical Archaeologist* 29: 70-86.

1970 The Phenomenon of American Archaeology in the Near East. Pp. 3-40 in *Near Eastern Archaeology in the Twentieth Century: Essays in Honor of Nelson Glueck*, ed. J. A. Sanders. Garden City, NY: Doubleday.

1974 Principal advisor and editorial consultant, *Great Peoples of the Bible and How They Lived*. Pleasantville, NY: Readers Digest Association.

Yadin, Y.
1958-61 See *Hazor I, II, III-IV*.

1960   New Light on Solomon's Megiddo. *Biblical Archaeologist*
       23: 62-68.
1963   *The Art of Warfare in Biblical Lands in Light of Archae-
       ological Study.* Trans. M. Pearlman. New York: McGraw-
       Hill.
1972   *Hazor.* London: Oxford University.
1973   A Note on the Stratigraphy of Israelite Megiddo. *Journal*

of Near Eastern Studies 32: 330.

Yeivin, S.
1971   The Benjamite Settlement in the Western Part of Their
       Territory. *Israel Exploration Journal* 21: 141-54.

Zayadine, F.
1966   Early Hellenistic Pottery. *Annual of the Department of
       Antiquities of Jordan* 11: 53-64.

1a. Tell el-Fûl from the north in 1964.

1c. The excavation staff for the 1964 campaign.

In the center is Professor James L. Kelso (holding his hat). To the right are Howard Jamieson and Delbert Flora. Back row: third from left, John Holt; on right is Umhau Wolf. Absent are George Nickelsburg, John Zimmerman, and Oliver Unwin. The director, Paul W. Lapp, took the photograph.

1b. Looking east at Tell el-Fûl in February 1968.

Note the modern houses encroaching upon the mound and the frame and foundation for the West Bank palace which King Hussein was building before the outbreak of the 1967 war.

1d. The top of the mound looking south as excavation begins.

In the background are the standing remains of the Iron I fortress and the north side of the Iron II revetment, with Jerusalem in the background to the south and west beyond. Work has begun in Areas I, II, and III in the foreground.

2a. Small trench on the north side of the Period II tower.

Foundation trench for the fortress can be seen sloping to the corner of the tower at the base of the fairly straight line of stones. L. XIII-10, 11, 12 have been removed. For a close-up photograph, see Lapp 1969: pl. 3.

2b. The northwest corner of the Period II tower.

Stones and fill (L. XIII-14, 15) to the south of the buttress have not yet been removed. Meter stick in right background is on Period III **peel. (cf. fig. 13, p. 24).**

2c. Poor base of Period II tower as seen on the west face at the northwest corner.

Corner buttress to left, Iron II peel wall to right. L. XIII-14, 15 stones and fill removed.

2d. Looking east at Iron I (Period II) Wall S and floors beyond.

Floor XVII-12 (Period II) lies on the east side of Wall S just behind the upper meter stick. Floor XVII-8 of Period I is the darker area in center back. On the left there was Hellenistic disturbance at the north end of Wall S (L. VII-3N, 5a, 18a, and XVII-3).

158

3a. Looking south at Wall S.
Period II Floor XVII-12 to east.

3b. Trench T on either side of Wall S.
L. XVII-14 debris below Floor XVII-12 removed to east. Debris VII-20, 21 removed to bedrock on the west.

3c. Looking south where Wall S has been removed in Trench T.

Wall S rests on chalky layer L. VII-21 (Period II) above L. VII-22 (Period I).

3d. Looking east at Iron II revetment wall west of Fortress.
The wall has been dismantled down to the step on which the meter stick lies.

4a. Looking toward the Fortress, south of Wall S and east of the West Casemate.

South end of Wall S in the foreground. The east-west aligned stones directly beyond may have been a part of Wall S. A deposit at the foot of the revetment, (L. II-46) far south in the photograph, also contained Iron I pottery (cf. pl. 5a). Long inner West Casemate wall is to the right. The socket in the center of the photograph is on Floor II-12/VII-16, Area Q; Hellenistic Fill II-43, Floor II-44, and Fill II-45 have been removed below.

4b. Looking south at a substantial section of the outer East Casemate wall.

Excavated just north of Albright's eastern excavations. Deposits on the east side (L. XXIV-8, 9, 11, 12) attested to its Iron II construction.

4c. Looking east toward the Fortress remains.

From top to bottom, the meter sticks rest on 1) Period III peel against the Period II tower, 2) Period III "mid-wall," 3) Period III revetment (cf. pl. 3d), and 4) outer Hellenistic wall. Debris XIII-2 which has been removed from between the upper peel wall and the mid-wall was from Period II. Cf. section e-f, plan 7.

4d. Looking south along the Iron II peel against the Period II Fortress wall.

5a. Looking east along the north face of the Iron II revetment.

Upper meter stick on revetment stones, L. II-22. South wall of Area P, L. II-2, 2E (with middle meter stick) at foot of revetment. The few sherds from the removal of L. II-2 were Iron II (Period III) and the soil below (L. II-46) contained only Period II sherds. The lower meter stick rests on IV B Floor II-40.

5b. The West Casemate walls going north from the Iron II revetment.

Most southern Room L not yet cleared; Room M cleared to plastered Floor II-25; Room N not cleared; Room O cleared of Hellenistic debris, L. II-14.

5c. Looking north into Room L.

Floor II-30 on left; down to Floor II-36 on right. Forty-cm-wide north-south Wall II-32 on left next to outer West Casemate wall.

5d. Looking west into Room N at III A plastered Floor II-19.

Debris east and below the floor (L. II-27, 34) has been removed to bedrock.

6a. Looking south at the northern end of preserved West Casemate.

Foreground meter stick on farthest north preserved portion of outer West Casemate. Smaller stick on same wall, upper courses removed. Removal of lower courses uncovered Period III sherds. Opening to Cistern 2 between casemate walls. Hellenistic debris removed.

6b. Looking south at Cistern 2 and channel leading to it.

Higher wall to the right is the outer West Casemate with channel wall next to it. Iron II and Iron I debris was removed from the channel (L. VII-15W).

6c. Looking north in Area P.

On north is Wall P/Q, on west is inner West Casemate, on south is Wall II-2, and unexcavated debris is on east. Paving stones of Floor II-5 in north over evidence of a Period IV B oven. Debris II-9 has been removed down to surface visible in the rest of the enclosed area.

162

7a. Looking west in Area Q at the bottom part of a Hellenistic cooking-pot just above Floor II-44.

Inner West Casemate is in the back. The cooking-pot (no. 163) is on an earlier floor than the one the socket was on (cf. pl. 4a).

7b. Looking north in Area Q at a Hellenistic incurved-rim bowl found just above the later Hellenistic Floor VII-16.

The bowl (no. 73) was from a later occupation than the cooking-pot shown in pl. 7a and is contemporary with the door socket (pl. 4a).

7c. Looking west in Room M, the "Little Plastered Room."

Plaster Floor II-25 and drain to Room F in northwest corner.

163

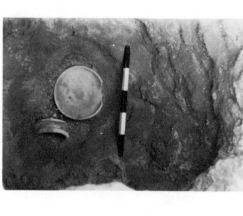

8a. Looking south into the Northeast III Building.
Foundation Trench XVI-10 along the west wall. L. XVI-11, 12 are
removed from between walls; L. XVI-13 stones still in the south.

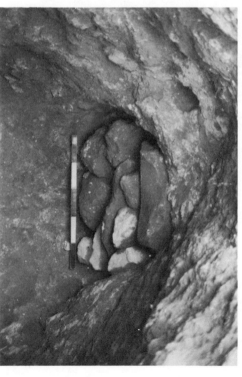

8c. Looking down and south at the vessels in Silo 28.
Vessels nos. 69, 91.

8b. Looking south toward the northern end of the Northeast
III Building.

Ashy debris, perhaps representing the 587 B.C. destruction was found
between the west wall and the oblique wall in the rear of the
photograph (L. IX-14). Silo 28 was in the depression to the left, west
of the east wall of the Northeast III Building. Silo 27 opening is in
back of the right meter stick. The left meter stick is placed in the
ruins of a Hellenistic oven.

8d. Looking southwest in Silo 28 at the packing in the
passageway (L. IX-19).

9b. Silo 21 before the cap has been removed.

9d. Broken humped cap partially covering Silo 26.

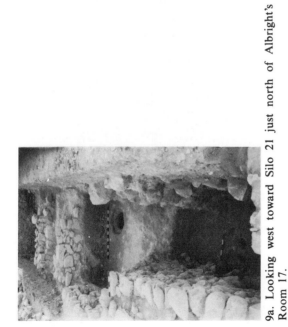

9a. Looking west toward Silo 21 just north of Albright's Room 17.

Silo 22 is in left foreground. The subsurface IV B debris (L. XXI-3) from around it has been removed.

9c. The tilted cap of Silo 25, looking south.

165

10a. Looking west at the excavations north of Albright's work on the east side of the mound. Silo 23 is in the right background, with Area XX ext. rock cuttings in the foreground. Silo 21 is in the back on the left with Silo 22 barely discernible by the wall in the left foreground.

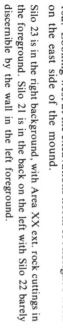

10c. Looking down from the west at Silo 23 with the bedrock construction above.

10b. Looking west at the blocking and cut into the scarp above Silo 23.

10d. The Mid-Field silos from the northeast. North to south, Silos 36, 38, 39 and Silo 37 to the west.

11a. Looking east in Room E.

Revetment wall to south, Wall E/F to east, and Wall D/E to north. Note small stone construction of the III B Walls E/F and D/E compared to the III A casemate walls. The diagonal line of stones is a prerevetment construction of Iron I. L. I-44 inside the stone line against the revetment and L. I-45 outside the stone line have been removed.

removed to bedrock. The triangular cut on the east wall 140 cm north of the revetment may have been Albright's cut.

11b. Looking southeast in Room E before the removal of L. I-44 and I-45 and the west balk.

L. I-27 north of the stones and L. I-26 south of the stones have been removed.

11c. Looking south in Room D toward Wall D/E.

L. I-14 has been removed, as has L. I-16 from the depression north of Wall D/E. At left is Wall D/G. L. I-18 to north or I-43 in Room D not yet removed.

11d. Looking east in Rooms D and G.

Photographed the same time as pl. 11c. L. I-18 is not yet removed. In Room G L. I-14 is removed to L. I-20. In Room J (upper left) are L. I-19, 22, and 21.

167

12a. Period III basin complex in Room G.

The installation was set against the outer West Casemate wall. The debris of L. I-35 has been removed.

12b. Looking from Room J south, with doorways to Room G and Hellenistic basins in Room F in the background.

The Period III plastered basin complex is in Room G, and L. I-29 has been removed to the plastered floor in Room J. Poor supporting Wall F/G is behind middle meter stick; north-south Wall E/F-D/G, to west.

12c. Looking north in Room F beneath Hellenistic Basins *b* and *d*.

Note Pit I-49 against the revetment and the supporting crosswall I-48 for the Hellenistic basins.

13b. Looking south at the IV B occupation in Rooms F-G and J.

Hellenistic basins in south in Room F; L. I-20 removed in Room G but Period III basins of L. I-35 not yet revealed. L. I-22 is removed in southern Room J. Partition Wall I-23 barely visible in lower right. **One would have stepped up through the doorways of Wall J/G into Room G.**

13d. Wall J/K going west over Silo 40.

L. XII-13 basin is on the north side of the wall. The low rectangular stone at the **west end of Wall J/K is probably the sill of a doorway.** The west wall of Room J is going south into the balk. The regularly **patterned rock scree on the south is apparently fall from Wall J/K.** The surface L. I-sub 29 has a grinding stone on its northwest corner.

13a. Looking down and north at the Hellenistic basins against the revetment in Room F.

13c. Looking east at plastered face of outer West Casemate wall and plastered floor in the southern part of Room J.

L. I-22 has been removed in Room J.

169

14a. Looking south in Area K at basin complex.

The poor circular wall (L. XII-20) enclosed L. XII-12 which revealed Basin XII-13. L. XII-19 has been removed in L. XII-21 west and north of Wall XII-20. Wall J/K in south over Silo 40. The fallen wall south has not yet been excavated.

14b. Rooms R, T, and U toward the west.

Channel VI-27 in Room R with subscree debris VI-25 to the south removed to floor. Further east in Room R Fill VI-23 for the earliest Hellenistic floor removed to bedrock. In Room T the thin north-south wall and lower deposits (L. XI-18-21) not yet removed. North of Room T is Floor XI-7 of Room TV. Area U is to the far west beyond Wall H. East-west Wall U/Z in far west.

14c. North wall of Area Uw going west over Silo 43.

Continuation of Wall U/Z in pl. 14b.

14d. Looking north at Wall R/RE with upper Hellenistic Floors VI-10, 11, 9 on either side.

Stone cup, no. 148, visible just to the left of the south end of Wall R/RE. Cistern I is in the balk to north behind meter stick. Perhaps Wall R/RE connected with the wall to north covering the cistern after upper layers of Hellenistic debris had collected in the cistern, or perhaps stones of the connecting wall collapsed into the cistern accounting for some of the stones in its upper layers.

170

15a. Looking west at Wall R/RE in foreground with lowest Hellenistic floors on either side.

In Room R are seen Floor VI-18, 16, and in Room RE, Floor VI-15. To the west the "garden fence" has not yet been removed. In back: south, Room T; north, Room TV.

15b. Looking north at Wall H.

Small meter sitck in front is on Stone D with Stones C, B, and A to south. North of the east-west Wall U/Z is Floor XV-10 in Area Zs, contemporary with Floor XV-8 in Area U south of the wall.

15c. Looking east at Wall H in Area U.

Stones A-D have been removed. In the forground is Pit XV-17.

171

16a. Looking down and north into Silo 42 with opening to settling basin in the bottom.

16c. Looking south into Rooms V, CR, and CRn.
Rockfall III-14 south of Wall V/CR-CRn over Cistern 1 is removed exposing L. III-19. "Garden fence" went north and west of Cistern 1 under which was Pottery Cache X-8. In right foreground Floors X-8, 9 have been removed.

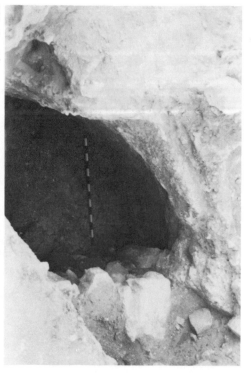

16b. Looking south in Area Z at bedrock channel complex, Silo 41 opening, and Wall H.

Channel XIV-24 leads to round depression L. XIV-22. Wall H is founded on a later phase Hellenistic floor (L. XIV-sub 9) than the doorway to the east on bedrock.

16d. Looking east-northeast at Cistern 1 opening.

172

17c. Looking east-southeast at the passage in the Cistern 1 mid-wall.

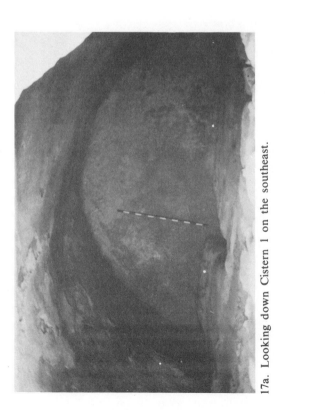

17a. Looking down Cistern 1 on the southeast.

17b. Looking east-southeast at the mid-wall face of Cistern 1.

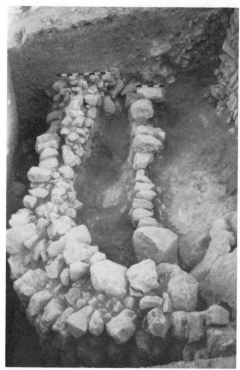

18a. Looking south at the Hellenistic "tower." Cf. fig. 25, p. 64.

18b. Looking north at casemate Rooms EC-1 and EC-2 between the East Casemate walls.

The stone basin in EC-1 is over Silo 34. Debris in the northwest corner of EC-2 is the Iron II deposit (L. V-89, 90) which demonstrated the Period III date of the casemate walls. Buttress V-66 is seen in the north at the left.

18c. Silo 34 mouth and plug in Room EC-1.

18d. Looking south along the inner East Casemate wall and the Hellenistic walls built against it.

The Late Phase Hellenistic wall is removed in the foreground revealing the Early Phase construction of the Hellenistic House.

174

19a. Floor cut into bedrock in the west end of Room A.

Capped Silo 30 cut below the Early Phase IV B Hellenistic floor.

19b. Looking east in Room A at Silos 30, 31, and 32 cut into bedrock beneath the early IV B floor.

In the east beyond the north doorway (cf. pls. 19c and 20c), Early Phase Floor V-32 and fill beneath (L. V-54) have not yet been removed.

19c. Silo 32, which was beneath the Early Phase floor, in front of doorway in the north wall of Room A.

Note socket on right (cf. pls. 19d and 20c).

19d. Early Phase IV B floor in Room A, looking toward the east where Late Phase constructions have not been removed.

The Late Phase east wall (L. V-53) rests on the Late Phase floor (L. V-21). Note the Early Phase floor extending over the east side of Silo 31 (cf. pl. 20a). Silo 30 is below floor level. The socket toward the east rests on the floor (cf. pl. 20c). Silo 32 not yet revealed.

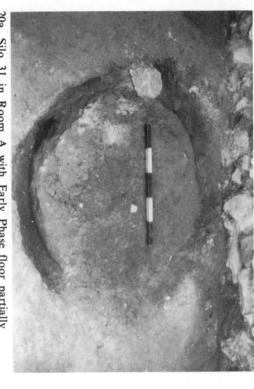

20a. Silo 31 in Room A with Early Phase floor partially covering its cap on the east side.

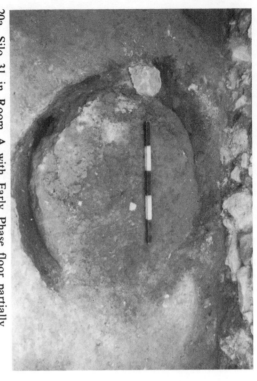

20c. The Early Phase IV B doorway in the north wall of Room A.

The socket sets on the Early Phase floor. On the right edge of the photograph fill (L. V-29) for the later floor and the Late Phase east wall (L. V-53) can be seen.

20b. The basin or drain opening in the bottom of Silo 31.

20d. Looking west-northwest at the Late Phase IV B floor in Room A and the Early Phase floors in Rooms B and C.

In the southwest corner of Room B Silo 29 is hardly visible.

21b. Looking east at Early Phase Floor VIII-15 in Room C.

Hellenistic terrace wall (L. VIII-21) is against inner East Casemate wall in the east. The floor (L. VIII-15) is above Period III debris (L. VIII-16, 18, 19). In the foreground is Room B (pl. 21a). In the Late Phase Fill VIII-9 covered Wall B/C.

21d. Looking southeast at Iron II Wall V-37 going into south balk in Room C.

Wall V-37 is below the floor (L. V-sub 10) on which the east Hellenistic wall is set. The stone scree which covered it can be seen in the south balk. To the west of Wall V-37, Period III occupation Debris V-50 was removed.

21a. Looking north in Room B at the hard-packed Early Phase floor on bedrock.

Foundation Trench VIII-14 is cut into the floor (L. VIII-20) on the west of Wall B/C, and Trench VIII-10 is on the east.

21c. Looking north at Wall A/B-C over capped Silo 33.

Note channel leading to the silo to the west of Wall B/C. Iron II Wall V-37 goes beneath Wall A/B-C in Room C.

177

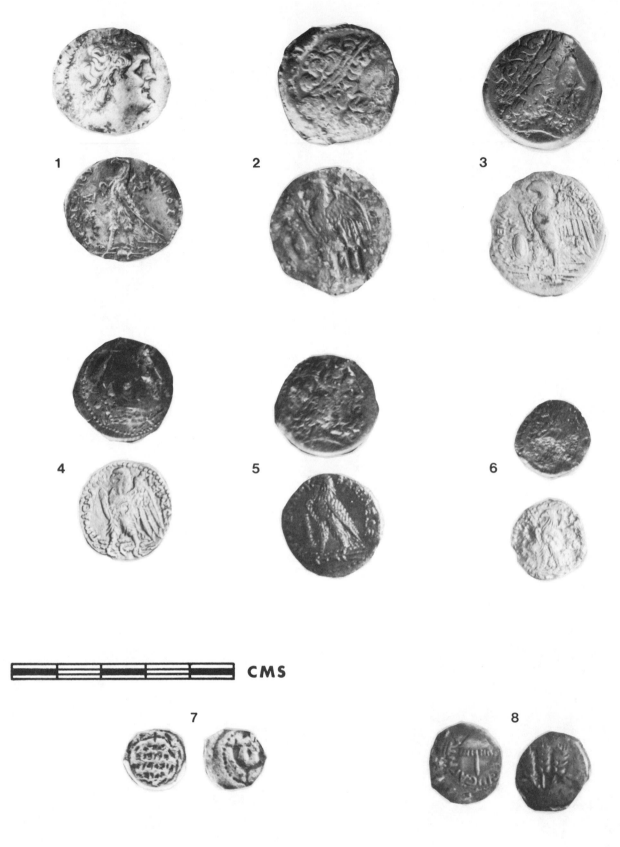

CMS

22. Coins from the 1964 Campaign. Ptolemaic, nos. 1-6;
Maccabean, no. 7; Herodian, no. 8.

1 = reg. no. 113, 2 = 8, 3 = 12, 4 = 3, 5 = 24, 6 = 25,
7 = 5, 8 = 19.

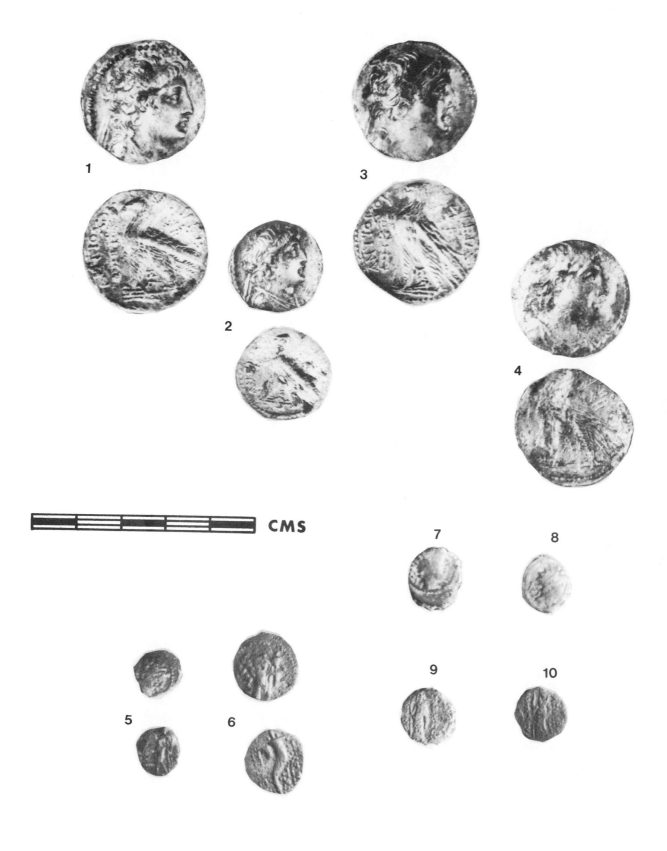

CMS

23. Seleucid Coins from the 1964 Campaign.

1 = reg. no. 15, 2 = 16, 3 = 17, 4 = 18, 5 = 13, 6 = 4, 7 = 21, 8 = 22,
9 = 10, 10 = 70.

24. Stone objects.

1 = reg. no. 147, 2 = 149, 3 = 150, 4 = 145, 5 = 2, 6 = 153, 7 = 154,
8 = 152, 9 = 156, 10 = 157, 11 = 151, 12 = 148, 13 = 158.

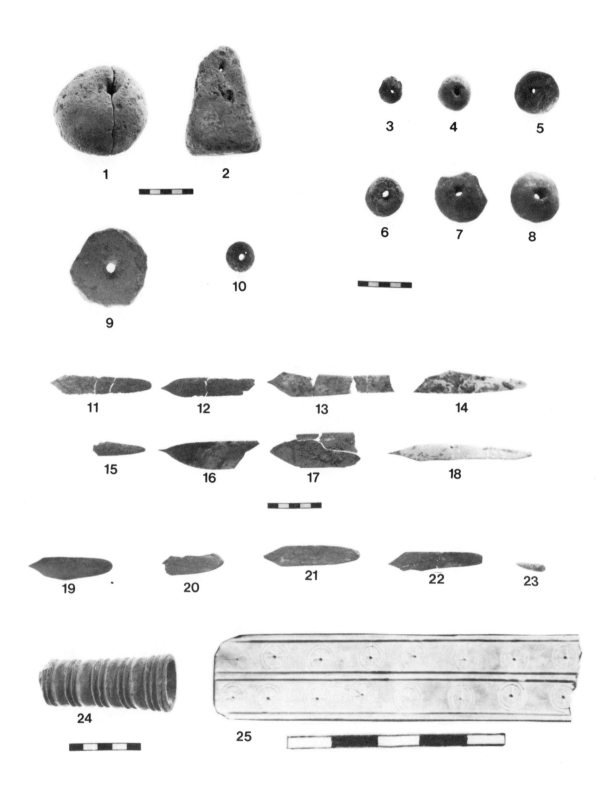

25. Loom weights, nos. 1-8, spindle whorls, nos. 9, 10, bone
spatulas, nos. 11-23, bone knife handle, no. 24, and ivory
inlay, no. 25.

1 = reg. no. 95, 2 = 134, 3 = 27, 4 = 28, 5 = 26, 6 = 83, 7 = 111, 8 = 112,
9 = 80, 10 = 9, 11 = 30, 12 = 31, 13 = 32, 14 = 33, 15 = 39, 16 = 41,
17 = 44, 18 = 45, 19 = 104, 20 = 105, 21 = 106, 22 = 107, 23 = 127,
24 = 77, 25 = 159.

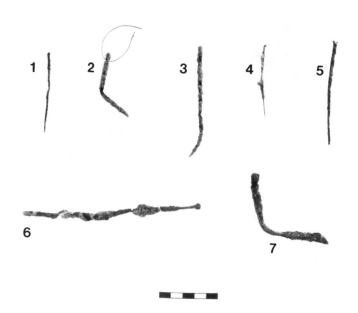

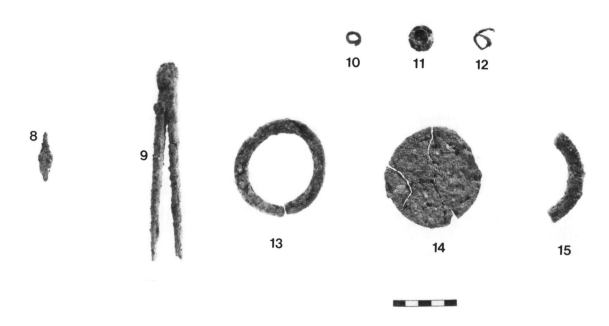

26. Metal artifacts.

1 = reg. no. 43, 2 = 51, 3 = 97, 4 = 100, 5 = 133, 6 = 36, 7 = 74, 8 = 78,
9 = 37, 10 = 6, 11 = 47, 12 = 99, 13 = 40, 14 = 42, 15 = 101.

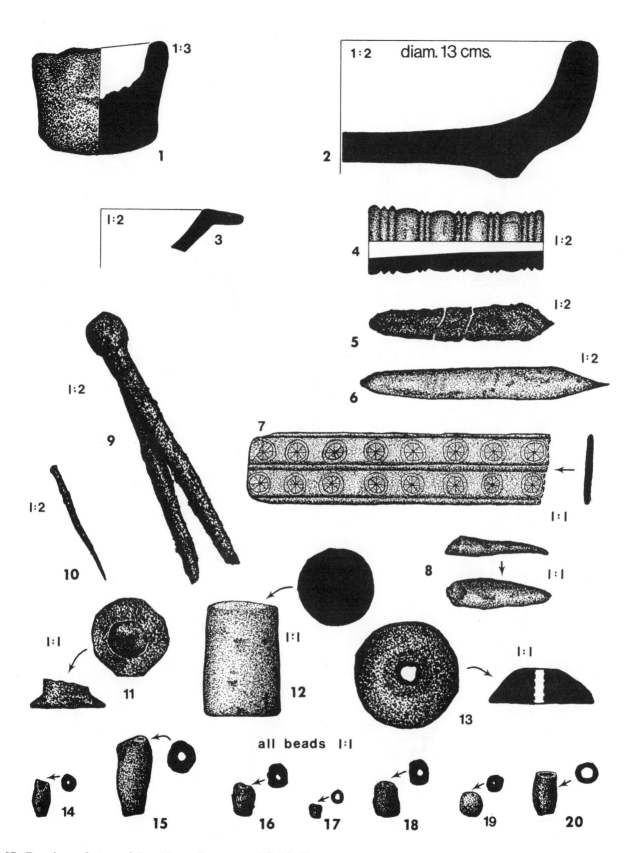

27. Drawings of some of the objects. Stone, nos. 1-3, 12, 13,
bone, nos. 4-8, metal, nos. 9-11, beads, nos. 14-20.

1 = reg. no. 148, 2 = 158, 3 = 82, 4 = 77, 5 = 30, 6 = 45, 7 = 159,
8 = 127, 9 = 37, 10 = 43, 11 = 47, 12 = 81, 13 = 9, 14 = 35, 15 = 38,
16 = 46, 17 = 49, 18 = 53, 19 = 98, 20 = 132.

183

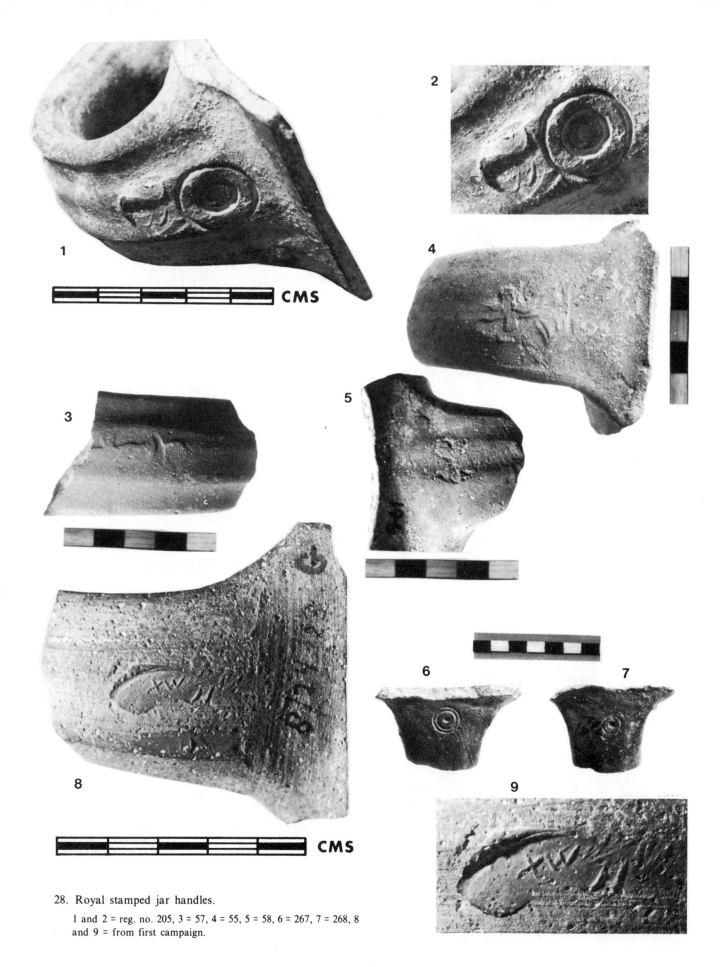

CMS

CMS

28. Royal stamped jar handles.

1 and 2 = reg. no. 205, 3 = 57, 4 = 55, 5 = 58, 6 = 267, 7 = 268, 8 and 9 = from first campaign.

184

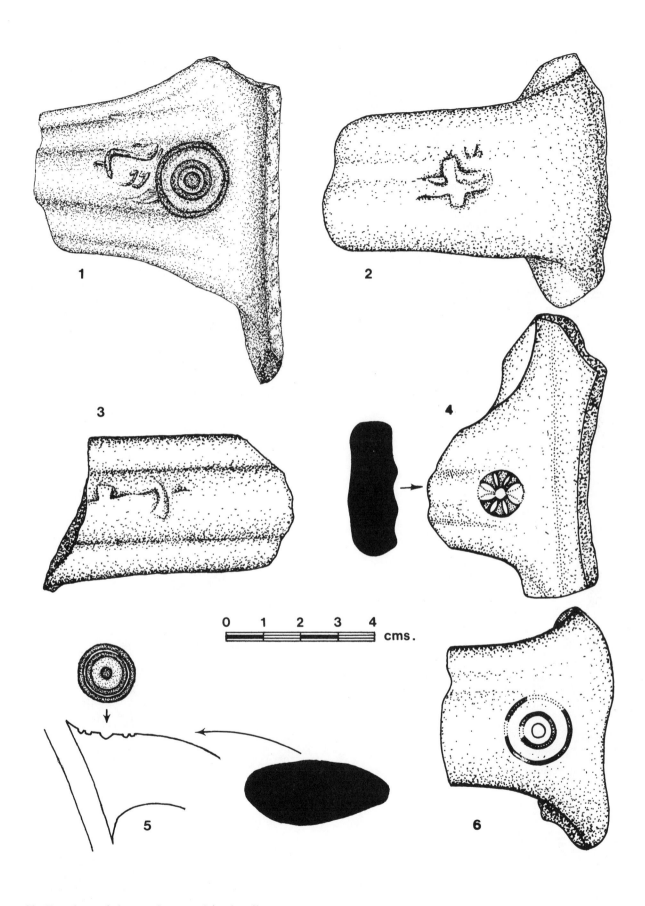

29. Drawings of the royal stamped jar handles.

1 = reg. no. 205, 2 = 55, 3 = 57, 4 = 58, 5 = 267, 6 = 268.

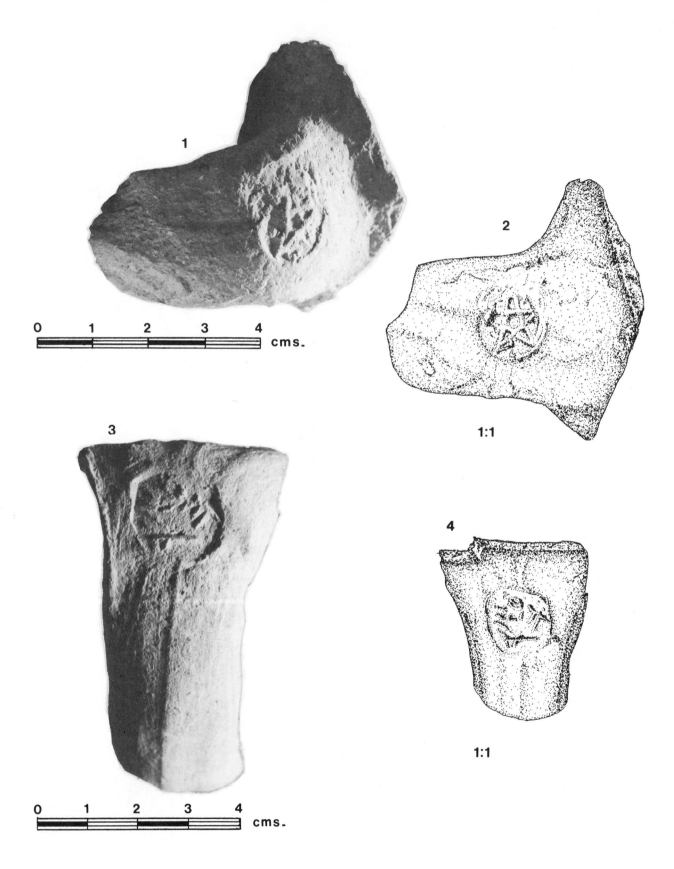

0 1 2 3 4 cms.

1:1

1:1

0 1 2 3 4 cms.

30. A *yrslm* handle and a *yhd*-plus-symbol handle.
   1 and 2 = reg. no. 203, 3 and 4 = 204.

31. An ostracon, reg. no. 1.

　　1. The ostracon (photo by Dorothy Olsen). 2. The inscription on
the ostracon (photo by Dorothy Olsen). 3. Hand copy of the
ostracon (drawing by Jeannine M. Schonta).

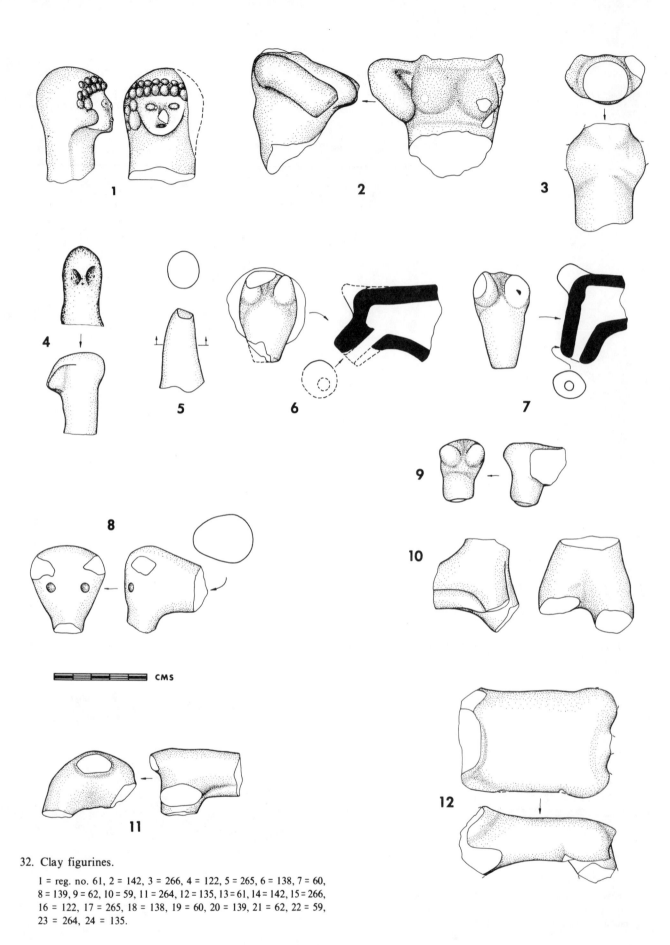

32. Clay figurines.

1 = reg. no. 61, 2 = 142, 3 = 266, 4 = 122, 5 = 265, 6 = 138, 7 = 60,
8 = 139, 9 = 62, 10 = 59, 11 = 264, 12 = 135, 13 = 61, 14 = 142, 15 = 266,
16 = 122, 17 = 265, 18 = 138, 19 = 60, 20 = 139, 21 = 62, 22 = 59,
23 = 264, 24 = 135.

13　14　15

16　17　18　19

20　21　22　23

Scale for figs 13-24

CMS

24

Pl. 32 continued.

189

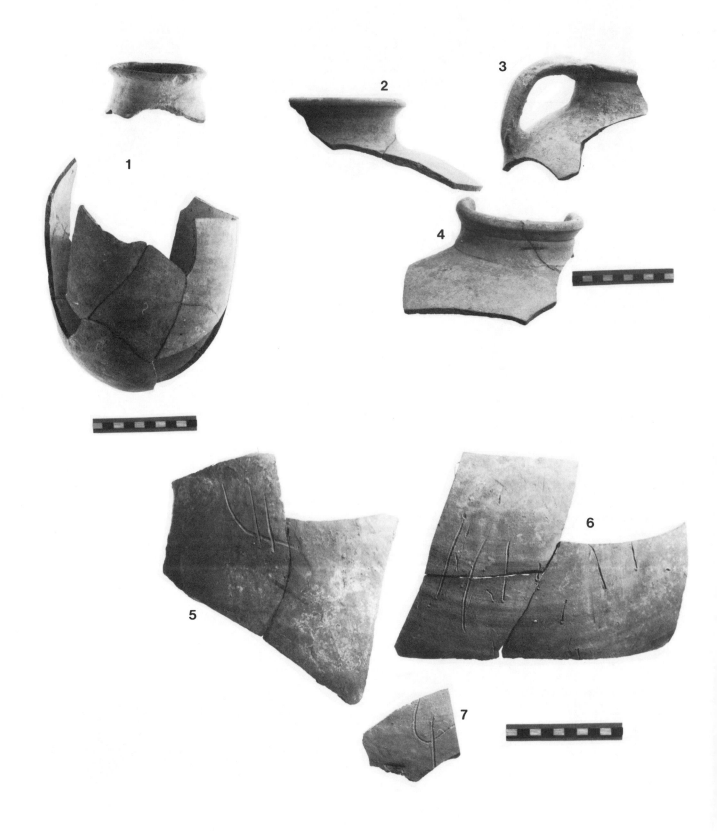

33. Period III B jars and jugs and marked sherds.

1 = reg. no. 206, 2 = 269, 3 = 270, 4 = 271, 5 = 272, 26 = 273, 7 = 54.

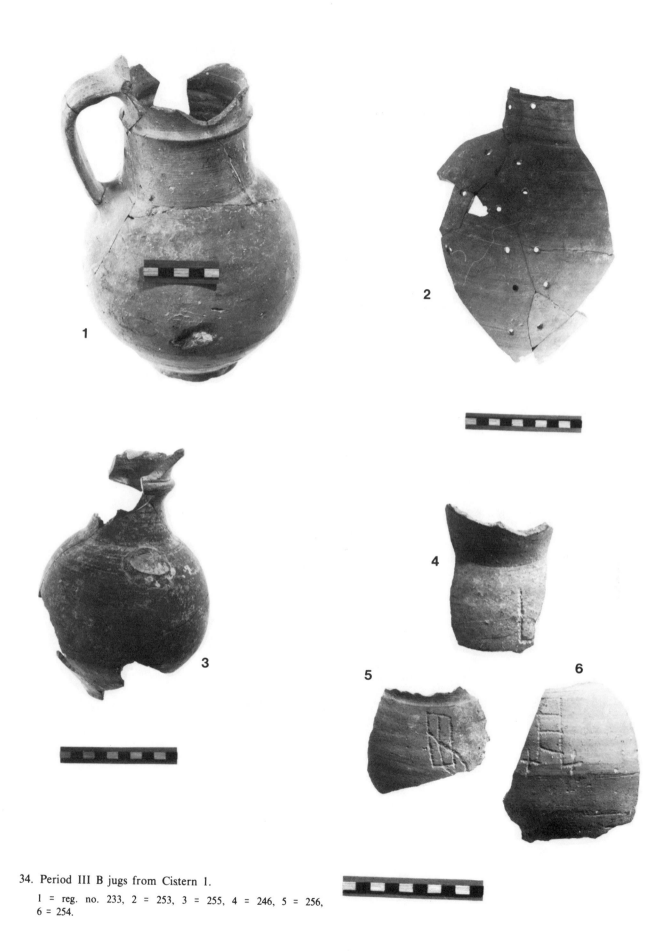

34. Period III B jugs from Cistern 1.

1 = reg. no. 233, 2 = 253, 3 = 255, 4 = 246, 5 = 256,
6 = 254.

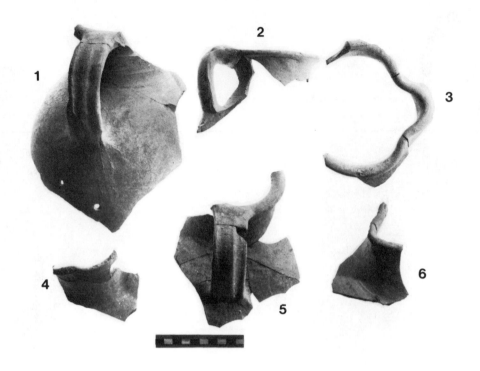

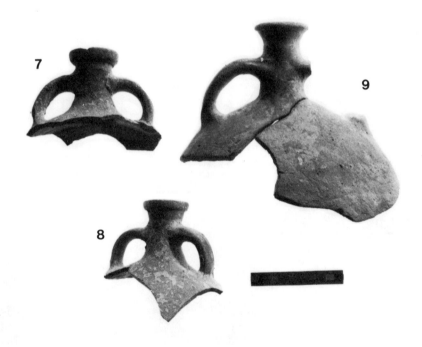

35. Period III B jug and flask rims and handles.

1-9 = reg. nos. 274-282.

36. Period III juglets.

1 = reg. no. 211, 2 = 284, 3 = 210, 4 = 209, 5 = 214.

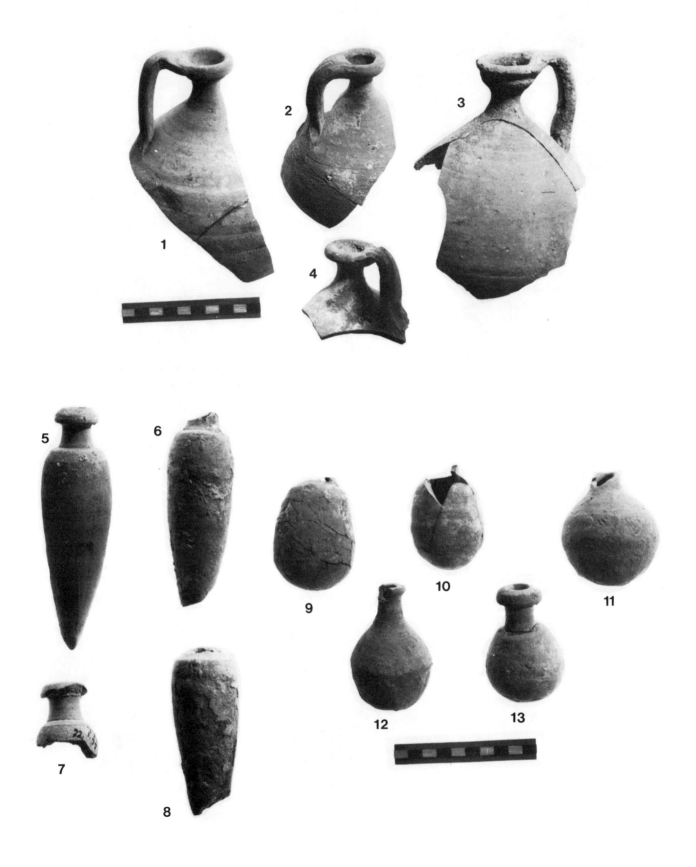

37. Period III B juglets and bottles.

1 = reg. no. 285, 2 = 286, 3 = 126, 4 = 287, 5 = 71, 6 = 213, 7 = 216,
8 = 215, 9 = 172, 10 = 212, 11 = 215, 12 = 137, 13 = 173.

38. Period III B large bowls. ·
    1 = reg. no. 143, 2 = 69, 3 = 228, 4 = 217.

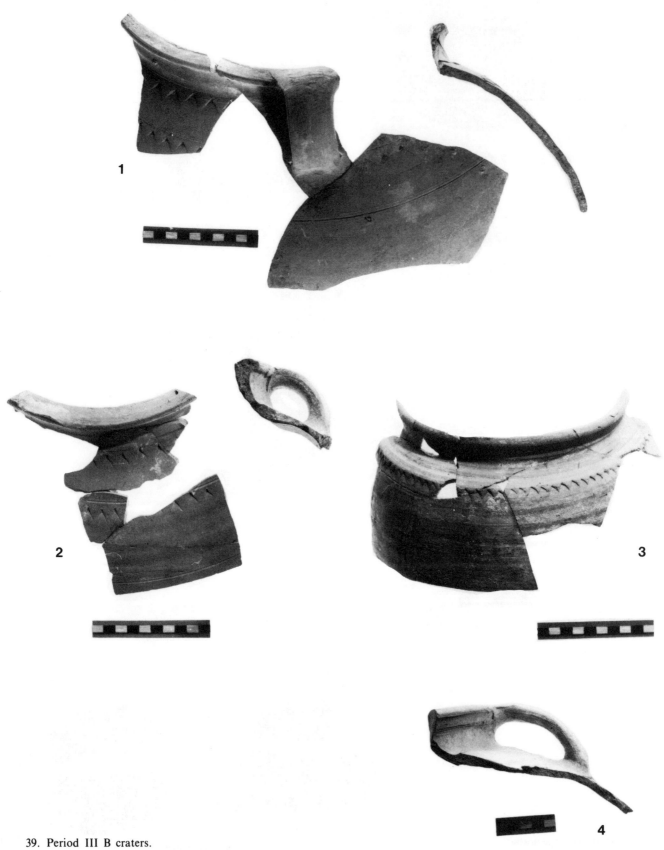

39. Period III B craters.

1 = reg. no. 259, 2 = 260, 3 = 258, 4 = 261.

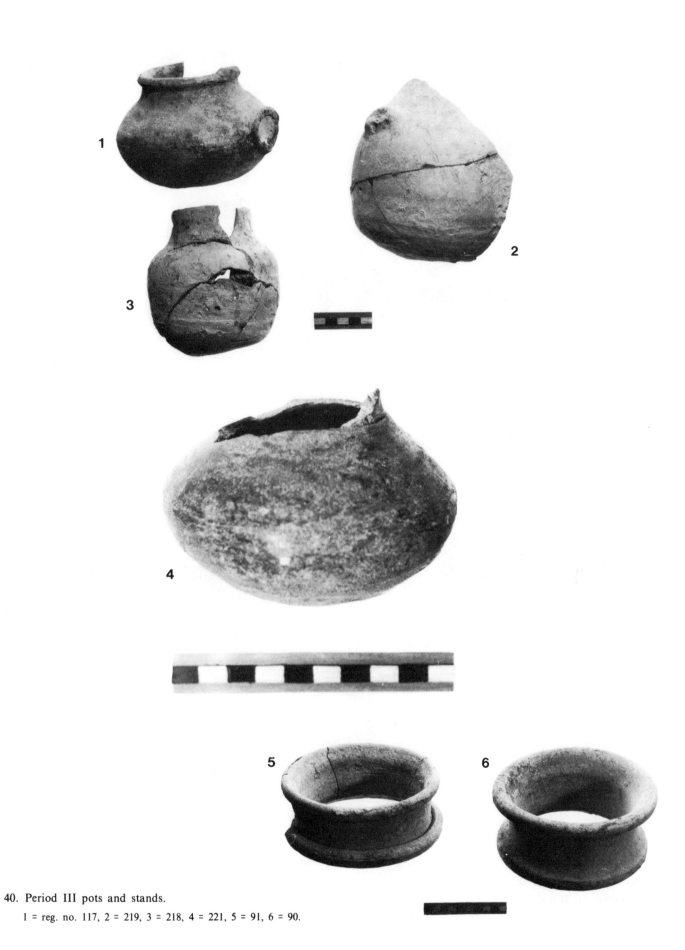

40. Period III pots and stands.

1 = reg. no. 117, 2 = 219, 3 = 218, 4 = 221, 5 = 91, 6 = 90.

41. Period III cooking-pots.

1-10 — marked handles from Silo 36, 11 = reg. no. 88, 12 = 160,
13 = 288, 14 = 289.

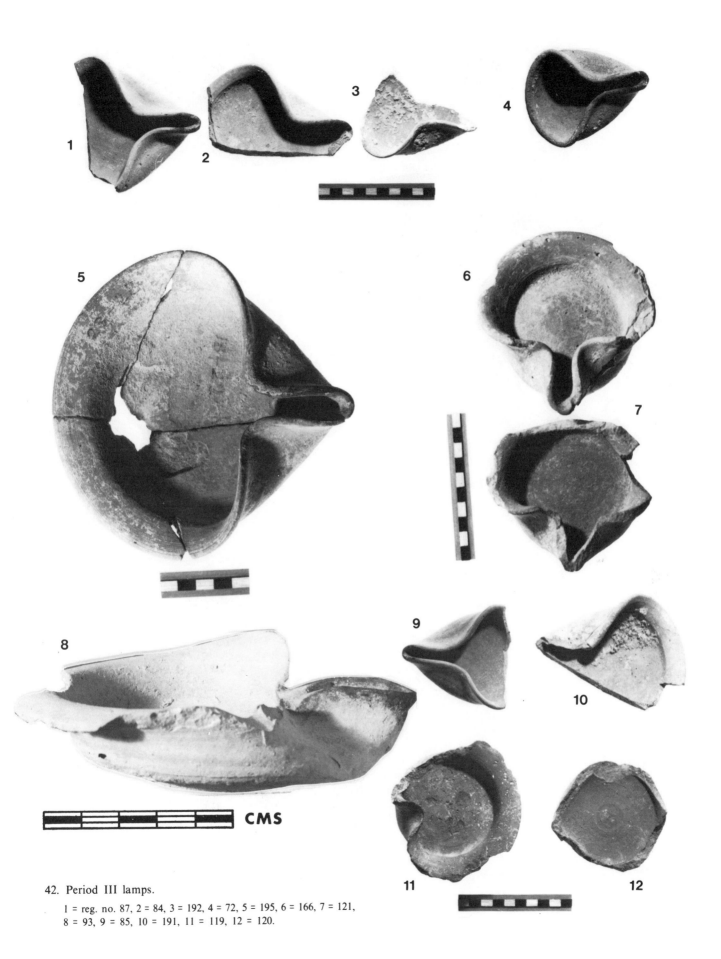

CMS

42. Period III lamps.

1 = reg. no. 87, 2 = 84, 3 = 192, 4 = 72, 5 = 195, 6 = 166, 7 = 121,
8 = 93, 9 = 85, 10 = 191, 11 = 119, 12 = 120.

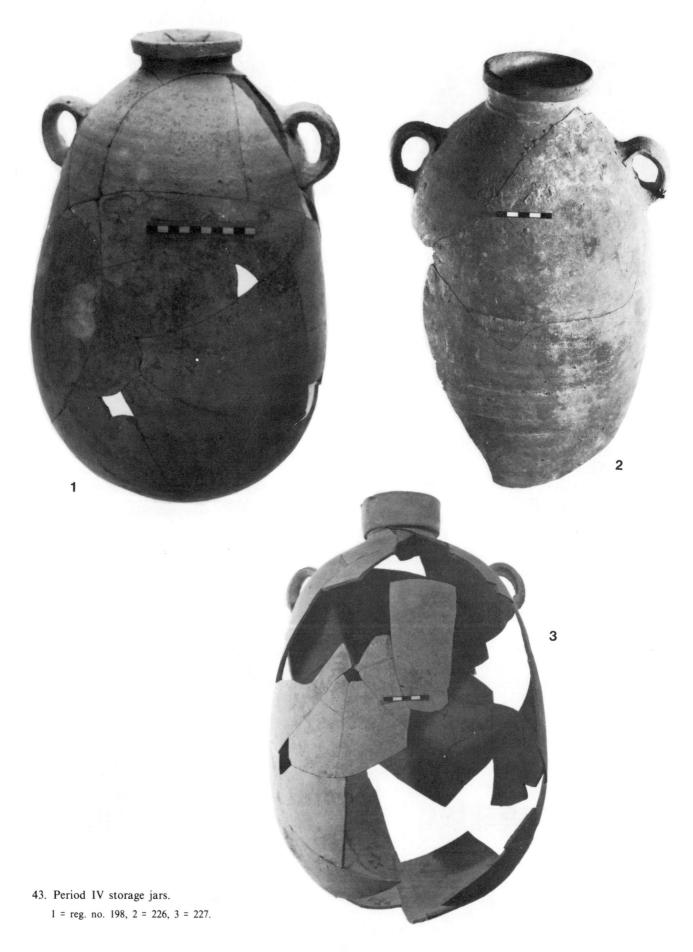

43. Period IV storage jars.
   1 = reg. no. 198, 2 = 226, 3 = 227.

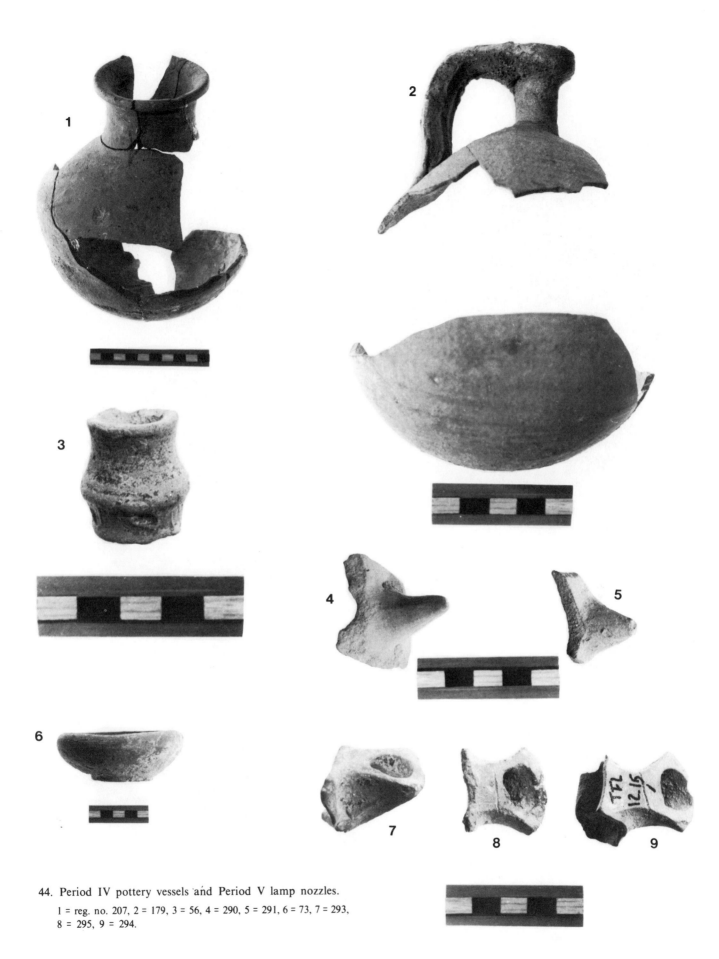

44. Period IV pottery vessels and Period V lamp nozzles.
1 = reg. no. 207, 2 = 179, 3 = 56, 4 = 290, 5 = 291, 6 = 73, 7 = 293, 8 = 295, 9 = 294.

45. Period IV cooking-pots.
   1 = reg. no. 162, 2 = 92, 3 = 116, 4 = 220, 5 = 169, 6 = 170, 7 = 89.

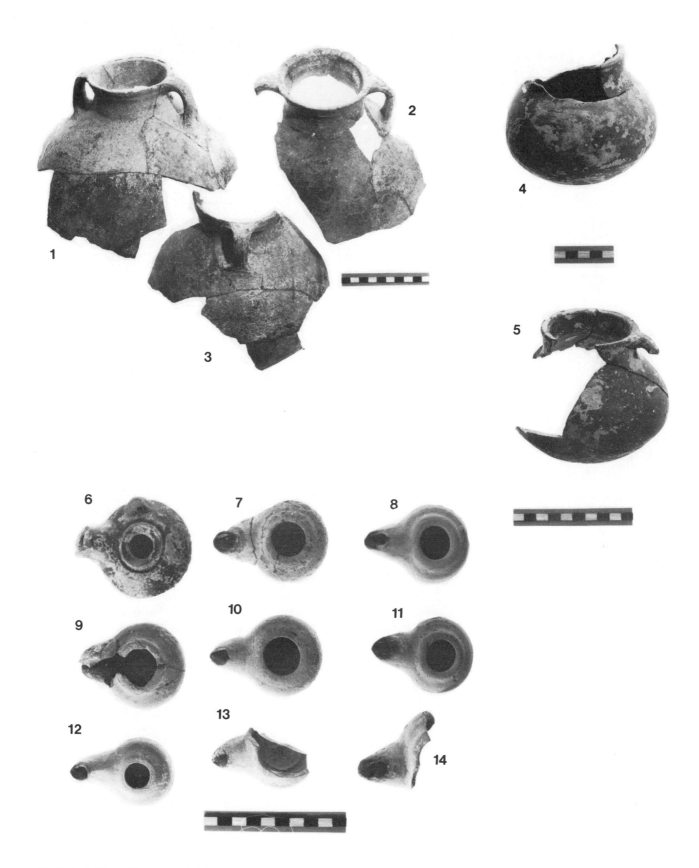

46. Period IV cooking-pots and lamps.

1 = reg. no. 296, 2 = 292, 3 = 283, 4 = 146, 5 = 164, 6 = 118, 7 = 66,
8 = 63, 9 = 67, 10 = 136, 11 = 65, 12 = 64, 13 = 68, 14 = 197.

Pl. 47

MIDDLE BRONZE AND PERIOD I POTTERY
See pp. 79-80

	Locus	Stratum	Ware
1a 1b	IV-unstr.	—	2.5 YR 5/6 red, 10 YR 6/3 pale brown to 6/4 light yellowish brown core; many small, medium, and large crystalline and some white and gray incl.; cl; handmade
2	XXIII-13	I	5 YR 5/2 reddish gray, 10 YR 5/1 gray core; many small to medium and some large white incl.; ffl
3	XIX-2ext	III A	10 YR 6/3 pale brown, 5 YR 6/4 light reddish brown core; many small and medium white and dark incl.; ffl
4	XVI-5	III B	5 YR 7/4 pink, 10 YR 7/3 very pale brown core; many small and few medium white and gray incl.; ffl
5	XIII-2	II	5 YR 6/4 light reddish brown, 10 YR 5/2 grayish brown core; many small to medium and few large white and few small and medium brown incl.; ffl
6	VII-3b	II	5 YR 6/6 reddish yellow, 10 YR 5/2 grayish brown core; many small and few medium white and few dark incl.; ffl
7	XIII-2	II	5 YR 7/4 pink, 7.5 YR 7/4 pink surfaces, 10 YR 5/1 to 4/1 gray to dark gray core; many small to some large white, black, brown, and gray incl.; ffl
8	XXIII-13	I	5 YR 7/6 reddish yellow, 10 YR 6/1 light gray core; many small to large white, gray and some brown incl.; ml
9	XVII-8	I	5 YR 6/4 light reddish brown core, 10 YR 6/4 light yellowish brown toward ext., 7.5 YR 8/4 pink ext. surface, 10 YR 5/2 grayish brown toward int., 7.5 YR 7/2 pinkish gray int. surface; many small to medium white and some gray and brown incl.; ffl
10	XXIII-13	I	5 YR 7/3 pink; many small to some medium white and few gray incl.; fl
11	XXIII-13	I	10 YR 6/4 light yellowish brown; some small brown and white incl.; fl
12	XIX-2ext	III A	7.5 YR 7/4 pink; many tiny white and some medium gray and brown incl.; ffl
13	I-unstr.	—	10 YR 5/1 gray core, 7/3 very pale brown with 7.5 YR 6/4 light brown toward surfaces; many small and medium and few large gray incl.; ffl; 2.5 YR red slip top of rim; 5 YR 6/4 light reddish brown paint on ext. surface
14	XVII-14	I	2.5 YR red, 10 YR 4/1 dark gray core; many small to medium white and grayish incl.; ffl
15	VII-20	I	7.5 YR 6/4 light brown, N4/ dark gray core; many small to some to some medium gray incl.; ffl

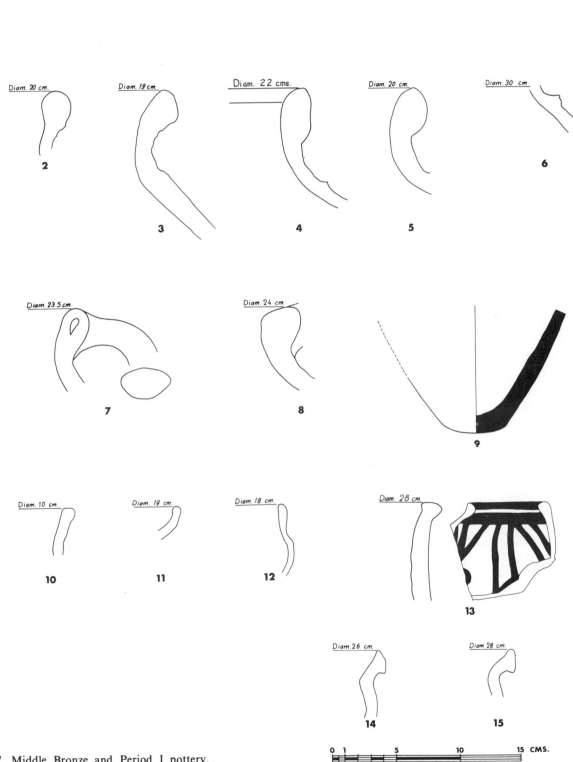

47. Middle Bronze and Period I pottery.

Pl. 48

PERIOD II POTTERY
See pp. 80-81

	Locus	Stratum	Ware
1	XIII-2	II	5 YR 7/3 pink, 10 YR 5/1 gray core; many small to medium gray, some white, and few brown incl.; ffl
2	XVIII S-36	pre-III A	7.5 YR 7/2 pinkish gray, 10 YR 4/1 dark gray core; many small to few medium white incl.; ffl
3	XVIII S-36	pre-III A	5 YR 7/4 pink, 10 YR 7/3 very pale brown core; many small and few medium white and gray incl.; ffl
4	VII-5b	III B	7.5 YR 6/4 light brown, 10 YR 5/2 grayish brown core; many medium and large white and gray incl.; ffl
5	XVII-4	II	7.5 YR 8/4 pink, 7/2 pinkish gray core; many tiny white and few brown incl.; ffl
6	XIII-2	II	2.5 YR 5/5 light red, N3/ very dark gray core, 5 YR 7/4 pink next to core; many small to medium white and gray incl.; ffl
7	XIII-2	II	2.5 YR 6/6 light red, N5/ gray core; many small to few medium white and brown incl.; ffl
8	VII-3b	II	5 YR 7/4 to 7/6 pink to reddish yellow, 10 YR 6/3 pale brown core; many small to large white and gray and some brown incl.; ml
9	XIII-10	II	10 YR 7/4 very pale brown, 7/2 light gray core, 5 YR 7/4 pink ext. surface, 7.5 YR 7/4 pink int. surface; many small to some large dark brown and very light brown incl.; ffl
10	XIII-2	II	2.5 YR 6/6 light red; many small white and few small to medium brown incl.; ffl
11	VII-3b	II	2.5 YR red, N4/ dark gray core; many small and few medium white incl.; ffl
12	XIII-2	II	5 YR 5/4 reddish brown, 5/3 reddish brown core; many small to some medium and few large white and dark brown incl.; ffl
13	XIII-2	II	5 YR 7/5 pink/reddish yellow, 5/1 gray core; many small to some medium white, gray, and few brown incl.; ffl
14	XIII-2	II	5 YR 7/5 pink/reddish yellow; many small to medium and few large white, some gray and few brown incl.; ffl
15	XIII-2	II	5 YR 6/4 light reddish brown, 10 YR 4/1 dark gray core; many small to medium white and few gray incl.; ffl
16	XIII-2	II	2.5 YR 5/6 red, N4/ dark gray core, 10 YR 7/4 very pale brown around core; many small to medium white or grayish incl.; ffl
17	XVII-4	II	2.5 YR 5/6 red, 10 YR 4/2 dark grayish brown core; many small and some medium white and gray incl.; ffl
18	XVII-4	II	5 YR 6/6 reddish yellow, 10 YR 5/1 gray core; many small and medium white incl.; ffl; slightly raised ridge on rim with diagonal grooves
19	XIII-15	II	Not available
20	XIX-unstr.	—	2.5 YR 6/6 light red; many small and medium white incl.; ffl
21	XIX-2ext	III A	5 YR 6/6 reddish yellow; many small and some medium white and few large white and brown incl.; ffl

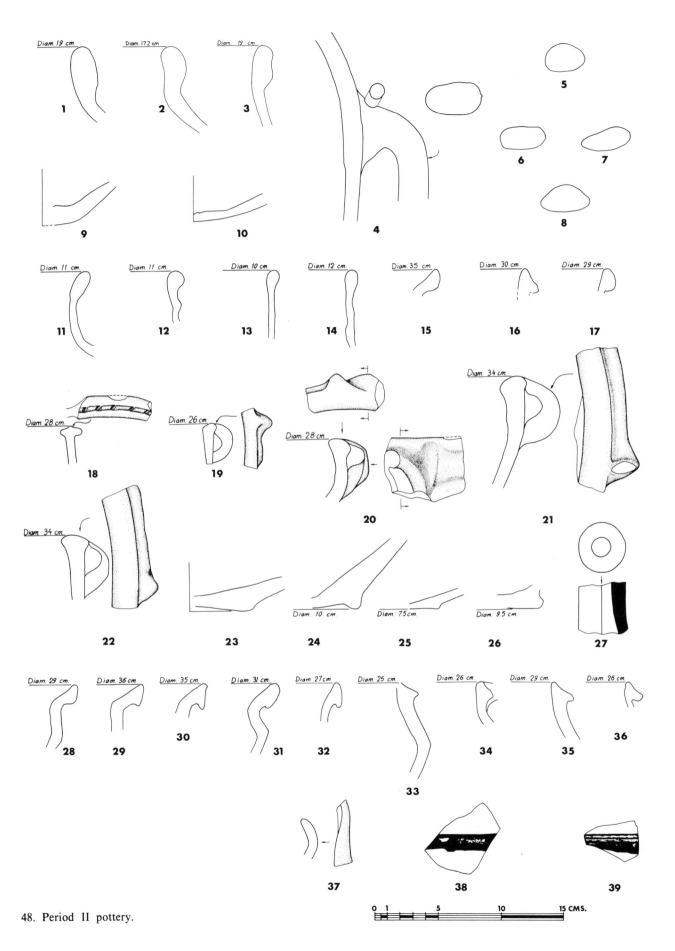

48. Period II pottery.

Pl. 48 cont.

22	XXIII-8	IV	5 YR 6/3 light reddish brown; many small and some medium white and brown incl.; ffl
23	XIII-2	II	2.5 YR 6/6 light red, 5 YR 5/1 gray core, 10 YR 7/3 very pale brown around core; many tiny white and some small to few medium black and brown incl.; ffl
24	XIII-10	II	5 YR 4/4 reddish brown, 10 YR 6/2 light brownish gray core; many small to medium and few large white incl.; ffl
25	XIII-10	II	2.5 YR 5/6 red, 10 YR 5/1 gray core, 10 YR 7/5 very pale brown/yellow around core; many small to medium gray and few white incl.; ffl
26	XVII-4	II	75 YR 7/4 pink, 10 YR 6/4 light yellowish brown core; some small white and brown and few medium brown incl.; ffl
27	VII-5b	III B	5 YR 5/6 yellowish red; many small white and some medium white and gray incl.; ffl
28	XIII-2	II	10 YR 7/4 very pale brown, 4/1 dark gray core, 5 YR 6/4 light reddish brown around core; many small to some medium white incl.; ffl
29	XVII-4	II	5 YR 5.5/6 reddish yellow/yellowish red, 10 YR 5/2 grayish brown core; many small to medium white and gray incl.; ffl
30	XIII-2	II	5 YR 5/6 yellowish red, 10 YR 4/2 dark grayish brown core; small and medium many white and some brown incl.; ffl
31	XIII-10	II	5 YR 6/4 light reddish brown, 10 YR 6/4 light yellowish brown core; many small to medium light gray incl.; ffl
32	XIII-10	II	5 YR 5/4 reddish brown, 5 Y 3/2 dark olive gray core; many small to medium white and many tiny crystalline incl.; ffl
33	XIII-11	II	5 YR 6/4 light reddish brown, 10 YR 4/1 dark gray core, 10 YR 6/4 light yellowish brown around core; many small to medium white and gray incl.; ffl
34	XIII-11	II	7.5 YR 4/2 to 4/4 brown to dark brown surfaces, 10 YR 2/1 black core, 2.5 Y 4/2 dark grayish brown around core; many small to medium white incl.; ffl
35	XIII-15	II	As 48:33 above
36	XIII-2	II	2.5 YR 5/6 red, N4/ dark gray core, 10 YR 7/4 very pale brown around core; many small to medium white or grayish incl.; ffl
37	VII-5b	III B	Not available
38	XX-7	IV	2.5 YR 4/4 reddish brown sandwiched (6 layers) with N5/ gray; medium and small white incl.; 2.5 YR N2.5/ black over 5 YR 8/4 pink surface
39	XX-7	IV	2.5 YR 5/8 light red; few medium and small white and very few medium black incl.; 2.5 YR N2.5/ black over 5 YR 8/4 pink surface

Pl. 49

PERIOD III JARS
See pp. 88-89

	Locus	Stratum	Ware
1	XVIII S-36	pre-III A	5 YR 4/4 reddish brown, 2.5/1 black core, 7/6 reddish yellow ext. surface; medium white incl.; fcl
2	XVIII S-36	pre-III A	5 YR 4/3 reddish brown, 7/4 pink ext. surface; mcl
3	XVIII S-36	pre-III A	5 YR 4/4 reddish brown, 7/4 pink ext. surface; very small white incl.; ml
4	XVIII S-36	pre-III A	5 YR 7/4 pink; very small white incl.; ml
5	XVIII S-36	pre-III A	7.5 YR 6/2 pinkish gray, 8/4 ext. surface; few white incl.; fl
6	XVIII S-36	pre-III A	5 YR 4/1 dark gray, 8/1 white ext. surface; small white incl.; mcl
7	XVIII S-38	pre-III A	2.5 YR 4/4 reddish brown, 5 YR 7/4 pink ext. surface; mcl
8	XVIII S-39	pre-III A	2.5 YR 6/4 light reddish brown, 5 YR 8/3 pink ext. surface; small and some large white incl.; mcl
9	II-35	III B	Not available
10	XVI-4	III B	Not available
11	III-24 C-1	IV	5 YR 5/6 yellowish red, 10 YR 5/2 grayish brown core; many small and some medium white incl.; ffl
12	XVIII S-36	pre-III A	10 YR 7/1 light gray, 5 YR 7/3 pink ext. surface; medium white incl.; ffl
13	XVIII S-38	pre-III A	5 YR reddish yellow, 10 YR 5/2 grayish brown core; many small and some medium white and gray incl.; ffl
14	V-90	III A	10 R 6/6 light red; many small and medium white and some brown incl.; ffl
15	II-29	III B	10 R 5/8 red, 5 YR 7/4 pink ext. surface; small white incl.; ml
16	XVI-5	III B	Not available
17	III-24	IV	5 YR 6/6 reddish yellow, 2.5 YR 5/6 red core; many small and some medium white, some medium gray and dark incl.; ffl
18	XVIII S-36	pre-III A	5 YR 7/6 reddish yellow, 8/3 pink ext. surface; large white incl.; mcl
19	XVIII S-36	pre-III A	5 YR 7/6 reddish yellow, 7/3 pink ext. surface; small white incl.; mcl
20	XVIII S-36	pre-III A	5 YR 7/4 pink, 3/1 very dark gray core, 7/3 ext. surface; very small white incl.; mcl
21	XVIII S-36	pre-III A	2.5 YR 5/4 reddish brown, 6/4 light reddish brown ext. surface; small white incl.; ml
22	XVIII S-36	pre-III A	5 YR 7/4 pink, 7/3 pink ext. surface; very small white incl.; ml
23	XXIV-12	III A	7.5 YR 7/6 reddish yellow, 6/6 reddish yellow core, 8/2 pinkish white ext. surface; small white incl.; ml
24	XXIV-8	III A	5 YR 8/4 pink; small white incl.; ml
25	I-45	III	Not available
26	XIX-2ext	III A	5 YR reddish yellow, 10 YR 6/1 gray core; many medium and some large white incl.; ffl
27	XIX-2ext	III A	5 YR reddish yellow, 10 YR 6/4 light yellowish brown core; many small and some medium white and few brown incl.; ffl
28	V-90	III A	7.5 YR 5/6 red, 5 YR 5/4 reddish brown core; some medium white and brown incl.; fl

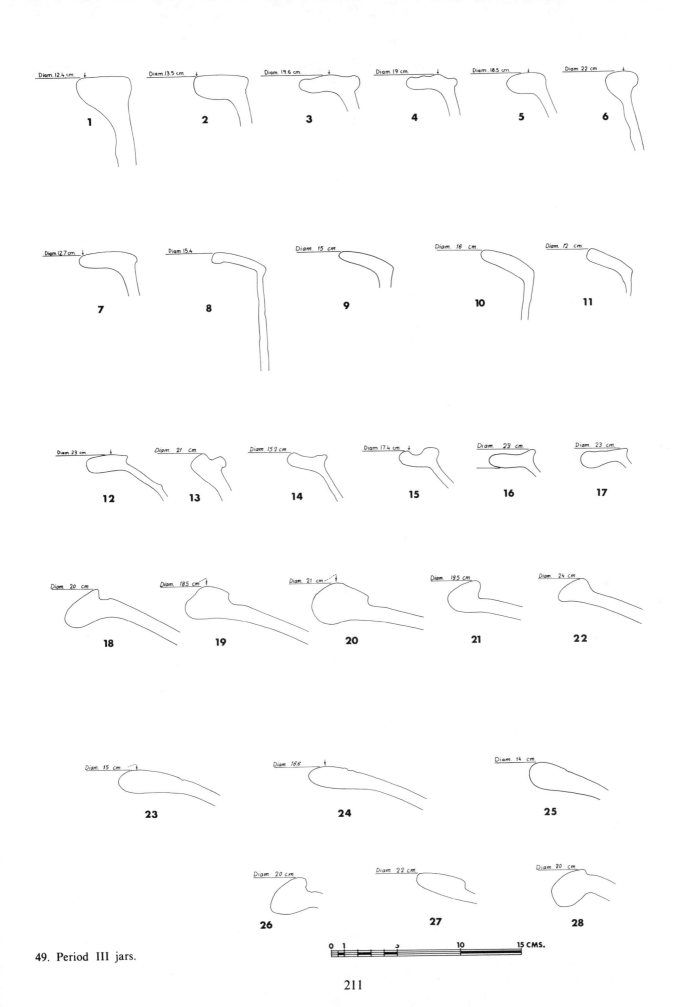

49. Period III jars.

Pl. 50

PERIOD III JARS
See pp. 89-90

	Locus	Stratum	Ware
1	I-49	III A	10 YR 8/2 white; ffl
2	VIII-16	III A	5 YR 7/3 pink; many small and some medium white and some brown incl.; ffl
3	VIII-19	III A	5 YR 6/6 reddish yellow, 10 YR 6/2 light brownish gray core; many small and medium white and some large white, brown, and gray incl.; ffl
4	XXIV-12	III A	5 YR 4/1 dark gray, 6/3 light reddish brown toward ext.; many small to some medium white and brown incl.; ffl
5	XXIV-11	III A	5 YR 6/3 light reddish brown; many small and medium white and gray incl.; ffl
6	XXIV-11	III A	10 YR 6/3 pale brown, 6/2 light brownish gray core; very many tiny and some small white and brown, and very few medium white incl.; cl
7	XIX-2ext	III A	7.5 YR 6/4 light brown, 10 YR 6/2 light brownish gray core; many small and some medium white and gray incl.; ffl
8	XIX-2ext	III A	10 YR 5/2 grayish brown; many small and some white and gray incl.; ffl
9	II-15	III A	7.5 YR 7/8 reddish yellow, 8/4 pink ext. surface; small white incl.; ffl
10	II-15	III A	10 YR 8/6 yellow, 8/4 very pale brown toward ext. surface; small white incl.; ffl
11	II-15	III A	5 YR 5/3 reddish brown; some small and medium white and few small brown incl.; ffl
12	II-35	III B	7.5 YR 6/2 pinkish gray, 5/4 brown toward surface; medium white incl.; ffl
13	II-29	III B	10 YR 5/1 gray; some small and medium white and grayish incl.; fl
14	II-31	III B	5 YR 6/4 light reddish brown, 10 YR 6/3 pale brown core; many small and few medium white and some medium gray incl.; ffl
15	XVI-4	III B	Not available
16	IX-14	III B	Not available
17	XVI-5	III B	10 YR 5/1 gray; many small and medium white and grayish incl.; ffl
18	IX-14	III B	2.5 YR 6/6 light red, 10 YR 6/2 light brownish gray core; many small and some medium white and very few large brown incl.; ffl
19	IX-7	III B	Not available
20	I-45	III B	Not available
21	I-45	III B	Not available
22	I-45	III B	Not available
23	I-45	III B	Not available
24	I-45	III B	Not available
25	I-45	III B	Not available
26	I-35	III B	2.5 YR 6/4 light reddish brown; many small to medium white, brown, and few black incl.; ffl
27	I-35	III B	2.5 YR 5/4 reddish brown; many small and few medium white incl.; ffl

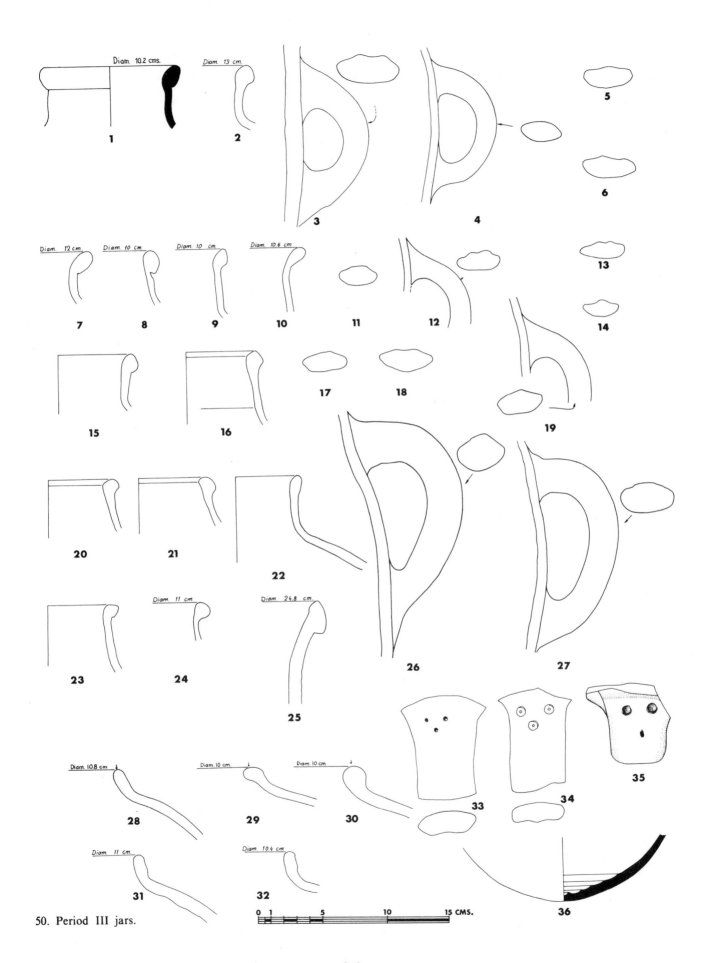

Diam. 10.2 cms.

Diam. 13 cm.

Diam. 12 cm.

Diam. 10 cm.

Diam. 10 cm.

Diam. 10.6 cm.

Diam. 11 cm.

Diam. 24.8 cm.

Diam. 10.8 cm.

Diam. 10 cm.

Diam. 10 cm.

Diam. 11 cm.

Diam. 10.4 cm.

50. Period III jars.

0 1   5   10   15 CMS.

Pl. 50 cont.

28	XVIII S-36	pre-III A	5 YR 8/2 pinkish white, 8/1 toward ext. surface; small white incl.; ml
29	XVIII S-36	pre-III A	5 YR 8/3 pink, 8/1 ext. surface, 3/1 very dark gray core; ml
30	XVIII S-36	pre-III A	5 YR 6/4 light reddish brown, 8/3 pink ext. surface, 5/1 gray core; small white incl.; mcl
31	XVIII S-38	pre-III A	10 YR 5/1 gray and 10 R 5/6 red; very many tiny and few small white, and some medium brown incl.; cl
32	XVIII S-38	pre-III A	2.5 YR 6/6 light red; many small and medium white and grayish incl.; ffl
33	XVIII S-36	pre-III A	10 R 6/1 reddish gray, 6/3 pale red ext. surface; medium white incl; mcl; 3 punched holes
34	XVIII S-36	pre-III A	5 YR 7/2 pinkish gray, 8/1 ext. surface; small white incl.; ml; 3 punched holes
35	XVIII S-39	pre-III A	5 YR 4/1 dark gray; medium and large white and dark incl.; 2 punched holes
36	XVIII S-39	pre-III A	2.5 YR 6/8 light red; small white incl.; ml

Pl. 51

PERIOD III JARS
See p. 90

	Locus	Stratum	Ware	Reg. no.	Photo pl.
1	X-8	III B	5 YR 5/1 gray, 2.5 YR 5/2 weak red toward surface; very many medium and small white incl.	271	33:4
2	X-8	III B	10 YR 5/1 gray core, 5 YR 5/6 yellowish red toward ext. surface, 10 YR 5/3 toward int. surface; many small and some medium white and few medium gray incl.; ffl		
3	X-8	III B	5 YR 7/6 reddish yellow, 5/3 reddish brown core; many small and medium white incl.	269	33:2
4	X-8	III B	2.5 YR N5/ gray, 6/6 light red toward surfaces; medium and small white incl.		
5	III-30 C-1	III B	2.5 YR 5/6 red, 10 YR 5/1 gray core; many small and few large white and few medium brown incl.; ffl		
6	III-30 C-1	III B	5 YR 6/4 light reddish brown ext., 10 YR 6/2 light brownish gray int.; very many tiny to small white and some brown, and few large brown and white incl.; cl		
7	III-30 C-1	III B	5 YR 6/6 reddish yellow near surfaces, 10 YR 6/2 light brownish gray around core, 2.5 YR 5/6 red core; many small and some medium white, and few brown incl.; ffl		
8	III-30 C-1	III B	5 YR 6/3 light reddish brown, 10 YR 6/2 light brownish gray core; many small and some medium white, and few brown incl.; ffl		
9	III-30 C-1	III B	10 YR 6/4 light yellowish brown, 5/2 grayish brown, 2.5 YR 6/6 light red; many small and some medium white, and some medium grayish incl.; ffl		
10	III-30 C-1	III B	5 YR 6/3 light reddish brown, 10 R 4/1 dark reddish gray core; many small to few medium white and dark brown incl.; fl		
11	III-30 C-1	III B	5 YR 6/6 reddish yellow; many small and few medium white and some brown incl.; ffl		
12	X-8	III B	5 YR 6/4 light reddish brown, 5/1 gray core; many medium and small white incl.		
13	III-30 C-1	III B	5 YR 7/6 reddish yellow, 10 YR 7/2 light gray core; many small and some medium white and few dark incl.; ffl		
14	III-30 C-1	III B	7.5 YR 5/4 brown, 10 YR 5/1 gray core; many small and medium white and few large brown incl.; ffl		
15	III-30 C-1	III B	5 YR 6/6 reddish yellow, 10 YR 6/2 light brownish gray core; some small white and many medium and some large gray incl.; ffl		

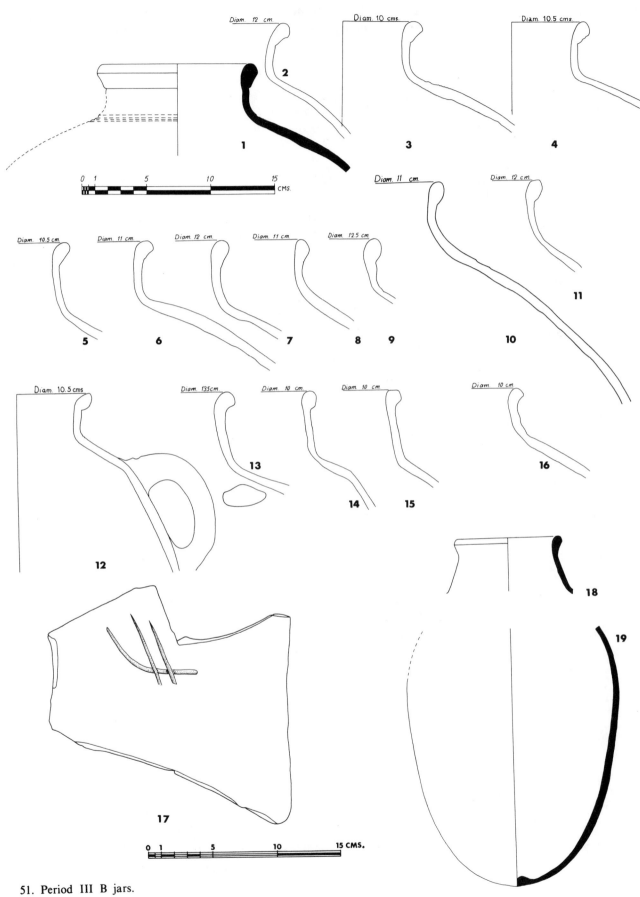

51. Period III B jars.

16	III-30 C-1	III B	5 YR 6/4 light reddish brown, 10 YR 5/2 grayish brown core; many small and some medium white and grayish incl.; ffl		
17	III-30 C-1	III B	7.5 YR 6/4 light brown; many small white and some red incl.; incised detail on ext. surface	272	33:5
18 & 19	III-30 C-1	III B	5 YR 4/4 reddish brown, 4/1 dark gray core; few large and medium and many small white incl.; ffl	206	33:1

Pl. 52

PERIOD III JARS
See p. 90

	Locus	*Stratum*	*Ware*	*Reg. no.*	*Photo pl.*
1	XII-28 S-40	III B	10 YR 8/2 white; very small white incl.; fl		
2	XII-28 S-40	III B	5 YR 8/4 pink; small white incl.; ml		
3	XII-28 S-40	III B	7.5 YR 8/2 pinkish white; small white incl.; fl		
4	XII-28 S-40	III B	7.5 YR 8/4 pink; small white incl.; fl		
5	XII-28 S-40	III B	10 YR 8/2 white; small incl.; ml		
6	XII-28 S-40	III B	5 YR 8/2 pinkish white; very small incl.; fl		
7	XII-28 S-40	III B	5 YR 8/4 pink; fl		
8	XII-28 S-40	III B	10 R 5/6 red, 4/1 dark reddish gray toward core; many medium and small white incl.; ml		
9	XII-28 S-40	III B	2.5 YR N4/ dark gray, 10 R 5/6 red toward surfaces; many medium and small and few large white incl.; fcl		
10	XII-28 S-40	III B	2.5 YR N4/ dark gray, 4/4 reddish brown toward surfaces; many small and medium white incl.; fcl		
11	XII-28 S-40	III B	5 YR 6/6 reddish yellow; few large gray and white and many medium and small white incl.; ffl		
12	XII-28 S-40	III B	10 R 5/6 red, 4/1 dark reddish gray core; many small to few medium white incl.; ffl; incised marks on ext. surface	273	33:6
13	III-28 C-1	III A-B	2.5 YR 6/6 light red, N6/ gray toward center; many small and medium white incl.	201	
14	III-28 C-1	III A-B	10 R 6/6 light red; very many medium and small white incl.	199	
15	III-28 C-1	III A-B	5 YR 4/4, 5/4 reddish brown, to 5/1 gray; large medium and many small white incl.	200	
16	III-28 C-1	III A-B	2.5 YR 6/6 light red, 7.5 YR 6/2 pinkish gray toward center; many medium and small white incl.	202	
17	III-24 C-1	IV	5 YR 5/6 yellowish red, 6/4 light reddish brown core; many small and some medium white, and few medium brown incl.; ffl		

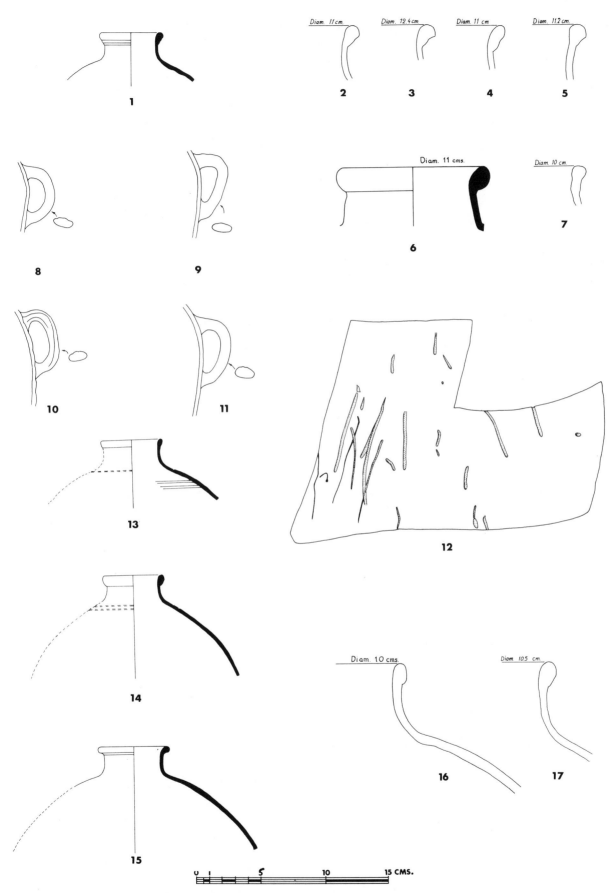

Diam. 11 cm.

Diam. 12.4 cm.

Diam. 11 cm

Diam. 11.2 cm.

Diam. 11 cms.

Diam. 10 cm.

Diam. 10 cms.

Diam. 10.5 cm.

15 CMS.

52. Period III jars.

Pl. 53

PERIOD III JUGS
See p. 90

	Locus	Stratum	Ware	Reg. no.	Photo pl.
1	III-30 C-1	III B	5 YR 4/4 reddish brown, 4/2 dark reddish gray int. surface, 7.5 YR 7/2 to 5 YR 7/2 pinkish gray ext. surface; many small and medium and few large white incl.; ffl	231	
2	III-30 C-1	III B	7.5 YR 6/4 light brown, 8/4 pink to 5 YR 6/1 gray int. surface, 7/3 pink to 5/1 gray ext. surface; many small, medium, and some large white, and very few gray incl.; ffl	233	34:1
3	III-30 C-1	III B	7.5 YR 5/4 brown, 5 YR 7/4 pink toward surfaces; many medium to few large black and white incl.; ffl	234	
4	III-30 C-1	III B	2.5 YR 5/6 to 4/6 red; many small to medium and few large white, with few medium gray and brown incl.; ffl	237	

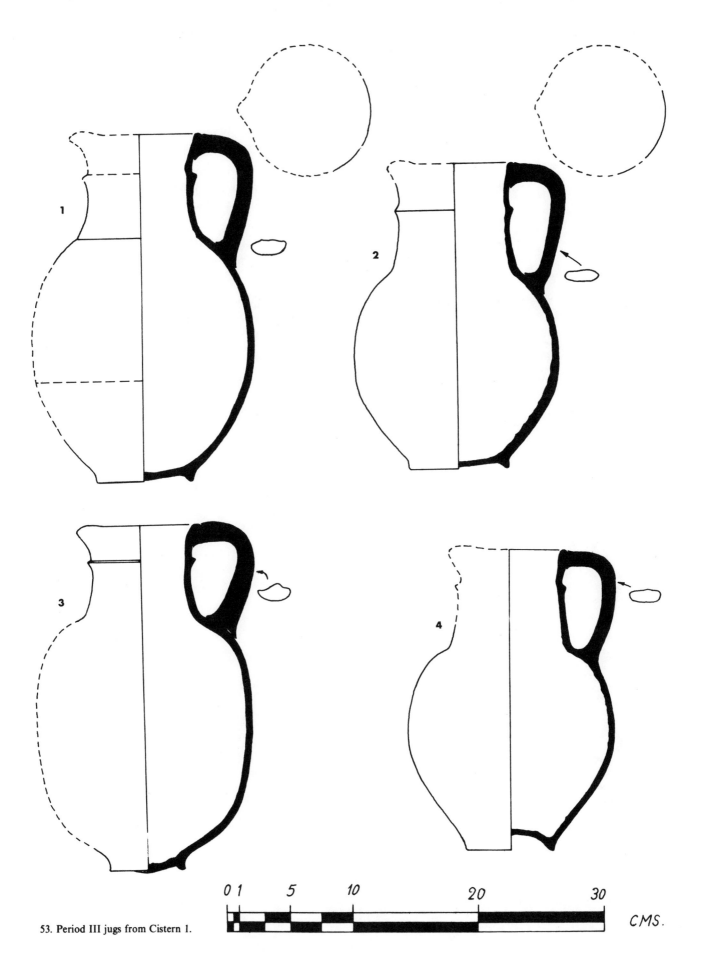

53. Period III jugs from Cistern 1.

0 1   5   10   20   30

CMS.

Pl. 54

PERIOD III JUGS
See p. 90

	Locus	Stratum	Ware	Reg. no.	Photo pl.
5	III-30 C-1	III B	10 YR 3/2 very dark grayish brown to 2.5 YR 2/0 black; many medium, some small and large white incl.; ml	238	
6	III-30 C-1	III B	10 YR 6/4 light yellowish brown to 5/4 yellowish brown, 2.5 YR 5/6 red toward surfaces; many small and few medium white and brown incl.; ffl	240	
7	III-30 C-1	III B	2.5 YR 5/6, 4/6 red, 6/6 light red to 10YR 5/1 gray to 6/3 pale brown ext. surface; many small, medium, and large white incl.; ffl	241	
8	III-30 C-1	III B	10 YR 5/3 brown, 5 YR 6/6 reddish yellow toward ext. surface; many small and some medium white incl.; ffl	244	

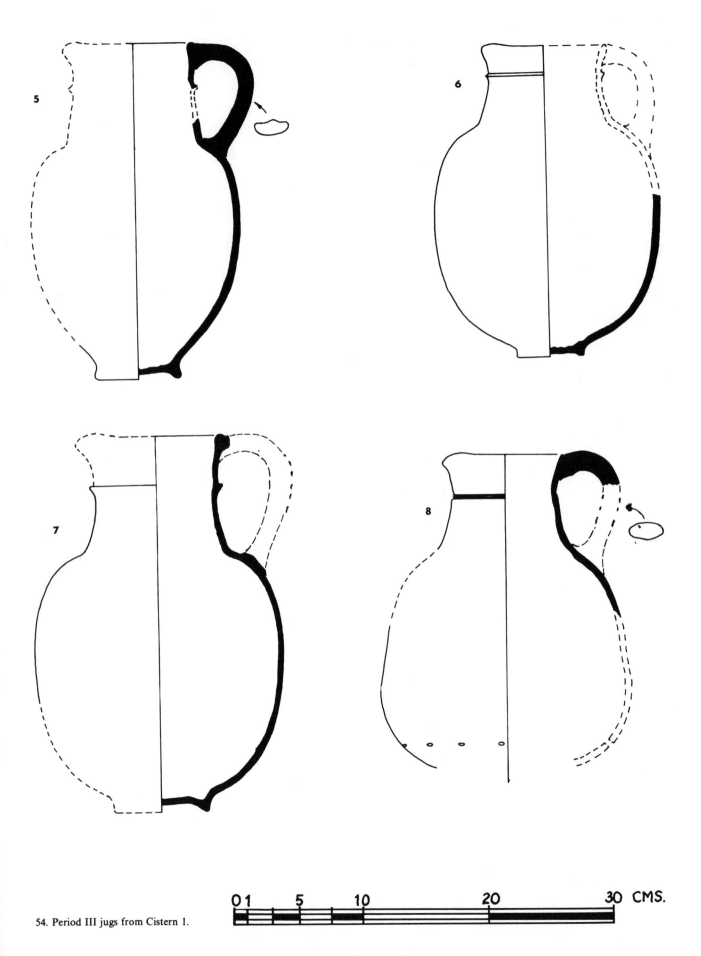

54. Period III jugs from Cistern 1.

0 1   5   10   20   30 CMS.

Pl. 55

PERIOD III JUGS
See p. 90

	Locus	Stratum	Ware	Reg. no.	Photo pl.
9	III-30 C-1	III B	10 YR 5/3 brown to 5/2 grayish brown toward int., 2.5 YR 5/6 red toward ext.; many small to some medium and few large white incl.; incised lines on shoulder	246	34:4
10	III-30 C-1	III B	2.5 YR 5/6 red; many medium and small white incl.; ffl; punctured holes for mending length of jug	253	34:2
11	III-30 C-1	III B	7.5 YR 6/4 light brown; medium and small and few large white incl.; ml; incised detail on shoulder	254	34:6
12	III-30 C-1	III B	2.5 YR 5/6 red, 5 YR 5/3 reddish brown toward center; medium and small white incl.; ffl	255	34:3
13	III-30 C-1	III B	5 YR 4/3 reddish brown; small and few large and medium white incl.; incised detail from shoulder of jug	256	34:5

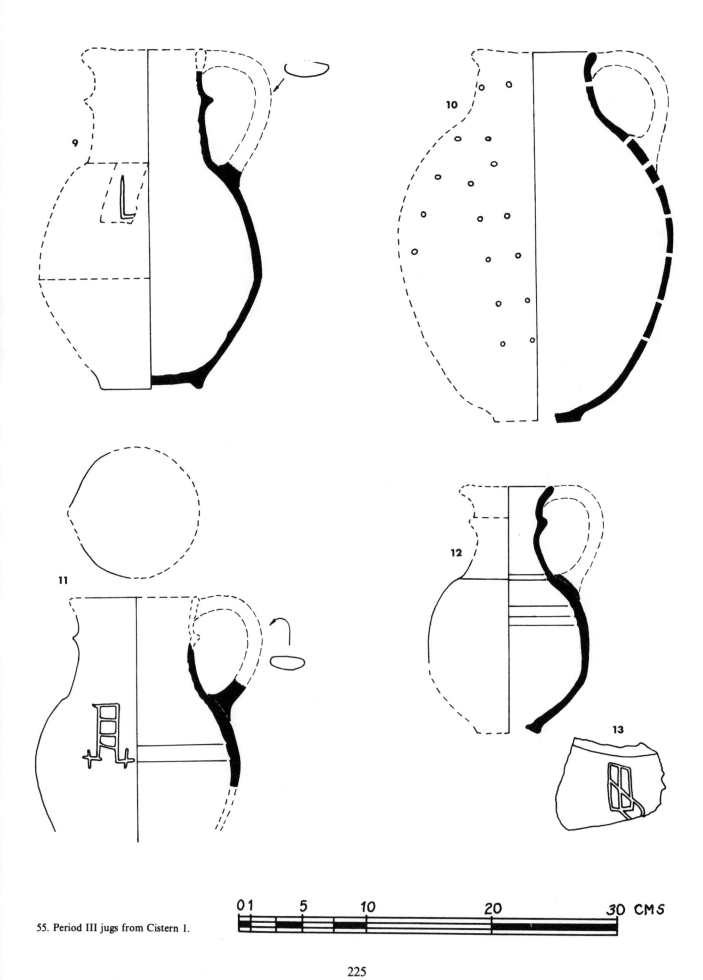

55. Period III jugs from Cistern 1.

0 1   5   10   20   30 CMS

Pl. 56

PERIOD III JUGS
See p. 90

	Locus	Stratum	Ware	Reg. no.	Photo pl.
14	III-30 C-1	III B	10 YR 6/4 light yellowish brown, 7/1 to 7/2 light gray int. surface, 7/3 very pale brown to 6/3 pale brown ext. surface; some small to medium and few large white and black incl.; ml	232	
15	III-30 C-1	III B	7.5 YR 7/4 pink to 6/4 light brown; many small, some medium and few large white and brown incl.	235	
16	III-30 C-1	III B	2.5 YR 5/6, 4/6 red; many small, some medium and few large white and black incl.; ml	236	
17	III-30 C-1	III B	7.5 YR 5/4 brown, 7/2 pinkish gray to 6/4 light brown; some small, many medium, and few large white incl.; ml	239	
18	III-30 C-1	III B	10 YR 5/2 grayish brown core, 7.5 YR 5/4 brown toward surfaces, 5 Y 6/2 light olive gray patching on ext.; many small, some medium, and few large white incl.; ffl	242	
19	III-30 C-1	III B	2.5 YR 5/2 grayish brown core, 7.5 YR 6/4 light brown to 5/4 brown toward surfaces; many small white and very few medium and large white and brown incl.; ml	243	
20	III-30 C-1	III B	2.5 YR 4/8 red; many small, some medium, and few large white incl.; ml	245	
21	III-30 C-1	III B	10 YR 4/2 dark grayish brown core, 2.5 YR 5/6 toward surfaces; many small, some medium and large white incl.; ffl	247	
22	III-30 C-1	III B	2.5 YR 4/6 red to 7.5 YR 5/4 brown; many small, medium, and large white incl.; ml	248	
23	III-30 C-1	III B	2.5 YR 4/8 red; many small to some medium white incl.; ffl	249	
24	III-30 C-1	III B	7.5 YR 6/4 light brown core, 5/2 brown toward surfaces; many small, some medium, and large incl.; ml	250	
25	III-30 C-1	III B	7.5 YR N6/ gray to 6/4 light brown, to 2.5 YR 6/6 light red int.; medium and small white incl.; ffl	251	
26	III-30 C-1	III B	2.5 YR 6/6 light red; few large and medium and medium white incl.; ml	252	
27	III-30 C-1	III B	5 YR 5/6 yellowish red; few small and large white and medium and large gray incl.; ml	257	

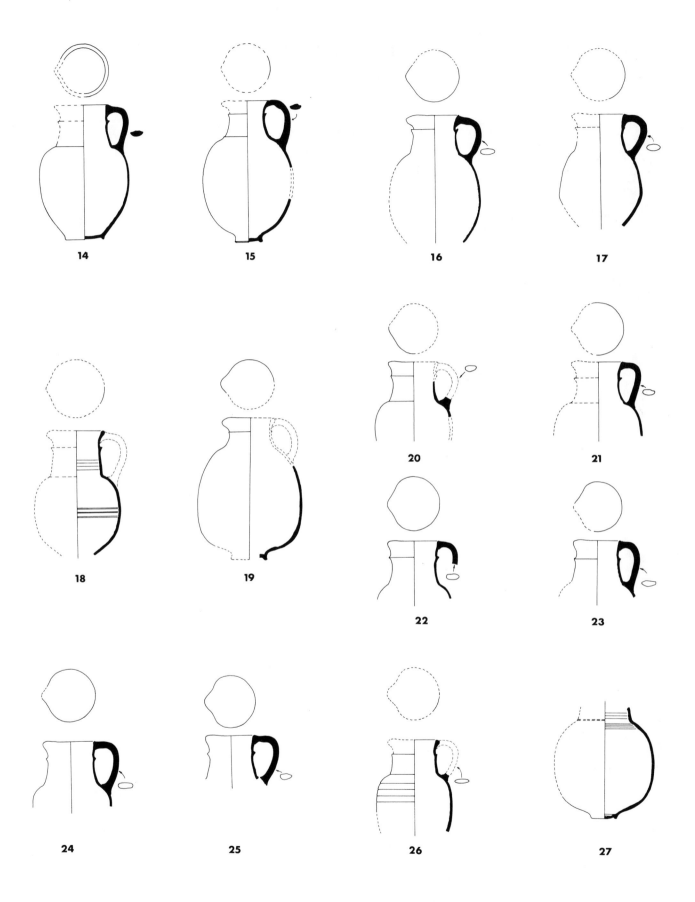

14 **15** **16** **17**

18 **19** **20** **21**

22 **23**

24 **25** **26** **27**

56. Period III B jugs from Cistern 1.

0 1   5   10   20   30 CMS.

Pl. 57

PERIOD III JUGS
See pp. 90-91

	Locus	Stratum	Ware
1	XVIII S-36	pre-III A	2.5 YR 5/6 red, 7.5 YR 8/2 surfaces; small white incl.; ffl
2	XVIII S-36	pre-III A	10 YR 8/1 white with some 5 YR 7/4 pink, 5 YR 5/6 yellowish red surfaces; small white incl.; ffl
3	XVIII S-36	pre-III A	7.5 YR 7/2 pinkish gray, 2.5 YR 4/6 red surfaces; small white incl.; ml
4	V-90	III A	10 YR 5/2 grayish brown, 5 YR 5/4 core; many small and some medium and very few large white and brown incl.; ffl
5	XIII-8	III A	5 YR 8/4 pink to 7/8 reddish yellow; ffl
6	XVI-5	III B	Not available
7	II-32	III B	Not available
8	IX-7	III B	5 YR 6/4 light reddish brown; many small and some medium and few large white and brown incl.; ffl
9	II-35	III B	Not available
10	II-30	III B	2.5 YR red; some small and medium white and dark incl.; fl
11	XVI-5	III A	Not available
12	XIII-8	III A	5 YR 8/4 pink to 7/8 reddish yellow; white incl.; mcl
13	XIX-2ext	III A	5 YR 6/4 light reddish brown, 10 YR 5/1 gray core; many small and medium white and some medium and few large brown incl.; ffl
14	XIX-ext	III A	5 YR 6/4 light reddish brown, 10 YR 5/2 grayish brown core; some small and medium white and grayish incl.; ffl
15	XVI-5	III B	Not available
16	XVI-5	III B	Not available
17	I-45	III B	Not available
18	XIX-2ext	III A	5 YR 6/3 light reddish brown, 10 YR 6/1 gray core; many small and some medium white and very few large brown incl.; ffl
19	XVI-4	III B	Not available
20	XIX-2ext	III A	7.5 YR 6/4 light brown; many small and medium white and some grayish incl.; ffl
21	XVIII S-36	pre-III A	7.5 YR 8/2 pinkish white; ml
22	XVIII S-36	pre-III A	5 YR 7/4 pink; ml
23	VII-10b C-2	III A	5 YR 7/4 pink; many tiny white and some medium white and gray incl.; ffl
24	XVI-5	III B	2.5 YR 5/6 red, 10 YR 5/4 light yellowish brown core; many small and some medium white, and few brown incl.; ffl
25	XIX-2ext	III A	5 YR 7/4 pink; very many small white and some brown incl.; cl

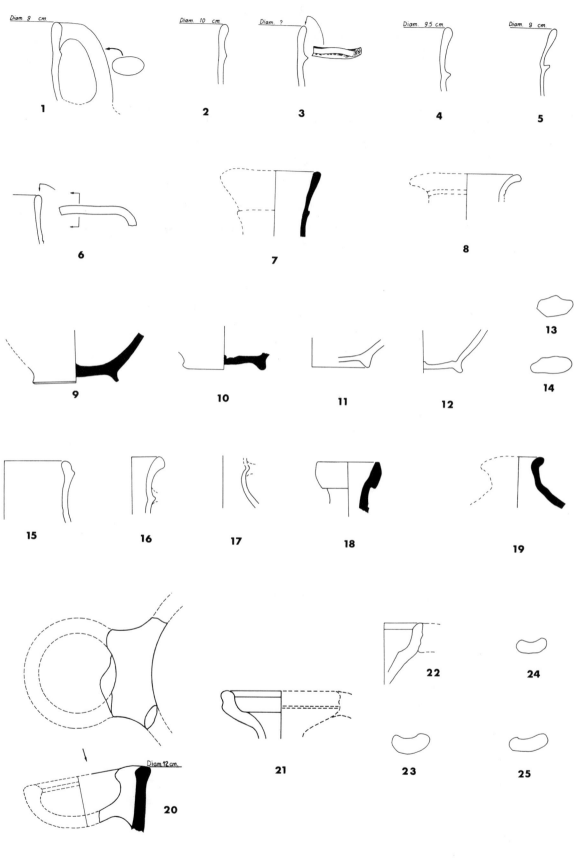

Diam. 9 cm.   Diam. 10 cm.   Diam. ?   Diam. 9.5 cm.   Diam. 9 cm.

1   2   3   4   5

6   7   8

9   10   11   12   13   14

15   16   17   18   19

Diam. 12 cm.

20   21   22   23   24   25

57. Period III jugs.

0   1   5   10   15 CMS.

Pl. 58

PERIOD III B JUGS
See p. 90

	Locus	Stratum	Ware	Reg. no.	Photo pl.
1	X-8	III B	5 YR 6/6 reddish yellow, 10 YR 4/1 dark gray core; many small and medium white and few dark incl.; ffl	270	33:3
2	III-30 C-1	III B	10 R 6/8 light red; few small white incl.; ffl	275	35:2
3	III-30 C-1	III B	5 YR 5/8 yellowish red, 10 YR 5/3 brown core; medium and many small white incl.; ffl	274	35:1
4	III-24 C-1	IV	10 R 5/8 red; many medium and small white incl.; ffl		
5	III-30 C-1	III B	5 YR 6/6 reddish yellow to 4/8 yellowish red toward center; medium and small white incl.; ffl	278	35:5
6	III-30 C-1	III B	5 YR 6/4 light reddish brown to 6/1 gray; many medium to small white incl.; ffl	279	35:6
7	III-30 C-1	III B	5 YR 6/6 reddish yellow, 2.5 YR 5/8 red toward surfaces; many medium and small white and few medium gray incl.; ffl	276	35:3

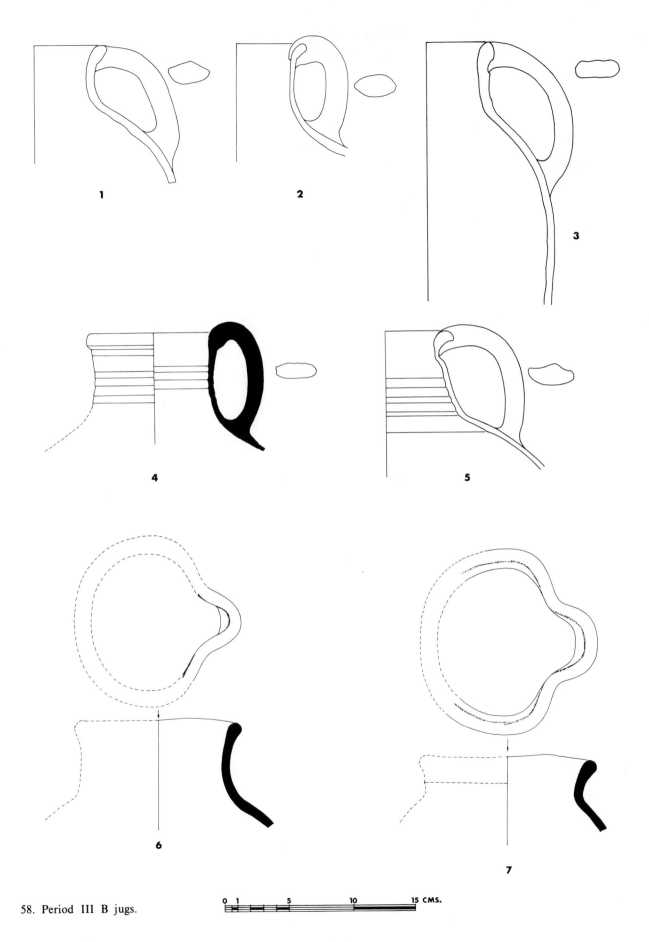

58. Period III B jugs.

Pl. 59

PERIOD III B FLASKS
See p. 91

	Locus	Stratum	Ware	Reg. no.	Photo pl.
1	III-30 C-1	III B	2.5 YR N4/ dark gray with 4/6 red core; many medium and small white incl.; ffl	280	35:7
2	III-30 C-1	III B	As 59:1 above	281	35:8
3	X-8	III B	7.5 YR 6/4 light brown to 6/8 reddish yellow; many medium and small white incl.; ffl	282	35:9
4	III-22 C-1	IV	5 YR 5/1 gray, 6/4 light reddish brown toward ext. surface; large and many small white incl.; ffl	125	
5	III-28 C-1	III A-B	Not available		

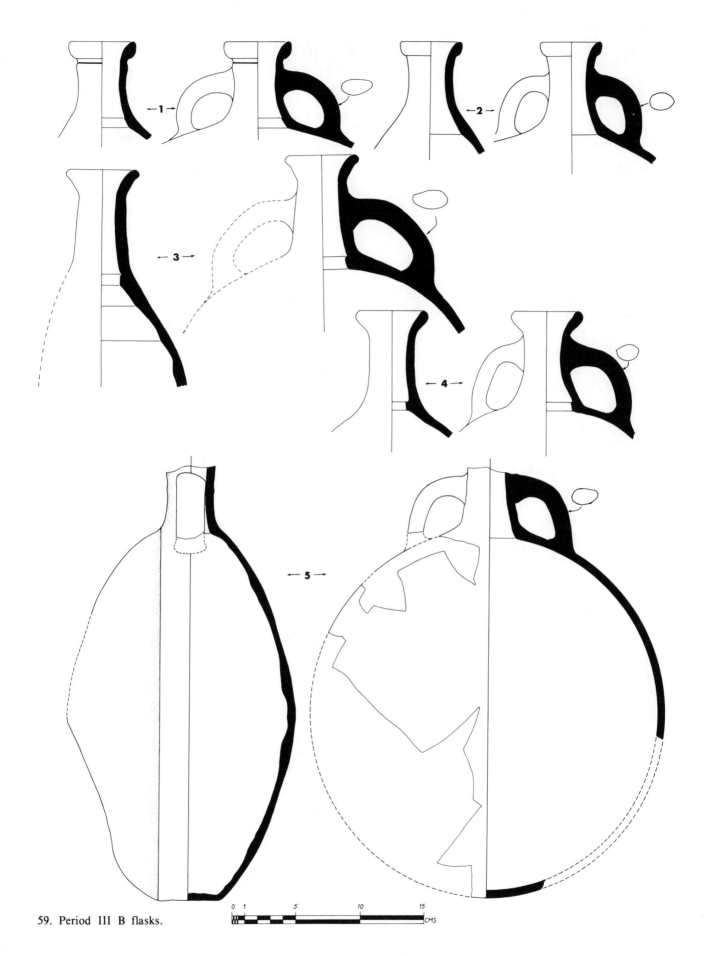

59. Period III B flasks.

Pl. 60

PERIOD III JUGLETS
See p. 92

	Locus	Stratum	Ware	Reg. no..	Photo pl.
1	XVIII S-36	pre-III A	5 YR 7/4 pink; ffl; slip, vertically burn.		
2	XVIII S-36	pre-III A	7.5 YR 7/4 pink; some large incl.; ml; slip, vertically burn.		
3	XVIII S-36	pre-III A	5 YR 8/4 pink; ml; slip, vertically burn.		
4	XVIII S-36	pre-III A	5 YR 8/3 pink, 10 YR 8/1 white toward ext. surface; ml		
5	XVIII S-36	pre-III A	7/5 YR 8/4 pink; ffl		
6	III-24 C-1	IV	Burnished vertically	211	36:1
7	XVIII S-36	pre-III A	2.5 YR 6/6 light red; ffl; slipped	284	36:2
8	III-30 C-1	III B	2/5 YR N 4/ dark gray, 7.5 YR 5/4 brown ext. surface; few large and medium and many small white incl.; ffl	210	36:3
9	III-24 C-1	IV	2.5 YR 5/8 red, N5/ gray toward center; medium and small white incl.; ffl	209	36:4
10	III-22 C-1	IV	2.5 YR 4/6 red, 7.5 YR 5/2 brown toward int. surface; many medium and small white incl.; ffl		
11	III-24 C-1	IV	2.5 YR N3/ dark gray; few very small white incl.; ffl	214	36:5
12	II-17	III A	5 YR 6/2 pinkish gray, 2.5 YR N3/ very dark gray surfaces; many small white incl.; ffl		
13	XVIII-unstr.	—	2.5 YR N2.5/ black; medium and small white incl.; ffl		

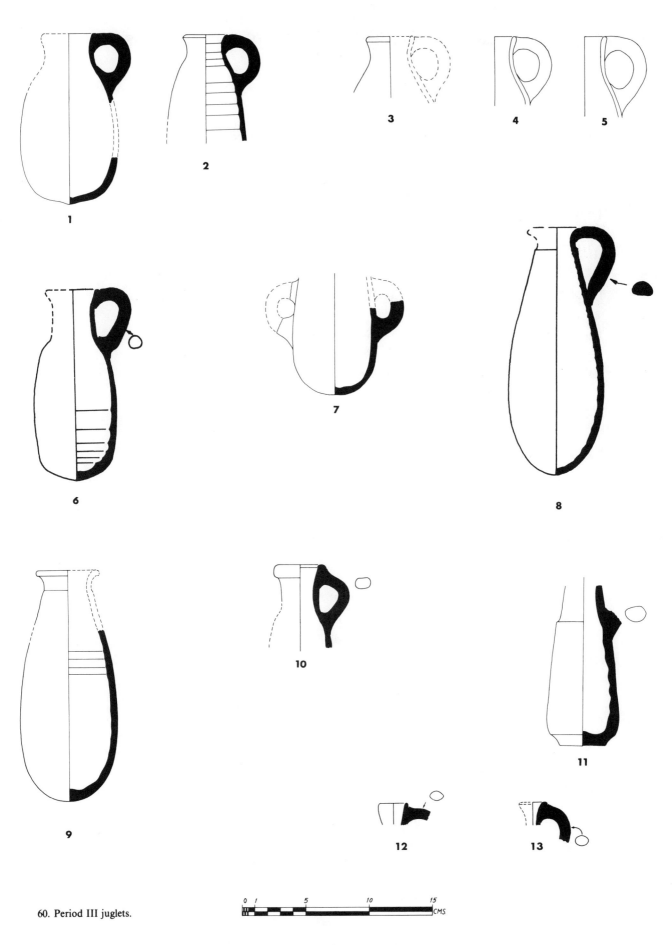

60. Period III juglets.

235

Pl. 61 PERIOD III B GLOBULAR JUGLETS AND BOTTLES
See p. 92

	Locus	Stratum	Ware	Reg. no.	Photo pl.
1	III-24 C-1	IV	5 YR 4/8 yellowish red; many medium and small white incl.; ffl		
2	III-24 C-1	IV	2.5 YR N4/ dark gray, 5/6 red toward ext. surface; many medium and small white incl.	285	37:1
3	III-24 C-1	IV	2.5 YR 6/4 light reddish brown, N5/ gray toward int. surface; many medium and small white incl.; ffl	126	37:3
4	III-20 C-1	IV	2.5 YR N5/ gray, 5/4 reddish brown toward ext. surface; many medium and small white incl.; ffl	286	37:2
5	III-24 C-1	IV	2.5 YR 5/6 red, N6/ gray toward surfaces; many medium and small white incl.; ffl		
6	III-24 C-1	IV	2.5 YR N5/ gray, 5/4 reddish brown toward ext. surface; medium and small white incl.	287	37:4
7	III-24 C-1	IV	2.5 YR 6/6 light red, 10 YR 5/1 gray core of handle; many small white incl.; ffl		
8	II-23	IV B	2.5 YR 6/6 light red; many small and some medium white and some brown and gray incl.; ffl		
9	III-24 C-1	IV	2.5 YR 4/8 red, N6 gray toward ext. surface; many medium and small white incl.; ffl		
10	I-45	III B	2.5 YR 4/6 red; many medium and small white incl.; ffl	216	37:7
11	III-24 C-1	IV	Complete: 5 YR 6/6 reddish yellow ext. surface; small white incl.; ffl	71	37:5
12	III-22 C-1	IV	2.5 YR 5/2 weak red to N4/ dark gray; many medium and small white incl.	213	37:6
13	I-47	IV B	2.5 YR 6/6 light red; medium and large gray incl.; ml	215	37:8
14	V-unstr.	—	2.5 YR 6/6 light red; many small and some medium white and few medium gray incl.; ffl		
15	III-24 C-1	IV	10 R 5/6 red; few small white incl.; ffl	173	37:13
16	III-24 C-1	IV	7.5 YR 5/2 brown; few large and medium dark and many medium and small white incl.; ml	212	37:10
17	III-24 C-1	IV	2/5 YR 5/6 red; ffl	172	37:9
18	XXII-11 S-43	IV A	7.5 YR N7/ light gray, 5 YR 6/3 reddish brown toward surfaces; many small white and few gray and red medium incl.; ffl	137	37:12
19	VI-25	IV B	7.5 YR 8/6 reddish yellow; medium and few large red and few medium and small white incl.; ffl	141	37:11
20	I-14	IV B	10 YR gray; many small and few medium white and very few medium brown incl.; ffl		
21	VIII-unstr.	—	2.5 YR 6/6 light red; many small and few medium white and brown incl.; ffl		

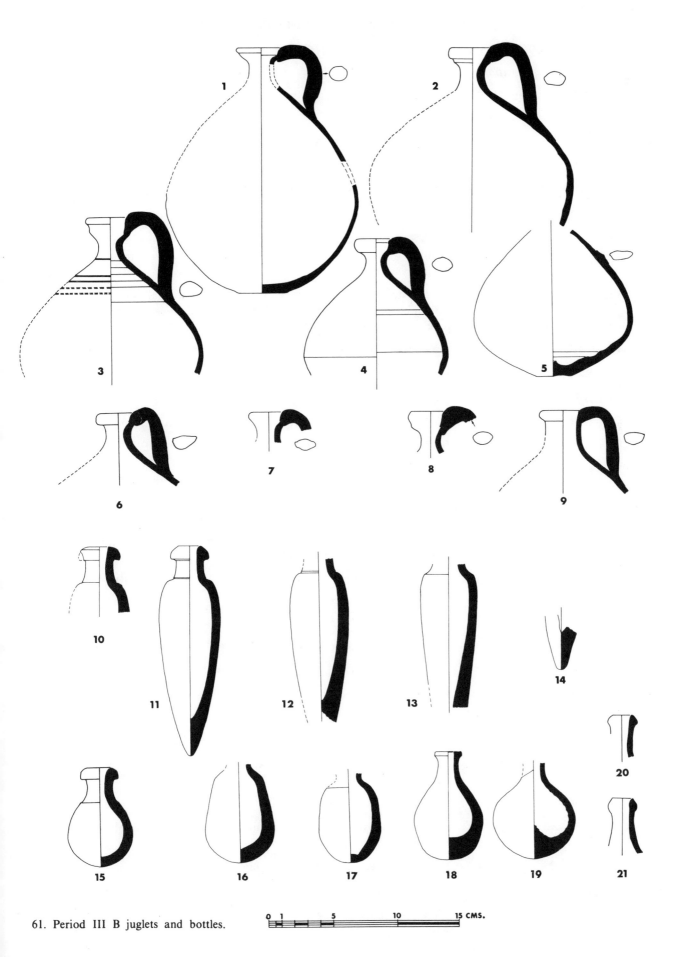

61. Period III B juglets and bottles.

Pl. 62

PERIOD III A BURNISHED BOWLS
See p. 93

	Locus	*Stratum*	*Ware*
1	XVIII S-36	pre-III A	2.5 YR 6/6 light red; ml; burnished inside and rim
2	XVIII S-36	pre-III A	5 YR 8/1 white; ffl
3	XVIII S-36	pre-III A	10 R 6/4 pale red, 10 YR 8/1 ext. surface; ml; burnished inside and rim
4	XVIII S-36	pre-III A	10 YR 6/6 light red; ml; burnished inside and rim
5	XVIII S-36	pre-III A	5 YR 7/4 pink; ml; burnished inside and rim
6	XVIII S-36	pre-III A	10 R 6/3 pale red; ml; wide burnishing inside and rim
7	XVIII S-36	pre-III A	2.5 YR 6/6 light red; 5 YR 6/6 reddish yellow core; some small and medium white, gray and brown incl.; fl; 2.5 YR 6/6 light red burnished slip on int. surface
8	XVIII S-36	pre-III A	5 YR reddish brown to 5/6 yellowish red; many small and some medium white and brown incl.; ffl; 2.5 YR 6/6 light red slip ext. surface, 5 YR 7/4 pink slip int. surface
9	I-49	III A	5 YR 5/6 yellowish red; small white incl.; ml; burnished inside and rim
10	XVIII S-36	pre-III A	10 R 6/4 pale red; ml; burnished inside and rim
11	XVIII S-36	pre-III A	As 62:10 above
12	XVIII S-36	pre-III A	7.5 YR 8/2 pinkish white; ml; burnished inside and rim
13	XVIII S-36	pre-III A	10 R 6/6 light red; ml; burnished inside and rim
14	XXIV-8	III A	7.5 YR 8/4 pink; ml; burnished inside and rim
15	XXIV-8	III A	10 R 6/4 pale red; ffl; burnished inside and rim
16	XXIV-8	III A	10 R 6/4 pale red; ffl; burnished slip inside and rim
17	XVIII S-36	pre-III A	10 R 6/4 pale red, 10 YR 8/1 white toward ext. surface; ml; burnished inside and top of handle and rim
18	XVIII S-36	pre-III A	5 YR 7/4 pink, 10 R 5/4 weak red ext. surface; ml; burnished inside and rim
19	XVIII S-36	pre-III A	5 YR 7/3 pink; ffl; burnished slip inside and rim
20	XVIII S-36	pre-III A	5 YR 8/1 white; few large incl.; ml; burnished but mostly rubbed off
21	XVIII S-36	pre-III A	7.5 YR 8/4 pink; ml; burnished inside and rim
22	XVIII S-36	pre-III A	10 R 6/4 pale red; ml; burnished inside and rim
23	XVIII S-36	pre-III A	2.5 YR 5/6 red; ffl; burnishing int. and on rim
24	XVIII S-36	pre-III A	10 R 5/4 weak red; fl; burnished red slip int. and on rim
25	XVIII S-36	pre-III A	2.5 YR 5/6 red, 5 YR 7/3 pink ext. surface; ml; burnished slip inside and top of rim
26	XVIII S-36	pre-III A	10 R 5/2 weak red; ffl; burnished inside and on top of rim
27	XVIII S-36	pre-III A	2 YR 6/6 reddish yellow; some small and medium white and brown incl.; fl; 2.5 YR 5/6 red slip int. surface
28	XVIII S-36	pre-III A	10 R 4/4 weak red, 5 YR 8/1 white ext. surface; ml
29	XXIV-8	III A	7.5 YR 8/4 pink, 6/2 pinkish gray toward int.; ffl
30	XVIII S-36	pre-III A	5 YR 6/6 reddish yellow, 10 YR 5/3 brown core; some small and medium white and gray incl.; ffl

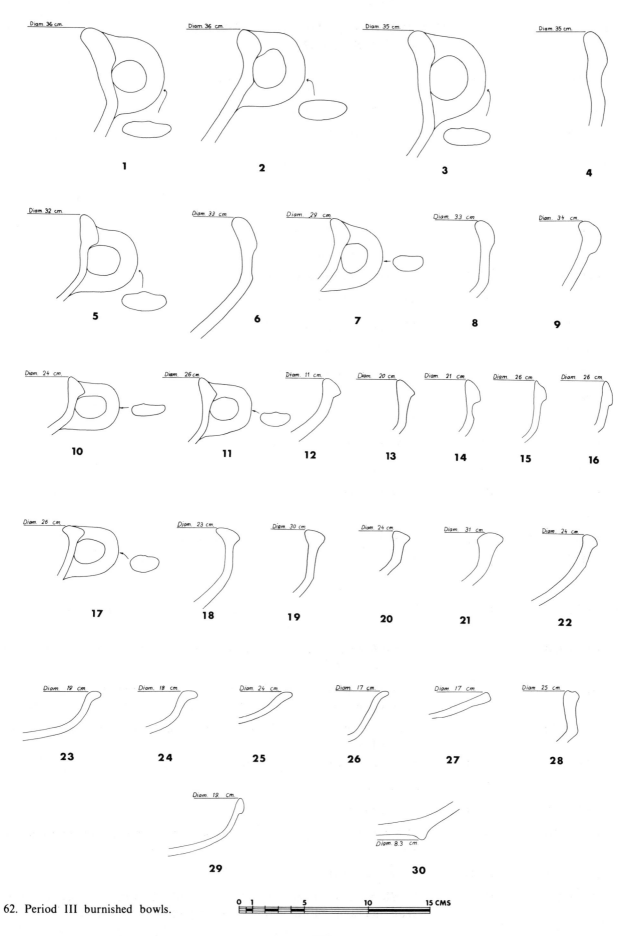

Diam. 36 cm. **1**

Diam. 36 cm. **2**

Diam. 35 cm. **3**

Diam. 35 cm. **4**

Diam. 32 cm. **5**

Diam. 33 cm. **6**

Diam. 29 cm. **7**

Diam. 33 cm. **8**

Diam. 34 cm. **9**

Diam. 24 cm. **10**

Diam. 26 cm. **11**

Diam. 11 cm. **12**

Diam. 20 cm. **13**

Diam. 21 cm. **14**

Diam. 26 cm. **15**

Diam. 26 cm. **16**

Diam. 26 cm. **17**

Diam. 23 cm. **18**

Diam. 30 cm. **19**

Diam. 24 cm. **20**

Diam. 31 cm. **21**

Diam. 24 cm. **22**

Diam. 19 cm. **23**

Diam. 18 cm. **24**

Diam. 24 cm. **25**

Diam. 17 cm. **26**

Diam. 17 cm. **27**

Diam. 25 cm. **28**

Diam. 19 cm. **29**

Diam. 8.3 cm. **30**

62. Period III burnished bowls.

0 1 5 10 15 CMS

Pl. 63

PERIOD III BURNISHED BOWLS
See pp. 93-94

	Locus	Stratum	Ware
1	XVI-5	III B	Burnished interior and rim
2	XVI-5	III B	Burnished interior and rim
3	XVI-4	III B	Burnished interior and rim
4	XVI-5	III B	Burnished interior and rim
5	XVI-5	III B	Burnished interior and rim
6	II-32	III B	Burnished interior and rim
7	II-35	III B	Burnished interior and rim
8	I-45	III B	Burnished interior and rim
9	XVI-5	III B	Burnished interior
10	XVI-6	III B	Burnished interior and rim
11	XVI-4	III B	Burnished interior and rim
12	I-45	III B	Burnished interior and rim
13	I-45	III B	Burnished interior and rim
14	I-35	III B	Burnished interior and rim
15	I-45	III B	Burnished interior and rim
16	I-45	III B	Burnished interior and rim
17	II-35	III B	Burnished interior and rim
18	II-35	III B	Burnished interior and rim
19	II-29	III B	10 R 6/4 pale red; fl; burnished slip inside and outside
20	II-31	III B	7.5 YR 8/4 pink; fl; burnished inside and outside
21	I-35	III B	Burnished interior and rim
22	III-22 C-1	IV	5 YR 5/2 reddish gray to 4/3 reddish brown; many small, some medium, and few large white incl.; ffl
23	III-29 C-1	III A-B	2.5 YR 6/6 light red; many tiny white, some small gray, and few small and medium brown incl.; ffl
24	III-22 C-1	IV	5 YR 6/6 reddish yellow, 10 YR 6/3 pale brown core; some small and few white and gray incl.; fl; 2.5 YR 5/6 red burnished slip int. and ext. surfaces
25	III-22 C-1	IV	10 R 6/6 light red, 10 YR 5/2 grayish brown core; very many tiny and some small white incl.; ffl
26	I-35	III B	Burnished interior and exterior
27	II-32	III B	Not available
28	XVI-6	III B	Burnished interior
29	III-22 C-1	IV	10 YR 6/3 pale brown; some small and few medium white and grayish incl.; fl
30	IX-14	III B	Burnished interior
31	III-22 C-1	IV	2.5 YR 5/6 red ext. surface to 5 YR 6/4 reddish brown int. surface; many small and some medium white and grayish incl.; ffl

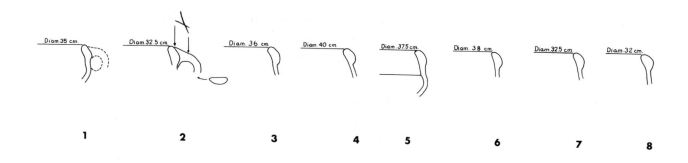

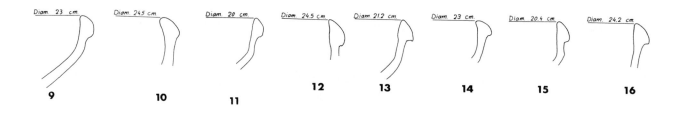

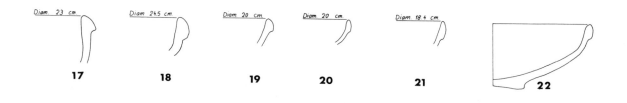

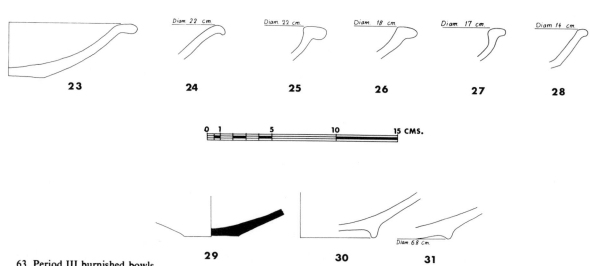

63. Period III burnished bowls.

Pl. 63 cont.

32	III-22 C-1	IV	2.5 YR 5/6 red, 10 YR 6/4 light yellowish brown; some small and medium white and gray incl.; ffl
33	III-22 C-1	IV	5 YR 5/6 yellowish red, 10 YR 6/4 light yellowish brown core; some small and medium white, and some small gray incl; ffl
34	XVI-4	III B	Burnished interior
35	III-22 C-1	IV	5 YR 5/6 yellowish red; some small and few medium white, and few small gray incl.; fl; 2.5 YR 5/6 red burnished slip int. surface
36	III-22 C-1	IV	5 YR 5/6 yellowish red; few small white and medium brown incl.; fl
37	III-22 C-1	IV	10 YR 5/2 grayish brown, 5/1 gray core; few small white and some small gray incl.; fl
38	III-22 C-1	IV	5 YR 5/6 yellowish red, 10 YR 5/1 gray core; some small white and gray incl.; fl
39	III-22 C-1	IV	2.5 YR 5/6 red; many small and some medium white and few brown incl.; ffl
40	III-22 C-1	IV	2.5 YR 6/6 light red, 10 YR 7/3 very pale brown core; few medium white, some small brown, and very few large grayish incl.; ffl; 2.5 YR 5/6 red burnished slip int. and ext.
41	III-22 C-1	IV	5 YR 6/6 reddish yellow, 10 YR 6/3 pale brown core; few small white and some small brown incl.; fl
42	XVI-5	III B	Burnished interior and exterior
43	I-45	III B	Burnished interior and rim
44	IX-7	III B	Burnished interior and rim
45	IX-7	III B	Burnished interior
46	XVI-4	III B	Burnished interior
47	XVI-5	III B	Burnished interior
48	XVI-4	III B	Burnished interior

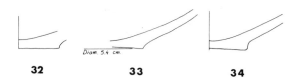

32   **33**   **34**

Diam. 5.4 cm.

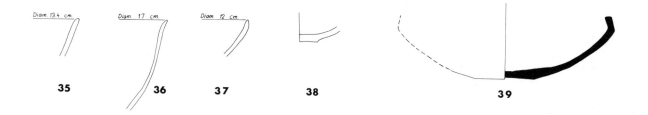

Diam. 13.4 cm.   Diam. 17 cm.   Diam. 12 cm.

35   **36**   **37**   **38**   **39**

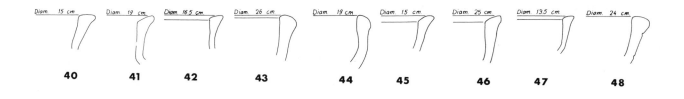

Diam. 15 cm. Diam. 19 cm. Diam. 16.5 cm. Diam. 26 cm. Diam. 19 cm. Diam. 15 cm. Diam. 25 cm. Diam. 13.5 cm. Diam. 24 cm.

40   **41**   **42**   **43**   **44**   **45**   **46**   **47**   **48**

0 1   5   10   15 CMS

Pl. 63 cont.

Pl. 64

PERIOD III BOWLS
See pp. 93-94

	Locus	Stratum	Ware	Reg. no.	Photo pl.
1	XVIII S-36	pre-III A	10 R 5/4 weak red, 5/2 weak red int. surface; ml		
2	XVIII S-36	pre-III A	5 YR 7/4 pink, 10 R 5/6 red int. surface; some medium incl.; ffl		
3	XVIII S-36	pre-III A	5 YR 8/4 pink; ffl		
4	XVIII S-36	pre-III A	2.5 YR 6/4 light reddish brown; some small and few medium white and brown incl.; fl		
5	I-49	III A	5 YR 7/4 pink; small incl.; ml		
6	I-49	III A	10 YR 8/2 white; small white incl.; ml		
7	I-49	III A	5 YR 8/4 pink; fl		
8	XIX-2ext	III A	2.5 YR 5/6 red; many small and some medium white incl.; ffl		
9	I-49	III A	5 YR 7/4 pink, small white incl.; ml		
10	XVIII S-36	pre-III A	5 YR 7/4 reddish yellow; ml		
11	XVIII S-36	pre-III A	7.5 YR 6/4 light brown; many small and some medium white and gray incl.; ffl		
12	XVIII S-36	pre-III A	5 YR 8/1 white; ml		
13	XVIII S-36	pre-III A	10 YR 8/3 very pale brown; ml		
14	XVIII S-36	pre-III A	10 YR 7/1 light gray; ml		
15	I-49	III A	7.5 YR 6/2 pinkish gray; black and beige striations int. surface; fl; metallic		
16	II-29	III B	7.5 YR 8/2 pinkish white; ml		
17	IX-13 S-28	III B	2.5 YR 4/8 red, 7.5 YR 6/2 pinkish gray surfaces; small and few large and medium white incl.	69	38:2
18	III-22 C-1	IV	10 YR 4/1 dark gray; some small and medium white and grayish incl.; fl		
19	III-28 C-1	III A-B	10 R 5/8 red, 5/1 reddish gray core; many medium white incl.; ffl	143	38:1
20	IX-7	III B	Not available		
21	III-22 C-1	IV	7.5 YR N5/ gray, 5/4 brown toward surfaces; medium and small white incl.	263	
22	III-22 C-1	IV	2.5 YR 5/6 red; many small and some medium white and grayish incl.; fl		
23	III-20 C-1	IV	2.5 YR 6/6 light red; many small and some medium white, and few medium brown incl.; ffl		
24	III-22 C-1	IV	2.5 YR 5/6 red to 10 YR 6/4 light yellowish brown; many small and some medium white and few gray incl.; ffl		
25	III-22 C-1	IV	10 R 6/6 light red; many small and some medium white and few medium brown incl.; ffl		

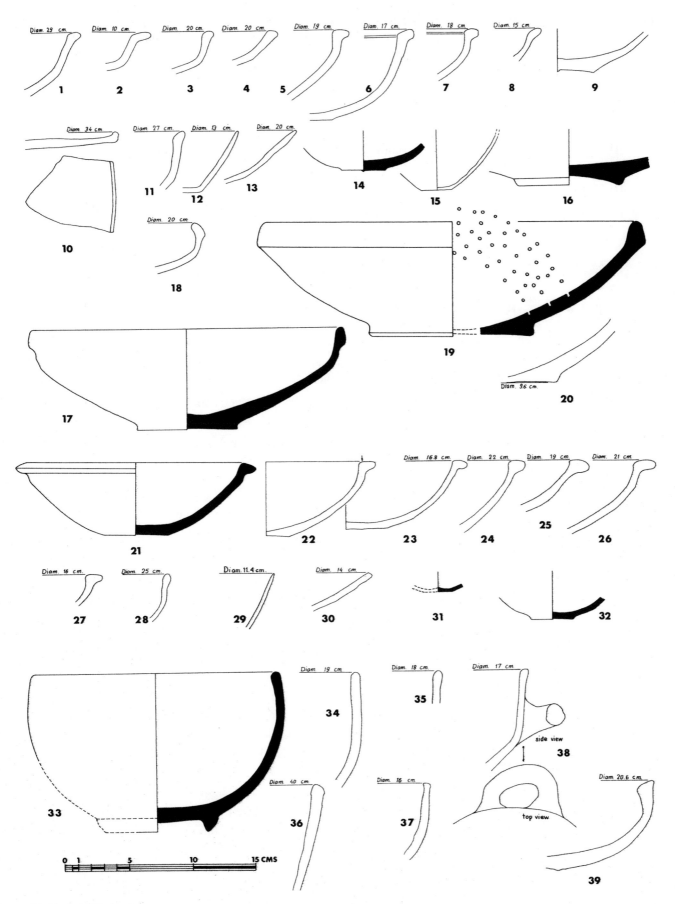

Diam. 29 cm. **1**
Diam. 10 cm. **2**
Diam. 20 cm. **3**
Diam. 20 cm. **4**
Diam. 19 cm. **5**
Diam. 17 cm. **6**
Diam. 18 cm. **7**
Diam. 15 cm. **8**
9
Diam. 34 cm.
10
Diam. 27 cm. **11**
Diam. 13 cm. **12**
Diam. 20 cm. **13**
14
15
16
Diam. 20 cm. **18**
19
Diam. 9.6 cm. **20**
17
21
22
Diam. 16.8 cm. **23**
Diam. 22 cm. **24**
Diam. 19 cm. **25**
Diam. 21 cm. **26**
Diam. 16 cm. **27**
Diam. 25 cm. **28**
Diam. 11.4 cm. **29**
Diam. 14 cm. **30**
31
32
33
Diam. 19 cm. **34**
Diam. 18 cm. **35**
Diam. 17 cm.
side view **38**
top view
Diam. 40 cm. **36**
Diam. 16 cm. **37**
Diam. 20.6 cm. **39**

0 1 5 10 15 CMS

64. Period III bowls.

245

Pl. 64 cont.

26	III-22 C-1	IV	2.5 YR 5/6 red with 10 YR 5/2 grayish brown near surfaces and core; many small and few medium white and some medium brown incl.; ffl	
27	I-35	III B	Not available	
28	II-31	III B	5 YR 8/2 pinkish white; ffl	
29	XVI-5	III B	Not available	
30	III-22 C-1	IV	5 YR yellowish red; some small and few medium white and some small gray incl.; fl	
31	III-22 C-1	IV	Not available	
32	III-22 C-1	IV	5 YR 6/6 reddish yellow, 10 YR 5/2 grayish brown core; some small white and gray, and very few medium white incl.; fl	
33	III-22 C-1	IV	7.5 YR N7/ light gray, 6/4 light brown toward surfaces; many medium and small white incl.; ffl	262
34	III-29 C-1	III A-B	7.5 YR 6/4 light brown, 5 YR 6/6 reddish yellow core; many tiny and few medium white, and some brown incl.; ffl	
35	III-22 C-1	IV	10 YR 6/3 pale brown; some small and few medium white and grayish incl.; fl	
36	III-22 C-1	IV	5 YR 6/6 reddish yellow; many small and medium white, and few medium brown incl.; ffl	
37	III-22 C-1	IV	5 YR 6/4 light reddish brown to 10 YR 5/2 grayish brown; many small and some medium white, and few gray incl.; ffl	
38	III-21 C-1	IV	2.5 YR 6/6 light red, 2.5 YR 6/4 light reddish brown core; many small and some medium white and brown incl.; ffl	
39	III-22 C-1	IV	5 YR 5/3 reddish brown; many small and few medium white and some medium brown and gray incl.; ffl	

Pl. 65

PERIOD III B LARGE BOWLS AND CRATERS
See pp. 93-95

	Locus	Stratum	Ware	Reg. no.	Photo pl.
1	III-30 C-1	III B	5 YR 5/6 yellowish red, 10 YR 5/4 yellowish brown core; many medium to small white incl.; ffl	217	38:4
2	III-30 C-1	III B	2.5 YR 5/4 reddish brown, 10 YR 4/1 dark gray core; many medium and small white, and few crystalline incl.; fl	228	38:3
3	III-30 C-1	III B	2.5 YR 6/6 light red, 5 YR 6/4 light reddish brown core; many small and medium white and grayish incl.; ffl		
4	III-30 C-1	III B	10 YR 5/1 gray, 5 YR 5/3 reddish brown core; very many tiny, some small, and few large brown and white incl.; cl		
5	III-29 C-1	III A-B	2.5 YR 5/8 red with some 5 YR 6/3 light reddish brown; many medium and small white and few medium red incl.; ffl	259	39:1
6	III-29 C-1	III A-B	2.5 YR N4/ dark gray with 6/8 light red surfaces; handle—7/5 YR 6/2 pinkish gray with 2.5 YR 6/8 light red surfaces; few large and many medium and small white incl.	260	39:2
7	III-28 C-1	III A-B	2.5 YR 4/6 red; few large, many medium white incl.; fl; 0.5-cm.-wide horizontal burnishing ext.	258	39:3
8	III-29 C-1	III A-B	2.5 YR 5/6 red unevenly fired to N5/ gray; few large white, gray and dark red, and many medium and small white incl.	261	39:4
9	III-30 C-1	III B	2.5 YR light brownish gray, 7.5 YR 6/4 light brown core; many small and some medium white and few medium brown incl.; ffl		
10	III-30 C-1	III B	10 YR 5/2 grayish brown, 2.5 YR 6/6 light red core; many small and some medium white and brown incl.; ffl		
11	III-30 C-1	III B	7.5 YR 6/4 light brown, 10 YR 6/1 gray core; many small and some medium white and few brown incl.; ffl		
12	III-30 C-1	III B	10 YR 6/3 pale brown, 6/2 light brownish gray core; many small and some medium white, and few gray incl.; ffl		
13	III-24 C-1	IV	5 YR 6/1 gray to 6/4 light reddish brown toward surfaces; few large white and brown, and many medium and small white incl.; impressed circle design on shoulder		

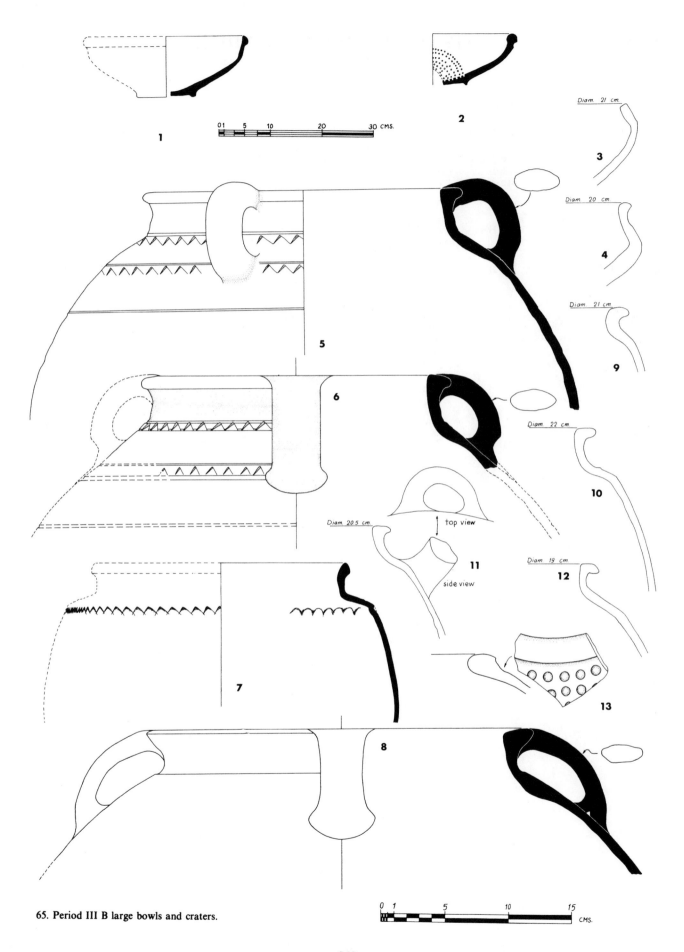

65. Period III B large bowls and craters.

249

Pl. 66

PERIOD III POTS AND STANDS
See p. 95

	Locus	Stratum	Ware	Reg. no.	Photo pl.
1	XVIII S-36	pre-III A	5 YR 7/4 pink; ml; red slip on ext.		
2	XVIII S-36	pre-III A	2.5 YR 6/4 light reddish brown; ffl; slip on ext.		
3	XVIII S-36	pre-III A	2.5 YR 6.2 pale red; ffl		
4	VII-10b C-2	III A	2.5 YR N3/ very dark gray; many small white incl.	221	40:4
5	III-31 C-1	III B	7.5 YR 5/2 brown; many small white incl.; ffl; lower part burnt	117	40:1
6	III-30 C-1	III B	5 YR 4/4 reddish brown; many small and medium white incl.	219	40:2
7	III-24 C-1	IV	2.5 YR 6/2 pale red; few medium and large and very many small white incl.; ffl; air pockets throughout section	218	40:3
8	XXIV-8	III A	5 YR 8/4 pink; ffl		
9	IX-13 S-28	III B	Complete: 5 YR 8/2 pinkish white surfaces with 10 YR 3/3 dark brown blotches showing through; small white and dark incl.; ffl	90	40:6
10	IX-13 S-28	III B	7.5 YR 6/4 light brown; few medium white incl.; ffl	91	40:5

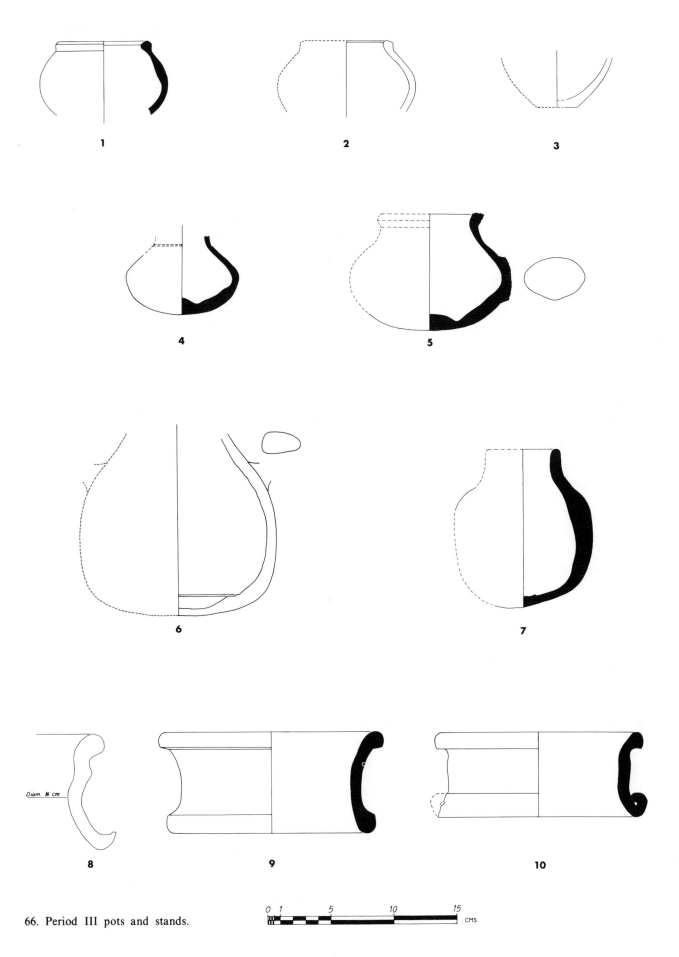

66. Period III pots and stands.

Diam. 16 cm

0 1   5   10   15   CMS.

Pl. 67

PERIOD III COOKING POTS
See pp. 95-97

	Locus	Stratum	Ware	Reg. no.	Photo pl.
1	XVIII S-36	pre-III A	Not available		
2	XVIII S-36	pre-III A	2.5 YR 3/6 dark red, 10 R 5/2 weak red surfaces; incl.; fcl		
3	XVIII S-36	pre-III A	10 R 5/4 weak red; few incl.; ml		
4	XVIII S-36	pre-III A	10 R 5/4 weak red, 3/3 dusky red core; few incl.; ml		
5	XVIII S-36	pre-III A	10 R 6/6 light red; ml		
6	XVIII S-38	pre-III A	10 R 5/4 weak red; incl.; fcl		
7	XVIII S-36	pre-III A	10 R 6/6 light red; medium and large incl.; fcl		41:9
8	XVIII S-36	pre-III A	2.5 YR 4/4 reddish brown to 4/8 red; medium and small white and dark incl.		41:2
9	XVIII S-36	pre-III A	2.5 YR 4/6 red; white and crystalline large and medium incl.; fcl		41:7
10	II-15	III A	2.5 YR 5/6 red; some small and medium white and grayish incl.; ffl		
11	VII-10b C-2	III A	2.5 YR 5/6 red, 5 YR 4/4 reddish brown core; many small and medium white and grayish incl.; ffl		
12	XXIV-8	III A	5 YR 4/4 reddish brown, 2.5 YR 5/6 red around core, 5 YR 5/4 reddish brown core; some small white and gray incl.; fl		
13	XIII-8	III A	2.5 YR 5/6 red; ffl		
14	VII-10b C-2	III A	10 R 5/6 red toward top, to 10 R 3/1 dark reddish gray at bottom; ffl	88	41:11
15	XVIII S-38	pre-III A	10 R 6/4 pale red; ffl		
16	XVIII S-36	pre-III A	10 R 6/6 light red; small white incl.; ffl		
17	XVIII S-36	pre-III A	10 R 5/4 weak red, 2.5/1 reddish black core; ffl		
18	XVIII S-36	pre-III A	2.5 YR 4/6 red; few medium white and small white and dark incl.		41:10
19	XVIII S-36	pre-III A	10 R 5/6 red, 5/1 reddish gray core; ffl; handle—10 R 4/1 dark reddish gray		41:8
20	XVIII S-36	pre-III A	7.5 YR 5/2 brown; large, medium, and small white incl.		41:3
21	XVIII S-36	pre-III A	5 YR 6/4 light reddish brown, 4/1 dark gray core; ffl		
22	XVIII S-36	pre-III A	2.5 YR 4/6 red; small and few medium and large white incl.		41:6
23	I-45	III B	2.5 YR 4/6 red; few medium and small white incl.		
24	I-45	III B	Not available		
25	III-24	IV	2.5 YR 5/8 red, 5/4 reddish brown core; some small gray incl.; fl		

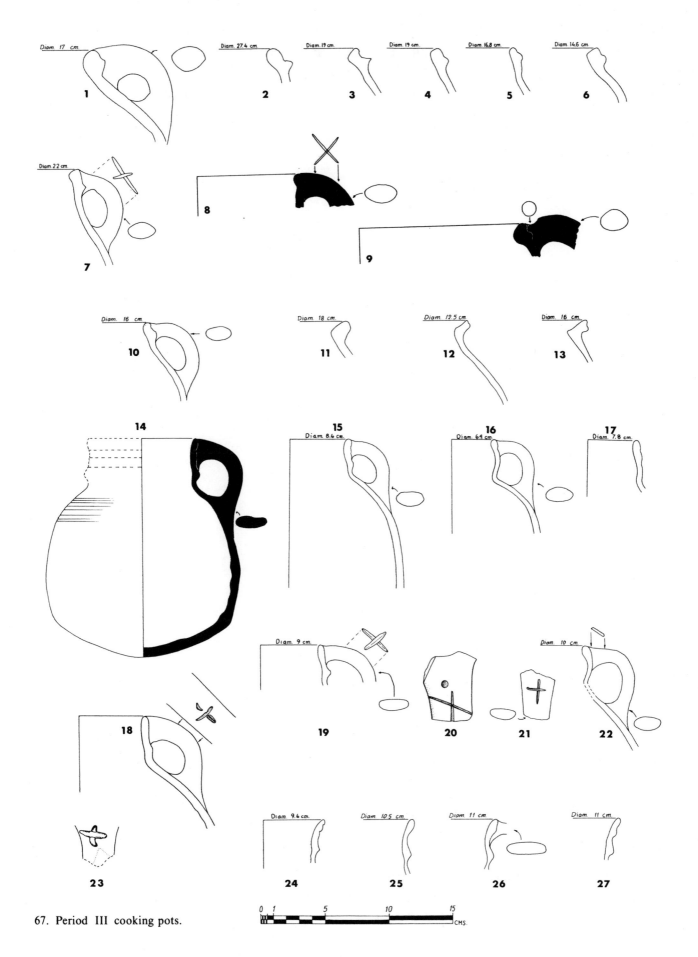

Diam. 17 cm.

Diam. 27.4 cm.

Diam. 19 cm.

Diam. 19 cm.

Diam. 16.8 cm.

Diam. 14.6 cm.

Diam. 22 cm.

Diam. 16 cm.

Diam. 18 cm.

Diam. 12.5 cm.

Diam. 16 cm.

Diam. 8.6 cm.

Diam. 6.9 cm.

Diam. 7.8 cm.

Diam. 9 cm.

Diam. 10 cm.

Diam. 9.6 cm.

Diam. 10.5 cm.

Diam. 11 cm.

Diam. 11 cm.

1 2 3 4 5 6 7 8 9 10 11 12 13 14 15 16 17 18 19 20 21 22 23 24 25 26 27

67. Period III cooking pots.

0 1 5 10 15 CMS.

253

Pl. 67 cont.

| 26 | III-24 | IV | 5 YR 4/8 yellowish red, 2.5 YR 5/4 reddish brown core; some small gray incl.; fl |
| 27 | III-24 | IV | 2.5 YR 4/8 red, 4/4 reddish brown core; few small gray incl.; fl |

Pl. 68

PERIOD III COOKING POTS
See pp. 96-97

	Locus	Stratum	Ware	Reg. no.	Photo pl.
1	III-28 C-1	III A-B	2.5 YR 4/6 red; many small and few medium white and gray incl.; ffl		
2	I-45	III B	7.5 YR 5/4 brown, 10 YR 3/1 very dark gray core; some small and medium and few large white and grayish incl.; ffl		
3	XVI-5	III B	Not available		
4	III-24 C-1	IV	2.5 YR 4/6 red; some small brown incl.; fl		
5	III-24 C-1	IV	5 YR 4/8 yellowish red, 5/4 reddish brown core of handle; some small white and brown and few medium brown incl.; fl		
6	V-90	III A	2.5 YR 5/6 red, 5 YR 4/3 reddish brown core; some small and medium white, brown, and gray incl.; fl		
7	V-90	III A	2,5 YR 5/6 red; some small white and brown incl.; fl		
8	I-45	III B	Not available		
9	II-35	III B	Not available		
10	XVI-4	III B	Not available		
11	II-35	III B	Not available		
12	III-24 C-1	IV	5 YR 5/6 yellowish red, 10 YR 5/1 gray core; many medium and large white and grayish incl.; ffl		
13	XXI-5 S-21	III	5 YR 5/6 yellowish red, 10 YR 5/2 grayish brown core; many small and medium white, brown, and gray incl.; ffl		
14	XXII-11 S-43	IV A	5 YR 4/6 yellowish red, 7.5 YR 4/2 dark brown core; medium white and gray, and small white and crystalline incl.		
15	XXII-11 S-43	IV A	7.5 YR brown, 10 YR 4/4 dark yellowish brown core; many small white incl.; ffl		
16	XII-24	IV B	2.5 YR 5/8 red, 10 YR 4/1 dark gray core; medium and small white incl.	174	
17	IX-13 S-28	III B	7.5 YR 3/2 dark brown to N3/ very dark gray; small white incl.	160	41:12
18	XII-28 S-40	III B	2.5 YR 5/8 red, 7.5 YR N4/ dark gray core; some small to medium white and gray incl.; fl	180	

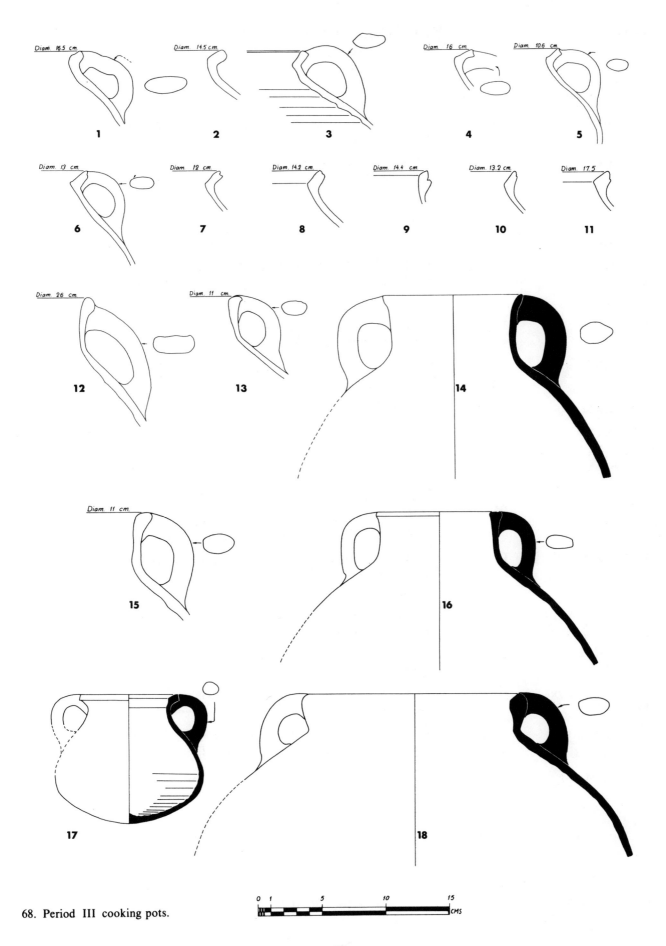

68. Period III cooking pots.

257

Pl. 69

PERIOD III B COOKING POTS
See p. 97

	Locus	Stratum	Ware	Reg. no.	Photo pl.
1	X-8	III B	5 YR 4/4 reddish brown, 2.5 YR N/4 dark gray core; few large, medium and small incl.; ffl		
2	III-30 C-1	III B	5 YR 4/8 yellowish red, 10 YR 5/1 gray core; some small white and brown incl.; fl		
3	III-30 C-1	III B	5 YR 4/4 reddish brown; some small and medium white and gray incl.; fl		
4	III-24 C-1	IV	5 YR 5/3 reddish brown; many small and medium white and brown, and very few large white incl.; ffl		
5	III-24 C-1	IV	5 YR 5/6 yellowish red; many small and medium white and dark incl.; ffl		
6	III-24 C-1	IV	10 YR 5/2 grayish brown; many small and medium white and gray incl.; ffl		
7	III-24 C-1	IV	5 YR 5/6 yellowish red, 7.5 YR 5/4 brown core; some small and medium white and grayish incl.; fl		
8	III-24 C-1	IV	2.5 YR 4/6 red, 10 YR 4/2 dark grayish brown core; some small and medium white and brown, and few large white incl.; ffl		
9	X-8	III B	2.5 YR 4/2 weak red to N4/ dark gray; many medium and small white and crystalline incl.; ffl		
10	III-24 C-1	IV	5 YR 6/6 reddish yellow, 10 YR 5/1 gray core; many small and medium white and gray incl.; ffl		
11	III-24 C-1	IV	5 YR 5/6 yellowish red, 10 YR 5/2 grayish brown core; some small and medium white incl.; fl		
12	I-45	III B	2.5 YR 4/4 reddish brown, N4/ dark gray core; medium and few large white incl.; ffl		
13	XVI-6	III B	Not available		
14	II-35	III B	5 YR 4/3 reddish brown, 4/1 dark gray core; few medium white incl.; ffl		
15	XVIII	III B	2.5 YR 5/6 red; some small and medium white, brown, and grayish incl.; ffl		
16	III-24 C-1	IV	5 YR 4/1 dark gray, many large and medium incl.	288	41:13
17	III-24 C-1	IV	7.5 YR 5/4 brown, 10 YR 5/2 grayish brown core; many small and medium white and gray, and very few large gray incl.; ffl		
18	III-24 C-1	IV	2.5 YR 5/6 red, 10 YR 5/1 gray core; many small and medium and few large white and gray incl.; cl	289	41:14
19	I-35	III B	Not available		
20	III-24 C-1	IV	5 YR 4/8 yellowish red; few small white incl.	222	

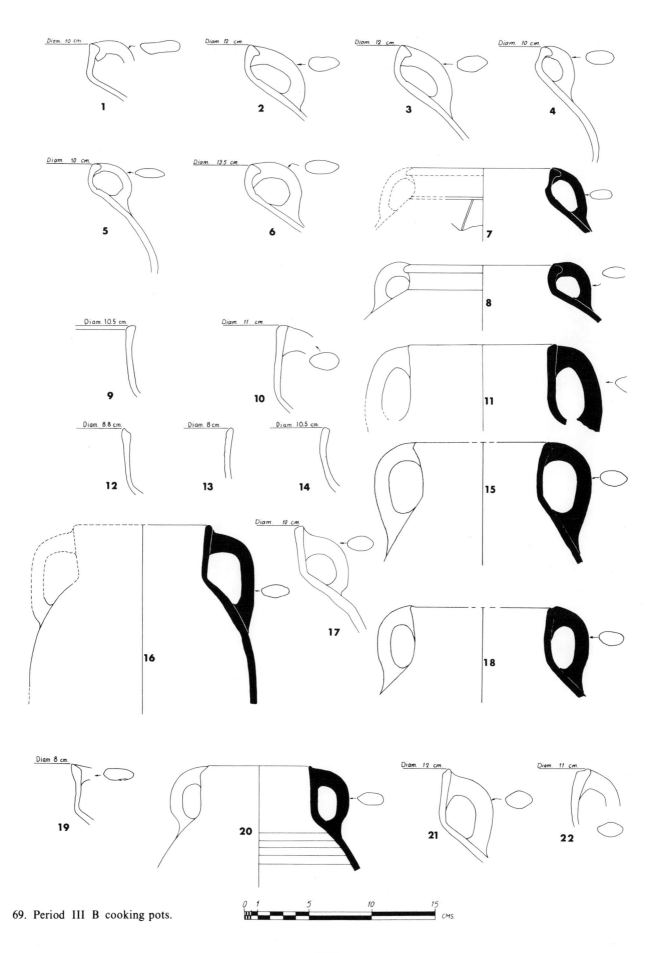

Diam. 10 cm.

1

Diam. 12 cm.

2

Diam. 12 cm.

3

Diam. 10 cm.

4

Diam. 10 cm.

5

Diam. 13.5 cm.

6

7

8

Diam. 10.5 cm.

9

Diam. 11 cm.

10

11

Diam. 8.8 cm.

12

Diam. 8 cm.

13

Diam. 10.5 cm.

14

15

16

Diam. 10 cm.

17

18

Diam. 8 cm.

19

20

Diam. 12 cm.

21

Diam. 11 cm.

22

69. Period III B cooking pots.

0 1   5   10   15
                                    CMS.

259

Pl. 69 cont.

| 21 | III-21 C-1 | IV | 10 YR 4/2 dark grayish brown; many small and some medium white and some gray incl.; ffl |
| 22 | III-22 C-1 | IV | 5 YR yellowish red, 10 YR 5/1 gray core; many small and some medium white and gray incl.; fl |

Pl. 70

PERIOD III LAMPS
See p. 98

	Locus	Stratum	Ware	Reg. no.	Photo pl.
1	XVIII S-38	pre-III A	2.5 YR 5/6 red; medium and small white incl.		
2	III-30 C-1	III B	10 R 6/8 light red; few large and medium and many small white incl.; ffl	191	42:10
3	III-24 C-1	IV	2.5 YR 5/6 red; many medium and small white incl.	87	42:1
4	III-22 C-1	IV	2.5 YR 6/6 light red; medium and small white incl.; burnt spout	84	42:2
5	III-30 C-1	III B	2.5 YR 6/8 light red; few medium and small white incl.; burnt spout	85	42:9
6	III-28 C-1	III A-B	10 R 6/6 light red, 6/1 reddish gray surfaces; many small white incl.; ffl; burnt spout	86	
7	III-28 C-1	III A-B	2.5 YR 4/6 red; medium and many small white incl.; ffl	194	
8	III-21 C-1	IV	2.5 YR 5/6 red; many medium and small white incl.	192	42:3
9	III-24 C-1	IV	Complete: 2.5 YR 6/6 light red, few large white and red incl.—surfaces	72	42:4
10	XX-5ext	IV	2.5 YR 5/8 red; medium and small white incl.	196	
11	XX-5ext	IV	2.5 YR 6/8 light red; medium and small white incl.		
12	XX-7	IV	2.5 YR 5/6 red; medium and small white incl.		
13	XX-unstr.	—	2.5 YR 5/8 red; few medium and small white incl.		

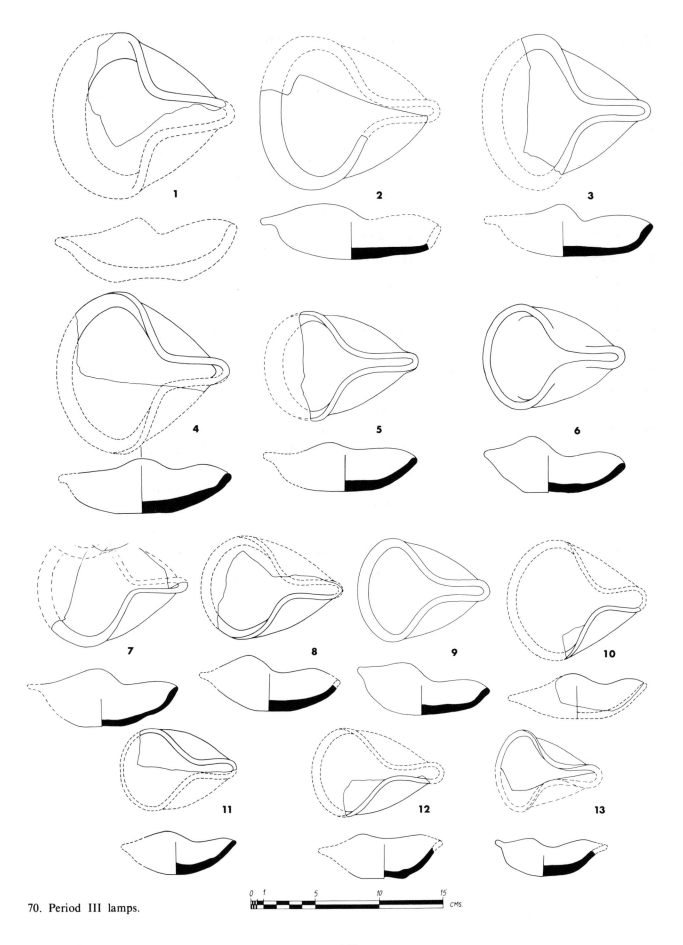

70. Period III lamps.

Pl. 71

PERIOD III LAMPS
See pp. 98-99

	Locus	Stratum	Ware	Reg. no.	Photo pl.
1	XVIII S-36	pre-III A	5 YR 7/4 pink; mfl	195	42:5
2	II-17	III A	7.5 YR 4/4 dark brown; 2.5 YR 3/6 dark red surfaces; large and small white, medium white and black incl.	140	
3	III-31 C-1	III B	7.5 YR 6/4 light brown; 5 YR 8/3 pink surfaces; medium and small white incl.	93	42:8
4	II-35	III B	Not available		
5	II-35	III B	Not available		
6	II-35	III B	Not available		
7	II-32	III B	Not available		
8	III-31 C-1	III B	2.5 YR 4/6 red; small, medium, and large white incl.; burnt spout	94	
9	III-31 C-1	III B	As 71:8 above	119	42:11
10	III-31 C-1	III B	2.5 YR 4/6 red; small, medium, and large white, medium and large gray incl.	120	42:12
11	III-31 C-1	III B	5 YR 6/6 reddish yellow; 5 YR 8/1 white to 5 YR 8/2 pinkish white slip; medium and large white and few gray incl.	165	
12	XXIV-unstr.	—	5 YR 6/4 light reddish brown, 5/1 gray core; medium and small white incl.; ffl	166	42:6
13	I-unstr.	—	2.5 YR 4/6 red; medium and small white incl.	121	42:7
14	III-24 C-1	IV	5 YR 7/6 reddish yellow; large, medium, and small white incl.	193	

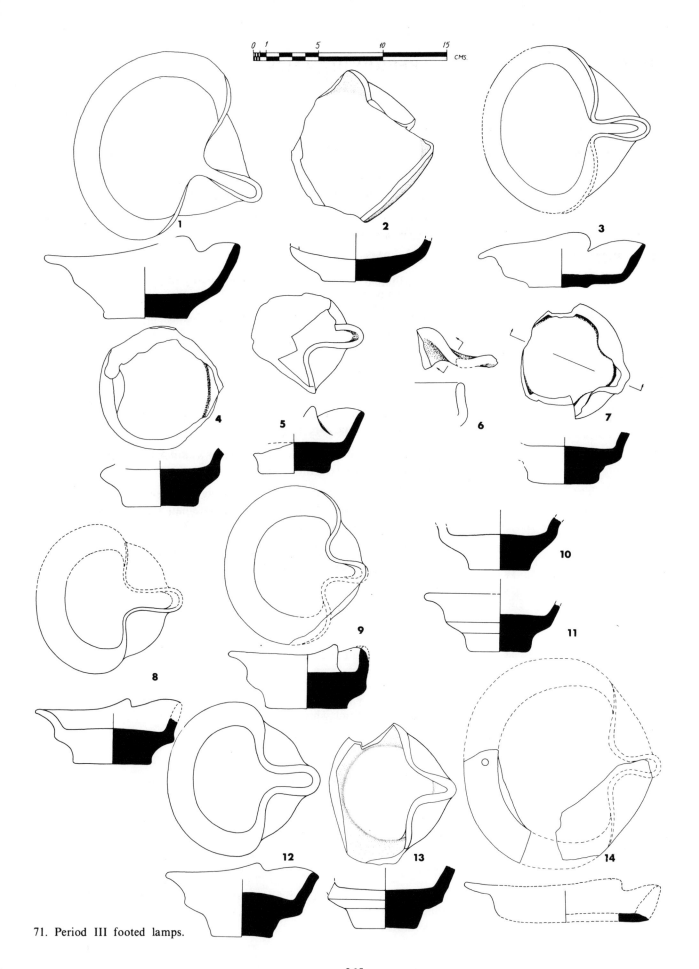

71. Period III footed lamps.

Pl. 72

PERIOD IV JARS
See p. 102

	Locus	Stratum	Ware	Reg. no.	Photo pl.
1	XX-4ext	IV C	7.5 YR 7/4 pink, 10 YR 7/3 very pale brown core; many small and some medium white and brown incl.; ffl		
2	XX-4ext	IV C	2.5 YR 6/8 light red; some small white and brown incl.; fl		
3	XX-4ext	IV C	2.5 YR 6/6 light red; some small and few medium white and brown incl.; fl		
4	XX-4ext	IV C	As 72:2 above		
5	XX-4ext	IV C	5 YR pink, 10 YR 7/2 light gray core; many tiny and small white and some brown incl.; ffl		
6	XX-4ext	IV C	7.5 YR 6/4 light brown, 10 YR 6/2 light brownish gray core; some small and medium white and few dark incl.; ffl		
7	XX-4ext	IV C	7.5 YR 6/4 light brown, N6/ gray core; 8/4 pink surfaces; many small to some medium white incl.; ffl		
8	XX-2ext	IV C	5 YR reddish brown, 10 YR 5/1 gray core; many small and some medium white and gray incl.; ffl		
9	XX-2ext	IV C	2.5 YR 6/8 light red; some small and few medium white and brown incl.; fl		
10	XX-2ext	IV C	5 YR 6/6 reddish yellow, 2.5 YR 6/6 light red core, 10 YR 5/2 grayish brown around core; few small white and brown incl.; fl		
11	XX-2ext	IV C	2.5 YR 5/6 red, 5 YR 5/2 reddish gray core; many small and medium white, and few large brown incl.; ffl		
12	XX-2ext	IV C	As 72:3 above		
13	XX-2ext	IV C	2.5 YR 6/6 light red; many small white and few medium brown incl.; fl		
14	XX-2ext	IV C	2.5 YR 6/8 light red, 5 YR 5/3 reddish brown core; some small white and grayish incl.; fl		
15	XX-5	IV B	7.5 YR 6/4 light brown, 10 YR 6/1 gray core; many small and medium white incl.; ffl		
16	XX-6	IV B	2.5 YR 6/6 light red, 5 YR 6/4 light reddish brown core; some medium white and brown incl.; fl		
17	XX-6	IV B	10 R 5/1 gray, 5 YR 5/4 reddish brown core; some medium white and brown incl.; fl		
18	VIII-8	IV B	5 YR 5/4 reddish brown; many small white and some small to medium brown incl.; ffl		
19	V-29	IV B	7.5 YR 6/4 light brown to 2.5 YR 5/8 red; few small, medium, large white and brown incl.; fl	181	
20	VI-24 S-42	IV B	7.5 YR 7/4 pink, 2.5 YR 5/6 red core, 5 YR 5/1 gray line around core; some white and few brown small to medium incl.; fl		

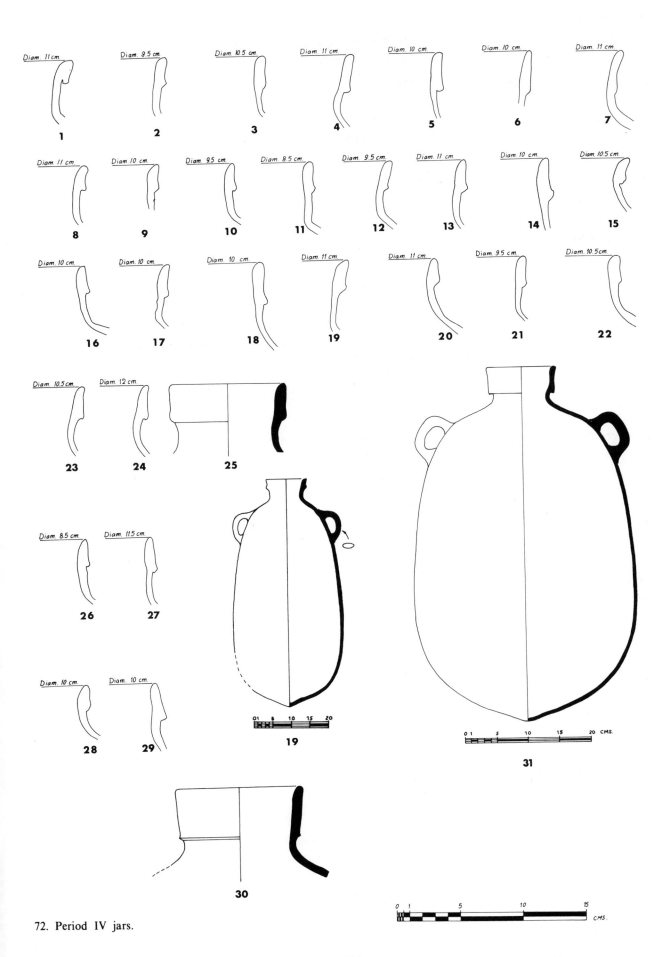

Diam. 11 cm.   1
Diam. 9.5 cm.   2
Diam. 10.5 cm.   3
Diam. 11 cm.   4
Diam. 10 cm.   5
Diam. 10 cm.   6
Diam. 11 cm.   7

Diam. 11 cm.   8
Diam. 10 cm.   9
Diam. 9.5 cm.   10
Diam. 8.5 cm.   11
Diam. 9.5 cm.   12
Diam. 11 cm.   13
Diam. 10 cm.   14
Diam. 10.5 cm.   15

Diam. 10 cm.   16
Diam. 10 cm.   17
Diam. 10 cm.   18
Diam. 11 cm.   19
Diam. 11 cm.   20
Diam. 9.5 cm.   21
Diam. 10.5 cm.   22

Diam. 10.5 cm.   23
Diam. 12 cm.   24
25

Diam. 8.5 cm.   26
Diam. 11.5 cm.   27

19

Diam. 10 cm.   28
Diam. 10 cm.   29

31

30

72. Period IV jars.

267

Pl. 72 cont.

21	V-13	IV B	10 YR 5/2 grayish brown, 5 YR 5/4 reddish brown core; some small and medium white and brown incl.; fl		
22	VI-12	IV B	2.5 YR 5/8 red, 5 YR 7/4 surfaces; many small to few medium white, and very few brown incl.; fl		
23	XVII-5	IV B	5 YR 6/4 light reddish brown, 2.5 YR 5/6 red core, 4/1 dark gray line around core; some small white, gray, and brown incl.; fl		
24	XVII-5	IV B	5 YR 6/4 light reddish brown, 2.5 YR 5/6 red core, 4/1 dark gray line around core; some small white and few brown incl.; fl (= 72:23?)		
25	XVII-3	IV B	2.5 YR 6/6 light red, 10 YR 5/2 grayish brown core; many small and some medium white, and few dark incl.; ffl		
26	XV-7	IV B	5 YR 6/6 reddish yellow, 6/2 pinkish gray core; some small white and few gray and brown incl.; ffl		
27	XV-11	IV B	5 YR 6/3 light reddish brown, 2.5 YR 5.4 reddish brown core; many small to few medium white, and few small to medium brown incl.; fl		
28	XII-12	IV B	7.5 YR 6/2 pinkish gray to 6/4 light brown, 5 YR 4/1 dark gray core; many tiny white and few small red incl.; ffl		
29	XII-12	IV B	5 YR 6/3 light reddish brown, 5/3 reddish brown to 4/1 dark gray core; some small to few medium white and dark brown incl.; fl		
30	II-12	IV C	2.5 YR 4/6, N4/ dark gray small core; few small white incl.		
31	XVIII S-37	IV C	Not available	227	43:3

Pl. 73

PERIOD IV JARS
See p. 102

	Locus	Stratum	Ware	Reg. no.	Photo pl.
1	XX-4ext	IV C	5 YR 7/4 pink, 10 YR 6/2 light brownish gray core; very many small and medium white and few brown incl.; ffl		
2	XX-4ext	IV C	10 YR 5/2 grayish brown from inside surface; 10 R 6/6 light red from outside surface; many small and medium white and brown incl.; ffl		
3	XX-4ext	IV C	5 YR 7/4 pink from outside surface, 10 YR 6/2 light brownish gray from inside surface; many small and medium white, and few medium and large gray incl.; ffl		
4	XX-2ext	IV C	2.5 YR 6/6 light red; some small white and brown incl.; fl		
5	XX-2ext	IV C	5 YR 7/4 pink; many small and some medium white and few gray incl.; ffl		
6	XX-2ext	IV C	5 YR 6/3 light reddish brown, 10 YR 6/2 light brownish gray core; many small and medium white and few brown incl.; ffl		
7	XX-2ext	IV C	5 YR 6/3 light reddish brown from outside surface, 10 YR 6/1 gray from inside surface; very many small and some medium and few brown incl.; cl		
8	VI-32	IV B	5 YR 7/6 reddish yellow, 10 YR 7/2 light gray core; very many small and some medium white and some medium brown incl.; ffl		
9	VI-24 S-42	IV B	5 YR 4/3 reddish brown to 4/1 dark gray; few medium and small incl.		
10	XI-18	IV B	5 YR 6/4 light reddish brown, 2.5 YR 6/6 light red; many small white and brown incl.; ffl		
11	XV-11	IV B	7.5 YR 6/4 light brown, 10 YR 6/2 light brownish gray core; many tiny white and some small to medium brown incl.; ffl		
12	XII-18	IV B	7.5 YR 7/4 pink, 2.5 YR 6/8 light red core; many small to few medium white and some small to few medium brown incl.; ffl		
13	XII-16	IV B	5 YR 7/3 pink toward ext., 7.5 YR N6/ gray toward int.; many tiny to some medium dark gray and white incl.; ffl		
14	XII-12	IV B	2.5 YR 6/6 light red, 5 YR 5/1 gray core; many small to few medium white, and very few brown incl.; fl		
15	I-9	IV B	7.5 YR 7/4 pink, 2.5 YR 6/6 light red core; many small white and some small to medium brown incl.; ffl		
16	I-8	IV B	7.5 YR 6/4 light brown, 10 YR 6/2 light brownish gray core; many tiny white and some small to medium brown and few gray incl.; fl		

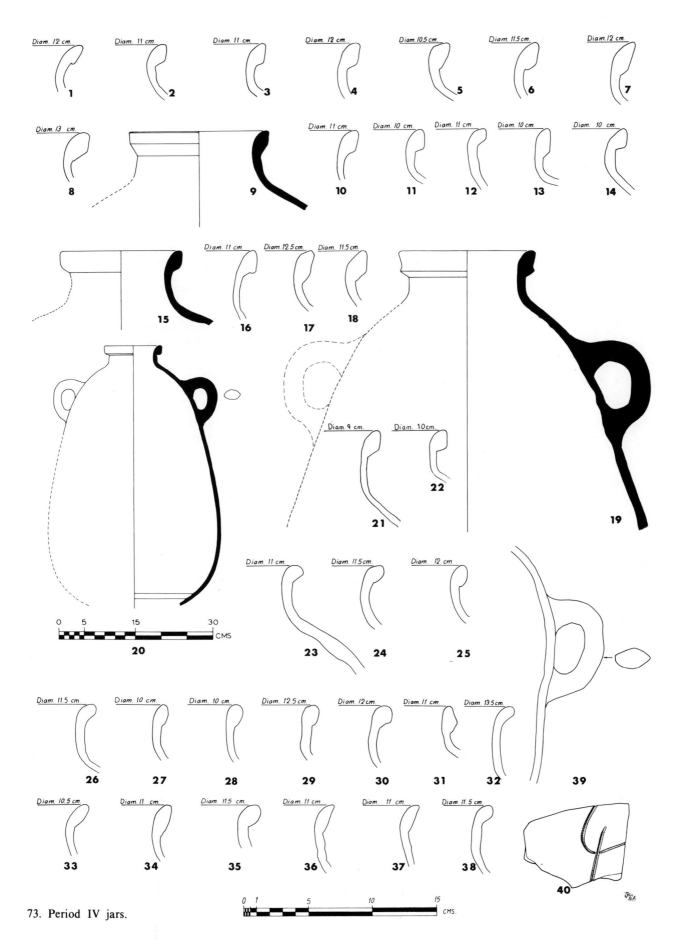

Diam. 12 cm.
1

Diam. 11 cm.
2

Diam. 11 cm.
3

Diam. 12 cm.
4

Diam. 10.5 cm.
5

Diam. 11.5 cm.
6

Diam. 12 cm.
7

Diam. 13 cm.
8

9

Diam. 11 cm.
10

Diam. 10 cm.
11

Diam. 11 cm.
12

Diam. 10 cm.
13

Diam. 10 cm.
14

15

Diam. 11 cm.
16

Diam. 12.5 cm.
17

Diam. 11.5 cm.
18

19

Diam. 9 cm.
21

Diam. 10 cm.
22

0 5   15   30
CMS
20

Diam. 11 cm.
23

Diam. 11.5 cm.
24

Diam. 12 cm.
25

39

Diam. 11.5 cm.
26

Diam. 10 cm.
27

Diam. 10 cm.
28

Diam. 12.5 cm.
29

Diam. 12 cm.
30

Diam. 11 cm.
31

Diam. 13.5 cm.
32

Diam. 10.5 cm.
33

Diam. 11 cm.
34

Diam. 11.5 cm.
35

Diam. 11 cm.
36

Diam. 11 cm.
37

Diam. 11.5 cm.
38

40

73. Period IV jars.

0 1   5   10   15
CMS.

271

Pl. 73 cont.

17	V-54	IV B	10 YR 5/2 grayish brown; very many small and medium white and brown, and some large brown incl.; cl		
18	VIII-8	IV B	7.5 YR 6/4 light brown, 10 YR 6/2 light brownish gray core; many tiny white and some small to medium brown and gray incl.; ffl		
19	III-14	IV C	5 YR 6/6 reddish yellow; many small white incl.		
20	III-27	IV	7.5 YR 6/4 light brown; medium and small white incl.	198	43:1
21	XVIII S-37	IV C	Not available		
22	XVIII S-37	IV C	Not available		
23	XXII-11 S43	IV A	2.5 YR 6/4 light reddish brown, 10 YR 5/1 gray core; many small to medium dark gray incl.; ffl		
24	XX-4ext	IV C	10 YR gray; many small and some medium white incl.; ffl		
25	VI-32	IV B	5 YR 6/2 pinkish gray, 5/1 gray core; many small to some medium white, and some small to few medium brown incl.; ffl		
26	XV-16	IV B	7.5 YR 7/4 pink, 2.5 YR 6/6 light red core; many tiny white and some small to medium brown incl.; fl		
27	XI-18	IV B	5 YR 6/6 reddish yellow, 10 YR 6/2 light brownish gray core; many small and medium white and gray incl.; ffl		
28	XI-21	IV B	5 YR 7/4 pink, 10 YR 7/2 light gray core; many small white and some brown and gray incl.; ffl		
29	I-8	IV B	5 YR 7/3 pink, 5/1 gray core; many small white and some small to large brown incl.; ffl		
30	I-8	IV B	5 YR 7/4 pink, 10 YR 7/2 light gray core; many tiny and some small white and gray incl.; ffl		
31	I-11	IV B	2.5 YR 6/6 light red; some medium white, brown, and gray incl.; fl		
32	I-11	IV B	7.5 YR 7/4 pink, 7/2 and 6/2 pinkish gray to 6/4 light brown core; many tiny white to few medium white and brown incl.; ffl		
33	I-11	IV B	10 YR 5/2 grayish brown; many small and medium white and brown incl.; ffl		
34	I-9	IV B	5 YR 6/1 gray; many small and medium white and brown incl.; ffl		
35	XII-23	IV B	5 YR 6/4 light reddish brown, 5/1 gray core; many small white and few brown incl.; ffl		
36	XII-23	IV B	10 YR 7/4 very pale brown, 2.5 YR 6/8 light red core; many small and few medium white, and some small brown incl.; fl		
37	XII-12	IV B	7.5 YR 6/4 light brown, 2.5 YR 6/6 light red core;		

Pl. 73 cont.

			many small to few medium white, and few brown incl.; fl		
38	XII-11	IV B	2.5 YR 6/6 light red; many small and medium white and brown incl.; ffl		
39	XVII-5	IV B	2.5 YR 6/8 light red, 10 YR 5/2 grayish brown core, 5 YR 7/6 reddish yellow ext. surface; some small to medium white, brown, and red incl.; ffl		
40	VII-10a C-2	IV B	5 YR 6/6 reddish yellow, 5/3 core; small white and medium white and dark incl.; incised marking	54	33:7

Pl. 74

PERIOD IV A JARS
See p. 102

	Locus	Stratum	Ware	Reg. no.
1	XIV-17 S-41	IV A	7.5 YR 7/4 pink, 2.5 YR 6/8 lihgt red core; medium and small white incl.	
2	XIV-17 S-41	IV A	7.5 YR 6/4 light brown; medium and small white incl.	183
3	XIV-17 S-41	IV A	7.5 YR 6/2 pinkish gray, 2.5 YR 6/8 light red toward surfaces; few large and small white incl.	186
4	XIV-17 S-41	IV A	7.5 YR 7/4 pink, 10 YR 6/3 pale brown core; few large white and gray, and many medium and small white incl.	187
5	XIV-17 S-41	IV A	2.5 YR 5/8 red; many medium and small white incl.	184
6	XIV-17 S-41	IV A	7.5 YR 6/4 light brown to 10 YR 6/1 gray to 2.5 YR 6/8 light red core; medium to small white incl.	185
7	XIV-17 S-41	IV A	5 YR 5/6 yellowish red, 7.5 YR 6/4 light brown core; many medium and small white incl.	188
8	XIV-17 S-41	IV A	7.5 YR 6/2 pinkish gray, 5 YR 5/8 yellowish red toward surfaces; few large and medium white and gray incl.	189

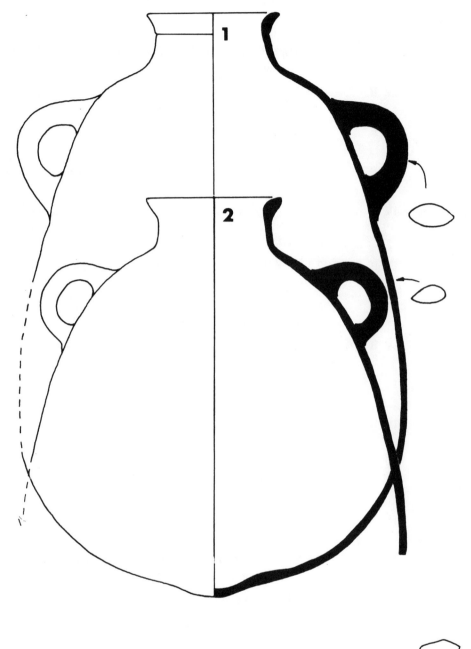

Diam. 12 cm. Diam. 11 cm. Diam. 12 cm. Diam. 10 cm.

3 **4** **5** **6** **7**

0   5   10 CM.

8

74. Period IV jars.

Pl. 75

PERIOD IV JUGS
See pp. 102-3

	Locus	Stratum	Ware	Reg. no.
1	VI-24 S-42	IV B	2.5 YR 6/6 light red, 5 YR 8/4 pink ext. surface, 5 YR 5/1 gray core of handle; some small to few large white incl.; fl	
2	VI-32	IV B	7.5 YR 6/4 light brown; many small to few medium white, and some small to few medium brown incl.; fl	
3	I-19	IV B	10 YR 5/6 red; many tiny white and some small to medium brown incl.; ffl	
4	I-19	IV B	10 R 5/6 red; many small white and few medium white and brown incl.; fl	
5	I-9	IV B	10 YR 7/3 very pale brown, 2.5 YR 6/6 light red core and most of inside surface; many small to some medium white and brown incl.; ffl	
6	XI-18	IV B	2.5 YR 6/8 light red; many small white and some small to medium brown incl.; fl	
7	XX-5	IV B	5 YR 6/4 light reddish brown, 6/2 pinkish gray core; many small white and few small to medium brown incl.; fl	
8	V-29	IV B	5 YR 6/6 reddish yellow, 10 YR 6/3 pale brown core; some small white incl; fl	
9	XII-18	IV B	2.5 YR 6/6 light red; some small and few medium white, and some medium brown incl.; fl	
10	XII-19	IV B	2.5 YR 6/6 light red, 10 YR 8/4 very pale brown ext. surface; many small to few medium white and brown incl.; fl	
11	VIII-14	IV B	2.5 YR 6/6 light red, 7.5 YR 6/2 pinkish gray core, 10 YR 8/4 very pale brown ext. surface; many small to some medium white and few brown incl.; ffl	
12	V-29	IV B	5 YR 6/6 reddish yellow, 10 YR 6/3 pale brown core; some small white and very few small brown incl.; fl	
13	XX-5ext	IV B	7.5 YR 7/4 pink, 2.5 weak red core; many small to some medium white, and some small to medium brown incl.; ffl	
14	VI-25	IV B	2.5 YR 5/8 red; very small white incl.	161
15	I-9	IV B	5 YR 6/6 reddish yellow, 6/2 pinkish gray core; small white and medium white and gray incl.	230
16	XI-18	IV B	2.5 YR 6/6 light red, 10 YR 6/4 light yellowish core of handle; many small and medium white and gray, and some large gray incl.; ffl	
17	XX-5ext	IV B	2.5 YR 6/6 light red, 7.5 YR 8/4 pink surfaces; many small to few medium white and brown incl.; fl	
18	II-24	IV B	10 R 6/6 light red; many small to some medium white incl.; fl	
19	XII-23	IV B	5 YR 7.5/4 pink surfaces, 2.5 YR 6/6 light red core; many tiny white, and some small to medium to very few large brown incl.; fl	

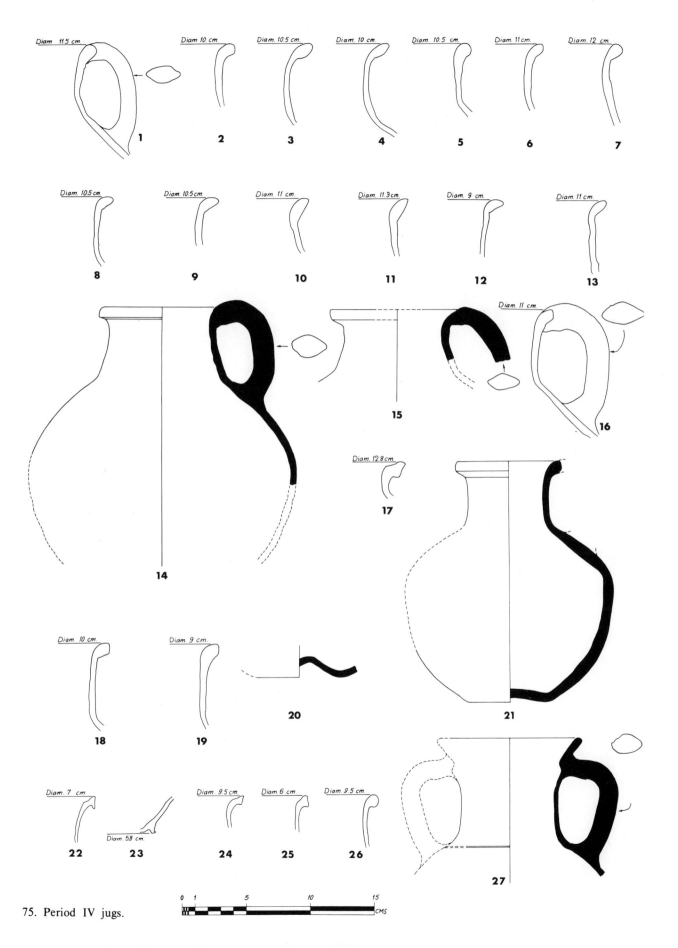

Diam. 11.5 cm. Diam. 10 cm. Diam. 10.5 cm. Diam. 10 cm. Diam. 10.5 cm. Diam. 11 cm. Diam. 12 cm.

1 2 3 4 5 6 7

Diam. 10.5 cm. Diam. 10.5 cm. Diam. 11 cm. Diam. 11.3 cm. Diam. 9 cm. Diam. 11 cm.

8 9 10 11 12 13

14 15 Diam. 11 cm. 16

Diam. 12.8 cm.

17

Diam. 10 cm. Diam. 9 cm.

18 19 20 21

Diam. 7 cm. Diam. 9.5 cm. Diam. 6 cm. Diam. 9.5 cm.

22 Diam. 5.8 cm. 24 25 26

23 27

75. Period IV jugs.

0 1 5 10 15
CMS

279

Pl. 75 cont.

20	XXI-4 S-22	IV B	2.5 YR 6/6 light red, 10 YR 8/4 very pale brown ext. surface; many small to some medium brown and white incl.; fl		
21	XXII-11 S-43	IV A	5 YR 6/6 reddish yellow, 4/1 dark gray small core; few large, many small and medium white incl.	207	44:1
22	XX-4ext	IV C	5 YR 8/4 pink, 7.5 YR 7/2 pinkish gray core; many tiny white and some tiny brown incl.; fl		
23	XX-4ext	IV C	5 YR 8/3 to 7/4 pink, 2.5 YR 5/6 red core; many tiny white and few brown incl.; fl		
24	XX-2ext	IV C	2.5 YR 5/2 grayish brown, 7.5 YR 7/4 pink surfaces, 10 R 6/8 light red to 4/1 dark gray core; many white and some brown tiny incl.; fl		
25	XII-18	IV B	2.5 YR 6/6 light red; some small white and brown incl.; fl		
26	VI-14	IV B	10 YR 6/2 light brownish gray, 2.5 YR 6/6 light red core; some tiny and few small white and some medium brown incl.; fl		
27	III-24 C-1	IV	10 R 5/8 red; few medium and small white incl.	229	

Pl. 76

PERIOD IV FLASKS AND JUGLETS
See p. 103

	Locus	Stratum	Ware	Reg. no.	Photo pl.
1	XXII-11 S-43	IV A	10 YR 5/1 gray; many small and medium white and gray and some large brown and gray incl.; ffl		
2	XXII-11 S-43	IV A	2.5 YR 6/6 light red, 10 YR 5/2 grayish brown core of handle; many small and some medium white and brown incl.; ffl		
3	XXII-11 S-43	IV A	2.5 YR 6/6 light red; some small and medium white and brown incl.; fl		
4	XX-5ext	IV B	10 YR 6/1 gray; many small and medium white and some large gray incl.; ffl		
5	VI-24 S-42	IV B	5 YR 5/8 yellowish red, 5/1 gray core; few large gray and few small white and crystalline incl.	208	
6	II-unstr.	—	10 YR 6/4 light yellowish brown, 4/1 dark gray around core, 5 YR 5/4 reddish brown core; some small to medium white and few brown incl.; fl		
7	IX-12 S-28	IV B	5 YR 7/4 pink, 5/4 reddish brown core, 10 YR 5/2 grayish brown around core; many small and some medium white and few medium brown incl.; ffl		
8	XX-2ext	IV C	2.5 YR 6/6 light red; many small and medium white and some large brown incl.; ffl		
9	XVIII S-37	IV C	10 R 6/6 light red; many small and some medium white and brown incl.; ffl		
10	I-9	IV B	2.5 YR 6/8 light red to N6/ gray; small white incl.		
11	I-unstr.	—	2.5 YR 6/8 light red to 5 YR 5/1 gray; medium and small white, and very few medium dark incl.		
12	V-unstr.	—	5 YR 7/4 pink; some small white and few brown incl.; fl		
13 & 14	VI-24 S-42	IV B	10 R 5/8 red; many small white incl.; ffl	179	44:2
15	VI-12	IV B	2.5 YR 6/6 light red, 10 YR 5/1 gray core of handle; some small and few medium white and gray incl.; fl		
16	VI-14	IV B	5 YR 6/6 reddish yellow, 10 YR 6/2 light brownish gray core of handle; many small white and few brown incl.; fl		
17	XII-12	IV B	10 YR 8/3 very pale brown, 5 YR 7/4 pink core, 10 YR 7/1 light gray core of handle; few small white and brown incl.; fl		
18	VII-5a	IV B	10 YR 8/3 very pale brown; some small and medium white, brown, and gray incl.; fl		
19	III-14 C-1	IV C	5 YR 7/2 light gray; some small and medium white and few brown incl.; fl		

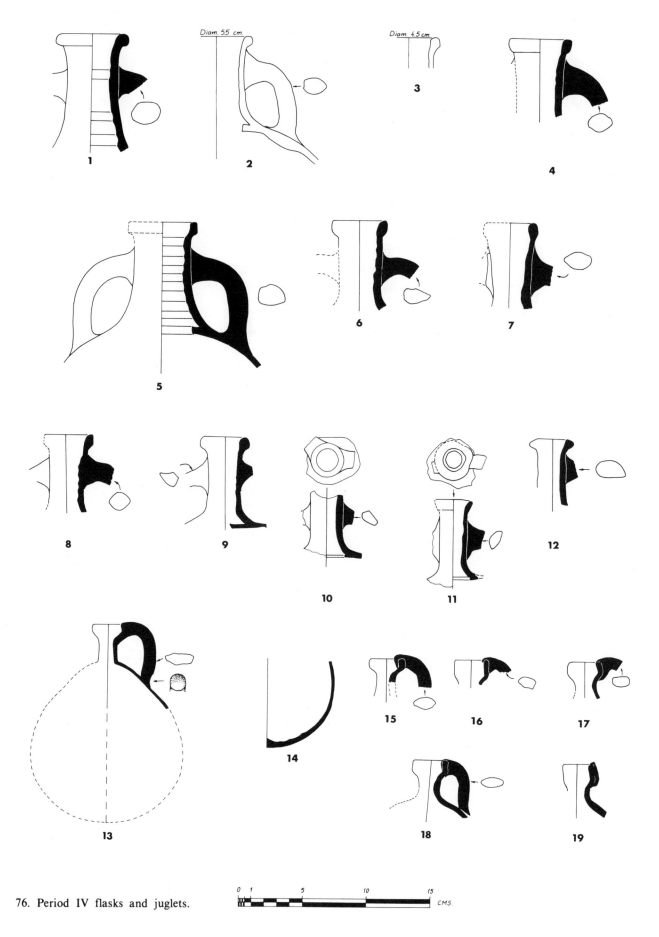

Diam. 55 cm.

Diam. 4.5 cm.

76. Period IV flasks and juglets.

Pl. 77

PERIOD IV POTTERY
See pp. 103-4

	Locus	Stratum	Ware	Reg. no.	Photo pl.
1	XX-5	IV B	5 YR 6/4 light reddish brown; many small and some medium white and dark incl.; ffl		
2	XII-18	IV B	2.5 YR 5/6 red, 5/2 weak red core; some small white incl.; fl		
3	I-11	IV B	10 YR 5/1 gray; many small and medium white incl.; ffl		
4	XX-4ext	IV C	10 YR 5/1 gray; many small and medium white and gray incl.; ffl		
5	XV-3	V	2.5 YR 6/6 light red; some small white and brown incl.; fl		
6	XVIII-unstr.	—	5 YR 7/4 pink; fl		
7	III-24 C-1	IV	7.5 YR 6/4 light brown; many small and medium white, gray, and brown incl.; ffl		
8	VI-28 S-42	IV B	7.5 YR 6/4 light brown, 10 YR 6/2 light brownish gray; many small and medium white and gray incl.; ffl		
9	VI-15	IV B	2.5 YR 6/6 light red; many small and medium white incl.; ffl		
10	XXII-11 S-43	IV A	10 YR 5/2 grayish brown, 2.5 YR 6/6 light red; many small and medium white and brown incl.; ffl		
11	I-18	IV B	10 YR 4/2 dark grayish brown, 5 YR 5/4 reddish brown core; almost no incl.; vfl		
12	XX-5	IV B	Complete but rim chipped: 7.5 YR 7/4 pink; very small white incl.; ffl; 2.5 YR 4/4 reddish brown paint poorly preserved	56	44:3
13	XII-19	IV B	5 YR 7/6 reddish yellow; few small white incl.	291	44:5
14	I-unstr.	—	5 YR 6/6 reddish yellow to 7.5 YR 6/4 light brown; medium and small white incl.	290	44:4
15	VII-15E	IV B	Complete: 2.5 YR 6/8 light red surfaces; few small white and dark incl. on surface; ffl	73	44:6
16	V-32	IV B	2.5 YR 5/6 red, 5 YR 4/1 dark gray surfaces; some small to medium white incl.; fl		
17	V-29	IV B	5 YR 6/6 reddish yellow, 10 YR 5/2 grayish brown core; some small white and gray incl.; fl		
18	XX-5	IV B	10 YR 6/3 pale brown; many small and medium white and very few large brown incl.; ffl		
19	III-20 C-1	IV	10 YR 7/2 light gray to 7.5 YR 6/4 light brown; many small and medium white and some brown, and very few large brown incl.; ffl		
20	XVII-5	IV B	2.5 YR 6/8 light red; some small white and brown incl.; fl		

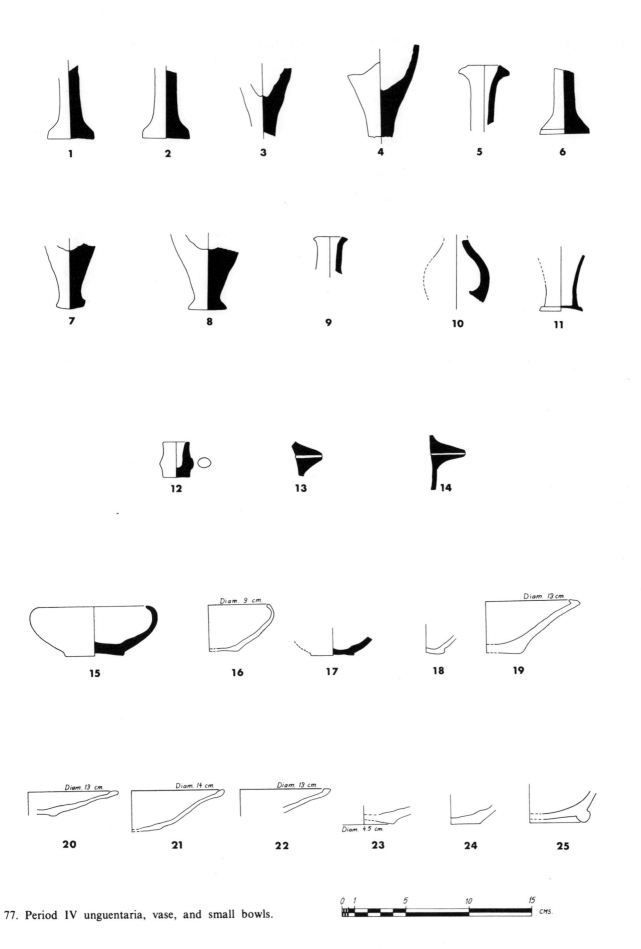

77. Period IV unguentaria, vase, and small bowls.

285

Pl. 77 cont.

21	V-32	IV B	2.5 YR 5/8 red; many small and some medium white, and few medium brown incl.; ffl
22	III-20 C-1	IV	2.5 YR 6/6 light red, 10 YR 6/2 light brownish gray core; some small and medium white incl.; fl
23	I-19	IV B	5 YR 6/6 reddish yellow, 10 YR 6/4 light yellowish brown core; some small and medium white and brown incl.; fl
24	XI-18	IV B	2.5 YR 6/6 light red; many small and medium white and brown incl.; ffl
25	VIII-unstr.	—	5 YR 6/6 reddish yellow; vfl; 2.5 YR N 2.5/ black paint int. and ext. to base and black rings bottom base

Pl. 78

PERIOD IV COOKING POTS
See p. 104

	Locus	Stratum	Ware	Reg. no.	Photo pl.
1	V-21	IV B	2.5 YR 4/6 red; few small white incl.; ffl	162	45:1
2	VI-24 S-42	IV B	Complete: 10 R 4/6 red ext. surface except where blackened by use; ffl	92	45:2
3	XIV-12	IV B	2.5 YR 4/6 red; few medium small white incl.	169	45:5
4	V-8	IV B	2.5 YR 4/6 red; medium and small, and few large white incl.	170	45:6
5	V-21	IV B	2.5 YR 5/6 red, N5/ gray core of handle; some small white incl.; fl		
6	VI-24 S-42	IV B	2.5 YR 5/4 reddish brown, 10 YR 4/1 dark gray core; many small to medium gray or white incl.; ffl		
7	XII-12	IV B	2.5 YR 5/8 red, 5/2 weak red core; many small to few medium white incl.; fl		
8	XVII-5	IV B	5 YR 5/4 to 4/4 reddish brown; very many small white and dark incl.; cl		
9	XVIII S-37	IV C	2.5 YR 4/6 red; some small white and gray incl.; fl		
10	XX-2ext	IV C	10 YR 5/2 grayish brown; some small and medium white and gray incl.; fl		
11	XXII-11 S-43	IV A	5 YR 4/4 reddish brown, 10 YR 4/1 dark gray core; many small to medium white and some black incl.; ffl		
12	I-29	IV C	5 YR 5/6 yellowish red, 10 YR 4/1 dark gray core; many small to some medium crystalline and few white incl.; ffl		
13	XXI-3	IV B	10 YR 5/6 yellowish brown, 4/1 dark gray core; many small black and few white incl.; fl		
14	VI-24 S-42	IV B	2.5 YR 5/6 red, 5 YR 4/1 dark gray core; many small to some medium white and few black incl.; fl		
15	V-29	IV B	Not available		
16	III-27 C-1	IV	2.5 YR 4/4 reddish brown; white and very small crystalline incl.; ffl	220	45:4

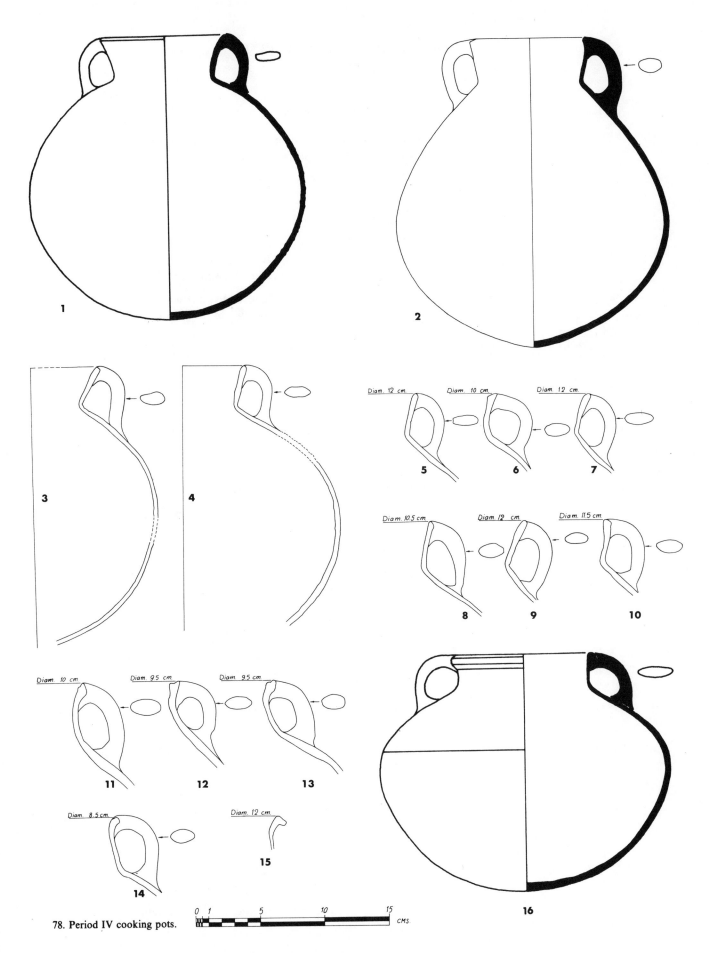

1

2

3

4

Diam. 12 cm. **5**

Diam. 10 cm. **6**

Diam. 12 cm. **7**

Diam. 10.5 cm. **8**

Diam. 12 cm. **9**

Diam. 11.5 cm. **10**

Diam. 10 cm. **11**

Diam. 9.5 cm. **12**

Diam. 9.5 cm. **13**

Diam. 8.5 cm. **14**

Diam. 12 cm. **15**

16

78. Period IV cooking pots.

0 1   5   10   15   CMS.

Pl. 79

PERIOD IV COOKING POTS
See p. 104

	Locus	Stratum	Ware	Reg. no.	Photo pl.
1	XXII-11 S-43	IV A	Complete: 2.5 YR 4/4 reddish brown ext. surface; some white large, medium, and small incl.; ffl	116	45:3
2	II-12	IV C	2.5 YR 4/6 red, 10 YR 5/3 brown core; very few very small white incl.	89	45:7
3	V-34 S-30	IV B	2.5 YR 5/8 red, 4/4 reddish brown core; some small white and grayish incl.; fl	168	
4	VI-24 S-42	IV B	5 YR 4/8 yellowish red, 10 YR 3/3 dark brown core; many small to medium light gray and few black incl.; ffl		
5	XII-18	IV B	5 YR 6/6 reddish yellow, 5/4 light reddish brown core; many small and some medium white and grayish incl.; ffl		
6	VI-25	IV B	2.5 YR 5/8 red to 7.5 YR 5/4 brown; few medium and small white incl.	146	46:4
7	VI-25	IV B	2.5 YR 4/8 red, 5 YR 5/3 reddish brown core; small, medium, and large white incl.	164	46:5
8	VI-25	IV B	2.5 YR 5/8 red; many small and some medium white and grayish incl.; fl	175	
9	VI-25	IV B	5 YR 3/8 yellowish red; many small and medium white and brown incl.; ffl	176	
10	VI-25	IV B	5 YR 5/6 yellowish red; some small and medium white and gray incl.; fl		
11	VI-25	IV B	2.5 YR 5/8 red, 10 R 5/4 weak red core; some small white incl.; fl		
12	VI-25	IV B	2.5 YR 4/6 red, 7.5 YR 4/4 dark brown core; very few small white incl.; fl		
13	VI-25	IV B	2.5 YR 5/4 reddish brown, 7.5 YR 4/4 dark brown core; some small white and grayish incl.; fl		
14	VI-25	IV B	2.5 YR 5/4 reddish brown; some small and medium white and grayish incl.; fl		
15	V-57L S-33	IV A	10 R 3/4 dark red, 2.5 YR N2/ black core; large and medium white, and few medium crystalline incl.	296	46:1
16	V-57L S-33	IV A	2.5 YR 4/6 red, N4/ dark gray core; few small white and crystalline incl.	292	46:2
17	V-57L S-33	IV A	2.5 YR 5/4 reddish brown; very few crystalline incl.	283	46:3
18	V-57L S-33	IV A	5 YR 4/4 reddish brown; many tiny to few medium crystalline, and few dark brown incl.; ffl		
19	V-32	IV B	5 YR 4/6 yellowish red, 10 YR 3/2 very dark grayish brown core; some small and medium crystalline, and some white and gray incl.; ffl		
20	V-34 S-30	IV B	2.5 YR 6/6 light red; some small and medium brown, and few small white incl.; fl	178	

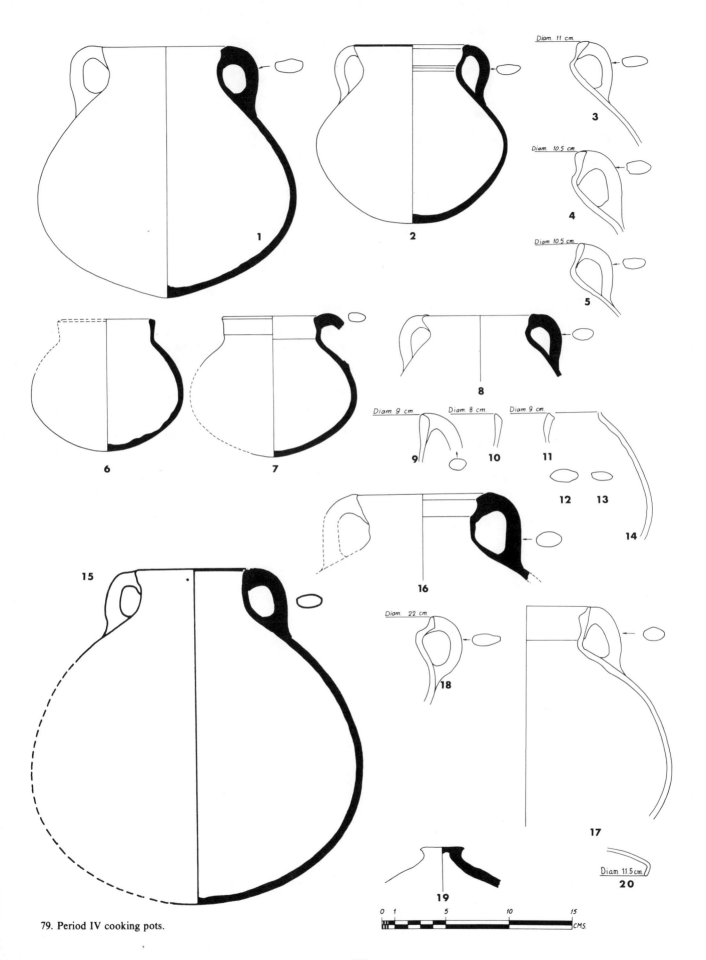

Diam. 11 cm.

Diam. 10.5 cm.

Diam. 10.5 cm.

Diam. 9 cm.

Diam. 8 cm.

Diam. 9 cm.

Diam. 22 cm.

Diam. 11.5 cm.

79. Period IV cooking pots.

0 1   5   10   15
                                         CMS.

291

Pl. 80

PERIOD IV LAMPS
See pp. 104-5

	Locus	Stratum	Ware	Reg. no.	Photo pl.
1	XXII-11 S-43	IV A	5 YR 8/4 pink; few or no incl.; ffl; 5 YR 3/3 dark reddish brown to 4/4 reddish brown; paint fairly well preserved	118	46:6
2	XXII-11 S-43	IV́ A	5 YR 6/6 reddish yellow; few medium gray incl.; 10 R 4/8 red paint poorly preserved top to carination running over below		
3	III-21 C-1	IV	5 YR 7/4 pink; few medium and large white incl.; ffl; burnt spout	63	46:8
4	III-20 C-1	IV	Complete: 5 YR 7/6 reddish yellow ext. surface; white incl.; ffl; burnt spout	64	46:12
5	III-22 C-1	IV	Complete: 7.5 YR 7/6 reddish yellow ext. surface; medium and small white incl.; ffl; burnt spout	65	46:11
6	III-22 C-1	IV	10 R 6/8 light red; small white incl.; ffl	66	46:7
7	III-24 C-1	IV	2.5 YR 6/6 light red; medium dark red and gray, and and small white incl.; fl	67	46:9
8	III-27 C-1	IV	2.5 YR 5/6 red, 5 YR 7/6 reddish yellow toward ext. surface; small white incl.; fl; burnt spout	197	46:14
9	XII-11	IV B	5 YR 6/8 reddish yellow; many small white incl.; ffl; burnt spout	68	46:13
10	XX-5ext	IV B	Complete: 5 YR 7/4 pink ext. surface; small white incl.; ffl; burnt spout	136	46:10
11	VI-13	IV B	7.5 YR 6/4 light brown to 2.5 YR 6/6 light red toward surface; few large dark and few medium dark and white incl.		

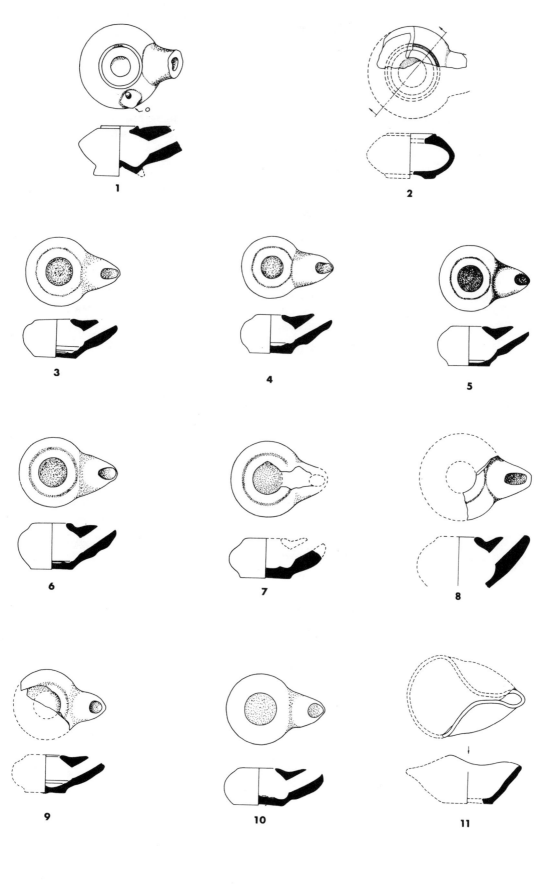

80. Period IV lamps.

Pl. 81

PERIOD V POTTERY
See p. 105

	Locus	Stratum	Ware	Reg. no.	Photo pl.
1	XII-7	V	7.5 YR 8/6 reddish yellow, 6/4 light brown core, 2.5 YR 6/8 light red line around core; some white and brown incl.; fl		
2	XII-9	V	2.5 YR 6/6 light red, 5 YR 6/2 pinkish gray to 5/1 gray core; some small white and brown incl.; fl		
3	VII-4	V	As 81:1 above		
4	XXII-3	V	7.4 YR 7/4 pink, 2.5 YR 5/6 red core, 10 YR 5/2 grayish brown line around core; many tiny white and few small brown incl.; ffl		
5	XVIII S-37 top	V	7.4 YR 7/4 pink, 2.5 YR 5/6 red core, 10 YR 5/2 grayish brown line around core; few tiny white and few small brown incl.; ffl		
6	V-unstr.	—	7.5 YR 6/4 light brown, N5/ gray core; some small white incl.; fl		
7	V-unstr.	—	2.5 YR 6/7 light red, 10 YR 5/2 grayish brown core; many tiny white, and few small to medium white and brown incl.; ffl		
8	XII-7	V	2.5 YR 6/6 light red, 5 YR 6/4 light reddish brown to 5/1 gray core; many tiny white incl.; fl		
9	XII-9	V	7.5 YR 6/4 light brown, 2.5 YR 6/6 light red core, 10 YR 5/2 grayish brown core of handle; many tiny white and some small to medium brown incl.; ffl		
10	XII-2	V	7.5 YR 6/4 light brown; some tiny white and few small to medium brown incl.; fl		
11	XII-3	V	2.5 YR 6/6 light red, 5 YR 6/4 light reddish brown core; some small white and brown incl.; fl		
12	XII-7	V	5 YR 6/6 reddish yellow; few small white incl.	293	44:7
13	XXII-2	V	5 YR 5/1 gray; few small white incl.; 5 YR 2.5/1 black paint	294	44:9
14	V-unstr.	—	2.5 YR 5/6 red; few small white incl.	295	44:8

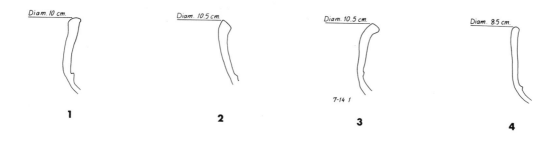

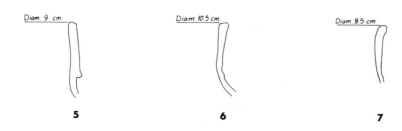

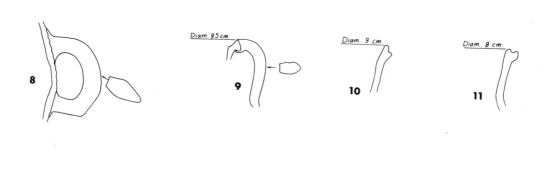

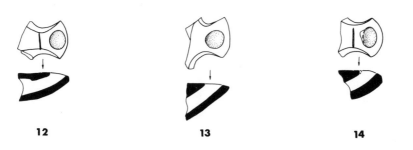

81. Period V pottery.

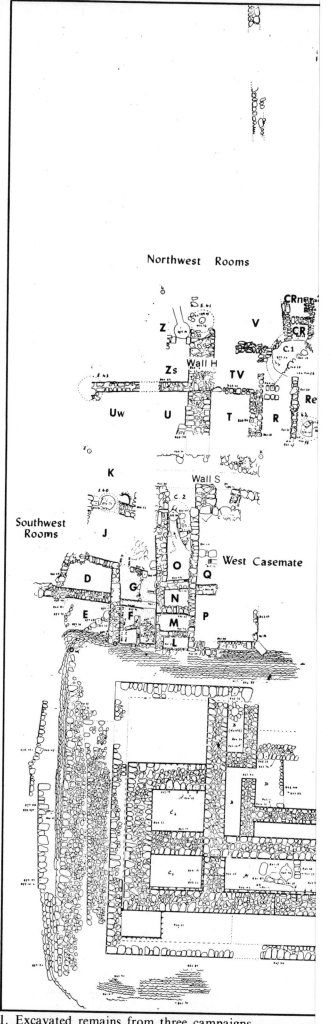

1. Excavated remains from three campaigns.

2. Excavated areas and sections of the 1964 campaign.

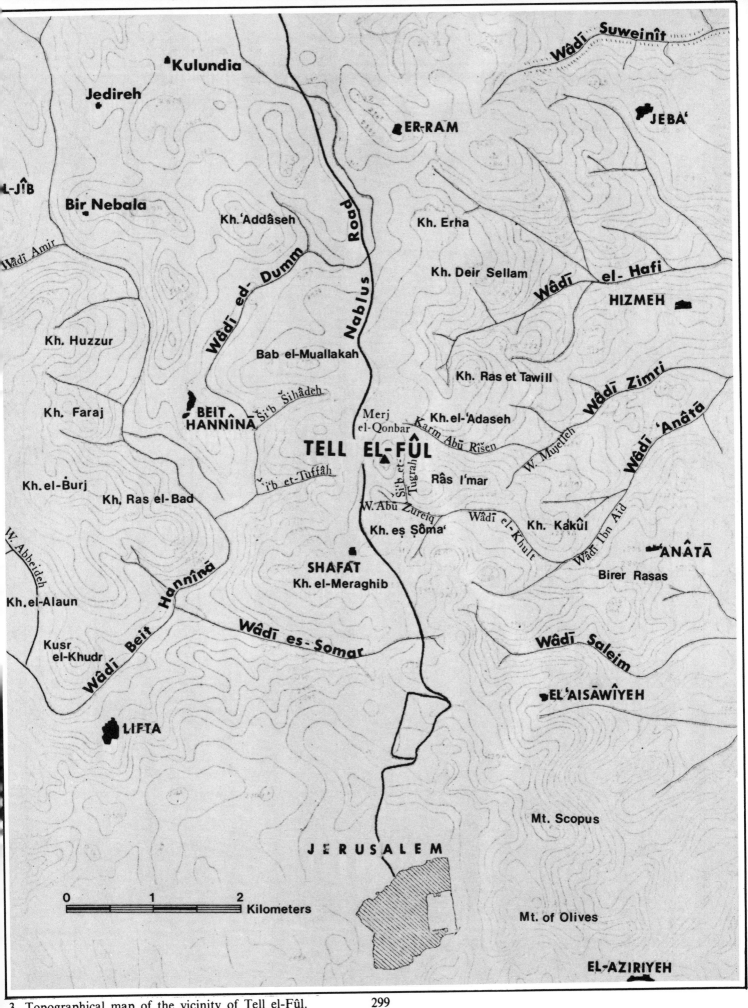

3. Topographical map of the vicinity of Tell el-Fûl.   299

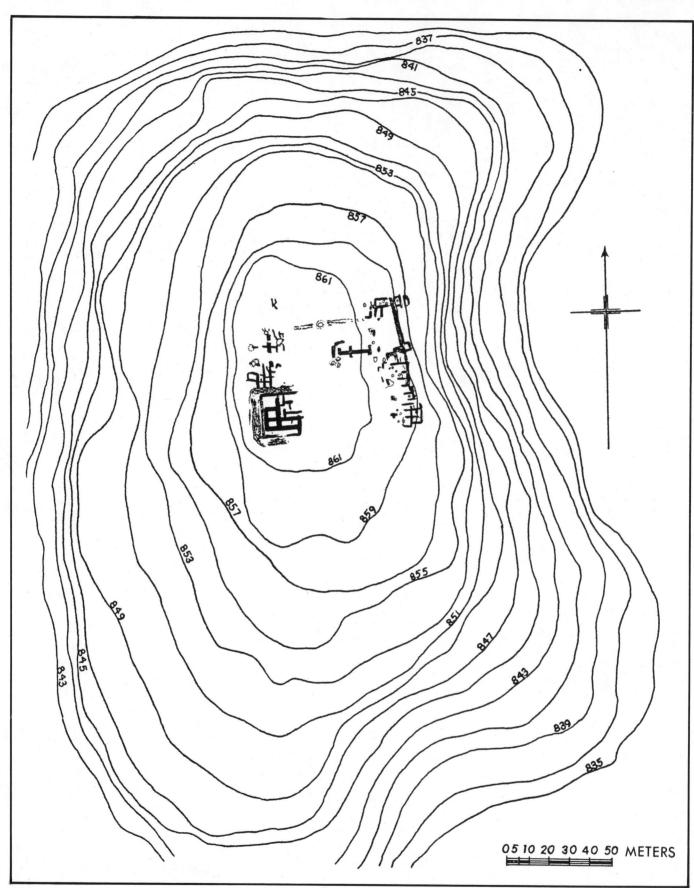

4. Topographical map of Tell el-Fûl showing excavated remains of the three campaigns.

A

(

L. X

L.XIV-5

rock
fall

5. Section n-s. North-south section on the west side o

Area XV

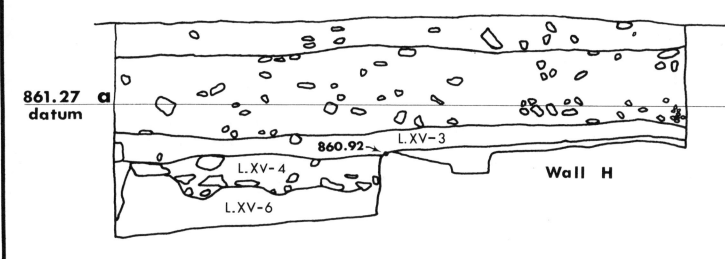

861.27 **a**
datum

860.92 →

L.XV-3

L.XV-4

L.XV-6

Wall H

Area XVII

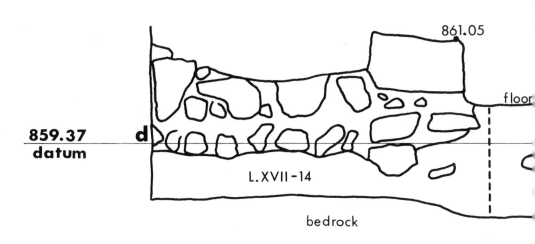

861.05

floor

859.37 **d**
datum

L.XVII-14

bedrock

6. Section a-b. West-east section of Areas XV, XI, VI, north face.
   Section c-d. East-west section of Trench T.

Se

Se

Sc

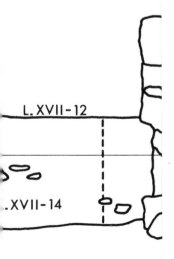

L. XVII-12

. XVII-14

e

h

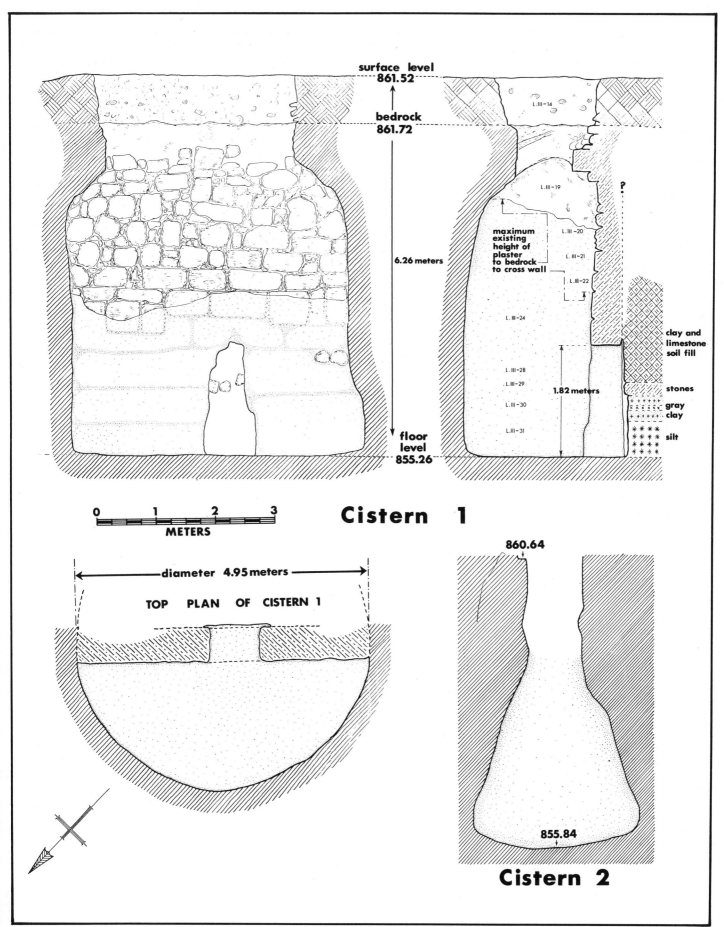

surface level
861.52

bedrock
861.72

L.III-14

L.III-19

maximum
existing
height of
plaster
to bedrock
to cross wall

L.III-20

L.III-21

L.III-22

6.26 meters

L.III-24

clay and
limestone
soil fill

L.III-28
L.III-29

1.82 meters

stones

L.III-30

gray
clay

L.III-31

silt

floor
level
855.26

0 1 2 3
METERS

Cistern 1

← diameter 4.95 meters →

TOP PLAN OF CISTERN 1

860.64

855.84

Cistern 2

10. Cisterns 1 and 2 plans and sections.

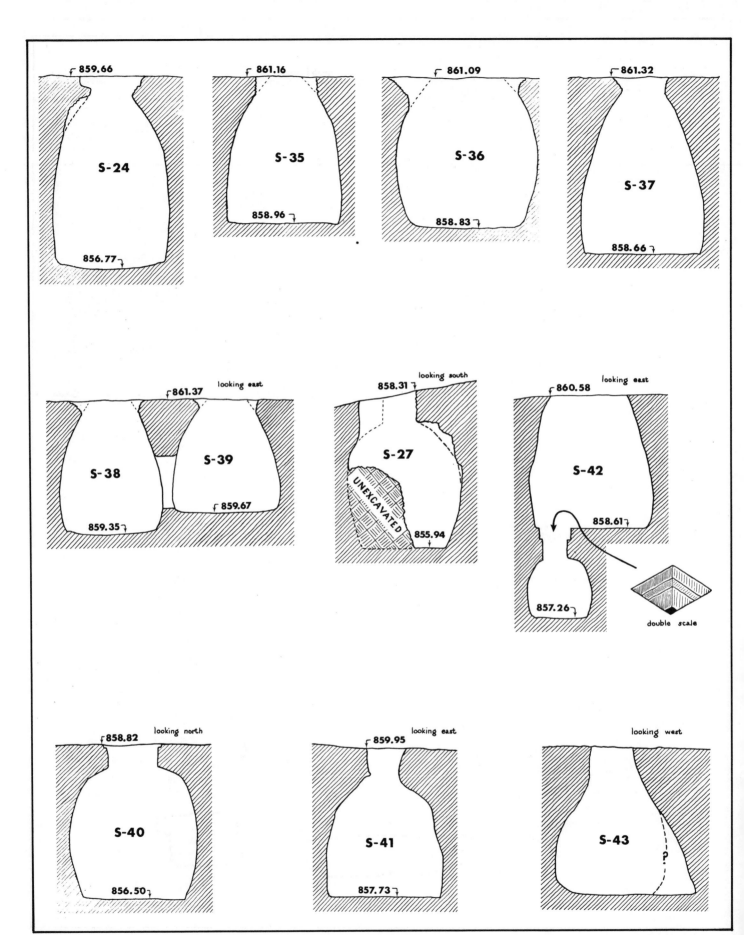

859.66

S-24

856.77

861.16

S-35

858.96

861.09

S-36

858.83

861.32

S-37

858.66

looking east

861.37

S-38

859.35

S-39

859.67

looking south

858.31

S-27

UNEXCAVATED

855.94

looking east

860.58

S-42

858.61

857.26

double scale

looking north

858.82

S-40

856.50

looking east

859.95

S-41

857.73

looking west

S-43

?

11. Silo sections.

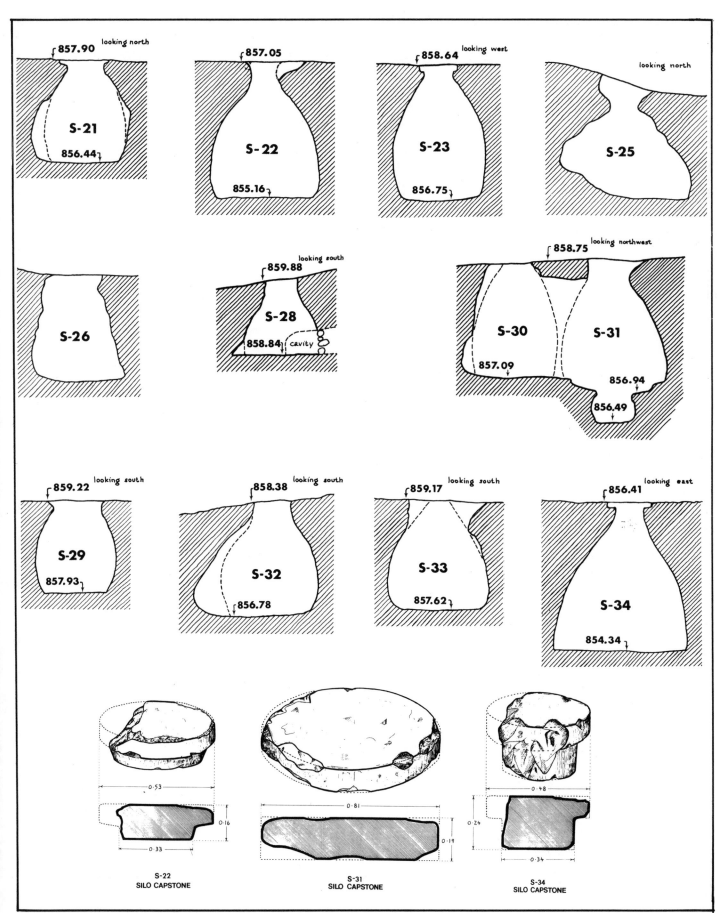

looking north
857.90
S-21
856.44

857.05
S-22
855.16

858.64 looking west
S-23
856.75

looking north
S-25

S-26

looking south
859.88
S-28
858.84 cavity

858.75 looking northwest
S-30 S-31
857.09
856.94
856.49

859.22 looking south
S-29
857.93

858.38 looking south
S-32
856.78

859.17 looking south
S-33
857.62

856.41 looking east
S-34
854.34

0·53
0·16
0·33
S-22
SILO CAPSTONE

0·81
0·19
S-31
SILO CAPSTONE

0·48
0·24
0·34
S-34
SILO CAPSTONE

12. Silo sections and caps.

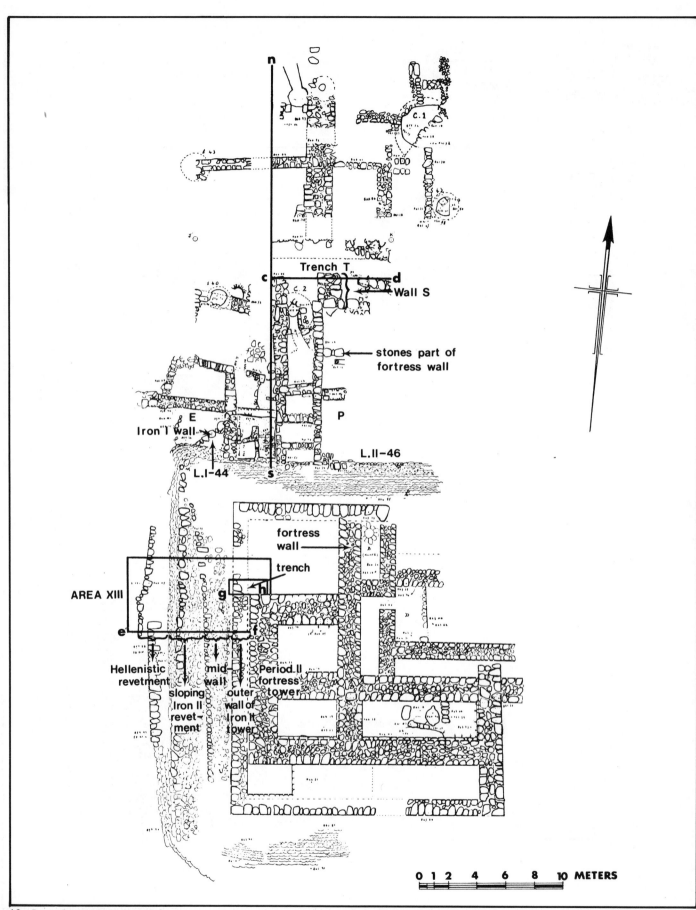

n

C.1

Trench T

c ─────────────── **d**

← Wall S

→ stones part of
fortress wall

E

Iron I wall

P

s

L.I-44

L.II-46

fortress
wall →

trench

AREA XIII

g **h**

e **f**

Hellenistic
revetment

sloping
Iron II
revet-
ment

mid-
wall

outer
wall of
Iron II
tower

Period II
fortress
tower

0 1 2   4   6   8   10 METERS

13. Iron I excavated remains.

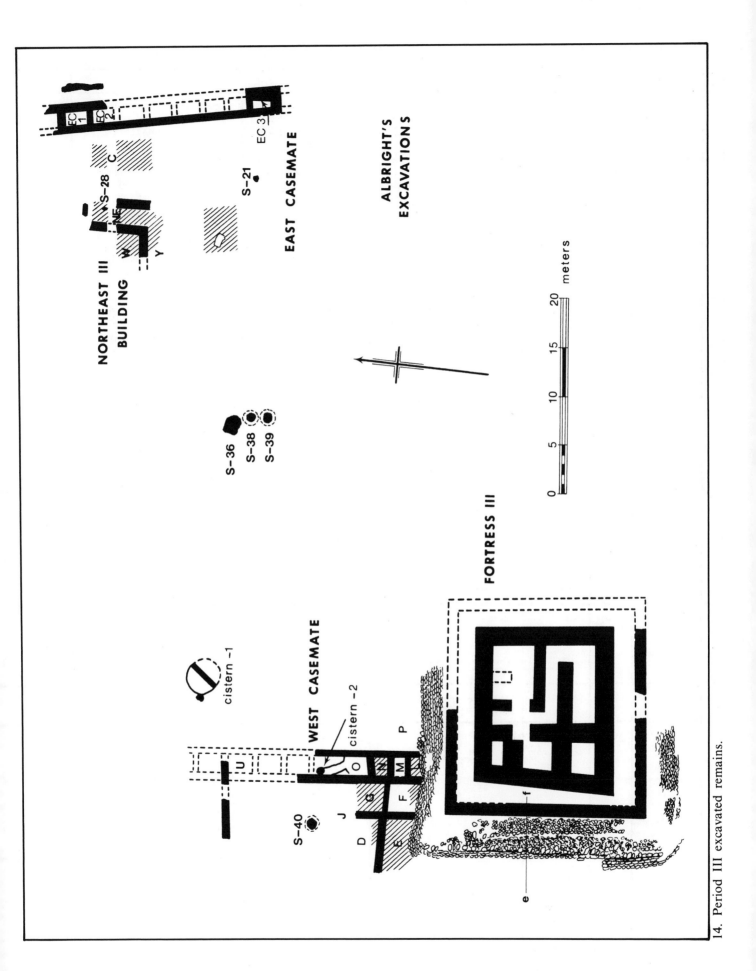

NORTHEAST III
BUILDING

EAST CASEMATE

ALBRIGHT'S
EXCAVATIONS

WEST CASEMATE

FORTRESS III

meters

14. Period III excavated remains.

No.	Locus	Plate	Metal	Type & Reign	Date	Obverse	Reverse	Ref.
3	II-sf.	22:4	AE	Ptolemaic Ptolemy III	246-221 B.C.	Head of Alexander the Great r., with horn of Ammon, clad in elephant's skin and aegis.	Eagle standing l. on thunderbolt, wings displayed; ΠΤΟΛΕΜΑΙΟΥ ΒΑΣΙΛΕΩΣ; between legs: Δ.	BMC, p. 57, n. 111 ff.
4	II-sf.	23:6	AE	Ptolemaic-Ace Antiochus IV	175-164 B.C.	Heads of the Dioscuis r., each surmounted by a star.	Cornucopia upright, containing fruit; on r. downward: [A]NTI.XEΩN´TΩN; on l. downward: ENΠT.ΛEM[AIΔI]; no monogram.	BMC, p. 128, n. 1 ff. Rev. Numism 1962, p. 25 ff.
5	VI-sub sf.	22:7	AE	Maccabean John Hyrcanus II	67-40 B.C.	Within a laurel-wreath tied at bottom: See fig. 35, p. 109.	Double cornucopia, filleted, with poppy-head between the horns.	
8	VIII-5	22:2	AE	Ptolemaic Ptolemy II probably	285-246 B.C.	Head of Zeus r.	Eagle standing l. on thunderbolt, wings displayed; ΠΤΟΛΕΜΑΙΟΥ ΒΑΣΙΛΕΩΕ; in field l. symbols or letters unclear; below, countermark in shape of trident—mint of Berytus?	
10	XIV-sub sf.	23:9	AE	Seleucid Antiochus IV Epiphanes	175-164 B.C.	Head of Antiochus IV r., diademed and radiate.	Hera, veiled, standing facing, wearing long chiton, r. resting on long sceptre; inscription nearly obliterated: [ΒΑΣΙΛΕΩΕ ΑΝΤΙΟΧΟΝ]; serrated edge.	Babelon, p. 74, n. 572 ff.
11	XXIII-sf.		AE	Roman	second half 4th century A.D.	Damaged and much worn.	Type: Emperor standing, holding shield.	Mint of Constantinople.
12	XIV-16 S-41	22:3	AE	Ptolemaic Ptolemy II	285-246 B.C.	Head of Zeus r.	Eagle standing l. on thunderbolt, wings displayed; usual inscription; in field l.: Σ; between legs: P.	BMC, p. 24, n. 19.
13	XIV-sub sf.	23:5	AE	Seleucid Antiochus III	224-187 B.C.	Head of Apollo r.	Apollo, nude, standing l., holding in r. arrow, l. resting on bow; [at r. ΒΑΣΙΛΕΩΕ; at l. ΑΝΤΙΟΧΟΝ]	Babelon, p. 54, n. 411 ff.
14	VII-15E		AE	Maccabean or Herodian		Prutah-size, typical cast-trunnions.	Details uncertain.	
15	V-67 S-32	23:1	AR tetradrachm 26 mm. 12.98 gr.	Seleucid Antiochus VII	136/135 B.C.	Bust of Antiochus VII r., diademed and draped.	Eagle standing on prow; at shoulder, palm branch; around beginning r. above: ΒΑΣΙΛΕΩΕ ΑΝΤΙΟΧΟΝ; in field l. A and club PE surmounted by monogram of Tyre; in field r. AΣ and date IOP = 177 = 136/135 B.C.; between eagle's legs: Σ.	Babelon, p. 142, n. 1101.
16	V-67 S-32	23:2	AR didrachm 21 mm. 6.33 gr.	Seleucid Antiochus VII	Unclear	Same type as preceding.		

15. The Coins from the 1964 Campaign.

No.	Locus	Plate	Metal	Type & Reign	Date	Obverse	Reverse	Ref.
17	V-54 lip of S-32	23:3	AR tetradrachm 27 mm. 12.97 gr.	Seleucid Antiochus VII	136/135 B.C.	Same as above no. 15 except:	Between eagle's legs: ℙ.	Babelon, p. 142, n. 1099 f.
18	V-54 lip of S-32	23:4	AR tetradrachm 26 mm. 13.21 gr.	Seleucid Antiochus VII	136/135 B.C.	Same as preceding, no. 17.		
19	XXII-3	22:8	AE	Herodian Herod Agrippa I	A.D. 42/43	Umbrella with fringe, beginning above on r. [BACIΛ]EΩCAΓPIΠA	Three ears of barley, issuing from between two leaves; across field date LS = 6 = A.D. 42/43.	BMC, p. 236, n. 1 ff.
20	XVIII-sf.		AE	Arabic		Clipped coin, nearly blank; traces of Kufic inscription.		
21	III-14	23:7	AE	Seleucid Antiochus IV	175-164 B.C.	Head of Antiochus IV r., diademed and radiate; behind head.	Hera, as no. 10 above; serrated edge.	
22	V-34 S-30	23:8	AE	Seleucid Antiochus IV	175-164 B.C.	Same as preceding.		
23	XVIII-sf.		AE	Seleucid Antiochus IV	175-164 B.C.	Same as preceding.		
24	XVIII-sf.	22:5	AE	Ptolemaic Ptolemy III	246-221 B.C.	Head of Zeus Ammon r.	Eagle standing l. on thunderbolt; ΠΤΟΛΕΜΑΙΟΝ ΒΑΣΙΛΕΩΕ; in field l. club.	BMC, p. 53, n. 68 ff.
25	VI-24 S-42	22:6	AE	Ptolemaic Ptolemy III	245-221 B.C.	Destroyed [Head of Zeus Ammon r.].	Eagle standing l. on thunderbolt; ΠΤΟΛΕΜΑΙΟΝ ΒΑΣΙΛΕΩΕ; cornucopia resting on eagles's l. wing; between legs ✳	BMC, p. 55, n. 95.
70	XXII-5	23:10	AE	Seleucid Antiochus IV	175-164 B.C.	Same as no. 10 above.		
113	XIV-26	22:1	AR tetradrachm 23/26 mm. 13.48 gr.	Ptolemaic Ptolemy II	253/252 B.C.	Head of Ptolemy I r.; diademed and wearing aegis.	Eagle standing l. on thunderbolt; ΠΤΟΛΕΜΑΙΟΝ [Σ]ΩΤΗΡΟΣ; in field l.: ΣΙ· in field r.: ΛΓ = 33 = ⳨ 253/252 B.C.	BMC, p. 30, n. 71 f.; Mint of Sidon.
128	XXIV-sf.		AE	Seleucid Antiochus III?		Very unclear, probably same as no. 13.		
130	VI-30 intrusive		AE	Umayyad	ca. A.D. 70	Details unclear.		
131	XI-18		AE	Ptolemaic Ptolemy III?		Much worn; probably same as no. 3.		